Criminals in the Making
Criminality Across the Life Course

John Paul Wright
University of Cincinnati

Stephen G. Tibbetts
California State University, San Bernardino

Leah E. Daigle
Georgia State University

SAGE

Los Angeles • London • New Delhi • Singapore

For information:

SAGE Publications, Inc.
2455 Teller Road
Thousand Oaks,
California 91320
E-mail: order@sagepub.com

SAGE Publications India Pvt. Ltd.
B 1/I 1 Mohan Cooperative
Industrial Area
Mathura Road,
New Delhi 110 044
India

SAGE Publications Ltd.
1 Oliver's Yard
55 City Road
London EC1Y 1SP
United Kingdom

SAGE Publications
Asia-Pacific Pte. Ltd.
33 Pekin Street #02-01
Far East Square
Singapore 048763

Printed in the United States of America

Library of Congress Cataloging-in-Publication Data

Wright, John Paul.
Criminals in the making : criminality across the life course/John Paul Wright, Stephen G. Tibbetts, Leah E. Daigle.
    p. cm.
Includes bibliographical references and index.
ISBN 978-1-4129-5519-5 (cloth)
ISBN 978-1-4129-5520-1 (pbk.)
    1. Criminal behavior. 2. Criminology. I. Tibbetts, Stephen G. II. Daigle, Leah E. III. Title.

HV6080.W74 2008
364.3—dc22   2007052935

This book is printed on acid-free paper.

08   09   10   11   12   10   9   8   7   6   5   4   3   2   1

Acquisitions Editor:	Jerry Westby
Associate Editor:	Deya Saoud
Editorial Assistant:	Eve Oettinger
Production Editor:	Astrid Virding
Copy Editor:	Liann Lech
Typesetter:	C&M Digitals (P) Ltd.
Proofreader:	Joyce Li
Indexer:	Molly Hall
Cover Designer:	Gail Buschman
Marketing Manager:	Jennifer Reed Banando

Brief Contents

Contents

Introduction

The life course is fraught with unpredictable moments that lead to sometimes surprising outcomes. For us, this book represents just one of those surprising outcomes. Born out of our displeasure with the current state of criminology and its reliance on theories that exclude the science of human development, we chose to take on the complicated and perhaps perilous effort to integrate the massive literature on human development with what is known about criminal behavior.

Students of complex behavior understand well the challenges in describing and explaining serious, recidivistic criminal behavior. Although the difficulties are numerous, we cite three that make the endeavor even more difficult. The first problem can be found in the way science operates. To make the complex understandable, science reduces information by categorizing findings into parts derived from a larger whole. As applied to the study of criminal behavior, many disciplines conduct research on the causes and consequences of criminal conduct. Psychologists study cognitive growth and its relationship to aggression, and behavioral geneticists study the influence of heritable genes on adult criminal conduct. Yet findings in one science rarely penetrate the other. This is especially true for criminology. Sound scientific findings relating genetic influences or cognitive growth to criminal conduct are surprisingly absent from most influential criminological theories. From our perspective, for criminology to rise above its current state of relying on empirically challenged theories, it must begin to incorporate reliable and valid findings well known to other disciplines.

Relatedly, the second problem that emerges is the sheer volume of information now known about human development. To say that there has been a boom in scientific research into various aspects of human evolution would be to understate the magnitude of growth in studies. Although not all of the information found in academic journals or disseminated at professional meetings is of the same quality, sorting through the multitude of studies found in psychology, sociology, child and adolescent development, and behavioral genetics is daunting and sometimes discouraging. Even as this book goes into publication, new studies are being published that will call into question old findings or push research into a direction different from its past.

The final problem is related to the nature of human development—that is, events and happenings that occur in our past affect our future as well as the views and perceptions of others around us. Human beings have the rather remarkable capacity to remember the slightest details of events that transpired years ago. We also base our current behavior on our subjective interpretation of the causes and consequences of those events. What this means is that our development is linked across time by our cognitive understanding of the past, which, in turn, can alter the choices we make to direct our future. In short, life does not follow a chapter-by-chapter guide, like a book inevitably will, but ebbs and flows across time with future reference points becoming objects of past concern. For our part, however, we are limited to a chapter-by-chapter approach that traces human growth across time.

The starting point of our book recognizes the union between biological development and the social environment. The past decade witnessed unparalleled scientific growth in our understanding of the brain, the central nervous system, neurotransmitters, hormones, and the heritability of traits related to crime and misbehavior. At no other time in history have scientists had available to them the tools to peer into the brain, watch the electrical energy inside the brain send its signals to the appropriate regions, or view firsthand how factors that disrupt this flow of electrochemical energy produce disturbances in behavior. These tools now exist, and their use has revolutionized the science of human development.

But merely recognizing that biological factors are related to crime is sure to cause some degree of trepidation in many criminologists. After all, almost every introductory criminology textbook begins its discussion of biology and crime with the recognition that biological theories have been used to justify Nazism, eugenics, and the gross oppression of various minority groups. What they fail to notice, however, is that the *ideas* from radical sociologists, who view humans as the mere products of society, have also been used to justify the death and destruction of millions of people. Their names are forever etched in history: Marx, Stalin, Pol Pot, and Mao Zedong.

Science cannot advance when it eschews facts—indeed, hard scientific facts—for the sake of political correctness or out of fear that the rich complexity of findings will be misunderstood by politicians, businesses, or laypeople. From our point of view, criminology now stands on the threshold of scientific acceptability, but it will be accepted as a science only if it begins to incorporate the important, scientifically valid findings from various disciplines. This includes those research findings that link biological development with human aggression and violence. We hope this book represents one small step in that direction.

So, do we believe that biology is all that matters? Of course not. Biology is only part of the crime equation. Biology interacts with and correlates with environment, and there is clear evidence that the social environment also influences our biology. Those tangible and intangible elements found in our environments help shape our thoughts, behaviors, and biological development. Thus, our approach to understanding crime is a *biosocial* approach—that is, we highlight the important interaction between healthy biological and social maturation.

Biosocial criminology views behavior as the product of complex interactions between biologically rooted influences and social environments that may, or may not, promote or inhibit certain behaviors. These factors likely change over time.

Certainly, social influences ebb and flow in their influence (think parents), but so do biological influences. The brain, for instance, develops rapidly from the time it is in the womb through much of the first part of life. During adulthood, however, synaptic pathways remain fairly stable in number and in efficiency until old age, when metabolic rates decline and pathways are pruned. It is this type of change across the life course, both biological and social, that our book traces. Life is dynamic and complex, and to appreciate what is truly remarkable about human behavior, you only have to recognize our unique adaptive abilities. These abilities clearly change over time.

Before we close our introduction, let us briefly explain why we went to the trouble to write this book. We were trained as traditional criminologists. Over time, we grew uncomfortable with the state of criminological theory and its rigid adherence to sociological dogma. Each of us, in his or her own way, sought out answers from other fields. When we looked beyond our traditional training, we began to see the utility and scientific necessity of incorporating biology and genetics into our understanding of the unfolding of lives. What we seek is consilience, or the unity of knowledge from diverse fields.

Our goals in this book are thus threefold:

1. Present the reader with an understanding of how humans develop, and how that development can go awry.

2. Link scientific findings from various fields, including neurology, molecular genetics, and behavioral genetics, to the development and maintenance of criminal propensity across time.

3. Detail many of the consequences accompanying faulty development, such as school failure.

In the end, our hope is that the reader will come away more informed about the development of criminal propensity and criminal behavior. We also hope that the reader will be forced to think more broadly about potential factors related to pathological behavior, and that the reader will have an appreciation for the complexity of human behavior. Finally, we hope the reader of this book will come away with a new appreciation of human growth and behavior. Many of the studies we cite in our book are new to criminology, as is much of the information we present. Time will tell if our work has any influence, but we do believe that one thing is certain: We have learned much from writing this book.

John Paul Wright

Stephen G. Tibbetts

Leah E. Daigle

Acknowledgments

M any people have aided in the production of this book. With immeasurable gratitude, we thank the research assistance of Jennifer Childress, Kevin Beaver, and especially Danielle Boisvert. We also want to thank the multitude of comments from the following reviewers:

Robert Apel
University at Albany, State University of New York

Matt DeLisi
Iowa State University

Joshua Freilich
John Jay College & The Graduate Center, City University of New York

Elaine Gunnison
Seattle University

Carter Hay
Florida State University

Lila Kazemian
John Jay College of Criminal Justice

Lisa M. McCartan
Le Moyne College

Wilson Palacios
University of South Florida

Craig T. Robertson
The University at North Alabama

Most importantly, we would like to thank Jerry Westby for believing in our vision of this book. He fully embraced our concept for this work and has supported us throughout this process. We would also like to acknowledge the staff at Sage who worked on this project, especially Deya Saoud. Sage has exhibited the highest level of professionalism and efficiency in preparing this book for publication.

I, John Paul Wright, would like to thank Francis T. Cullen for all of his years of academic and personal mentorship. I would also like to acknowledge Kevin Beaver, Matt Delisi, and Michael Vaughn for their encouragement and dedication to this field of study. I also want to recognize the pioneers in the field, whose work has informed much of my thinking: E. O. Wilson, David Rowe, Steven Pinker, Avshalom Caspi, Terri Moffitt, and Judith Rich Harris. Finally, I would like to salute Anthony Walsh and Lee Ellis, whose careers exemplify the scholarly pursuit of truth.

Stephen G. Tibbetts would especially like to thank Laura Wheeler at California State University, San Bernardino, who aided in selecting and copying many of the figures that appear in the chapters dealing with brain structure and functioning. He would also like to thank Julie Humphrey, currently a doctoral student at Indiana University of Pennsylvania, who edited and revised the sections on *The Jack-Roller*. Additionally, Stephen Tibbetts would like to thank Dr. Larry Gaines and Dr. Pamela Schram, both at California State University, San Bernardino, for their constant support and advice. They have both been invaluable mentors and friends throughout the writing of this book; no one could ask for better colleagues.

CHAPTER 1

Life Course Criminology

Life can only be understood backwards; but it must be lived forwards.

Søren Kierkegaard,
Danish philosopher (1813–1855)

Life Course Criminology

Criminology is once again exciting. After years of unproductive theorizing and bitter academic debates concerning the appropriateness of including evidence from other disciplines—namely biology—the life course paradigm has ignited a firestorm of research. This research has the potential to usher in a new era in criminology—an era where advances occur at a startling rate; the strength of evidence is measurable; and better, deeper questions are asked about the causes of criminal conduct. Criminologists, like their cousins in the older and more mature disciplines of psychology and biology, are starting to seek out and use research findings from various fields. Thus, the remarkable advances witnessed in brain imaging, genetics, and neuropsychology can now inform the study of crime and aggression instead of being continually scoffed at and ridiculed.

Although criminology has made considerable advances, it has yet to fully embrace interdisciplinary research. It is still reluctant to enter into the fields of genetics and biology, and criminologists still remain largely unaware of how these fields can supplement or change our understanding of the development of criminal behavior. Even so, the framework blending these disciplines has been established and used fruitfully in other fields. We hope that this book will serve as an avenue for criminologists to acquaint themselves with the utility of a biosocial perspective.

The life course perspective has been tremendously influential in contemporary criminology, yet researchers first realized its value during the initial part of the 20th century. Its roots can be found in the efforts of criminologists who did not have available to them the current arsenal of computer processors, statistical programs, and validated self-report methodologies. Instead, they examined in detail the life histories of convicted and nonconvicted individuals and, by doing so, took the first steps toward understanding criminal behavior (Glueck & Glueck, 1950). Perhaps the most important researchers of the times were Sheldon and Eleanor Glueck, who examined the developmental patterns of two groups of boys. One group had been convicted of crimes; the other remained free of convictions. Their analyses revealed that multiple risk factors propelled certain youth toward delinquency and adult crime. Their multifactor approach remains a vibrant and informative analytical approach today. In short, their efforts forged the way for modern scientific criminology and its emphasis on the developmental nature of human violence. Although their efforts would establish the framework for the scientific study of criminal conduct for decades to come, the road was still littered with problems, roadblocks, and obstacles.

Origins of Life Course Criminology

Perhaps surprisingly, the studies that hinted most at the importance of the life course in the development of human violence and aggression were cross-sectional cohort studies. The most notable of these cohort studies, the Philadelphia cohort study by Wolfgang, Figlio, and Sellin (1972), studied all boys born in 1945 who lived in the city from the ages of 10 to 18. From this longitudinal study, we first learned that a fairly small group of offenders was responsible for committing the majority of all criminal offenses. Wolfgang's analysis revealed that only 6% of this cohort was responsible for the majority (more than 80%) of the total number of offenses committed. Other studies soon followed that replicated these findings (Farrington & West, 1990; Shannon, 1982). Farrington and West (1990), using a sample of individuals from Great Britain, and Shannon (1982), who conducted a multicohort study in Racine, Wisconsin, both found that a relatively few "chronic" individuals were responsible for the majority of all reported violent and property offenses. For the 1949 cohort of the Racine, Wisconsin, study, for example, only 3% of males who had four or more felony contacts accounted for almost half of all contacts for the cohort (Shannon, 1982). Overall, these studies presented convincing evidence of the existence of a "career criminal," or of an offender whose criminal conduct remained frequent and continuous over lengthy periods of his life course.

Jumping forward in time, the late 1970s brought many important changes in criminology and criminal justice. The 1960s and 1970s were a period of massive social change; the country endured Vietnam, Watergate, the civil rights movement, and Kent State in a very short period of time. More importantly, the country witnessed substantial increases in crime and violence. Out of the cloud of social disorganization and the apparent failure of "liberal" social programs to ameliorate widespread social problems, a new, conservative approach to crime control took hold. Incarceration became a favored approach to controlling crime, and prison construction ballooned.

In large response to the substantial increases in incarceration, policymakers and academics desired to know how shifting larger proportions of the population into prisons and jails influenced the crime rates. Although the matter is still hotly contested, one core issue is not: The effectiveness of incarceration as a crime reduction tool relies on the type of offender incarcerated. Place in prison a high-rate offender, and you will reduce crime; conversely, incarcerating low-rate offenders does nothing to reduce crime rates. Moreover, the incarceration of high-rate offenders is cost-effective, meaning that the financial cost of keeping them locked up offsets the costs of the crimes they would commit if free. The same cannot be said of locking up low-rate offenders. Given the billions of dollars being spent to increase the available number of prisons, a natural question emerged: Are we reducing crime in a cost-effective manner? In due course, findings from the cohort studies emerged to inform these policy debates. It did not take long for researchers and policymakers to recognize the utility of studying "criminal careers and career criminals."

The Criminal Career Approach

Implicit in the criminal career approach is the presumption that offending behavior by individuals is not static; rather, individuals differ in their participation, initiation, frequency, and level of seriousness in offending (Blumstein, Cohen, Roth, & Visher, 1986). As such, criminal career research investigates the sequences, or stages, of offending over time (Blumstein et al., 1986). Individuals begin offending, escalate their offending, and reduce or terminate their offending. More importantly, individuals differ dramatically in the rate at which they commit crimes.

In addition to examining the frequency of offending, the criminal career approach also considers the duration of the criminal career. Examinations of duration have revealed that the typical criminal career is relatively short in length, with onset during adolescence and termination by early adulthood (Blumstein, Cohen, & Farrington, 1988). In fact, research has shown that involvement in minor forms of delinquency is quite common, with more than half of all juveniles participating in some type of misbehavior (Moffitt, 1993a). Despite the normative nature of delinquency, however, most individuals do not continue problematic behavior as adults (Nagin & Paternoster, 1991). Some individuals' criminal careers, however, do span across developmental periods. This fact—what criminologists term *behavioral stability*—will be addressed in detail in forthcoming chapters. The criminal careers paradigm was the first theoretical orientation to draw attention to time-stable differences in antisocial behavior. Those offenders who show the highest levels of behavioral stability generally begin their offending early in life, known as *age of onset,* and they are less likely to desist from offending until late in life (Loeber, 1982; Moffitt, 1993a; Petersilia, 1980). Recognizing the differences in frequency and length of a criminal career allows researchers to further differentiate which factors influence these features.

Although some offenders may have the same age of onset and may engage in crimes at similar rates, they may not commit the same types of crimes. Some offenders may limit themselves to property crimes, whereas others may be more versatile in their offending. Most notably, it has been found that versatility is linked to continuity in offending and antisocial behavior over the life course (Blumstein et al., 1986; Loeber, 1982; Loeber & Stouthamer-Loeber, 1996). For the majority of offenders, violence is just a small part of their behavioral repertoire. For other offenders, however, their viciousness knows no bounds.

The criminal career perspective thus laid the groundwork for understanding how individuals develop into serious offenders. It focused research attention on various dimensions of offending, such as the age of onset, that have yielded valuable criminological insights. More importantly, the criminal career perspective brought a multifactor, longitudinal approach to the study of criminal conduct. This perspective served as the bedrock for the more general life course paradigm of criminal offending.

What Is Life Course Criminology?

The life course is defined as the interconnection of trajectories that are influenced by societal changes and short-term developmental transitions (Elder, 1985). A trajectory is a pathway or state linked over at least one developmental period of the life course (Elder, 1985). Within trajectories, change is marked by life events called transitions (Elder, 1985). These transitions can maintain or alter an individual's trajectory. Significant changes that can alter a person's behavioral trajectory are termed *turning points*. Turning points can result in swift, dramatic changes or more gradual modifications in behavior across the life course (Elder, 1985; Sampson & Laub, 1990).

Because of the dynamic nature of the life course perspective, development is viewed as a continuous process. As such, transitions and turning points in any life stage may be consequential and worthy of study. Unlike previous sociological explanations of criminal behavior, those derived from the life course perspective devote attention to the interlocking nature of trajectories, transitions, and turning points in a variety of domains. Sociological, biological, and psychological factors influence each other reciprocally throughout a person's life. Stated differently, the forces that create human beings with unique traits, talents, and abilities work in conjunction with each other. Thus, changes in one domain of life can influence development in another domain (see Figure 1.1). By considering the interactive nature of trajectories and recognizing the effects that life events both within and outside an individual can have, criminal behavior is conceived as a response to a constellation of dynamic factors.

Life course analyses are based on two general principles. First, the potential effect of any life event is determined by its relation to other events and its timing in the life course (Elder & Rockwell, 1979). The same event, then, may have different effects depending on the characteristics of people's lives and the time in life when the event occurs. Second, the meaning and consequence of any event on an individual is related to the prevailing social context and the life history of that particular person (Elder & Rockwell, 1979). This principle suggests that similar events occurring during different social time periods may lead to different consequences. For example, an unmarried, adult woman becoming pregnant may have less costly ramifications today than it did 50 years ago, largely because contemporary women

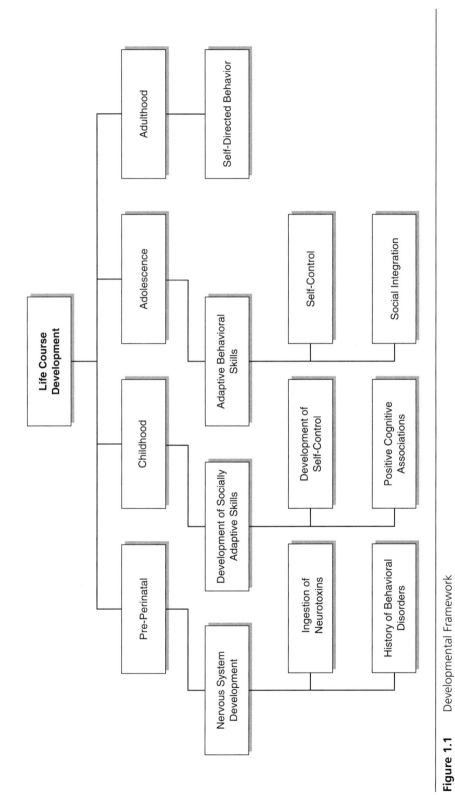

Figure 1.1   Developmental Framework

are better educated than in the past and have greater economic resources. Societal attitudes toward unwed mothers have also shifted substantially toward being more supportive and less isolating.

Taken together, these principles highlight the nonuniform response of individuals to similar social processes. Similar environments, for example, do not produce similar individuals; they create and highlight unique individual differences. Take, for example, two children living with abusive parents. One child may become highly aggressive and involved in criminal conduct, whereas the other child may dedicate his or her adult life to helping other abused youth. The differences in outcomes may be related to the sex of the youth, to the varying ages between the youth, or to personality differences in coping styles. The point is, individuals often respond to life events in ways that best suit them, and not our theories.

Concepts and Issues in Life Course Criminology

Like any theoretical perspective, the life course perspective emphasizes certain core constructs. One such construct focuses on the degree to which antisocial behavior is stable and the degree to which it is subject to change. To understand the competing explanations of stability and change in behavior, however, it is first important to distinguish between states and traits. States are similar to trajectories or pathways. A person's behavior at any given time may be determined by the state in which he or she is acting. Similar to trajectories, states are not always permanent and may be altered by transitions and turning points. Traits, on the other hand, are individual characteristics that persist over a person's life. Behaviors resulting from traits may change over the life course, but the traits themselves are not variable. As such, stable individual traits may manifest themselves in a variety of behaviors and situations over time.

States and traits thus form the bedrock of explanations of stability in criminal offending. Unlike stable trait arguments, *state dependence* refers to the ability of past behavior to influence future behavior (Nagin & Paternoster, 1991). This may occur, for example, when involvement in crime reduces a person's inhibitions against misbehavior, reduces his or her bonds to society, or increases his or her motivation to commit crime in the future.

Others, however, have proposed that this relationship is also indirect (Moffitt, 1993a; Sampson & Laub, 1995). In this sense, a person's involvement in antisocial behavior can limit future life choices, future chances, and future opportunities. Engaging in delinquency early in the life course may decrease a person's ability to maintain bonds to conventional society (i.e., completing high school), thus effectively restricting his or her future behavioral options (Sampson & Laub, 1995). Participation in crime and disrepute, the argument goes, "divorces" one from other legitimate opportunities. It is important to point out, however, that state dependence theorists do not view individual traits as unimportant; they merely place less emphasis on crime-producing traits and more emphasis on the varied consequences of criminal conduct that may ensnare individuals in a web of deviance (Sampson & Laub, 1995).

Other scholars, known as propensity theorists, view the relationship between past and future behavior as being caused by time-enduring individual traits. These traits, such as low self-control, propel people into interactions with criminal others, into criminal circumstances, and into criminal behavioral patterns. Instead of behaviors knifing off opportunities, as state dependence theorists argue, the traits of the individual account for both his or her reduction in social opportunities and his or her stable criminal behavior. As such, differences between people in their participation in crime and other antisocial activities are a direct result of *population heterogeneity* in the underlying propensity to engage in crime (Gottfredson & Hirschi, 1990). Because crime-related traits are considered unchanging over time, people with these traits will engage in antisocial and criminal behavior at higher rates throughout the life course than will those who do not possess those traits (Gottfredson & Hirschi, 1990).

Propensity theorists are also quick to point out that these traits, such as impulsivity and a lack of empathy, not only influence behavior, but they also affect the choices that people make (see Figure 1.2). A propensity toward antisocial behavior increases the likelihood that individuals will self-select themselves into situations where crime and aggression are more likely to occur (Gottfredson & Hirschi, 1990). Although they do not ignore the power of individual choice, proponents of state dependence believe that choices are made in response to underlying traits in conjunction with available opportunities. Notably, available choices are structured by the interaction of individual characteristics and the consequences of past behavior (Sampson & Laub, 1995).

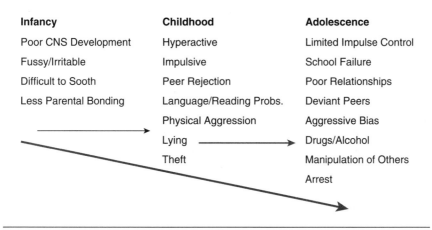

Infancy	Childhood	Adolescence
Poor CNS Development	Hyperactive	Limited Impulse Control
Fussy/Irritable	Impulsive	School Failure
Difficult to Sooth	Peer Rejection	Poor Relationships
Less Parental Bonding	Language/Reading Probs.	Deviant Peers
	Physical Aggression	Aggressive Bias
	Lying	Drugs/Alcohol
	Theft	Manipulation of Others
		Arrest

Figure 1.2   Stability and Change

Life Course Theories of Criminal Behavior

Our book is not primarily concerned with theory. Although we see theory as something useful, we also believe that criminology has too many theories. Even so, we provide a brief introduction of recognized life course-based perspectives. Interested readers should consult the original author's statements.

Gottfredson and Hirschi's General Theory of Crime. According to Gottfredson and Hirschi (1990), crime is caused by low self-control. To Gottfredson and Hirschi, heterogeneity in an underlying propensity to commit crime (i.e., low self-control) differs between individuals and thus accounts for why some people engage in crime and others refrain. And because those low in self-control are impulsive and hedonistic, they will engage in an array of risk-taking behaviors, what Gottfredson and Hirschi call *analogous behavior,* such as smoking, reckless driving, and cheating.

Gottfredson and Hirschi locate the cause of low self-control in the failure of parents to effectively monitor their children, recognize and label their children's misbehavior, and sanction that misbehavior. Thus, self-control is not an innate characteristic but a trait that emerges from familial interaction. Levels of self-control, they argue, are typically determined by age 8. Once established, an individual's ability to regulate his or her own behavior becomes a stable individual difference that has lifelong consequences.

Gottfredson and Hirschi (1990) contend that antisocial, risky, and impulsive behaviors are all manifestations of this underlying propensity. Not only will a person with low self-control be more likely to violate the laws of a community, but he or she will also be at an increased risk of engaging in other behaviors that, although legal, violate norms and reduce an individual's life chances. Stability in antisocial and aggressive behavioral patterns occurs not only because of persistent individual differences in self-control, but also because individuals with low self-control self-select themselves into situations and environments that correspond to and support their propensity. In doing so, individuals may persist in a deviant lifestyle over time, not because involvement at one time causes involvement at a later time, but because of the presence of an underlying propensity at *each* time.

Obviously, the theory of low self-control has been hotly debated, discussed, and dissected. Many of the objections to their theory are clearly ideological, in that numerous criminologists are simply antagonistic to individual, trait-based theories, regardless of the evidence. But Gottfredson and Hirschi's theory also offers many testable propositions that are contrary to "conventional criminological wisdom." For example, Gottfredson and Hirschi (1990; Hirschi & Gottfredson, 1995) contend that the effects of age on crime are invariant across time and place. In direct contradiction with developmental theories, the association between age and criminal offending, they argue, cannot be accounted for by historical, cohort, or individual characteristics. They further argue that because the cause of crime is the same across the life span, there is no need for longitudinal research designs; a person who is low in self-control will offend more relative to those with higher levels of self-control over time. Although a person may decrease in the level of offending or engage in other analogous behaviors rather than crime, his or her rate of offending will remain higher than the rate of those who possess higher levels of self-control (Gottfredson & Hirschi, 1990; Hirschi & Gottfredson, 1995).

It is important to note, however, that although the theory of low self-control is not specifically a developmental theory, the theory does have a developmental component. With its emphasis on the acquisition of self-control early in life, Gottfredson and Hirschi draw our attention to the factors that produce self-control and those factors that propel individuals low in self-control to continue to commit crime over lengthy parts of their lives. In addition, the development of a general theory of crime remains one of the only theories that can explain a range of maladaptive behaviors over the life course, including divorce, unemployment, and school failure, and thus it has helped to shape and inform current developmental theories of crime.

Sampson and Laub's Age-Graded Theory of Social Control. Sampson and Laub (1993) contend that a substantial amount of within-individual change in criminal behavior exists. It is this change in behavior that Sampson and Laub (1993) sought to explain. Similar to social control theory, they argue that an individual's bonds to institutions of informal social control influence criminality. When these bonds to society are weak or broken, an individual becomes free from the constraints of conventional society and, as a result, is more likely to engage in crime and delinquency than when these bonds to society are strong.

Sampson and Laub (1993) incorporate the central premise of social control theory into the life course perspective. In doing so, they draw attention to the presence, strength, and quality of informal social bonds and how these factors vary over time. For example, during adolescence, the major source of informal social control may be the school, whereas during adulthood, employment may become a dominant mechanism of informal social control. Accordingly, the development of these bonds represents potentially important and life-altering age-graded transitions. Movement through these transitions thus influences criminal involvement, moving some previously criminal individuals away from crime. In the adult life course, for instance, marriage and employment are particularly salient social bonds. Sampson and Laub (1993) argue that it is the quality of these bonds, rather than their mere presence, that keeps persons from engaging in crime. Specifically, it is not marriage itself, but a stable, strong marriage to which a person is committed that will help insulate a person from crime (Sampson & Laub, 1993). Attachment to meaningful employment, likewise, is more effective in changing criminal behavior than is simply being employed.

In addition to explaining change in offending behavior over time, this age-graded theory of social control is also applicable to the understanding of stability in behavior. Whereas Gottfredson and Hirschi (1990) adhere to a self-selection hypothesis, Sampson and Laub (1993) believe that involvement in deviancy has independent effects on informal social bonds through the process of *cumulative continuity*. As such, antisocial behavior generates consequences that have long-term, deleterious effects on a person's future life chances. Individuals without ample social skills, for instance, are unlikely to land good jobs that pay well. Unlike self-selection, in which the correlation between past and future criminality is said to be spurious, the accumulation of negative life experiences and its subsequent weakening of adult social bonds is thought to mediate the effect of prior misbehavior on future misbehavior. It is important to note that Sampson and Laub (1993) acknowledge that individual differences may influence a person's choices and how they select themselves into particular settings and behaviors. Although individual propensities may structure the decision-making process that underlies involvement in crime and deviancy, once engaged in, these behaviors have independent consequences on a person's conduct.

Developmental Trajectories and Typologies of Offenders

Taken together, Gottfredson and Hirschi's (1990) theory of low self-control and Sampson and Laub's (1993) age-graded theory of informal social bonds provide a general framework from which both stability and change in antisocial behavior can be explored. Other investigators, however, have recognized that individuals differ significantly in their rate of criminal offending, and that those who begin offending relatively early in the life course generally are the same individuals who offend across much of their life span (Nagin & Land, 1993). In light of this finding, some life course theorists have identified unique types of offenders based on the different trajectories they follow. These offender typologies are further characterized by unique sets of causal factors.

Moffitt's Theory of Adolescent-Limited and Life Course-Persistent Delinquents. Perhaps one of the most influential contemporary life course theories is Moffitt's (1993a) dual taxonomy of antisocial behavior. According to Moffitt (1993a), there are two qualitatively different types of offenders, each identifiable by a distinct offending trajectory. Not only are the characteristics of the trajectories different, each is determined by its own constellation of developmentally related factors.

The first type of offender, the adolescent-limited offender, engages in delinquency only during adolescence. These offenders typically do not begin to offend until reaching this stage of the life course. Adolescent-limited offenders engage mostly in minor forms of delinquency and then for only short periods of time. The life of the adolescent-limited offender is not riddled with antisocial behaviors, he or she is not committed to an antisocial lifestyle, and he or she typically does not commit a broad array of misdeeds. Instead, his or her antisocial behavior is situation-specific, suggesting that adolescence-limited offenders are decidedly prosocial in other contexts. Additionally, the antisocial behavior of the adolescent-limited offender rarely continues into adulthood.

Unlike adolescence-limited offenders, who temporarily participate in delinquency, the second type of offender is characterized as life course-persistent. These offenders exhibit antisocial tendencies very early in life and generally remain offenders throughout their adulthood. The types of crimes the life course-persistent offender commits are more serious than those committed by adolescence-limited offenders. Indeed, it is the extremity and frequency of their offending behavior, coupled with the fact that they offend across a variety of settings, that propels them toward high levels of continuity in their antisocial behavior. In short, life course-persistent offenders are committed to crime—that is, it is part of a lifestyle, or pattern of interactions, that emerges early in life and continues largely unabated for long periods across the life span.

Moffitt (1993a) further contends that each offending trajectory has a separate etiology. For the adolescence-limited offender, she identifies factors that produce a late age of onset. During adolescence, an individual undergoes various physical, emotional, and social changes. As the physical body begins to develop, adolescents are simultaneously expected to behave more like adults. Although adolescents are quickly maturing into young adults, they remain caught between demands that they act like adults while they remain separated from adult roles and institutions.

In this stressful, ambiguous position between adolescence and adulthood, adolescent-limited offenders choose alternative methods to gain adult status. They achieve adult status, according to Moffitt, by imitating the behaviors of their life course-persistent peers. Adolescent-limited offenders engage in delinquency, the argument goes, to acquire the mature status that life course-persistent delinquents appear to have achieved. They act like adults by drinking alcohol and experimenting with drugs, by partying and by committing minor acts of vandalism. Through their participation in these minor forms of delinquency, adolescent-limited offenders act autonomously in direct disregard to adult authority. Typically, at the end of adolescence, when persons are expected to become self-sufficient, the adolescent-limited delinquent is no longer compelled to mimic the antisocial behavior of life course-persistent youth to achieve mature status. Instead, they choose from various adult roles, such as employment, the military, or higher education. As such, the adolescence-limited offender desists from delinquency very quickly.

The etiology of the life course-persistent offender is quite different. Because of the earlier onset into delinquency and other antisocial activities, Moffitt (1993a) traces the sources of these behaviors to factors occurring before adolescence. Generally, antisocial behavior for this type of offender arises out of an interaction between individual characteristics and characteristics of the child-rearing environment. Moffitt identifies specific individual characteristics, such as hyperactivity and impulsivity, that predispose young children to aggression and violence. She argues that these traits result from neuropsychological deficits. The effects of these traits are omnipotent; they put children at risk for poor cognitive, emotional, and behavioral development (Moffitt, 1993a, 1997; Moffitt, Caspi, Dickson, Silva, & Stanton, 1996).

The second component of this interaction points to the child-rearing environment. First, it is important to note that youth are not born randomly across parents. Criminal parents, for example, are more likely to produce children who themselves mature to be criminals. Thus, parents who are hyperactive or impulsive (who lack self-control) are more likely to have children with these same traits. In disadvantaged familial environments, where inadequate parenting is common, problem behaviors stemming from the neuropsychological deficits of the child often fail to elicit appropriate responses from their parents. Because their early problem behaviors are not extinguished, a life course-persistent delinquent maintains an antisocial behavioral style through adolescence and well into adulthood. Involvement in delinquency and crime is thus viewed as part of the resulting constellation of problem behaviors that accompanies life course-persistent youths.

Adolescent-limited offenders are, for the most part, on the periphery of deviance, as they also have well-developed social skills and sufficient levels of self-control. The misbehavior of life course-persistent offenders, on the other hand, systematically mortgages their future opportunities. They generally do not have a supply of self-control and restraint and thus they tend to fail in school, are ostracized by prosocial peers, and tend to hang out with others of similar characteristics. The results have far-reaching effects: They are more likely to be divorced as adults; to drop out of school before acquiring their degree; to experience prolonged bouts of unemployment as adults; and to suffer from increased rates of disease, incarceration, and death.

Patterson's Early and Late Starters. A precursor to Moffitt's (1993a) dual taxonomy of offenders, Patterson's (1986) performance model for antisocial boys also identifies two groups of offenders. Similar to Moffitt's types, Patterson, DeBaryshe, and Ramsey (1989) distinguish their groups based in part on age of onset: late starters and early starters.

Late starters are individuals who do not begin to exhibit antisocial or delinquent behavior until adolescence. As previously noted, delinquency is quite common during this developmental period. From Patterson et al.'s point of view, delinquency occurs because of poor supervision by parents. Because of this inadequate level of supervision, adolescents are then vulnerable to friendships with other delinquent peers. In turn, delinquent peer networks then influence behavior. Specifically, these late starters begin to offend because of the deviant social networks they develop in response to the lack of appropriate parental safeguards.

Early starters, on the other hand, begin their antisocial behavior earlier, and their offending patterns exhibit a longer duration than do those of late starters (Patterson et al., 1989). This group of delinquents experiences poor parenting early in the life course, including poor parental management, limited or superficial supervision, and inconsistent discipline. Because of the deficiency in parenting, children's antisocial behaviors are not punished correctly. More importantly, parents tend to inadvertently reinforce the antisocial behaviors of their youth by not consistently recognizing inappropriate behavior and punishing it effectively. Instead, they tend to not be very consistent, nor do they make the punishment contingent on their child's bad behavior. And when they do punish the misbehavior of their child and act to sanction it, they do so in ways that only exacerbate the problems, such as striking out uncontrollably. Needless to say, these parent-child interactions produce a tremendous amount of conflict. Eventually, owing to the conflict, parents begin to redefine what they consider to be bad behavior, tacitly allowing their children to engage in subsequent deviancy (Patterson, 1980).

Because they are not equipped to handle the rules and social expectations found in schools, early starters are at a high risk of performing poorly in school and of being rejected by their peers. School failure, coupled with the development of delinquent peer relationships, sets a child on a path of delinquency. The coercive nature of parenting and the resultant negative competencies that develop are especially pertinent to those youths who are already at a risk for school failure. Individuals with a low IQ, for example, may be at an even higher risk for demonstrating early behavioral problems. Because of their cognitive deficiencies, children with low IQ may evoke poor parenting and may have limited abilities to form necessary social skills. Consequently, these children may develop a coercive interpersonal style that correlates with delinquency. In addition, children with low IQ are at an increased risk for early school failure, an identified risk factor for delinquency (Lynam, Moffitt, & Stouthamer-Loeber, 1993; Ward & Tittle, 1994).

Life Course Criminality

The astute reader will notice that most life course-based theories exclude any mention of biology or genetics. We will detail the reasons for this later, but for now, only Moffitt's dual taxonomy holds a role for biology—and then only for life course-persistent offenders. Our perspective—what we call *life course criminality*—readily incorporates biology, genetics, and socialization into a coherent model to understand how some individuals develop into serious offenders.

Our focus is on the development of criminality—or the propensity to engage in crime and other problematic behaviors—and how criminality plays out across an individual's life. Where our perspective differs from others can be found in our incorporation of biological and genetic influences into our explanation of criminality. Unlike general sociological perspectives, such as Sampson and Laub's, we see the unequal likelihood of engaging in criminal offending as an important within-individual element to explain. Some individuals will never get into trouble, and they have a difficult time with the thought of doing something that would bring about social rebuke. Other individuals, however, engage in behaviors that are dangerous, predatory, and pathological, and they do so across their lifetime (see Figure 1.3). Social rejection is of little deterrent value to them. Why people vary in criminal propensity, we believe, ought to be at the heart of criminological research, so it is here that we spend most of our time.

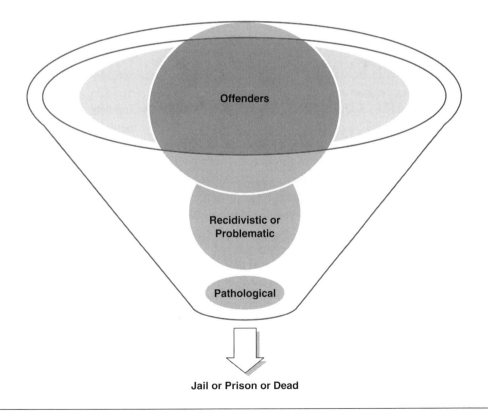

Figure 1.3   Filtering of Offenders

We believe that the evidence points to a complex mix of biological, genetic, and social variables in the creation and maintenance of criminality. Our biosocial perspective links variation in biological variables to environmental states and stimuli and seeks to explain how human organisms are affected by, and operate on, their immediate environment. Given criminology's reluctance to incorporate genetic or biological influences into theory, we must rely heavily on research from other disciplines. For most criminologists, much less their students, this information will be new.

By the time this book goes to press, some of the information contained within it will have changed. Research is published almost daily highlighting new findings—so much so that it is difficult to remain current in this area. This is a problem all three of us have had to deal with since we started this book. No matter, we start off the book with what we consider to be the most fundamentally important aspect to criminal and antisocial behavior—its stability over time and place. In Chapters 2 and 3, we examine the stability of antisocial behavior across time and place, as well as continuity in the processes that underlie stable behavioral patterns.

We then move on, in Chapters 4 through 8, to discuss how genetics and biology inform our understanding of criminal propensity. We detail how the central nervous system develops, especially the brain; how neurotransmission works; and how environmental factors can cause serious cognitive and neurological deficits that are related to criminal propensity. Moreover, unlike most texts on crime, we address biological and genetic differences between sexes. From our viewpoint, differences in brain structure and functioning and neuroendocrine responses are responsible for the dramatic differences we see in our daily lives between men and women, boys and girls.

With the stage set, we examine in Chapter 9 individual development in context and how certain risk factors, such as attention deficit hyperactivity disorder, make some individuals more susceptible to problem behaviors than others. Continuing with this theme in Chapter 10, we examine developmental factors in childhood, including social development, brain development, and language development. As we will show, many of the temperamental and behavioral routines linked to adult crime actually have their roots in childhood.

Major research findings are now showing why adolescence is such an important stage of development. In Chapter 11, we highlight these findings by linking amazing research on changes in adolescent brain structure and function to social development. Adolescence has always been recognized as a time when youth encounter numerous novel experiences. How effectively adolescents adapt to these novel experiences, including puberty and dating, will partly determine the quality and content of their adult lives.

Finally, our last chapter provides evidence that criminal behavior can change, and that it can change through targeted, policy-driven interventions. There is now a wealth of data that successful interventions can occur any time along the life course, that these interventions are multifaceted, and that they follow a "what works" agenda. For now, however, we turn to Chapter 2 and our focus on the stability of criminal behavior.

BOX 1.1   The Saga of Stanley: An Introduction

A classic case study, first published in 1930 by Clifford Shaw of the University of Chicago, resulted in a well-known book titled *The Jack-Roller: A Delinquent Boy's Own Story.* In this book, Shaw tells the story of a boy named Stanley, much of which was the result of Stanley articulately reporting details of key developmental events in his life to Shaw. Although written decades before life course theories became popular in criminological literature, Stanley's story provides one of the best representations of most of the various stages that are considered important in modern developmental/life course theories of criminality. Shaw and Stanley did an excellent job of documenting and analyzing these events; therefore, we have decided to use the story of Stanley's life to provide a true anecdote for many of the issues and factors that we cover in this book.

In each of the following chapters, we will review the relevant characteristics and events found in Stanley's case to the concepts and issues being discussed in the respective chapters. More importantly, we will discuss how such factors and episodes contributed to or inhibited Stanley's antisocial behavior. Our purpose for providing Stanley's story is to give readers more realistic, concrete examples of the often abstract and complex propositions that will be presented during our tour through various life stages. Additionally, reviewing the significant events that occurred in Stanley's life allows for a healthy exercise in applying developmental/life course theory, as well as providing a good, albeit unique, illustration of how key events (i.e., transitions), both positive and negative, are likely to have profound cumulative effects on individuals that will likely alter the long-term paths (i.e., trajectories) they take. Although no individual trajectory is the same, we believe it is beneficial to apply the concepts that we explore to an actual, carefully documented case. As Shaw (1930) notes, "Any specific act of the individual becomes comprehensible only in light of its relation to the sequence of past experiences in the life of the individual" (p. 13); hence, the importance of a detailed case study that follows the development of one individual over time.

Regarding the issues discussed in Chapter 1, it is important to note that the most accepted general theories of crime (such as low self-control), by themselves do not explain Stanley's antisocial behavior very well (this will become clear in later chapters), whereas a developmental/life course perspective appears to be much more valid in explaining his offending behavior. This conclusion is based on the details of Stanley's criminal career, which is not known to readers at this time, but it will become clear as we progress through the chapters. We ask that the readers bear with us, and then they can formulate their own conclusions regarding Stanley's criminality at the end of the book.

CHAPTER 2

The Stability of Criminal and Analogous Behaviors

Insanity: Doing the same thing over and over again and expecting different results.

Albert Einstein (1879–1955)

Sixty years of social science research has converged to show that many human characteristics emerge early in life and remain relatively stable from birth to death. Various human factors, including intelligence quotient (IQ), extraversion, impulsivity, and risk seeking, become apparent, visible, and measurable at very young ages. These factors, in turn, have been shown to continue to define individuals as they grow older. Take, for example, the emergence of IQ, or the general ability to learn. By age 4, people vary considerably, with some youths scoring fairly high and others scoring low. By the time they become adults, the differences between those who score low and those who score high are remarkably consistent over time. It is safe to say that youths with high IQs become adults with high IQs; youths with low IQs become adults with low IQs.

IQ, however, is not the only human characteristic that appears relatively stable across time. Various types of personality characteristics, such as impulsiveness and inattentiveness, also show remarkable degrees of stability over time (Caspi & Silva, 1995). At one level, it is rather easy to understand how biologically circumscribed factors that are strongly inherited and embedded in our DNA, such as IQ, can remain relatively stable across time. After all, factors related to brain functioning, such as the production of hormones, are largely determined by biological equations that unfold according to specific genetic sequences.

By extension, however, it is not so easy to understand how *behaviors,* especially criminal behaviors, can emerge early in life and remain relatively stable. The research has been hotly debated and contested. For some, the thought that "crime starts early in life and remains stable" evokes images of youngsters "born bad." These kids, the argument goes, will eventually develop into merciless criminals who will prey on society. For others, however, the idea that criminal behavior is stable overlooks the fact that people change, often in dramatic ways and sometimes for unforeseen reasons. Advocates of this position also question whether calling official attention to youths with early behavioral problems will serve only to label them as offenders when they have yet to commit a crime. Still, others question whether these findings are even real—that is, whether or not they are the product of scientists' obsession with numbers.

Critics of this research often cite three reasons to cast doubt on this important empirical finding. First, from a criminologist's point of view, crime is a behavior that is legally proscribed. Crimes and vices are illegal only because a political body has crafted a law proscribing certain conduct. Therefore, it makes no sense to describe infants or toddlers as criminals because they are incapable of engaging in behaviors proscribed by law. Relatedly, however, most laws also recognize intent as an important consideration. Most industrialized nations establish an age at which individuals are assumed to be capable of forming criminal intent. Young children are often statutorily exempted from legal consideration because of their inability to formulate intent or to appreciate the consequences of their actions. On its face, then, the idea that very young children can formulate criminal intent, much less engage in crime, appears ludicrous.

Second, not all cultures socially define specific behaviors as criminal. Some cultures, for example, value aggressiveness in males and thus do not view fighting between two competing males as worthy of social sanction. Even within cultures, subcultures form that define acts of violence as appropriate responses to perceived threats or as an instrumental method to achieve status and wealth. Thus, the recognition that the meaning of certain behaviors is socially constructed, or that these behaviors mean different things to different people in different contexts, makes measuring concepts such as crime or aggression meaningless.

Third, others point to the fact that class differences produce social inequality. Youths who grow up in poor neighborhoods do not have the opportunities to go to quality schools and do not have access to social networks that provide adequate jobs later in life. As a result, crime emerges as a way of dealing with the pressures of living in dire circumstances.

Yet the fact remains that almost all scientific data show that human aggression emerges very early in the life cycle and remains relatively stable over time. Certain individuals, regardless of the culture in which they live, demonstrate aggressive behavior as very young children, then as adolescents, and finally as adults. Although young children may not fully appreciate the consequences of their behaviors, nor be able to formulate intent, they are more than capable of acting aggressively—that is, they can pull hair, punch, kick, and injure others. We may not criminally sanction their behaviors, but if these behaviors are demonstrated in adolescence or adulthood, they will constitute assault. Thus, it is the patterned use of aggression with which we concern ourselves here, not whether a society defines a specific behavior as criminal.

Our view is that the evidence on the stability of criminal behavior is so strong that the relationship between past and future misbehavior constitutes one of the "brute facts" of crime; this fact should not be ignored because of the potential for social misuse, but should be understood so that the knowledge that comes from this area leads to efficient, humane interventions. Ultimately, understanding the developmental pathways that lead young children to stable, adult criminal behavior can serve to make society safer and to elevate the quality of life for youths who otherwise would have suffered the consequences that come with participation in crime. As we will discuss later, the lives of high-rate offenders are littered with personal failures, tragedies, and wasted time.

What Do We Mean by the Stability of Criminal Behavior?

In study after study, the variable that emerges as the strongest predictor of future criminal behavior is past criminal and delinquent behavior. Young children who tend to act impulsively, are difficult to manage, and are hyperactive are more likely to commit delinquent acts as adolescents. In turn, adolescents who engage in delinquency and criminal acts are more likely, as adults, to engage in criminal behavior. That is, over time, individuals who display a high propensity to commit crime are, *relative to other people*, far more likely to engage in illegal conduct.

Loeber (1982) defines the stability of criminal behavior as persistence in a behavior or style of interacting over time. This definition highlights two components important to understanding issues related to stability. The first component is time. The course of human development involves the passage of time, with developmental markers that are strongly age-related. For example, we understand that there are large developmental differences between a 2-year-old and a 16-year-old. These differences reflect the passage of time, measured in years, and the convergence of biological and psychosocial changes that have unfolded to produce a unique and identifiable individual. From this viewpoint, time, or age, is understood in terms of developmental sequences that place individuals along a continuum from least advanced to most advanced. Thinking about time in this matter draws attention to the developmental differences between people of differing ages. However, it also draws attention to the influence of past experiences on future behavior.

Relatedly, the second component of Loeber's definition of stability refers to the "persistence in a behavior or a style of interacting." Simply put, persistence refers to the continual demonstration of a behavior over time. When criminologists speak of persistent criminal behavior, for example, they are referring to individuals who engage in crime over a long period of time. Similarly, when Loeber highlights "a style of interacting," he is again referring to a consistent *pattern* of behavior and social interaction. Aggressive youths, for example, are more likely to attribute malicious intent to the social behavior of others when that behavior interferes with their goals. On the other hand, prosocial youths are more likely to interpret the exact same behavior differently (Caspi & Moffitt, 1993). This style of interaction can remain remarkably consistent over time and, in turn, affect the life course development of individuals.

Taken together, the stability of behavior draws our attention to the patterning of behaviors over time. Indeed, it is the stability of human behavior that makes our behaviors somewhat predictive. In order to better understand the concept of stability, think for a moment about how your own behaviors are routinized. At a broad level, you likely have a schedule that you follow—that is, you awake at a prescribed time; travel to a specific location, say, to school or to work; and along the way, you follow the same path day after day. This is routine, and knowing your routine, we can predict certain aspects of your behavior. At a more narrow level, knowing how often you have demonstrated aggression in the past gives us a decent ability to predict how frequently you will engage in aggressive behavior in the future. If, for example, you have a tendency to move from job to job because you continually fight with your boss, we know that you are more likely to leave the next job you acquire and to know that you will likely argue with your new boss as well. The point is, much of the way we spend our time is highly structured by the routines that we create. The same can be said about our behaviors. Aggressive interactional styles represent a pattern of behavior where aggression is used with a predictable degree of certainty.

How Is the Stability of Criminal Behavior Measured?

At first glance, it would seem an easy enough task to measure whether or not someone demonstrates stable criminal behavior patterns over time. Yet the measurement of stability is clouded by theoretical problems that relate to the interpretation of data, and by statistical problems that relate to the quantitative assessment of stability. In short, the measurement of stability is far from easy.

To assess behavioral stability, quantitative criminologists and those interested in the development of criminal behavior have typically turned to three sources of information. The first source comes from official records, such as arrest records. These data tell us, for example, how frequently a person has been arrested for a crime and his or her age when arrested. Logically, individuals with lengthy arrest records are assumed to demonstrate higher levels of stable criminal behavior.

Studies that employ official data to assess criminal stability are often found in the form of cohort studies. For example, Wolfgang, Figlio, and Sellin (1972) analyzed official records from individuals born in Philadelphia in 1945. And in a larger study, Shannon (1976) analyzed three birth cohorts born in Racine, Wisconsin, in 1942, 1949, and 1955. These studies, reviewed by Petersilia (1980), converge to show that the likelihood of ever being arrested at least once is quite high, but that about one third of individuals arrested only once were not arrested again (Petersilia, 1980). However, evidence of stability can be seen when the likelihood of being arrested multiple times is examined. In Petersilia's review, she reported that the likelihood of being arrested a third time, after two initial arrests, was very high—around 70%. The likelihood increased with each successive arrest so that the probability of being arrested a fourth time, after being arrested three times previously, was above .80, or 80%. Even so, Petersilia's review also found that a very small percentage of the overall cohorts examined experienced multiple arrests; typically less than 6% of any cohort. Thus, evidence from official data appears to show that a small percentage of any cohort remains criminally active over a long period of time and thus accounts for a large proportion of all reported crimes.

The second manner in which stability is assessed comes from direct observation. Research in this vein typically comes from psychology, where researchers observe children under specific circumstances over multiple occasions. For example, psychologists often watch how children interact with others while at play or in school. Differences between youths are noted and followed for the length of the study. In one such study, Cairns and Cairns (1994) made detailed observations of the classroom behavior of two cohorts of children from Grades 4 through 12. Their analyses, which included minute-by-minute accounts of aggressive behavior within the classrooms, revealed fairly high levels of aggression for certain youths.

Finally, perhaps the most common method of assessing stability comes from self-report measures of misbehavior. In general, this method involves asking people to report their involvement in a wide range of deviant and delinquent behavior across at least two points in time, either through the use of a survey or through a face-to-face interview. Once the data are collected, researchers correlate the scores to capture the *relative stability* of behavior over time (refer to Table 2.1 for greater detail). This method provides a reliable and valid measure of stability, but can be problematic. We discuss these issues in the next section.

Table 2.1   What Is a Correlation Coefficient?

Correlations are the most common measure of criminal stability. However, the correlation coefficient does not always present the most accurate picture of the stability of criminal behavior. For this reason, it is important to understand how criminologists typically use correlation coefficients, to understand their strengths, and to understand their weaknesses.

Suppose that we have collected self-report information from $N = 5$ people. Since we are interested in delinquency, we ask them to answer a series of questions about their involvement in misbehavior and since we are interested in the stability of behavior, we ask them these questions on twice a year, or at a six-month interval $(T_1 - T_2)$. Typical measures of delinquency include:

How often in the past six months have you:

Taken a car without the owners permission

Stolen something worth more than $50

Entered a building without the owners permission

Hit someone hard enough they needed medical attention

Sold hard drugs, such as heroin

Respondents then answer each question based on the follow response set:

T_1	T_2
1 = never	*1 = never*
2 = only once	*2 = only once*
3 = two to three times	*3 = two to three times*

4 = four to five times	*4 = four to five times*
5 = more than five times	*5 = more than five times*
Range = 5 to 25	*Range = 5 to 25*

Since there are five questions and five possible responses, the range of individual delinquency scores equals 5 to 25 (5×1 or 5×5). Those who score closer to 25 are relatively more involved in delinquency. Since there are N = 5 respondents, we sum each person's delinquency score for each period and divide by 5 to obtain an average (mean) delinquency score for the sample at each time period.

Analysts then employ a common statistical formula to calculate the degree of covariation between scores at Time period one and Time period two. The formula follows the form of:

$$\frac{\Sigma XY - NX}{\sqrt{[\Sigma X^2 - NX^2][\Sigma Y^2 - NY^2]}}$$

Correlations range from +1.0, showing a perfect, positive, linear relationship, to −1.0, showing a perfect, negative linear relationship. A correlation of 0 (zero) shows that the two variables are unrelated.

Correlations show us the direction and magnitude of the association between two variables, in this case, the correlation between T_1 delinquency scores and T_2 delinquency scores. Suppose we follow the calculations and derive a correlation of .80 between the two measures. Since the score is close to 1.0, this means that individuals who scored relatively high on delinquent behavior at T_1 also scored relatively high at T_2. Notice we use the term *relative* stability. This is because correlations only provide us with information about the movement of scores relative to prior scores. Suppose our N = 5 scores look something like this:

Time 1		*Time 2*	
Name	*Score*	*Name*	*Score*
(1) Tim	24	(1) Tim	22
(2) Steve	20	(2) Steve	18
(3) Mickey	8	(3) Susan	8
(4) Susan	7	(4) Mickey	6
(5) Bonnie	5	(5) Bonnie	5
Mean = 12.8		Mean = 11.8	

We see at both time periods, Tim and Steve report the most delinquent involvement, even though their scores decrease somewhat from one period to the next. Mickey and Susan, however, swap positions while Bonnie remains the most prosocial. Relative to Bonnie, Tim and Steve always score higher on the measures of delinquency. Also notice, however, that with each sample we have computed an average (mean) delinquency score. Relative to the mean, Tim and Steve always score above the mean for the sample while Bonnie, Mickey, and Susan always score below the mean. Hence the term *relative stability.*

Issues Related to the Measurement of Stability

To understand the relatively sophisticated analyses associated with most life course studies, especially as they relate to studies of stability and change, it is important to bring to the reader's attention the various theoretical and methodological issues underpinning these studies. We have already discussed the various methods used by criminologists to measure stability. In this section, we highlight in more detail both the theoretical and methodological issues that make the study of stability more complex than is realized by most criminologists.

According to Alwin (1994), there are six models, or assumptions, that guide studies of stability in behavior. The first is the *persistence* model, which holds that specific behaviors, traits, or dispositions are constant and unchanging across time. Advocates of this viewpoint would, for instance, point out that serious, recidivistic, adolescent offenders are highly likely to continue their offending well into their adult years. Thus, their aggressive behavior patterns are persistent across time.

Contrary to this perspective, other theorists maintain that human behavior is dynamic and often the product of situational inducements and pressures. Moreover, humans are remarkably adaptive and thus open to new experiences. This perspective, which Alwin labels *lifelong openness,* emphasizes the nature of intra-individual change over time and thus does not view traits and behaviors as strictly persistent.

Next, it is well documented that certain viewpoints change as people grow older. Youths are typically more likely to hold rather liberal political beliefs until they reach their mid- to late 30s, when their belief structures gradually shift to become more conservative. This perspective is one of *increasing persistence.* Simply put, behaviors and viewpoints become increasingly persistent, or stable, over time. This viewpoint is also similar to what Alwin refers to as the model of *impressionable years.* It is widely believed, for example, that after a period of rapid growth from infancy to early childhood, patterns of behavior emerge and then become fairly resistant to change.

Yet another viewpoint holds that the human life span is bifurcated; change occurs early in life, stability dominates midlife, and change again occurs late in life. Known as *midlife stability,* this perspective maintains that stability is most likely to occur during the middle years of the life span, but that stability is dwarfed by the constant change that occurred earlier in life and that will occur later in life.

Finally, Alwin's last model views behavior as becoming less persistent over time, hence the label *decreasing persistence.*

As you can tell, these models place varying emphasis on levels of stability and change across time, the direction of stability (increasing or decreasing), and the timing of stability and change (impressionable years). These themes are embedded in many studies of the development of aggressive behavior. In one example, Gottfredson and Hirschi theorize that levels of low self-control become apparent around age 8 and then become a stable personality characteristic. This is an example of the "impressionable years" model. Yet the important point to take away from Alwin is that it is not enough to assess the stability of a trait or behavior. What is necessary and more interesting is establishing the trajectories of stability.

Understanding these trajectories, or which model best "fits the facts," will help researchers better pinpoint the causes and correlates that predict or covary with stability and change across the life course. Characterizing the period from infancy through toddlerhood as a period of marked behavioral change is one thing; knowing the processes that place certain toddlers on a path toward stable aggressive behavioral patterns and others on prosocial trajectories is quite another.

Alwin (1994) also makes important differentiations between types of stability. These operative definitions of stability guide researchers in their efforts to analyze the stability of traits. Although Alwin lists four types of stability, we focus here on the two most relevant to criminological studies (p. 139):

1. Normative Stability: The preservation of a set of individual ranks on a quality within a constant population over a specified amount of time.

2. Molar Stability: The persistence of a behavior or behavioral orientation as expressed in the rate of change in that quality for an age-homogeneous cohort over a specified period of time.

Most studies on the stability of offending behavior over time are studies of normative stability. These studies generally follow over time a sample of individuals within a given age range (say, 11 to 17). Analysts will rank order individuals on their level of offending at Time 1 and then see how much, if at all, individuals have varied from their Time 1 scores at Time 2. As Alwin (1994) notes, this process does not take into account levels of stability associated with the aging process. In other words, 11-year-olds may have substantially different levels of stability on a trait or a behavior than a 17-year-old. When only aggregate levels of stability in a population are calculated, though, these differences are overlooked.

As the preceding discussion shows, levels of normative stability in the population mask varying levels of stability and change that occur within subgroups of the population. Chronological age, and the inherent understanding that chronological age is a reflection of developmental differences and processes, thus becomes an important marker by which developmental patterns can be charted and evaluated. That 11-year-olds report, on average, less exposure to delinquent peers than do 17-year-olds is important knowledge. That they will eventually reach similar levels as 17-year-olds shows the developmental nature of peer exposure and acquisition and strongly suggests that peer exposure levels eventually become normative, or stable, only at certain ages. The usefulness of this knowledge becomes even more apparent if we consider deviations within the age-homogeneous groups. If we can generally expect 11-year-olds to have an average, but low, level of delinquent peers, then 11-year-olds who are well above average in their number of delinquent peers may be on a very different life course pathway.

The above example of stability and change in delinquent peers also leads into our next set of issues. Peers—their presence and their behavior—are relatively easy to measure because there is an agreed-upon definition of what constitutes a peer. Researchers can assess peer relationships simply by asking subjects or informants to report on their number of friends and the characteristics of their friends. The important point for our purposes is that the measurement of friends does not change across time, partly because the concept of friends does not change over time. That is, the variable, or characteristic, of delinquent peers can be measured by the same set of indicators over time. The similarity of measures of an underlying construct across time is referred to as *homotypic continuity*.

Asendorpf (1992) makes a distinction between continuity and stability: Continuity refers to the "maintenance" of processes or functions, whereas stability refers to the consistency in rank order across time. In addition, "A trait is characterized by homotypic continuity if it can be operationalized by the same set of empirical indicators at different ages" (p. 122). Even so, when applied to the study of the stability of aggressive behavior, problems emerge that require a different approach.

As we mentioned earlier, the strongest predictor of future behavior is past behavior. Studies, covered later, consistently show that certain behavioral characteristics measured very early in life, such as acting impulsively and daringly, are substantively predictive of criminal behavior later in life. Yet we generally do not consider, do not label, and do not sanction the behavior of infants and toddlers as criminal. Thus, it would make no sense to measure the "criminal" behavior of young children with the same set of empirical indicators we use to measure truly criminal behavior in adults. However, given the clear associations between conduct early in life and conduct later in life, we have a strong reason to believe that they may be the product of the same underlying construct. What becomes necessary, then, is the use of *different* measures of the same underlying construct, namely, aggression, that are sensitive to differences in respondent age.

The use of age-sensitive measures of the same underlying, time-stable construct is referred to as *heterotypic continuity*. As we will address later, a substantial body of evidence shows considerable heterotypic continuity in behavior. Fussy, irritable infants are more likely to become toddlers who readily use force, such as hitting, pushing, and pulling hair. In turn, these youths are significantly more likely, barring any intervention, to become adolescents who participate in high rates of delinquent and possibly violent behavior. This process, with its roots found in infancy, extends into adulthood.

Outside of theoretical and definitional issues surrounding the study of stability, a number of analytical issues also must be considered when evaluating the validity of study findings. We address three of these issues in the next few paragraphs. First, it is well known to researchers of human development that the longer the interval between measurement waves, the lower the correlation. Cross-year correlations of criminal behavior, for instance, are typically very high, usually well above 0.60 to 0.70. These correlations will typically drop, however, when longer time spans are considered, say between Year 1 and Year 20. There is an apparent incongruity: Cross-year correlations are typically strong, but correlations between lengthy periods of measurement are considerably lower (Alwin, 1994; Asendorpf, 1992). It is tempting to interpret the drop in the correlations as evidence of behavioral change—after all, if the rank-order structure of individuals on a trait changes, the correlation coefficient will decline. Yet this interpretation may well be completely wrong for two reasons.

First, correlations are strongly affected by measurement error. The result of measurement error is to reduce the correlation between two variables. Within this context, however, error in measurement occurs over the course of many years. When this error is taken into account, it is not unusual to find that the correlations actually increase considerably (Alwin, 1994; Asendorpf, 1992). Conley (1984), for instance, found that the corrected annual level of stability in intelligence was 0.99, in extraversion and neuroticism it was 0.98, and in life satisfaction it reached 0.93.

Second, correlations are likely to fluctuate depending on the construct validity at the time the measurements are taken. Recall the discussion on heterotypic continuity—that measures of early behavior are necessarily different from measures of later behavior. If analysts examine the correlations between measures taken during infancy and early childhood and those taken later in adulthood, they likely will find somewhat small correlations. Again, is this evidence of behavioral change? Although we cannot rule out this possibility, it is equally likely that part of the explanation for the low correlation rests on the change in the construct validity of the concept being measured. Clearly, there is little definitional ambiguity in the measurement of violence committed by adolescents and adults. Yet toddlers also engage in acts of violence, apparently with some degree of regularity, but measurements taken during this time period are far more restricted and are thus less valid.

Relatedly, as discussed by Loeber and Hay (1997), offending rates are likely to fluctuate across time. High-rate offenders will reduce their level of offending, perhaps because of gaining a job or being incarcerated. When their situation changes, however, so may their rate of offending. This ebb and flow in offending rates is termed *periodicity*. The impact of periodicity on measures of delinquent and criminal involvement is to reduce the stability coefficient and thus to show change where it is questionable whether change has occurred. Studies have yet to determine precisely how much periodicity occurs. However, in one study conducted by Horney and her colleagues (Horney, Osgood, & Marshall, 1995), their results showed considerable movement into and out of offending depending on whether their study subjects were married, gained employment, or started using drugs. When their subjects gained employment, they generally reduced their participation in crime, but when their girlfriends or wives left them, their participation in crime increased. Stability coefficients fail to capture this variation and thus may tempt analysts into interpreting low correlations as evidence of change.

Empirical Findings on Stability

Early aggressive behavior is a substantial risk factor for later adjustment problems, including adult criminal conduct, automobile accidents, and mental illness (Hirschi & Gottfredson, 1994). In study after study, aggression that occurs early in the life course emerges as a robust predictor of problems that extend well into the adult years (Caspi & Bem, 1990; Huesmann, Eron, Lefkowitz, & Walder, 1984; Magnusson, Stattin, & Duner, 1983; Sampson & Laub, 1993; Wilson & Herrnstein, 1985). Indeed, virtually every study that includes measures of early problem behavior reveals that measurable individual differences, measured as early as 4 years of age and sometimes earlier, predict variation in frequent, serious adult criminal behavior. Using data from New Zealand, White, Moffitt, Earls, Robins, and Silva

(1990) found that antisocial behavior at age 11 predicted police contacts at age 15, and that "behavioral problems are the best preschool predictors of antisocial behavior at age 11" (p. 519). Similarly, in a study of a sample of children in state care who were followed through the age of 26, Zoccolillo, Pickles, Quinton, and Rutter (1992) found strong evidence that childhood conduct problems were related to a broad array of adult adjustment problems. A vast majority of youths classified as conduct disordered "showed pervasive social dysfunction as adults" (Fergusson, Horwood, & Lynskey, 1995, p. 379). As noted by Robins (1978), who summarized the results from her study of four male cohorts, "adult antisocial behavior virtually *requires* childhood antisocial behavior" (p. 611).

To date, literally thousands of studies report associations between early antisocial conduct and adolescent and adult behavior. The sheer volume of studies makes it a difficult task to review all the research in this area. Recognizing this problem, we chose instead to rely heavily on the published reviews of the stability literature and to highlight the important findings from those reviews. Readers requiring more information should consult the reviews we cite here.

Olweus (1979) is often credited with publishing the first review of empirical research on the stability of aggressive and criminal behavior. His review examined 16 separate longitudinal studies that included samples of children and adolescents from the United States, England, and Sweden and included reports dating back to 1935. These studies followed youths from a range of 2 years to 18 years, with sample sizes that ranged from 24 subjects to more than 400 subjects; an average of 116 subjects was used to calculate the correlation coefficients. The research subjects who comprise these studies were assessed through multiple methods, including direct observation by trained researchers, reports from teachers, clinical ratings, and reports from peers.

Overall, Olweus (1979) reported an average stability correlation of 0.63 between Time$_1$ and Time$_2$ aggressive behavior. That is, across all studies in his review, knowing a person's relative level of aggression at Time$_1$ accounts for almost 40% of the total variance in aggression at Time$_2$. Average levels, or means, however, can be highly influenced by extreme cases, or outliers. In this case, estimates of average levels of stability also can be influenced by other factors that can systematically increase or decrease the estimate of behavioral stability. For example, Olweus found that the magnitude of the stability correlation dropped substantially when the interval between Time$_1$ and Time$_2$ was increased—that is, when the follow-up period was extended. If researchers initially evaluate youths at 2 years and then again at age 3 and once more at age 10, they are likely to find a strong correlation from age 2 to age 3, but then a sharp drop in the size of the correlation from age 2 to age 10. For this reason, Olweus *disattenuated* the stability coefficients.

Although a more complete understanding of statistics is necessary to understand disattenuation, think of any test as composed of three parts: a true score, or a score that you would actually obtain without the influence of any error; an observed score, or the score that you earned; and error, which includes the influence of factors not captured by the observed score. The larger the difference between the true score and the observed score, the greater the error in measurement. As this applies to disattenuated correlations, error, which is present at Time$_1$, accumulates over time, or with an increased interval between follow-up periods, and thus has the effect of reducing the estimate of stability. Disattenuation simply corrects for this problem by accounting for the error in the measurement of aggression over time.

When Olweus applied this standard to his studies, he found that the average stability correlation increased from 0.63 to 0.79. That is, knowing a youth's relative level of aggression at $Time_1$ accounts for almost 64% of the variance in aggression at $Time_2$. Moreover, when Olweus examined whether the source of the evaluation influenced the measure of stability, he found that the average stability associated with direct observations was 0.81, and that associated with the use of teacher ratings was 0.79. He concluded that, at least over short periods of time, the source of the evaluative information was not associated with the measures of stability. Hence, he concluded that evidence collected from varying sources and from different countries, using varying definitions of aggression, and employing different lengths of follow-up and diverse age groups, converged to show that aggressive behavior is relatively stable over time. To give some impression of how stable aggressive behavior is over time, Olweus also made the case that aggression is as stable as IQ—one of the most studied individual traits in the world and the one trait that shows substantial stability across time and settings.

Three years after the publication of Olweus's seminal review, Loeber (1982) published his review of the research literature on the stability of aggression over time. Outside of including more studies in his analysis, Loeber evaluated specific hypotheses drawn from prior research on stability. More specifically, Loeber hypothesized the following:

- Youths who engage in extremely high rates of misbehavior early in life are more likely to continue over time to engage in antisocial conduct.
- Youths who show antisocial behavior across settings, such as school and home, are more likely to continue their antisocial conduct.
- Youths who engage in a variety of antisocial acts, as opposed to a limited number of acts, are at increased risk of continuing antisocial behavior into the future.
- The earlier the onset of antisocial behavior, the more likely it is to continue.

Following Loeber, we review each hypothesis sequentially.

First, are children who display high levels of antisocial conduct more likely to persist over time in their misbehavior? Loeber refers to this as the density hypothesis, largely to emphasize the difference between youths in the frequency of their antisocial behavior. According to Loeber (1982), "The results support the notion that youths who are extremely antisocial early in life continue to be antisocial later in life" (p. 1434).

For example, analyzing data from the National Youth Survey, Loeber (1982) found that youths with high levels of self-reported delinquency were very likely (probability equaled 0.59) to continue their offending into the next year. At the other end of the continuum, those who reported the lowest levels of delinquent involvement at $Time_1$ were substantially more likely to report very low levels at

Time$_2$ (probability equaled 0.75). Thus, youths at the high and low ends of the delinquency continuum were the most likely to remain stable. Data from Patterson (1982) and Lefkowitz, Eron, Walder, and Huesmann (1977) also reveal similar patterns. Lefkowitz et al. analyzed children from third grade through a 10-year follow-up. At the end of the 10 years, they had peers rate the child's aggression. Overall, they found a 10-year stability of 0.38, which is rather modest. Patterson, however, reanalyzed Lefkowitz et al.'s data and found that all the youths who initially scored above the 95th percentile scored above the median 10 years later. Finally, Osborn and West (1978), who followed a group of London boys, found that those rated "very troublesome" by their teachers at age 8 to 10 were very likely to become recidivistic criminals by the age of 19 and to continue their offending through the age of 24. As Loeber notes, only 5.8% of the remaining boys became recidivists.

Finally, analyzing data from a cohort of New Zealand youths born in 1972 and 1973, Moffitt (1990) identified and analyzed a group of boys who scored above the mean on misbehavior at ages 3, 5, 7, 9, 11, 13, and 15 years of age. Moreover, she relied on the reports of various agents, including self-reports, reports from teachers, and parental reports. Although the subgroup of boys constituted less than 6% of the overall sample, Moffitt found that much of the stability in the overall sample was driven by the very consistent misbehavior of this small group of youths. Overall stability coefficients were substantially reduced when these frequent, stable offenders were removed from the analysis.

In summary, it appears that youths who demonstrate very high levels of antisocial behavior, or conversely, very low levels of antisocial behavior, are the youths whose behavioral patterns are the most likely to remain stable over time. It is important to note, moreover, that prosocial behavior appears to have the strongest degree of stability across time. This fact has eluded most criminologists, largely because of their focus on antisocial and criminal conduct. That the extremes of antisocial and prosocial behavior appear the most immune to change, however, is not disputed.

Second, do youths who misbehave across settings, such as home or school, show higher levels of stability? Perhaps unsurprisingly, the data appear to support this hypothesis. Research shows that youths who misbehave regardless of context generally appear to be the same youths who have a high frequency of antisocial conduct. That is, youths who misbehave at home, in the classroom, at church, and in the neighborhood are more likely to continue misbehaving into the future and across contexts than are youths whose behavior problems are isolated within a single context. Certain adolescents, for example, may show behavioral problems only while in school, but others may demonstrate antisocial conduct across a range of settings.

Evidence of this fact comes from diverse sources. Using reports from teachers to measure conduct within a school setting, and reports from parents to measure conduct within the home, Mitchell and Rosa (1981) found that when the joint reports of parents and teachers were used to predict outcomes, their predictions were stronger than if they relied on the reports of parents or teachers separately. Using parent reports, Mitchell and Rosa found that 14.3% of children who were stealers ultimately became recidivistic stealers. The corresponding number for teachers was 45.5%. However, when combined, parent and teacher reports correctly identified

71.4% of recidivistic stealers. Similar results were found when Mitchell and Rosa examined lying, a subtle form of aggression. Half of the youths identified through the use of combined parent and teacher reports became recidivistic liars, compared to only 11.9% identified by parents and 25% identified by teachers. In another study, Pulkkinen (1982) studied 196 Finnish men and found that a combined peer- and teacher-rated aggression measure correlated at 0.31 with the number of criminal offenses measured at age 20.

Third, is the variety of antisocial acts a better predictor of future misbehavior than any single act? Loeber (1982) refers to this possibility as the variety hypothesis to highlight the diversity of antisocial acts within the behavioral repertoire of the individual. Certain youths, for instance, may steal when the opportunity presents itself. Other youths, however, will steal, commit arson, push others around, and get into fights.

This tendency to engage in a broad spectrum of deviant and criminal acts is referred to as the *generality* of deviance. Several studies, for instance, show that older adolescent and adult criminals commit multiple types of crimes—everything from selling narcotics to burglary to auto theft (Hirschi & Gottfredson, 1994). Moreover, their versatility in offending and preference for risky behaviors extends consequences into other domains of their life, as they are also far more likely than average individuals to commit suicide, abuse their children, and be involved in motor vehicle accidents (Jessor, 1998). This general tendency, or pattern, to behave in risky ways, such as not wearing a seat belt while driving recklessly, stands in stark contrast to the popular image of criminals who *specialize* in committing certain types of crimes, such as bank robbery. Although some data show that certain individuals prefer to commit limited types of crimes, such as narcotics distribution and other economically related crimes, the vast majority of serious and frequent offenders are characterized by a general tendency to commit a wide variety of crime (Farrington, 1982; Farrington, Snyder, & Finnegan, 1988; Gottfredson & Hirschi, 1990).

Available data also seem to support the hypothesis that individuals who engage in a diverse assortment of criminal and risky behaviors are far more likely to exhibit the highest levels of temporal stability in their conduct. Chronic adolescent offenders are significantly more likely to become frequent offenders as adults (McCord, 1983), to be arrested as adults (Sampson & Laub, 1993), and to have been rated as highly aggressive as young children (Robins, 1966; Stattin & Magnusson, 1989; West & Farrington, 1977). Analyzing data from the Cambridge Study of Delinquent Development, a prospective study of 411 London males, Farrington (1991) found that almost half of the males rated as highly aggressive at ages 8 and 10 were still the most aggressive at age 32 (compared to only one third of the remaining sample). Moreover, his analyses also revealed that youths rated as highly aggressive (between the ages of 8 and 10 or 12 and 14) were significantly more likely to be convicted of a violent crime as an adult; to have committed domestic abuse; to have suffered long periods of unemployment; to be heavy smokers; to have driven repeatedly while intoxicated; to be heavy drinkers; and to report committing a wide variety of crimes, from auto theft to vandalism to fraud. More recent analyses of his Cambridge data confirm these results.

Fourth, are those who experience an early onset of aggressive and criminal behavior more likely to continue their offending into the adult years? This hypothesis rests on the assumption that the onset of misbehavior represents an important dimension to understanding the duration of a criminal career. The earlier a career starts, the argument goes, the longer it will last and the more serious, in terms of adult crime, it will become. Age of onset thus focuses attention on three specific aspects of offending: timing, duration, and severity (Loeber & LeBlanc, 1990).

Turning again to findings drawn from Farrington's Cambridge data, it appears that the earlier the onset of aggressive and criminal behavior, the longer the individual will be involved in crime and the more serious the types of crimes committed. For example, Farrington (1991) found that youths convicted before the age of 16 constituted a group of highly active offenders as adults. This small group of youths, which contains only 23 out of the initial 411 males studied by Farrington, were convicted more than five times each and accounted for almost half of all crimes reported by the entire sample (similar results were found by Elliott, 1994, in his analysis of data from the National Youth Survey). Upon further analysis, Farrington found that 11 males were first convicted between the ages of 10 and 11, 6 were convicted between the ages of 12 and 13, 6 between the ages of 14 and 15, and another 6 at the age of 15 (see Loeber, 1982). Not only were those males who were convicted prior to age 16 more criminally involved as adults their crimes also tended to be more serious. Also, it appears that the earlier in life an arrest occurs, the higher the rate of offending over time. Youths whose first arrest occurred before the age of 13 had a rate of crime two to three times higher than that of youths arrested later in life (Cohen, 1986). Moreover, the duration of their offending also appears substantially longer—that is, individuals with an early age of onset are more active, or chronic, in their offending, and they offend over a relatively longer period of time (DeLisi, 2005; LeBlanc & Fréchette, 1989).

The studies mentioned thus far have relied primarily on measures of arrest, or official intervention. Although somewhat suitable, valid, and reliable, these measures fail to capture the precise timing when youths actually begin to offend. We know, for example, that the odds of being arrested are driven by the type of crime committed, with more serious crimes having an increased likelihood of arrest, and by the frequency with which a person offends, with higher-rate offenders more likely to be arrested (Blumstein et al., 1986). Self-report data, on the other hand, offer researchers a way to assess the age of onset without reliance on official records. For instance, Tolan (1987) asked a sample of youths between the ages of 15 and 18 to indicate when, after age 9, they had committed certain minor offenses, such as vandalism and theft. He then established two groups, an early-onset group, before the age of 12, and a late-onset group. Comparisons made between the groups revealed that the early-onset group had a rate of self-reported offending 3.5 times higher than the late-onset group. More revealing, when Tolan categorized the types of self-reported criminal behaviors by severity, he found that early-onset offenders engaged in serious felonies at a rate eight times higher than that of late-onset offenders. Similar findings were detected by Fréchette and LeBlanc (1979), who found that early starters had a rate of offending 2.5 times higher than a group of late starters. The differences became larger over time, thus showing that the earlier the age of onset, the higher the rate of self-reported offending and the longer the duration of the criminal career.

Other studies, however, point to an even earlier age of onset than that measured by Tolan or through studies that rely on official data. When the behaviors of preschool youngsters have been examined, for instance, researchers often find that hyperactive, impulsive youths who show marked behavioral deficits and signs of conduct disorder are the very youths most likely to show high levels of behavioral stability through life. In one study of hyperactive preschoolers who were followed up at age 6, researchers found that the highest levels of stability were for those whose misbehaviors were severe and across multiple settings (Schleifer et al., 1975).

As Campbell, Shaw, and Gilliom (2000) note, recent studies conducted on even younger children show that aggressive behaviors, or what they refer to as *externalizing behaviors,* are relatively stable from toddlerhood to above age 5 (Cummings, Iannotti, & Zahn-Waxler, 1989; Pierce, Ewing, & Campbell, 1999). In one such study, Caspi and Silva (1995) had the behaviors of 3-year-olds observed through the use of "testers," who evaluated the children using a series of psychological tests. They found that a range of variables, such as low impulse control and negative responsivity—what they characterized as a "lack of control"—predicted problem behaviors well into the future—that is, through ages 9, 11, 13, and 15 years. In another study of clinically referred youths, Speltz, McClellan, DeKlyen, and Jones (1999) found that 71% of 4-year-old boys diagnosed with Oppositional Defiance Disorder (ODD) were again classified with ODD 2 years later. And in two studies of nonclinical children, Campbell (1990, 1997) reported that more than 50% of a sample of children with behavioral problems remained stable from age 3 through middle childhood.

Summarizing the literature on the stability of problem behavior, Campbell et al. (2000) state that "the results of studies of young children with externalizing problems beginning as early as age 2 or 3 years indicate moderate to strong continuity when symptoms of disruptive behavior are frequent, relatively severe, and pervasive" (p. 474). Interestingly, Loeber (1982) reached similar conclusions. He notes that "early onset of delinquency is predictive of a chronic offense pattern, characterized by a large volume of crimes committed by a small proportion of youths" (p. 9). These youths tend to engage in more serious crimes and, before their first arrest, already display high rates of antisocial behavior at school, probably also in their family home, and in the neighborhood. Thus, numerous studies show that the earlier the onset of problem behavior—whether it is measured through the use of official records, such as arrest; direct observation; or maternal reports—the higher the likelihood that the problem behaviors will continue over time (stability), and that these behavioral patterns will become frequent and pervasive (chronicity and generality) (for an excellent review of issues related to the age of onset, see Farrington et al., 1990). We will discuss this issue in more detail in later chapters.

Thus far, we have seen that problem behaviors are more likely to persist when they occur early in the life course, when they are frequent, and when they are pervasive. Yet another important piece of information concerning the stability of aggressive behavior is mostly missing from published reviews—that is, highly aggressive behavior is found not only within individuals across settings, but within families across generations. Simply put, crime appears to be a consistent feature of some families. Known as *intergenerational continuity,* research in this vein seeks to establish the degree of similarity between aggressive behavioral patterns in one generation and the next.

Although the mechanisms that translate crime from one generation to the next are likely complicated and varied, basic research in this area demonstrates that criminal parents are more likely to have offspring who themselves engage in delinquent and criminal behavior (Farrington, 1978). This empirical relationship was found in Glueck and Glueck's (1950) analysis of two groups of boys, 500 delinquents and a matched group of 500 nondelinquents; in Farrington's analysis of 411 males from his Cambridge Youth Development Study (1978); and in McCord and McCord's (1959) analysis of Boston youths. But the most powerful evidence to date comes from the research of Huesmann et al. (1984), who studied 600 subjects, their parents, and their children over the course of 22 years. Like most studies, Huesmann and his colleagues found significant levels of stable aggressive behavior across subjects and across time. More importantly, however, their research also showed that aggressive behavioral patterns measured early in the life course, at age 8, predicted variation in levels of aggression of their offspring 22 years later. Indeed, the measures of stability were stronger across generations than they were across individuals within generations. For this reason and others that we will cover later, we believe the evidence shows that higher levels of criminal stability can be expected from youths born into families where aggression and criminal behavior have been normative features of life across generations.

Review of the Stability of Problem Behavior

The above review, along with reviews already published (Campbell et al., 2000; Loeber, 1982; Olweus, 1979), arrive at similar conclusions. Considerable stability exists in behavior, but levels of stability are higher for certain youths. As mentioned earlier, the highest level of stability can be found in very prosocial youths. Children who demonstrate substantial signs of compliance behavior, who regularly negotiate the complex interchanges between themselves and their peers, and who recognize and adjust to the varying behavioral regulations that differentiate contexts show substantial stability in their behavior.

At the other end of this spectrum, however, are the youths who show very early signs of behavioral maladaptation. Their behavioral problems manifest very early in life, as early as ages 2 to 3; manifest across behavioral settings, including the family, the preschool, and the neighborhood; and are frequent and pervasive. That is, youths who show early signs of inappropriate aggressive behavior, who show aggressive behavior across a variety of places and periods of time, and who show a general inability to regulate their own conduct are substantially more likely to manifest behavioral problems as adolescents and to engage in a wide variety of frequent criminal acts as adults.

It is important to point out, however, that the proportion of youths who follow the path from early to later problem behavior (often referred to as life course persistent) is fairly small. Several studies converge to show that only 5% to 6% of youths from any cohort demonstrate such high levels of stability across time. Analysis of data on children from Montreal revealed that only 5% became chronically aggressive (Nagin & Tremblay, 1999), whereas data from New Zealand showed that about 7% followed a life course-persistent trek from ages 3 to 18. Similar patterns were detected by Shaw, Owens, Vondra, Keenan, and Winslow (1996), who found that only 6% of children in their sample became persistent aggressive youths. Taken together, these findings point to a relatively small group of children who show very early and very serious signs of behavioral problems as those most likely to become serious, violent adult criminals. It is also important to note that although the absolute magnitude of the correlation between behaviors measured early in life and behaviors measured later in life may vary considerably, when more appropriate statistical techniques are used that account for the error in measurement that occurs over time, correlation coefficients reflect very substantial levels of stability across time in aggressive behavior.

BOX 2.1   The Continuing Saga of Stanley: Stability and Change

Stanley was born and raised in the inner city of Chicago. His offending shows a great deal of stability, starting at age 6. Stanley was picked up by police seven times during the year in which he was 6 years old (which included offenses of running away and begging for food). Furthermore, official records show that 31 offenses (the variety of these acts will be reviewed later) were recorded by Chicago police before he turned 18. Periods of time in which Stanley was not actively picked up by police generally represent the times that he was institutionalized or was inhibited by other activities (e.g., work). Therefore, this pattern of behavior tends to support more general theories of crime that claim that an individual who has certain dispositions toward committing crime will be likely to do so if given the opportunity. Given Stanley's locale (inner-city Chicago [the "Loop"]), he had plenty of opportunity to commit a variety of crimes, which he often did.

However, a general perspective of Stanley's offending career is lacking in providing answers to why he did not commit offenses at certain times when he had the opportunity. Although readers do not yet know the details of these episodes, in the following chapters we will examine periods in which Stanley was influenced by life events and he chose not to engage in offending. Such observations of an individual who previously demonstrated a high propensity to commit crime, but chooses not to engage in illegal behavior, provide strong support for the developmental/life course perspective of criminality. Ultimately, the case of Stanley will show that this type of theoretical framework is more valid in understanding his offending (or nonoffending) over time than is a more static, general perspective of criminality.

Stanley's case is particularly beneficial because his biological, psychological, and environmental characteristics have been recorded, and these factors (especially with his insightful recollection of additional details) can be used to build a better understanding of the stability and changes in his offending trajectory. Such factors will be examined in subsequent chapters.

Conclusion

All complex systems seek out stable operating parameters. Human beings are no different in this regard. From birth to death, many of our traits and characteristics will remain relatively stable. Our read of the available evidence tells us that the signs of serious criminality emerge early, are multifaceted, and can show remarkable resistance to change. Undoubtedly, some youths will evolve off this pathway, but for those who do not, they are likely to continue to demonstrate behavioral problems across a broad swath of their life course. But what causes relative rank order stability in criminality? We tackle that question in the next chapter.

CHAPTER 3

Continuity in Antisocial Potential

You can travel along 10,000 miles and still stay where you are.

Harry Chapin, *Sequel*

Past behavior predicts future behavior. Indeed, as we found out in the previous chapter, past behavior is the strongest predictor of future behavior known to social scientists. Still, although the available evidence shows clearly that stable behavioral patterns are characteristic of most people, little is known about the mechanisms that produce and maintain these behavioral patterns. Many scientists, however, point out that underlying observable misbehaviors is a latent, or unobservable, multifactorial tendency to continually violate social norms and laws. This general tendency, or what we call *criminality,* resides within individuals and is subject to multiple influences. What causes continuity in criminality is a crucial question in the study of crime, however, because understanding continuity has deep theoretical, practical, and personal implications.

First, if criminality is immune or resistant to change, then theories that point to categorical differences between offenders and nonoffenders are necessary to explain delinquency and crime. That is, if antisocial behavior, once established, remains a defining behavioral characteristic for certain youths, then the causes of crime will have to differentiate offenders from those who refrain from offending. Offenders, for example, likely have personality characteristics that differ significantly from nonoffenders. These differences, in turn, may appear early in the life course and become stable interpersonal characteristics that predispose some toward crime. Thus, theories that do not address the varying developmental trajectories that lead to crime may be invalid. Theories that do not account for stable individual differences may be empirically unfounded.

Second, at a more practical level, stable antisocial patterns of conduct may imply that planned interventions, such as Head Start and other rehabilitative efforts, are likely to be less than effective in reducing criminal behavior. Or, conversely, these findings may translate into the need to intervene early, before the consolidation of criminality can take place and before a pattern of criminal conduct can materialize. Moreover, if we can accurately and reliably assess factors that lead to an early onset of problem behavior, then interventions can be focused on those at greatest risk for later misconduct.

Third, appreciating stable differences in criminality naturally draws attention to the life course development of chronically troublesome youths. Criminally motivated adolescents do not do well in school; they do not appear to learn at similar rates as other youths, and they have problems with peer relationships and substance abuse. In short, the life course of antisocial youths is replete with problems that place them at increased risk for later adult crime, adult unemployment, early death, suicide, and imprisonment.

Finally, by examining the *continuity* of criminality over time, we may be better able to separate causes at one time period from correlates at another. This approach is referred to as the *stepping stone approach* because it recognizes that previous experiences and behaviors serve as the template for future experiences and behaviors. When faced with novel environments, for example, humans often draw on past experiences with similar environments to guide them. As such, causes of behavior at one point in time may be mere correlates at a future time period.

Continuity

Continuity is not the same thing as stability. Recall from Chapter 2 that stability refers to the relative consistency over time in rankings of delinquency and crime. Certain children score relatively high on measures of misbehavior over time, whereas others score consistently low. Continuity refers to the psychological structures, traits, or learned behaviors that carry forward from one developmental time period to the next. Continuity can also refer to the relative consistency in personality traits (Asendorpf, 1992) and how these dispositions relate to how decisions and choices are made over time. Finally, because continuity reflects the influence of prior experiences and traits, it reflects the "strength of previously achieved states, and therefore the probability of their repetition; it implies sameness, familiarity, and predictability" (Siegel, 1999, p. 219).

Continuity can be observed at any point along the life cycle. Children, for example, learn from and adapt to their immediate social environment. They learn, for instance, whether their environment is dangerous and packed with risks. They learn whether their environment is responsive to their needs and wants, and they learn how to manipulate their environment in ways that may increase their satisfaction and safety. As they age and are exposed to a greater number of social contexts, contexts that may be radically different from their initial learning environment, they import psychological structures and behavioral expectations formed from past experiences (continuity).

To illustrate this point, consider a toddler who has spent the past 4 years being socialized by his emotionally hostile and neglectful mother. Regardless of his pre-existing traits, the child has likely learned that his environment was unresponsive to his physical and psychological needs. In turn, the child acted out by throwing temper tantrums to gain the attention of his mother and to have basic needs met, such as being fed. This process was sustained and replicated over time. Later, at age 5, the child is placed in a day care center where nurturance, support, and direction are available and consistent. Although the environments may be very different, the child may still act out because he has carried with him psychological expectations (memories) about his home environment, and because he has acquired behaviors consistent with his expectations (Siegel, 1999). In turn, his behavior may be the subject of scorn and punishment by his caregivers, who hold different expectations for their environment.

As the above example shows, continuities in behavior, personality traits, and psychological functioning propel individuals into interactions with varying environments and with a wide range of individuals (who themselves have environmental expectations and accompanying behaviors). Continuity thus occurs at the level of the individual trait, at the level of social relationships, and at the level of the social environment. Continuity may be demonstrated at any level and may interact with any other level.

Heterotypic, Homotypic, and Cumulative Continuity

Is there a connection between a 2-year-old's kicking and slapping of others and an 18-year-old who engages in physical assaults, commits rape, or belongs to a gang? Is there a connection between a child who throws a temper tantrum and adult unemployment? The answers might surprise you.

Casual observations, as well as controlled studies of young children, highlight the fact that many behaviors demonstrated by toddlers would be sanctioned as "criminal" if committed by someone older. Toddlers are well known for their ability to pull hair, punch, and kick (assault and battery), their curiosity and willingness to play with matches (arson), and their unrestrained motivation to make other children's toys their own (theft). Toddlers, by most accounts, are the most criminal group in society!

Of course, we do not label the misbehavior of young children as worthy of criminal sanction. Our unwillingness to officially label the conduct of young children as "criminal," however, does not mean that their early antisocial behavior is unrelated to their future criminal behavior. As they grow older and acquire greater muscle mass and physical dexterity, for example, their criminality becomes more noticeable because it creates greater risks to others (Loeber & LeBlanc, 1990). A punch, a slap, or a kick put forward by a 2-year-old is *qualitatively* different from the same behavior committed by a physically well-developed 18-year-old male. The point is, over time, certain youths will continue to engage in fights with other youths, continue to steal, and continue to act in ways that are dangerous to themselves and others. These *very same* behaviors are demonstrated by young children and thus may serve as precursors to more serious forms of antisocial behavior later in life. In short, for some youths, there is continuity in their antisocial behavior over time.

Continuity over time in the same types of behaviors, such as hitting, kicking, and punching, or traits, such as intelligence or impulsivity, is referred to as *homotypic* continuity. Homotypic continuity refers to "sameness" or "similarity" over time. A trait or behavior shows homotypic continuity if it can be measured by the same set of indicators over time. To continue with the example of the antisocial 2-year-old who shows a continuous pattern of antisocial behavior through the age of 18, we can measure his aggression at 2 and his aggression at age 18 by some of the same indicators: frequency of fighting, stealing, and lying, for example.

As people age, however, they acquire a broader range of behaviors. In particular, antisocial adolescents and adults will engage in a wide variety of illicit and imprudent behaviors in which young antisocial children cannot participate. They will, for instance, experiment with and become addicted to drugs or will drive recklessly—behaviors typically out of the domain of young children. This tendency for antisocial youths to engage in a broad pattern of delinquent and criminal conduct is referred to as the *generality* principle. Numerous studies show that antisocial teens and adults report committing a broad range of illegal and imprudent behaviors (Elliott, 1994). Those who report selling drugs are also likely to report committing burglary and employing the services of prostitutes. In contrast, few offenders "specialize," or restrict their offending to a few isolated acts (Gottfredson & Hirschi, 1990; Hirschi & Gottfredson, 1994).

The generality of offending highlights the diverse types of antisocial behaviors in which criminally motivated adults and adolescents engage. Just because antisocial children have yet to fully mature and do not have opportunities to commit certain types of crimes does not mean that their early antisocial conduct is unrelated to their future pattern of imprudent and illegal conduct. When behaviors or traits take different forms over time, but are caused by the same underlying characteristic, they are referred to as *heterotypic*. Continuity in criminal behavior appears to be heterotypic—that is, continuities in antisocial conduct can be measured and assessed using *different* behavioral items that are representative of an underlying trait.

The differences between homotypic and heterotypic continuity are illustrated in Figure 3.1. Both forms of continuity are concerned with similarities over time, as evidenced from the focus on different age periods. The upper panel showing homotypic continuity in behaviors highlights an example of identical behaviors expressed over a 16-year developmental period. The lower panel also focuses on the same 16-year developmental period, but it includes two important differences. The first noticeable difference is that the behaviors change over time. Although still considered antisocial, if not criminal, the behaviors expressed at age 18 are not the same as those expressed earlier. The second difference, however, is what ties together early misbehavior (lying, stealing, etc.) to later misbehavior (drug abuse, theft, etc.)—that is, an underlying antisocial trait (criminality) that is responsible for the expression of aggressive and imprudent behavior at each developmental period.

Certain behaviors and traits are obviously homotypic, like kicking and punching. These behaviors can be expressed repeatedly over time and across a variety of behavioral contexts. And because these characteristics are present very early in life, they

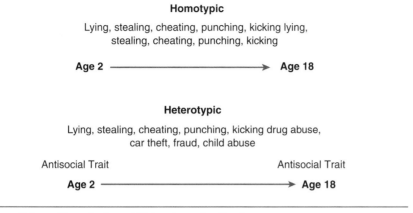

Figure 3.1   Homotypic and Heterotypic Continuity

may provide the foundation for other behaviors; kicking turns into walking as gross motor functions are refined, for instance. From an evolutionary viewpoint, they may also be the rudimentary methods that allow for self-protection and thus for survival. However, as youths age, they generally reduce in frequency their use of overt aggression—that is, they stop kicking and punching to get what they want (Tremblay et al., 1999). For chronically antisocial youths, though, there is a strong degree of continuity to their behavior. In kindergarten, they will punch and kick other kids when provoked or when they desire something. In junior high school, they will punch and kick others, including teachers and other authority figures. Their aggression, or at least their methods of aggression, can be traced backwards in time.

Early, chronic, antisocial conduct, however, often branches into other forms of antisocial behavior. Children who kick and punch in grade school may expand their repertoire of antisocial behavior to include a full range of imprudent and aggressive behaviors as adolescents or adults. For example, they may be more inclined to verbally abuse and assault their classmates and teachers; they may be more inclined to lie, steal, and cheat; they may be more inclined to use violence instrumentally and expressively. Thus, the expansion of antisocial behaviors beyond those homotypic antisocial behaviors draws attention to the possibility that antisocial conduct emanates from a central antisocial trait that is responsible for the breadth of antisocial behaviors. Antisocial behavior expands over time as opportunities for deviance broaden and as the individual's physical and cognitive capacities mature. Heterotypic continuity thus draws our attention to the linkages between the diverse manifestations of antisocial behaviors.

All antisocial conduct generates consequences. Some of these consequences are immediate, some are short-term, and some extend consequences that are prolonged and life altering. When young children display high rates of misbehavior, they are likely to be excluded by other, more prosocial children. They are likely to stir the ire of teachers, to be labeled as deviant, and to fail in school. Of course, failing in school and dropping out before obtaining a high school degree set the conditions for economic hardship well into the adult years. And participating in criminal behavior as a young adult can land a person in jail, prison, or the morgue. Thus, the power of antisocial behavior is that it often creates interpersonal and social problems that mortgage further the life chances of antisocial individuals. Without an education, complex social skills, and the discipline and self-control necessary to avoid the pitfalls and obstacles present in life, many antisocial youths become enmeshed in the sticky web of consequences generated from their conduct. In scientific terms, this is called *cumulative* continuity.

Behavior is sustained by its consequences. Children who are hyperactive and temperamental tax the patience of the best parents, who then generally withdraw support and react with increased hostility (Patterson, 1980). Left unchanged, the child's temperament will cause him or her to become isolated from other children, depriving the youth of age-appropriate role models and opportunities for prosocial growth. The net consequence of the child's interactional style is that his or her development becomes embedded in social relationships characterized by negativity, hostility, and aversive punishment. Of course, the texture of life is composed of routine, day-to-day interactions with others. When these interactions are predominantly negative and aversive, as they are when aggressive youths and adults interact with others, they tend to generate feelings of anger and resentment. Misbehavior and lack of acknowledgment of social rules of civility can cut off immediate and future opportunities for prosocial advancement. In this way, aggressive interactional styles accumulate consequences that only further embed youths in a lifestyle characterized by disrespect and disrepute.

State Dependence and Population Heterogeneity

How does antisocial behavior affect the lives of antisocial people? From the state dependence perspective, antisocial behavior generates a range of immediate and future consequences that alters the likelihood of future misbehavior. These consequences, or reactions, potentially limit future opportunities for prosocial growth while they simultaneously increase the possibility for future antisocial conduct. Thus, the future state of the individual is altered by previous states, linking prior misbehavior to future misbehavior.

In more concrete terms, the state dependence perspective draws attention to the personal impact of antisocial and criminal behavior on the lives of offenders. It is not difficult to envision how participation in crime may affect individuals. For instance, as youths deepen their penetration in crime and deviance, their bonds to conventional society may weaken; working at McDonalds' and other conventional but rather low-status jobs becomes a subject of ridicule and contempt. The stress and strain they feel may increase as their precarious relationships with significant others crumble because of their lack of honesty and commitment. Or, similarly, as they become more skilled in the use of aggression as a mechanism to achieve their goals, they may realize increased incentives that accompany acting aggressively, such as a reputation for fearlessness, as well as the subtle rewards that often accompany misbehavior. Nagin and Paternoster (2000) note that crime "transforms the offender's life circumstances in such a profound way that it alters the probability that subsequent criminal acts will occur" (p. 118).

But if life events can alter the life of an offender for worse, the opposite is also true—discontinuity can be produced by changes in the life circumstances of aggressive and criminal individuals (Horney, Osgood, & Marshall, 1995). Life experiences have the potential to redirect the trajectories of offenders, regardless of their age and their prior experiences with aggression. Prior research identifies specific turning points in the life course that may alter the likelihood of future misbehavior. These turning points include the acquisition of quality employment (Sampson & Laub, 1993), marriage to a nondeviant spouse, or the psychological and physiological changes that accompany aging (Shover, 1996).

From the state dependence perspective, transitions in the life course occur when new roles, and the novel experiences that accompany these roles, adjust the probabilities of future misbehavior. Consider marriage to a nondeviant spouse as an example. Marriage to a nondeviant spouse may offer an offender desirable emotional support or new scripts from which prosocial behavior can be modeled and reinforced. It can also create the conditions under which broad and effective social control is exercised—that is, someone else becomes intimately connected to the ebb and flow of an offender's life. This person can exercise control over the choices the offender makes, manage his or her time, and monitor his or her whereabouts. Marriage may also disrupt previous behavioral routines, reduce the time offenders have to spend in pursuit of criminal enterprises, and limit or shatter preexisting networks to criminal others.

Contrast this perspective against those who argue that individual differences in human aggression are relatively stable across time and setting. Population heterogeneity theorists, such as Gottfredson and Hirschi, maintain that once individual traits related to aggression and crime, such as low self-control, become a defining personal characteristic, those with the traits (low self-control) will always be more likely to commit crime. Their point is that engaging in antisocial and criminal behavior has no direct causal impact on the likelihood of acting aggressively or committing crime in the future. Why? Because the individual traits (low self-control) that produce aggression and crime at one point in time remain relatively constant across time, thus producing crime and aggression well into the future.

But what of the life events that state dependence theorists point to as creating conditions for interpersonal change? According to Gottfredson and Hirschi, role transitions and novel experiences are not likely to alter individual capacities toward crime because individual traits are largely unchangeable. Individuals low in self-control may marry, but they are significantly more likely to marry a person with similar characteristics—that is, someone who is aggressive. They may enter into the labor market and, incidentally, land a quality job, but they are also significantly more likely to be repetitively late to that job, to be frequently absent from that job, and, ultimately, to have their employment terminated.

State dependence and population heterogeneity are not mutually exclusive concepts. Certain youths are almost always at higher risk of engaging in crime and deviance across their life course. They are irritable as infants, troublesome as toddlers, difficult as adolescents, and dangerous as adults. Still, their course in life is one littered with social and personal failures that serve only to embed them in situations and relationships that make the transition from antisocial to prosocial less likely. Viewed from this perspective, state dependence and population heterogeneity are complementary concepts that help to explain why certain individuals are at increased risk of becoming antisocial and why, after antisocial conduct emerges, their conduct remains relatively enduring.

Whether prior misbehavior causes future misbehavior is still a matter of empirical debate. However, one fact remains: Characteristics exhibited by individuals early in their lives are related to their future life course outcomes, such as their level of education, their occupational status, their experience with divorce, and their involvement in crime and disrepute (Caspi, Henry, McGee, Moffitt, & Silva, 1995). Even so, the various mechanisms that connect an individual's early personality and behavior to his or her adult life course remain largely speculative. Few theories of crime, moreover, offer insight into these important connections. Given these shortcomings and the obvious importance of understanding those connections, we next examine the multiple sources of behavioral continuity. As we will see, sources of continuity appear as diverse as the outcomes associated with involvement in crime and deviance.

Sources of Continuity

Criminologists have explored at least three possible sources of behavioral continuity. The first source can be found in the community in which youths are embedded. In theory, community-based influences, such as poverty or the presence of delinquent gangs, remain constant over long periods of time and thus exert a consistent influence on antisocial youths over time. Whereas sociologists have completed extensive research into neighborhood variables responsible for high rates of crime, little research has examined how the proximate causes of antisocial behavior are maintained within these neighborhoods. There are, however, the usual suspects. For example, one of the most enduring characteristics of high-crime neighborhoods is the presence of criminal gangs and, more precisely, the dense clustering of convicted felons into a limited geographic area. Ethnographic evidence reveals the influence these individuals have in socializing young people into "the way of the street" (Anderson, 1999). Youths, particularly males, learn from an early age that toughness and aggression serve important roles in defining their manhood. These youths, the argument goes, become embedded in relationships that promote "street culture" and thereby limit their opportunities for change in the future.

Neighborhood influences on *individual* conduct have been found to be rather minor when compared to other competing variables, however (Sampson & Groves, 1995). Most research into the role of neighborhood shows that macro-level variables account for very little of the explained variance in individual misbehavior. Still, neighborhoods that are riddled with crime and saturated with criminals stand in stark contrast to the neighborhoods populated by individuals of economic means who are often better educated and less inclined to commit crime. This stark contrast highlights the numerous opportunities and incentives for crime that exist in dilapidated, largely inner-city communities.

From our point of view, continuity in criminal behavior derived from neighborhood influence comes in two forms. The first substantive influence is the opportunity structure for crime so prevalent in crime-ridden neighborhoods. Opportunities for crime are omnipotent in these places. Consider, for example, that few people can afford alarms for their vehicles or private police forces to keep their homes and apartments safe. Within these neighborhoods, the rewards for crime, including the payoff and status that come from engaging in crime, provide meaningful incentives for the criminally motivated to remain active. Given the relative ease with which most crimes can be committed and the rampant opportunities for crime embedded in the structure of most inner-city neighborhoods, it is easy to see how crime can become an integral part of the environment in which criminals and noncriminals coexist.

Relatedly, the second source of continuity, and from our point of view the most important, comes from the often overlooked and obvious fact that criminals are more densely gathered in certain neighborhoods than in others. This fact should not be discounted because criminal adults can exert a strong, negative influence on the well-being of a neighborhood in general and on the socialization of young people in particular. If we recognize adult criminality as the endpoint of a lengthy process of social and personal failures, then we also have to understand that adult criminality isolates individuals from the very institutions that lead to successful adult transitions, such as school and work. Indeed, the majority of adult criminals typically are high school dropouts, have limited cognitive abilities, and have extensive arrest records and criminal histories. In short, they tend to shun the very institutions that lead to successful adult transitions, such as school and work, and they tend to demonstrate antisocial values and attitudes. These values and attitudes, particularly those that glamorize and rationalize violence, theft, and other forms of crime, are passed on from the "old heads" to the younger generation. Thus, the standard supports and controls that limit aggressive behavior are turned on their heads. Arrest is no longer feared. Harming others is interpreted as a sign of strength, and going to jail or prison becomes an expectation. Crime becomes a normal way of life, a cycle that perpetuates itself and becomes difficult to break (see Figure 3.2).

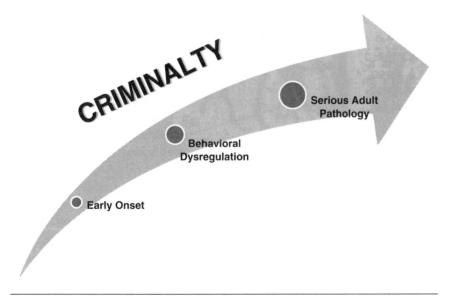

Figure 3.2   Pathway to Pathology

Genetic Continuity

Conventional wisdom suggests that genetic influences on behavior are permanent, unchanging across time. Quite the opposite is true, however. As we will discuss in future chapters, the influence that genes exert on behavior is dependent on a variety of factors. Reiss, Neiderhiser, Hetherington, and Plomin (2000) list three sources of variation that account for differential gene expression. First, a recent line of research has shown that intracellular operations that affect the encoding of amino acid sequences (DNA) and protein synthesis (RNA) influence the expression of genes. In turn, intracellular activities can be influenced by the presence of psychiatric drugs, fatigue, and stress (Glaser et al., 1990; Hyman & Nestler, 1993). Genes, it appears, are "turned on" during certain parts of the life course and "turned off" at other parts; whether they are on or off depends in part on the behavior of the individual and the source of environmental stimulation.

Second, Reiss et al. (2000) note that genetic expression is most likely to occur in environments that are conducive to the expression of specific traits. They note that as children pass through the highly structured environment of elementary school and into the less structured environment of high school, genetic differences are likely to become more obvious. As the environment shifts, so does the expression of genes.

Finally, Reiss and his colleagues maintain that genes may be responsible for the slow accumulation of deficits over time. These rather small effects build slowly over time and become obvious only later in life, when the full force of their influence on individual differences can be measured reliably.

Clearly, the influence of genes on behavior is more complex than typically realized. The complexity of the relationship makes research into this area difficult to complete, time consuming, and controversial. Yet major advances in behavioral genetics were made during the last part of th 20th century. These advances have shed light onto the role that genetic influences have in creating individual differences in aggression and in the maintenance of aggression over time. By far, the most important study to date comes from Reiss et al.'s (2000) analysis of data from 720 pairs of same-sex siblings and their parents. Theirs is one of the first true large-scale, genetically informed investigations into genetic influences on stability and change in behaviors.

With that said, their analyses revealed what has become common knowledge in certain academic communities—that genetic inheritance plays a powerful role in influencing behaviors such as aggression and sociability. They found, for instance, that genetic influences accounted for 67% of the variance in aggression at Time 1 and 68% 3 years later! More importantly for our purposes, Reiss and his colleagues (2000) also found that "genetic factors accounted for 69 percent of the stability of antisocial behavior across three years of adolescent development" (p. 222). Most of the stability in behavior across the 3 years of this study was due to continuity in genetic expression. Still, this leaves 31% of the variance in aggression not explained. Although it would be tempting to say that any variance left over should be accounted for by changes in environment that produce changes in levels of stability, that, too, would be somewhat false. Further analysis revealed that changes in genetic expression also produced changes in environment, not vice versa. For instance, youths who were once socially inhibited, shy, or withdrawn and who had become more bold, vocal, or gregarious selected themselves into new and different environments.

Whereas there is clear evidence showing that genes produce measurable traits and that they are also responsible for continuity, virtually nothing is known about the mechanisms that promote changes in genetic expression. That is, why and how do genes change the expression of traits related to criminal behavior? For now, we will have to wait for evidence to accumulate.

Person-Environment Interactions

What should be clear by now is that environment or context is viewed as an important source of continuity in behavior. Whether the source of continuity is found in the relationships that are created and maintained within neighborhoods or within the complex architecture of genes, context exerts some role in the maintenance of antisocial behavior. It should not be surprising, therefore, that the third possible source of continuity in antisocial behavior is the interaction that occurs between the individual and his or her immediate environment.

The fact that individuals help create their environment is of little doubt. The individual acts and the environment responds in kind. This process of stimulus and response plays out daily in our own lives, but is more apparent when we examine the lives of antisocial youths and adults. Aggressive individuals, whether they are young at heart or old in age, often create the very conditions that further embed them in a lifestyle of crime and disrepute. How? Their behavior often breaches the boundaries of good taste and conventionality dictated by most environments. In turn, their environment responds to these breaches in conduct in ways that isolate the individual from the environment or in ways that reinforce the negative behavior.

Consider how the rules for conduct vary across environmental domains. In elementary school, for example, students are expected to follow the instructions of their teachers without hesitation; they are expected to walk to other classrooms or to the bathroom in straight lines and to remain silent in the process. They are expected to raise their hand to speak and to exercise the necessary self-control to wait until the teacher calls on them before they ask their question. If we turn our attention to the adult domain of work, we can also extract several simple expectations—that is, arrive to work daily and on time, work at a steadfast pace until break, do not take longer at break than allowed, and get along with your coworkers. Of course, by definition, aggressive and antisocial people, young and old, violate these behavioral guidelines time and again. An antisocial youth will talk without being called on by the teacher and the antisocial adult will fail to show up to work. Their improper behavior is the stimulus.

Now, consider how the environment reacts as the response. Elementary school teachers may quickly label the child as a "problem" and single out the youth for extra supervision and increased sanctions. And, of course, workers who rarely show for work can expect to be counseled or their employment terminated. In each case, it is easy to see how the conduct of the individual was complicit in shaping the environment and his or her future life chances. We call this *interactional continuity*.

Interactional continuity refers to the constant interchange that occurs between an individual and his or her immediate social environment. The work of Gerald Patterson and others at the Oregon Social Learning Center demonstrates how the process of interactional continuity unfolds within families. The stimulus-response process occurs when an antisocial youth, most often the son, acts in a way that coerces the parent(s) to react with anger and an increase in aggression. That is, the male acts out, and the parent(s) escalate the confrontation by further acting out. This standoff is often remedied when the parents withdraw from the fight, thereby reinforcing the antisocial conduct of their son. Patterson refers to this as a "coercive" family process. He has demonstrated empirically that by breaking the cycle of coercive exchanges, usually by altering the response of the parents, the overall level of aggression experienced within the household is decreased.

As should be evident, interactional continuity likely involves the confluence of personality traits, expectations, and self-concepts that merge in time and space to promote and validate antisocial conduct (Caspi, Bem, & Elder, 1989). Social scientists have identified several types of interactional continuity, with each type emphasizing something unique about the stimulus-response sequence. What they share, however, is the understanding that individuals interact with their environment; thus, these styles of interaction are also referred to as *person-environment interactions*. We address each type of interactional continuity, or person-environment interaction, below.

Evocative Person-Environment Interactions

A quick example illustrates this type of interaction: Imagine walking into a bar or tavern populated by members of the Hell's Angels motorcycle club. Once inside, you locate the largest biker in the crowd and calmly walk up to him and spit into his face. What do you believe will happen next? Will he buy you a drink so you can discuss your unprovoked aggression? Will he recoil in horror and leave the scene? Most likely, and in short order, you will be used to mop the floor, undoubtedly leaving behind some of your teeth!

Why? It takes no stretch of the imagination to understand that your aggressive action provoked a spark of violence that brought to you pain and misery. In essence, your behavior, as wreckless and as short-sighted as it was, increased the probability that you would become a "victim" of crime and violence. In short, you evoked, or provoked, a response from your immediate environment.

Although the example is brash, it does highlight the reciprocal dynamics that underscore this type of person-environment interaction. We can also see this type of dynamic occur on a more limited scale, however, and in much more regulated environments. A surplus of empirical studies now confirm that infants who are fussy and difficult to soothe tend to evoke feelings of stress, pressure, anger, and anxiety from even the best of parents (Chess & Thomas, 1977). In turn, parents of these difficult children tend to alter their parenting styles to supply less support, spending less time nurturing the child. You might say that these parents "parent from a distance," primarily because they tend to reduce their control and oversight of the child as he or she ages and becomes even more difficult to manage (see Maccoby & Jacklin, 1983). In this way, continuity in difficult and antisocial behavior is maintained as the fussy infant grows into a "terrible toddler" and then into a "troubled teen." At each stage, the child's misbehavior helps to craft his or her environment.

Provocation can be a powerful force. It can arouse anger and other destructive emotions, it can move people to violence, and it can cause the social isolation of the provocateur. Provocation is so powerful that "once hostility and aggression become significant components in the lifestyle of individuals or become woven into the coercive exchanges of a family or group, it can gain a stranglehold on relationships" (Cairns & Cairns, 1994, p. 89). This stranglehold creates enormous stress and a variety of angry emotions that flow from evocative personal exchanges. Aggressive children provoke angry reactions from their parents, resentment from teachers, and fear and anxiety from their less aggressive peers. The results are predictable: Coercive exchanges mortgage future life opportunities, "including grade failure, school suspension, and expulsion" (Cairns & Cairns, 1994, p. 89); result in fewer positive parent-to-child interactions (Buss, Block, & Block, 1980); and create social isolation through peer rejection.

Proactive Person-Environment Interactions

The tendency for people to associate with similar others appears to be a "social law." It can be found in just about every study, and it does not appear to vary much across cultures or time periods (Warr, 2002). This tendency is known by several names, including "propinquity" (Cairns & Cairns, 1994); "birds of a feather" (Glueck & Glueck, 1950); "self-selection" (Gottfredson & Hirschi, 1990); "social homophily" (Reiss & Farrington, 1991); and, in the case of dating and marriage, "assortive mating" (Rutter & Quinton, 1984).

The theme found in each term is a recognition that individuals make choices about who they wish to have as friends, who they wish to date, for whom they wish to work, and who they wish to marry. These choices are not necessarily random, but emerge as an expression of the complex of traits, characteristics, and behaviors held by the individual. Thus, individuals proactively interact with their immediate social environment by exercising choices that are themselves circumscribed by their own individual characteristics. Through their choices, individuals become the architects of their own environment. They can create social opportunities and forge meaningful alliances, or, conversely, they can create the very conditions that lead to a life of economic hardship, interpersonal turmoil, and trouble with the law.

There can be little doubt that the process of proactive involvement occurs; people are not wholly passive, reactive agents who simply allow outside circumstances to affect their lives. The evidence in favor of self-selection is just too strong and too convincing. Moreover, the evidence in favor of self-selection becomes stronger when relatively older cohorts of people are analyzed and compared to younger cohorts.

As individuals mature, three processes emerge. First, their self-regulatory abilities surface and reach a relatively stable level. Most youths gain and exercise sufficient levels of self-control and impulse inhibition, but a minority will continue to act impulsively and without much forethought to the consequences of their behavior. Second, they escape the oversight of parents and teachers. Standard sources of guidance and conformity are temporarily replaced by the omnipotent effects of peers (Warr, 2002). Third, their preferences and tastes solidify and become more obvious (Scarr, 1988). They form their own opinions, have their own values, and express their own preferences. In combination, then, as individuals mature, they begin to distinguish themselves based on their own innate abilities to regulate their own behavior and on their preferences for associating with others who hold similar values and attitudes.

In total, this process of becoming an adult, what Freud termed *individuation,* begins early in the life course when children select themselves into and out of specific same-sex play groups (Cairns & Cairns, 1994). It is obvious when adolescents elect to join certain cliques to the exclusion of others (Warr, 2002), and it is clear in the highly differentiated environment of adult employment where acceptance is based on the acquisition of educational credentials and the exercise of social judgment (Sampson & Laub, 1993; Shover, 1996). Thus, as adolescents make the transition to adulthood, some will choose to enter the military, some will elect to continue with their education, and others will choose to work at relatively low-wage jobs with little economic security or social status. The point is, the process whereby individuals act to create their own environment grows only stronger across the lifespan, when their true attitudes, feelings, motivations, traits, and characteristics begin to more completely inform their perception of available choices and alternatives. Perhaps this is also why human behavior becomes more stable over time (Caspi & Bem, 1990).

The best documented evidence in favor of self-selection comes from research into peer group formation. Criminologists have long known that associating with delinquent peers is a strong, substantive predictor of involvement in crime (Elliott, Huizinga, & Ageton, 1985; Warr, 2002). But how are delinquent peers chosen? And how are individuals chosen by the peer group? The process is not random—that is, peers within the same classroom, school, or neighborhood do not associate with each other piecemeal. Instead, they "choose activities that are compatible with their own predispositions and select companions who are similar to themselves" (Caspi & Moffitt, 1995, p. 490). For example, evidence from the Carolina Longitudinal Study found that when peer networks were disrupted by changes in classrooms, peer networks reshuffled but were very similar to the original networks.

Social homophily is thus what occurs when a person seeks out and actively matches his or her traits to the characteristics of the group. Social homophily implies similarity, sameness, and evenness within a cluster of friends. The process that creates social homophily can best be viewed when delinquent and aggressive youths select themselves into nonconforming peer groups. They accomplish this literally by shopping around. They try one group, sometimes to be met by rejection, and stop "shopping" only when they find a group that will reinforce their own attitudes, values, and behaviors.

Contrary to popular and academic notions, delinquent youths are capable of forming meaningful friendships (Hirschi, 1969). Like any friendships, they are subject to the ebb and flow of shifting allegiances, but although antisocial youths may shift their allegiances and terminate friendships, their newly founded peer group will closely resemble their old group. Stable friendship types thus emerge and function to solidify individual antisocial characteristics. In an elegant analysis of the influence of stable pairs of friends, Cairns and his colleagues found that stable peer dyads were similar in their tendencies to drop out of school (Cairns, Cairns, & Neckerman, 1989) and in their tendency to commit suicide (Cairns & Cairns, 1994). In their more elaborated analyses, Cairns and Cairns also found that peer groups are generally homogeneous in terms of their level of aggression (male and female), their popularity (females), their academic abilities (females), and their attractiveness (males and females). According to Cairns and Cairns (1994),

> Groups tend to form along any salient characteristic where similarity can be defined. This holds for sex, age, race, smoking, failing a grade, aggression, doing well in class, playing football, or being a cheerleader. Once clustered, contagious reciprocity in behaviors and actions appears, creating new types of similarities among cluster members. (p. 114)

The extent to which self-selection is prominent in the lives of adults can be seen in studies of adults and their selection of mates. These studies show that married partners tend to be more similar than different, especially in terms of physical characteristics, cognitive abilities, values and attitudes, and personality traits (Caspi & Moffitt, 1995; Epstein & Guttman, 1984). Contrary to the conventional wisdom that opposites attract, it appears to be the case that individuals prefer friends and partners with similarities to which they can relate; values and attitudes that correspond with their own; and behaviors that reinforce, not challenge, their own style of interacting (this is known in the literature as phenotypic selection, compared to social homogamy, where mates are selected because they share the same social environments). Data from Farrington's Cambridge Study in Delinquent Development indicate that 83% of males with convicted wives were themselves convicted of a crime, compared to only 35% of males with unconvicted wives (Farrington, Jolliffe, Loeber, Stouthamer-Loeber, & Kalb, 2001). Moreover, 61% of convicted fathers were married to convicted mothers, compared to only 23% of fathers married to unconvicted mothers.

Yet if there is cause to be concerned about assortative mating, it can be found in the fact that aggressive individuals are far more likely to marry others with similar predispositions. Aggressive men, for example, are far more likely to marry aggressive and antisocial women than they are to marry conforming women. The consequences are threefold: First, marriage, often a key adult transition, may generate increases in criminal behavior if one spouse reinforces the antisocial behavior of the other spouse. In this case, males who marry antisocial females may increase their involvement in crime, and vice versa. Thus, instead of deflecting criminal men off of deviant pathways, marriage to a criminal spouse further embeds them in a lifestyle of disrepute.

Second, married couples tend to share genetically inherited traits that are related to criminal involvement. Thus, if they have children, they are more likely to pass on these traits to their children. One such trait for which there is considerable evidence of heritability and a correlation to criminal behavior is novelty seeking—that is, the desire to seek out new and thrilling experiences. Studies of twins reveal that novelty seeking is about 40% heritable (Hamer & Copeland, 1999). Similar studies across cultures also show that husbands and wives typically correspond closely in novelty seeking, and that when differences in novelty seeking become measurable, so does conflict within the marriage (Hamer & Copeland, 1999).

Modern behavioral genetics has discovered that many personality traits are highly heritable. What they generally have been unable to accomplish, however, is to pinpoint specific genes matched to specific traits. Novelty seeking, though, is the exception. Scientists have found that variation in the D4DR dopamine receptor gene corresponds directly to an individual's tendency to seek out thrills and novel situations. In essence, the length of the D4DR gene, caused by variation in the base pairs that code for amino acids, corresponds closely to a person's desire to engage in thrill-seeking behavior (Benjamin et al., 1996). The evidence has been found in mice and in various human populations across the world.

Finally, aggressive parents tend to produce relatively large families. Their kids, in turn, are significantly more likely to be criminal (West & Farrington, 1977). We will cover the various reasons for this in later chapters, but for now, we note that a minority of families account for a majority of arrests and convictions. Again turning to Farrington's data, he and his colleagues found that 1% of his families ($n = 4$, containing 33 people) accumulated 448 convictions (18% of all convictions). Half of all criminal convictions were accounted for by only 6% of the families in his study ($n = 23$). Very similar trends were found in the Pittsburgh Youth Study. Eight percent of all families ($n = 117$) included 597 arrested persons (for an average of 5 arrested persons per family!).

Assortive mating and assortive pairing pose a serious problem for criminologists. Individuals actively seek out others with similar characteristics, so it becomes difficult to discern cause from effect. Because peer groups are formed largely through propinquity and social homophily, some argue that peer groups represent only an extension of an individual's traits. Therefore, the group cannot be the cause of behavior because the behavior formed temporally prior to the formation of the group. Much the same argument is applied to the ability of marriage to influence the lives of deviant men. Because antisocial men are more likely to select antisocial women as mates, it is very unlikely that marriage per se will reduce offending. Finally, when individuals with similar traits marry or have children, issues concerning heritability further complicate matters.

Although it may be useful to pit self-selection against socialization as an alternative explanation for certain outcomes, including associating with delinquent peers, it is also wholly unrealistic. From our point of view, the fact that people select themselves into environments and networks that match many of their traits and characteristics should not be used as evidence that socialization, or the effects produced from within these environments, is unimportant. Self-selection may disproportionately place some people at increased risk for crime and deviance, but associations with criminal others often produces results independent of individual characteristics.

Reactive Person-Environment Interactions

The final person-environment interaction concentrates on the manner in which people process social information. It has long been recognized that people exposed to the same environment view it, experience it, and react to it differently. This process is well recognized by police officers, detectives, and other investigators. As is often the case, eyewitnesses to the same crime will often give very contrary and conflicting descriptions of both the sequences of events and those who allegedly perpetrated the crimes. Perhaps this is why in one study of 110 men set free from prison for crimes they were convicted of but did not commit (including men who were on death row and who came within hours of execution), more than two thirds were convicted because of faulty eyewitness identification!

This tendency for people to selectively interpret their cues from their environment is longstanding. There is an old saying that captures well this perspective: "We don't see things the way they are, we see them the way we are." Translated for our purposes, events, experiences, and environments are not interpreted the same across people. One person may see and experience anger and resentment at the sight of a child being paddled, whereas another may experience satisfaction at the thought that the parent is correcting the child's behavior. Same event, different interpretation.

But how does this apply to the study of aggression and continuity? To see the connection, we first have to recognize that aggressive individuals see the world through a different lens than do nonaggressive individuals. Research consistently finds that aggressive youths interpret their world fundamentally differently than do prosocial youths. First, they are much more likely to see their world as aggressive— that is, to see aggression in the social cues that emanate from the environment. Sudden eye movements, glances, or prolonged stares from others are sometimes seen as signs of provocation. Second, aggressive people, almost by definition, view aggression and violence as an effective, if not preferred, tool to resolve problems (Boldizar, Perry, & Perry, 1989). Verbal and physical altercations are not to be avoided, but instead are the means through which a tough reputation can be built and maintained. Third, aggressive people often respond with socially inappropriate responses to novel experiences and environments. When they come across a new or novel situation, they tend to rely on previous encounters where aggression was effective. Whether or not aggression was an appropriate response the first time is irrelevant—it was effective and thus is more likely to be used when novel situations are encountered. Social scientists call this *attributional bias*. Individuals with a hostile attributional bias are substantially more likely to see the world as hostile and to see people in their world as worthy of caution and suspicion.

These points lead us to a single question: Why? Why do aggressive people view the world as though it is hostile, unforgiving, and dangerous? Why this particular attributional bias? Obviously, it may simply be the case that aggressive people are more likely to live in neighborhoods where violence is omnipotent, and they simply learn to counteract aggression by acting aggressively. Some authors certainly view this as the case (Anderson, 1999).

Still, if this is true, it cannot explain very well why young children comprehend their world as hostile and aggressive. Yet we know that children vary greatly on this dimension. Some hold this bias, but many others do not, and many children who live in stressful and violent neighborhoods do not exhibit this worldview. Moreover, simply recognizing that dangerous places produce dangerous people tells us nothing of the mechanisms involved. The question thus moves from Why? to How?

To answer this question, we turn to work in social information processing. There is an especially large research base on social information processing, particularly on the information processing of children and young adults. This research has yielded valuable insight into the actual cognitive processes that contribute to an aggressive attribution bias, and it offers important contributions to understanding why continuity in aggressive behavioral patterns exists and is so difficult to change.

All individuals filter information; information is received, recognized, classified as important or unimportant, stored, and retrieved when necessary. Because there is so much social information, though, we cannot process all of it, and thus we reduce the volume by prioritizing and categorizing information. Information that is immediately relevant, such as "snakes are dangerous," is given a higher priority than, say, how Dickens began *A Tale of Two Cities*.

Filtering, however, is subject to individual bias. This bias is built into the manner in which we cognitively assess information and react to it. First, we should recognize that the initial information we have, or with which we are provided, sets the framework from which we will view all other information. This is referred to as a *primacy effect*. The first information to which you are exposed is the most important. Second, as if the primacy effect was not difficult enough to overcome, we also seem to anchor our opinions around this information. Thus, once our opinions and views are established, we are very reluctant to abandon them. This is called an *anchoring bias*. Finally, as we mentioned before, people are not passive victims of their environments; they actively engage their environment and thereby become important architects of their own design. In terms of exposure to social information, we bring with us a *confirmatory bias* that seeks to include information with which we agree or that fits our worldview, and we reject information and facts that are inconsistent with our worldview.

These broad principles of social information processing should not be underestimated. Let us give you a quick example that illustrates the power of these biases: It was not too long ago that most of the world's population believed the world to be flat. They were told it was flat, their parents and teachers instructed them that it was flat, and other authority figures proclaimed it was flat (primacy effects). In effect, the world being flat was common knowledge and passed the common sense test (anchoring bias). And when evidence emerged that proved the world to be spherical, not flat, it had to be wrong. After all, if the world were round you would fall off of it because you could not stand on it upside down! And can you not see the edge of the world off in a distance (confirmatory bias)? The power of social information processing is that it creates our environment—that is, we have a powerful tendency to act upon what we view to be "true," and to avoid the complexities that might complicate our worldview. Or, as Thomas and Thomas stated in 1928, "If men define situations as real, they are real in their consequences" (p. 572). The Thomases, we believe, were on to something.

Kenneth Dodge, from Vanderbilt University, was also on to something. Dodge is best known for his work on the social information processing of young children, and, more specifically, his five-step model of social information processing. According to Caspi and Moffitt (1995), "Research has shown that aggressive behavior may be related to biases or deficits in processing information at any step and in different combinations of steps" (p. 486).

The first process involves the encoding of information. This process is influenced, however, by the biological traits of the person, by his or her prior experiences, and by the multiple social cues available in the immediate environment. Encoding, however, involves searching the environment for social information and social cues. These cues come in the form of facial expressions, mannerisms, glances, and other subtle verbal and nonverbal points of information. As Caspi and Moffitt (1986) note, aggressive individuals do not appear to seek out very much information from their environment before attributing hostility (see also Dodge & Newman, 1981).

Second, information is then processed through a representation process. This step involves the actual interpretation of cues by drawing on past experiences, immediate affective states, and prior decision making. In this step, aggressive children have been found more likely to attribute hostility toward the intentions of others and to situations where social cues are more ambiguous (Dodge, 1980; Steinberg & Dodge, 1983).

The next step involves the response search process. In essence, when presented with a social event, such as someone pointing at them, individuals have to elect from a possible list of alternative actions. Evidence consistently shows that aggressive youths generate considerably shorter lists of alternative responses (Slaby & Guerra, 1988) and that they are much more likely to elect an aggressive response (Dodge, 1986).

The fourth step involves selecting a response. From the list of alternative responses, individuals have to select one or more options. If their options are already limited in number, the chances are increased that they will select an option with which they are familiar. Still, choosing between options also involves recognizing and calibrating the possible consequences of choosing one option over another. Relying on past experiences and past consequences, individuals elect to pursue one behavior as opposed to another. As you might expect, the evidence shows that aggressive youths are significantly more likely to choose an aggressive response in situations where the social cues accurately indicated aggressive potential, where the social cues were ambiguous as to intent, and where the social cues were nonaggressive (Cairns & Cairns, 1994). This step, which requires a decision to be made, is strongly influenced by the biological traits of the individual, especially if the youth is hyperactive or impulsive. These youths simply spend less time thinking about the consequences of their conduct, and they are less accurate in matching past experiences to their immediate social environment.

Finally, the last step involves the actual enactment process. Even here, though, all is not equal. Aggressive youths are typically less verbal and much larger in size than their same-age peers (Beaver & Wright, 2005; Wilson & Herrnstein, 1985). These factors influence their ability to have their intent correspond directly with their behavior. For example, if youths cannot verbally manipulate a complex social situation, they may choose instead to manipulate it physically (Caspi & Moffitt, 1995). Their advantages in physical size and their corresponding strength may make the choice to act physically more likely.

Aggressive youths and aggressive adults thus see the world through a different lens. Their world is one where aggression and violence are necessary, where aggression and violence are more than just options from a long list of potential alternatives. In their world, aggression and violence are *preferred* options—choices that often bring about an effective conclusion to conflict and where their concept of self is strengthened when employed instead of reduced. And as their experience with aggression grows, as they rely on it with more frequency, they begin to form a pattern of cognition that supports and justifies the use of violence. Thus, they are propelled down a path of increasing behavior maladaptation that, ironically, makes the use of aggression and violence more likely in the future.

BOX 3.1   The Continuing Saga of Stanley: Early Onset and Chronic Offending

Stanley started committing offenses very early (age 6), and these offenses increased in frequency and severity as he aged, which fits a chronic offender's profile. Most individuals who are arrested at early ages are at a significantly higher risk of becoming life course-persistent offenders (Moffitt, 1993a; Tibbetts & Piquero, 1999) and are more likely to continue committing serious offenses into adulthood. Early onset of offending is typically considered to be an arrest before the age of 14 (for a review, see DeLisi, 2006), which is supported by many studies showing that the earlier the arrests begin, the more likely that the individual will become a chronic, persistent offender. Generally speaking, the earlier the first contact with police, the higher the likelihood that the individual will become a persistent offender. Given Stanley's very early criminal activity, almost any prediction model would have classified him as a likely candidate for becoming a chronic, serious offender.

Stanley obviously was at high risk for a persistent trajectory of criminal offending. Both developmental/life course perspectives and general theories of crime (e.g., Gottfredson & Hirschi, 1990; Wilson & Herrnstein, 1985), as well as numerous empirical studies (Farrington, 1987; Moffitt, 1993a), would predict that this early pattern of offending would result in a criminal career that would last throughout the life course. However, we will see that, despite Stanley's early and frequent delinquency, his offending did not persist into adulthood.

Stanley's offending, we shall see in later chapters, diminished after certain life events, but most individuals who exhibit such early, chronic offending do not show such desistence from crime. Thus, it is important to examine individual trajectories of offending (as well as the transitions that influence such long-term propensities) that do not depend on just one or more latent traits as proposed by most of the general theories, but rather depend on numerous factors and key life events as highlighted by the life course/developmental perspective.

Conclusion

Individuals act on, interact with, and are influenced by elements in their social world. Although it would be a mistake to believe that individuals are the complete architects of their environment, it would be an equal mistake to believe that they are merely passive receptors of culture or socialization. Instead, as we have endeavored to explain, there is a complex interaction that occurs every time an individual engages in a behavior, especially an antisocial behavior. This interaction can be understood through a biosocial approach that links individual traits and characteristics to environmental stimuli.

CHAPTER 4

Genetics and Crime

Adapt or perish, now as ever, is nature's inexorable imperative.

H. G. Wells (1866–1946)

If there has been a revolution in modern science, it can be found in the journals that hold the studies linking various biological characteristics to human behavior and traits. Diverse fields, including neuropsychology, behavioral genetics, and molecular chemistry, report daily an almost endless array of important discoveries. These findings have removed any doubt that certain biological features of human beings influence adaptive—or, conversely, maladaptive—behavioral styles (see Figure 4.1).

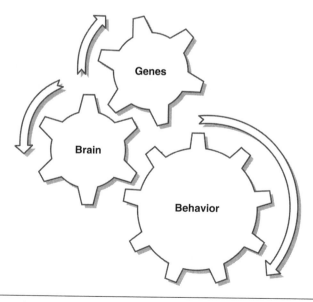

Figure 4.1   Connections

The influence of these various findings has yet to fully penetrate criminology. Indeed, as we have stated before, linking biological functioning to criminal behavior is still intellectually unpopular among many criminologists. The tide may be turning, but to understand the current state of affairs, we cover in this chapter, just briefly, the history of biological thought applied to criminal behavior. We trace the theorizing that linked variation in biological factors to misbehavior and the resulting exclusion of biology from the criminological vernacular. For decades, it remained widely unpopular and potentially dangerous to one's career to discuss the role and functions of biology, yet contemporary science has uncovered too much evidence for biology to continue to be ignored. Thus, after we examine the pitiful history of biology and crime, we begin an examination of the "new" biological thinking on human development.

Early Biological Explanations

Early biological theories were developed in what criminologists call "the positivist school of thought." This school of thought focused on the structure of the human body. Instead of tracing criminal behavior to rational decision making, positivists traced the causes of criminal behavior to inborn biological traits. Simply put, positivists believed that criminals possessed certain biological characteristics that made them inferior to law-abiding persons.

Early positivist researchers based much of their work on observations, so it should not be surprising that early biological positivists proposed that criminals could be identified via their specific bodily characteristics. Lombroso (1876) is probably best known for his view that criminals represented some "atavistic" throwback to human evolution. According to Lombroso, scientists could uncover truly atavistic differences through systematic measurement of physical characteristics. This "atavistic man" body type was generally characterized by a sloping forehead, disproportionately long arms, excessively large ears, twisted nose, abnormal amounts of skin wrinkling, and extra fingers or toes. Persons who fit this body type, approximately one third of all criminals, were considered to be born criminals (Lombroso-Ferrero, 1972). In addition to this criminal type, other types of criminals were also identified by Lombroso. Despite this recognition, these other types—the insane criminal and those criminals motivated by passion—were not seen as being the true criminal type and were subsequently viewed as less serious by Lombroso.

Lombroso, who today is viewed as the father of positivistic criminology, was not alone in his belief that biology was a key determinant of criminal behavior. In addition to Lombroso's work, others linked behavior to facial features as well as to the shape of a person's head (e.g., Franz Gall, 1758–1828). Physical characteristics aside, early positivists also believed that mental defects were a biologically rooted indicator of criminal propensity (Goddard, 1914; Hooten, 1939). Theoretically, persons who suffered from mental defects or were of limited intellect were not thought to be able to distinguish between right and wrong or lacked internal controls over their behavior (Goddard, 1914).

We have to remember that early positivists did not have the technical or scientific knowledge available to modern criminologists. This makes it all the more remarkable that positivists also speculated that criminal propensity was passed down through generations. Although positivists' knowledge of genes and genetics was highly limited, they did, nonetheless, believe that criminal behavior could have a genetic foundation and that criminal propensity could be transferred across generations within families (Lombroso-Ferrero, 1972). Early genealogical studies were largely supportive of this view and did show that crime, like other factors (intelligence, alcoholism), is concentrated in some families and not in others (Dugdale, 1877).

Biological Rejection

Biological explanations of criminal behavior dominated the late 19th and early 20th centuries. However, changes in society during the early 1900s instigated a move away from individual explanations of crime to explanations that focused solely on environmental factors. This shift arose out of a more optimistic view toward crime and criminals. Instead of criminal behavior being predetermined by individual factors, structural theories arose that focused attention on environmental sources of variation. From these viewpoints, individuals committed crimes not because they possessed particular biological characteristics that inevitably led them to criminal involvement, but because of their exposure to criminogenic social environments.

During the 1920s and 1930s, urban areas underwent tremendous population growth. Instead of providing lucrative job and housing opportunities for the new city residents, however, cities deteriorated. People were forced to work in unsafe factories and live in tenement housing, creating an environment in which families became entrenched in poverty.

Two major criminological theoretical developments, the Chicago school and strain theory, were born during this period. Both the Chicago school and Merton's strain theory located the causes of crime outside of the individual. For the Chicago school theorists, characteristics of the environment, in particular of urban slums, created a breakdown of societal norms, thus implicitly permitting persons to engage in criminal acts. This breakdown or disorganization fostered the development of delinquent networks that reinforced criminal rather than conventional values (Shaw & McKay, 1942).

For strain theorists, on the other hand, crime resulted from an inability to attain the conventional goals of society through legitimate means. Much like the Chicago school, Merton's (1938) propositions identified societal aspects, namely, the lack of legitimate opportunities for all of its members and the pervasive belief in the American Dream, as the primary forces behind crime. Although most citizens desired the prosperity of the American Dream, according to Merton, some simply were not afforded the opportunity to achieve the dream. With these opportunities blocked, individuals would seek out alternative ways to get what they desired.

These two theoretical schools of thought, and the theories derived from them, would dominate the field of criminal justice and criminal justice policy alike through the 1960s and 1970s. These perspectives helped to ideologically underpin the "war on poverty," and they helped to justify massive spending on social welfare programs aimed at reducing blocked opportunities and dysfunctional neighborhoods.

The 1960s and 1970s were also known for the civil rights movement, the women's rights movement, and the anti–Vietnam War movement. The collective influence of these events is easy to understate, but it is safe to say that they influenced every aspect of American society—especially academia. The language of oppression and discrimination captured the social sciences, and alleviating the conditions of the poor and disenfranchised became the focus of many scholars. Unfortunately, this also meant discarding and attacking ideas that might have been used, or were used, to justify the oppression of minority groups. It was during this time period when the rejection of biological explanations of crime occurred. After all, if criminal conduct could be "caused" by genes or other biological factors and these factors were disproportionately concentrated in minority groups, then someone might use this information to justify a new eugenics movement, or worse. No longer would biology play center stage and guide research. As time would tell, these forces would practically eliminate biological research into human behavior in the United States.

The New Study of Biology and Behavior

Fortunately, other sciences continued the march toward understanding how human biology influences development across the life course. Psychology, psychiatry, genetics, and neuropsychology, in particular, have brought to light many scientific findings showing the interconnections between environment and biology. It is largely these insights that we present. Before moving forward, however, it might serve us well to understand some of the basics behind human genetics and biology.

Deoxyribonucleic acid (DNA) is the foundation of life because it contains all necessary information for the creation of human beings. DNA contains genes, half of which you obtain from your father and half of which you obtain from your mother. These genes are located on chromosomes, of which all healthy humans have 22 pairs plus two sex-determining chromosomes (or 46 total in number). Males will have a Y chromosome; females will have an X chromosome.

Genes are regions on DNA that contain necessary hereditary information. Alleles are different versions of the same gene. Current estimates place the number of genes in the human genome between 19,000 and 25,000. Other plants and animals have more genes than we do. DNA is coiled in the now famous shape of the double-helix. The two strands of DNA are connected through hydrogen bonds to associated bases. When two bases are attached, it is referred to as a nucleotide. The four bases are adenine (A), thymine (T), guanine (G), and cytosine (C). Chemically, A can bond only with T, and G can bond only with C. Thus, a strand of base pairs may look like the following:

ATCGATA

TAGCTAT

There are at least 3 billion base pair sequences in the human genome. Of these sequences, 1% to 10% differ between individuals, or between 3 million and 30 million base pairs. It is important to note that only about 1.5% of the overall human genome codes for proteins; the rest of the genome has no coding function, or it is involved in the regulation of chromosomes, or it has been turned off by evolution.

Every individual trait is heritable, which means that it can be influenced by genes. Genes, however, do not cause criminal or pathological behavior (Rowe, 2002). Instead, genes, code for the amino acid sequences of proteins that form cell structures, constitute hormones and neurotransmitters, and regulate certain cell activities (Plomin, 1990). Proteins, as a result, do not cause behavior. They do, however, affect the way in which a person responds to his or her environment. It is also important to note that environmental stimulation can also elicit specific protein production (Walsh, 2002). What is inherited, then, is not behavior, but a tendency or a predisposition to behave in certain ways in response to environmental cues (Walsh, 2002). The expression of this tendency is itself dependent upon the situational and environmental factors present, in that these stimuli may cause protein production (Walsh, 2002). In other words, it is possible to have a genetic predisposition that is never expressed because of environmental constraints.

How, then, do genes influence behavior? One way in which genes influence behavior is through the amino acids for which they code (Plomin, 1990). Amino acids interact with other body components to produce behavioral responses to specific stimuli (Walsh, 2002). Genes can also activate and deactivate in response to their environment and in response to their own internal code. They can direct the construction of the human body, especially the brain and central nervous system. Genes monitor and regulate internal and external conditions. And genes also contribute to decision-making processes and to the interpretation of social cues. The influence of genes is far and wide.

Even so, no single gene has been identified that accounts for a large proportion of between-individual variation in behaviors found in any given population (Plomin, 1990). It is more likely the case that *polygeny,* or one behavior being influenced by many genes, is at work (Plomin, 1990). Conversely, genes do more than influence a single characteristic or behavior. One gene may have a variety of effects on a host of behaviors. This is known as *pliotropy* (Plomin, 1990).

Certain genotypes seem to be more, or less, at risk for criminality. Molecular studies have shown that specific genes are associated with traits linked to crime and offending, such as impulsivity, low self-control, and hyperactivity. However, these studies also show that single-gene influences are usually small and account for a limited amount of variance in the trait. Future research with more genes may show a cumulative or interactive effect, but for now, single-gene influences remain limited in their explanatory power. Research in the area of behavioral genetics, however, has provided consistent evidence in favor of genetic and environmental effects of human traits and behaviors.

The Behavioral Genetic Study of Criminality

Behavioral geneticists estimate the degree of heritability in a trait or characteristics. *Heritability* (h^2) is the proportion of phenotypic variance that can be attributed to genotypic variance within a population; it is a quantitative estimate of the extent of genetic influence on a behavior (Reiss et al., 2000). Another way of understanding heritability is that it represents the degree to which some trait is under genetic influence. These estimates range from 0 to 1, with 0 indicating no genetic influence and 1 representing total genetic influence.

Behavioral genetic studies calculate heritability, but they also estimate the influence of environmental effects on a trait. Environmental influences are decomposed into two parts: shared and nonshared environment (Reiss et al., 2000; Walsh, 2002). Environmental characteristics that operate to make persons who are exposed to them more alike are termed *shared* (Plomin, 1990). Within a family, those factors that are the same for all family members and produce similar effects among them are shared environmental characteristics (Rowe, 1985).

Conversely, those environmental factors that do not produce resemblances between family members are nonshared (Rowe, 1985). Nonshared environmental factors can be located both within and external to the family unit (Walsh, 2002). This property of the nonshared environment suggests that, contrary to traditional sociological principles, individuals within a family may experience quite divergent environments (Rowe & Plomin, 1981). These nonshared characteristics of the environment differentially affect individuals and are, consequently, responsible for the majority of environmental effects on children's behavior (Plomin & Daniels, 1987). Along with error in measurement, heritability and environmental effects together comprise variance in phenotypes within a population (Plomin, 1990).

The basis of behavioral genetics, then, is the determination of environmental influences, heritability, and any measurement error that is related to a particular trait or behavior within a specific population. Although this decomposition of variation into its component parts allows for the quantification of the separate influence of each, it does not speak to the specific influences within the environment that either facilitate genetic expression or influence behavior more directly (Rowe, 2002). Research identifying such influences has been completed, but behavioral geneticists are more concerned with determining which traits, behaviors, and characteristics are influenced by genes and, once known, the extent of their influence (Walsh, 2002).

Behavioral geneticists are quick to point out that environmental characteristics can have varying roles in the etiology of behavior. That is, the same environmental influence may differentially affect persons experiencing it. In some situations, a shared characteristic for one family may operate to create differences between siblings or parent-child pairs in another (Walsh, 2002). Because of the variability of effects of environmental variables, it is not possible to make general conclusions regarding the effects of heritability and environment on a range of outcomes. Instead, it is necessary to identify both the genetic and environmental influences themselves and the relative importance of each for explaining variation in behavior (Walsh, 2002).

In addition to providing evidence of a genetic basis, research has also illustrated the importance of gene-environment interactions. Not only can genetics increase or decrease the probability of particular characteristics occurring, genes can also increase a person's sensitivity to environmental factors. Many children, for example, appear to be very resilient to criminogenic environments. Partly because of their genome, they may simply be able to better handle the stresses and strains of living in poverty or of parental abuse and neglect. Other children are not so lucky. Their genomes may make them more sensitive to the stress and strain, and more reactive to parental abuse and neglect.

Genes further interact with environment through the mechanisms of choice. The decisions and choices a person makes are not divorced from his or her genetically related personal attributes. Rather, a person chooses options that correspond with, define, and reinforce his or her disposition (Paul, 1998; Plomin, 1994). Individuals may make choices haphazardly, impulsively, or without conscience. And individuals are very likely to make choices that reflect their proclivities and desires, including choices of friends and sexual mates.

tuate over time. The environment
it undergoes change over time.
es an environmental trigger, it is
ferentially according to the ever-
f genes and environmental influ-
nature of heritability estimates.
particular contexts, samples, and
lated. Recognizing that genes and
omental behavioral genetics exam-
ient (Plomin, 1990). Such research
of the components of variance in
ourse (Plomin, 1990). An example
ses with age is IQ (Plomin, 1990).
nshared environmental influences
e shared environment exerts less
o know that genes affect behavior;
nes and the environment in which

, first-degree relatives share half of
one quarter of their genes. If a trait
basis, logically it would be expected
ccording to level of genetic related-
t similarity. The effects of environ-
ney, too, can produce similarity or

nvironment and genetic influence,
se models measure the relationship
utcomes by determining the similar-
ing these similarities across a sub-
sample of pairs that vary in their level of genetic relatedness (Reiss et al., 2000).

Similarity in an outcome for individuals in a pair is calculated by either determining concordance for that measure or the intraclass correlation (Reiss et al., 2000). Pairwise concordance represents the proportion of pairs of relatives in which both members have a certain trait or behavior present (Reiss et al., 2000). A second type of concordance, proband concordance, represents the proportion of affected individuals in concordant pairs (Reiss et al., 2000). Concordance is typically calculated when the trait in question is measured using a dichotomous (yes/no) variable (Reiss et al., 2000).

When the trait under study is measured with a continuous variable and the difference on this trait can be quantitatively measured, a correlation coefficient (r) can be calculated (Reiss et al., 2000). The intraclass correlation represents the predictability of one pair member's value on a trait based on the other member's value and the extent to which the value is the same (Reiss et al., 2000). The value of r can range from −1 to 1, with values larger in magnitude representing a greater level of predictability (Reiss et al., 2000). Once the intraclass correlation is calculated, the values across subsamples of pairs with differing genetic similarity can be compared (Reiss et al., 2000). If a behavior or trait is influenced by genes, then the intraclass correlation would be higher for those pairs with greater genetic similarity (Reiss et al., 2000).

Family Studies. To estimate the effects of genetics and the environment on human behavior, it is often necessary to examine pairs of individuals who differ in their genetic relatedness. At the most basic level, if heredity influences an outcome, then pairs of individuals who are genetically similar should also be similar in the outcome variable (Plomin, 1990). Conversely, if heredity is not an influence, then genetic differences should not correspond with differences in the studied trait (Plomin, 1990). However, this type of study method does not recognize the influence of shared environmental factors. This omission is particularly salient when it is remembered that environmental resemblance often coexists with genetic resemblance (Plomin, 1990). Any resemblance found between related individuals, then, could be a consequence of shared environmental influences rather than genetic ones. The value of family studies should not be discounted, though. Their main contribution to behavioral genetics is the benchmarks and thresholds of heritability that they have provided (Plomin, 1990). Knowing the correlation between pairs of individuals for particular traits allows the researcher to estimate the maximum amount that can be attributed to genes (Plomin, 1990).

Twin Studies. Behavioral geneticists are able to obtain estimates of heritability by comparing intraclass correlations of monozygotic (MZ) twin pairs to same-sex dizygotic (DZ) twin pairs (Rowe, 1985). For MZ twin pairs, it is expected that they will evince twice the correlation than will DZ twin pairs, who share half their genes (Rowe, 2002). If a trait or behavior is not, however, influenced by genes, then there will be no appreciable difference between MZ and DZ twin pairs (Plomin, 1990). In such instances, environmental, rather than genetic, influence is implicated (Rowe, 2002). In addition to comparing the magnitude of correlations between MZ and DZ twin pairs, heritability estimates can also be derived by doubling the difference between MZ and DZ twin correlations.

BOX 4.1   Differences Between Monozygotic Twins

Monozygotic twins are formed when one egg is fertilized by one sperm that forms a zygote that later splits into two separate zygotes. Monozygotic twins are often referred to as identical twins; however, not all monozygotic twins are, in fact, genetically identical. In fact, research shows that many "identical" twins are discordant for handedness, meaning that one twin is right-hand dominant and the other is left-hand dominant (Sommer, Ramsey, Graafmans, Mandl, & Kahn, 2002). These and other differences between monozygotic twins sometimes can be explained by the developmental process of the twins in utero. Specifically, the timing that twinning occurs plays a role in dictating how similar the fetal environment will be for the twins. Differences in this environment and development may contribute to the differences that are sometimes found across monozygotic twins. Others argue that the twinning process itself—the separation of the zygote into two blastopheres—actually causes genetic changes that result in monozygotic twins being different from one another (Hall, 1996).

Monozygotic twins can be formed in several ways:

1. Early splitting of the zygote into two blastocysts can occur in which the resulting monozygotic twins will develop separately. Each will have its own placenta, chorion, and amniotic sac.

2. The zygote can also split later into two cell masses within one blastocyst. In this case, the twins may share a placenta and chorion, but may have their own amniotic sac.

3. The zygote can split even later during development so that the monozygotic twins share a placenta, chorion, and amniotic sac.

Because twin studies provide not only estimates of heritability but also estimates of environmental effects, they are useful tools. They also are more advantageous than family studies in that MZ and DZ twins have greater genetic dissimilarities than first- and second-degree relative pairs (Plomin, 1990). This difference provides for greater variability in pair correlations and in their differences across twin pairs (Plomin, 1990). Another way in which twin studies improve upon family studies is by limiting age and a portion of sample difference. That is, MZ and DZ twins are born at the same time and typically live in the same family, whereas first- and second-degree relatives are often of different age and family residence (Plomin, 1990). Reducing the differences between pairs helps ensure that the difference in correlation is a result of genetic rather than nonshared environmental influence (Plomin, 1990). It should be noted, however, that twin studies may also overestimate genetic influence if the environment of MZ twins is systematically different from that of DZ twins (Benson, 2002). Overestimation will occur when the greater similarity found between MZ twins occurs because of factors in their environment rather than their shared genes (Benson, 2002).

Adoption Studies. An additional type of study methodology employed in behavioral genetics research is the adoption study. Adoption studies are capable of examining both gene and shared environmental influences (Plomin, 1990). In these studies, both related individuals who are adopted and subsequently reared in separate environments and genetically unrelated individuals who are adopted and reared in the same familial environment are analyzed. Using these pairs of individuals allows heredity, in the case of adopted-apart relatives, and environment, in the case of adopted-together nonrelatives, to be assessed (Plomin, 1990).

Correlations for each type of pair are calculated and then compared to determine the resemblance of the pairs on an identified characteristic or behavior (Plomin, 1990). The correlation between related individuals who are reared apart reveals the degree of heredity, and the correlation between nonrelated individuals adopted together represents the influence of the shared environment (Plomin, 1990). That is, because related individuals who live in separate, nonrelated familial environments are not under the influence of shared environmental factors, any similarity evidenced is attributed to genetic relatedness (Plomin, 1990). Likewise, the similarity found between nonrelated persons living in the same family is considered to be under the influence of the shared environment because they are genetically unrelated (Plomin, 1990). For adoption studies in which identical twins are adopted into separate and uncorrelated families, heritability can be estimated directly from the value of the correlation coefficient, with a value of 0.8 suggesting that 80% of the variation in the variable in question is due to genetic variation (Plomin, 1990).

Another design using adoption methods is one in which parent-child pairs are examined for their similarity. Genetic influence in this type of design is estimated indirectly by comparing nonrelated parent-child pairs and nonadoptive or related parent-child pairs. Correlation between a nonadoptive parent and child can be due to genetic as well as to shared environmental factors (Plomin, 1990). Correlation between related or adoptive parent-child pairs, however, can be attributed only to shared environment (Plomin, 1990). When heredity is, in fact, influential for a certain trait or behavior, the correlation for nonadoptive parent-child pairs will be greater than that of adoptive parent-child pairs (Plomin, 1990). Much like twin studies, adoptive studies are not free from flaws. For example, it has been suggested that these studies overestimate the influence of genes. This overestimation occurs if adoptees are selectively placed into homes that have correlated environments and if the same factors in the environment that are correlated are also related to the trait of interest (Plomin, 1990). In light of this bias, consideration of such selective placement must be considered when employing adoptive methodologies.

Early Findings From Twin and Adoption Studies

Early research attempting to uncover the effects of genetics employed both twin and adoption methodologies. These initial studies found that most traits, like IQ, followed general genetic theory—that is, MZ twins had the highest concordance rates, followed by DZ twins and full siblings, followed by half-siblings, and then unrelated individuals (Plomin, 1990). This finding provided the benchmarks, known as the genetic cascade, to which other patterns of correlation or concordance could be compared (Reiss, 2001). In addition, findings from these early studies also revealed the importance of heredity across a range of outcomes, including crime.

Beginning in 1931 with Lange's twin study of criminality, evidence was found that, on average, MZ twins had higher concordance rates than DZ twins for criminal conduct (Lange, 1931). In Lange's study, MZ twins had a concordance rate of 77%, whereas DZ twins had a concordance rate of only 12%. Although this and other studies from this time period found substantial support for the influence of heredity, these studies were criticized for their small sample sizes and their grouping of twins as either MZ or DZ (Walters, 1992). In attempts to address these methodological weaknesses, others found smaller concordance rates (Christiansen, 1977; Dalgaard & Kringlen, 1976).

Using both a large sample size and easily identifiable MZ and DZ twins, Christiansen's (1977) Danish twin study was an important contribution to the literature on heredity and crime. This study used a sample size of 3,586 twin pairs born between 1881 and 1910 in Denmark. Assessing criminality through both penal and police records, Christiansen calculated concordance rates separately for both male and female twin pairs. For both sexes, MZ twin pairs had higher concordance rates for criminality than did the DZ twin pairs. With concordance rates of 0.35 for identical male twin pairs and 0.13 for fraternal twins, he concluded that criminality had a genetic basis. The majority of the twin studies conducted during this era echoed these conclusions, although the significant difference between MZ and DZ twin pairs was not found by all (see Dalgaard & Kringlen, 1976).

Other early twin studies investigated genetic influence on constructs related to criminal behavior. One construct, psychopathy, has been the variable of interest for a number of researchers. Despite using the Psychopathic-deviate (Pd) scale of the MMPI, different results have been amassed by several researchers. Whereas the concordance rates for adolescent twin pairs were found to be significantly different for MZ and DZ twins (Gottesman, 1963), adult twin pairs did not similarly evidence such a difference (Reznikoff & Honeyman, 1967). Equivocal results were also found for the genetic influence on children's psychopathic personality, with findings that both support the significance of heritability (O'Connor, Foch, Sherry, & Plomin, 1980) and show minimal influence (Owen & Sines, 1970).

Along with these twin studies, early adoption studies also tested the importance of genetic factors in the etiology of criminal behavior. Perhaps the most comprehensive data in this area derive from the Danish adoption studies, which include information on 14,427 children who were adopted between 1924 and 1947 (Mednick, Gabrielli, & Hutchings, 1984). Using court convictions as the outcome measure of criminal involvement, the researchers found support for a genetic link (Mednick et al., 1984). It was discovered that 20% of the adopted sons who had criminal biological parents and noncriminal adoptive parents, were themselves criminal. Furthermore, for full siblings raised in separate homes, there was a 20% concordance rate versus an 8.5% concordance rate for nonrelated siblings living in separate homes (Mednick et al., 1984). Later analysis on these same data revealed a genetic influence on chronic, nonviolent offending (Mednick, Gabrielli, & Hutchings, 1987). As noted by Gottfredson and Hirschi (1990), this and other, similar adoption studies are not able to address environmental influences that may also explain similarity in behavior. As such, it is likely that the adoptive households produced little variation in terms of their environment, thus limiting the ability of environmental effects to be identified (Benson, 2002). A study in which this particular criticism is addressed examined sets of identical twins who were reared apart.

In this study of 32 MZ twin pairs, the concordance rate for antisocial personality disorder was 29%, a rate similar to other twin studies (Grove et al., 1990).

Contemporary Studies

In a review of research that has been carried out to assess heritability across a range of outcome measures, Plomin (1990) found that a wide range of behavioral problems, personality disorders, and mood disorders are influenced by genes. Many of these disorders are indirectly related to criminal behavior. For example, schizophrenia and depression have been found to be influenced by genes, although schizophrenia appears to be related more strongly to genetics (Plomin, 1990). Depression and bipolar disorder both show a strong genetic influence in studies using the twin method, but less genetic influence is shown in adoption studies (Plomin, 1990). Other research supports the finding that genetics has a significant influence on depressive symptomology (Pike, McGuire, Hetherington, Reiss, & Plomin, 1996; Reiss et al., 2000). Genetics has also been found to be an important explanatory variable for the co-occurrence of depression and antisocial behavior (O'Connor, McGuire, Reiss, Hetherington, & Plomin, 1998). From a national sample of 720 same-sex adolescent siblings, O'Connor et al. (1998) determined that just under half of the variability in depressive symptoms and antisocial behavior is due to genetic influences.

Perhaps the most research on heritability has been targeted on cognitive abilities (Plomin, 1990). Early research focused primarily on the genetic basis of IQ. The finding that IQ is significantly influenced by heredity has been but a part of the long-term debate on the topic. Both adoption and twin data reveal that IQ has, in addition to an environmental basis, a genetic basis as well (Bouchard, 1987; Plomin, 1990). Overall, despite minor departures, the majority of this research estimates heritability to be at approximately 90% (Plomin, 1990). Also important, research on the heritability of IQ has provided evidence that the influences of genes fluctuate over time, with heritability in IQ increasing during childhood (Plomin, 1990). Other factors related to IQ have also been found to be explained by genetic influences (Nichols, 1978). Creativity, school achievement, and learning disabilities are also determined at least partially by genetics (Plomin, 1990). Notably, deficiencies in IQ and its corollaries are risk factors in the etiology of delinquency.

Personality characteristics have also been shown to have genetic roots. In fact, personality factors usually show strong, consistent heritability effects, ranging from 30% to 70% (Revelle, 1995). Traits such as alienation (0.48), control (0.50), and traditionalism (0.53), as studied through an adoption and twin combination method, are each highly heritable (Tellegen et al., 1988). A separate study of 707 sibling pairs was conducted to determine the extent to which genetics influences the three domains of positivity, negativity, and control. Of the 18 composite measures, all but three showed some genetic influence, with nonshared environmental influences also being evidenced (Plomin, Reiss, Hetherington, & Howe, 1994). Overall, approximately one quarter of the variance of the three outcome measures could be accounted for by genetic differences in the children (Plomin et al., 1994).

Temperamental factors also have genes to blame for at least part of their genesis. Rowe (1986) maintains that temperamental characteristics are one of the main areas influenced by genetic forces. Impulsivity, for example, is one aspect of personality that is heritable and subsequently related to delinquency and crime (Revelle, 1995). Temperament, when viewed as patterns of social responsiveness, has been found to be at least partially dependent upon genetics (Reiss et al., 2000). Perhaps most notable regarding temperament, it has the potential to evoke partic-ular responses from actors in the environment. That is, a genetically influenced trait of being "difficult" may serve to create responses from the parent that have implications for development (Reiss et al., 2000). In this sense, it is not that parents have an innate parenting style from which they always retrieve behavioral responses; rather, they react to their children depending upon their given genetic capacities and their environmental supports (Reiss et al., 2000).

Along with traits that are influenced by genes, behavioral precursors to delin-quency and crime have been integrated into behavioral genetics research. Three specific constructs that have been examined are hyperactivity, conduct disorder, and ADHD (Silberg et al., 1996). For boys and girls between the ages of 8 and 16, approximately 70% of the variation in hyperactivity is attributable to additive genetic effects (Silberg et al., 1996). Genetic effects are also consistently found for conduct disorder (Silberg et al., 1996). The influence of genetics on the occurrence of ADHD has also been confirmed in multiple twin studies, so much so that ADHD is now believed to be a purely genetic disorder (Barkley, 1998; Levy, Hay, McStephen, Wood, & Waldman, 1997).

Of further interest, Reiss et al. (2000) discovered that genetics also plays an important role in the stability of antisocial behavior. They found that stability coef-ficients for antisocial behavior were 0.61 and that the level of stability was largely attributable to genes (Reiss et al., 2000). Stability is created and/or sustained through genes and shared environmental influences, whereas change is created and/or sustained primarily through genes and nonshared environmental influ-ences. By finding that nonshared environmental influences can lead to change in behavior, behavioral genetics research has lent support for the developmental per-spective of crime. That is, despite or because of certain genetic characteristics, other influences, such as local life circumstances, will interact to determine the changes in a person's life.

In conclusion, this area of research has recognized the importance of both the environment and genetics. In doing so, behavioral genetics research has provided a mechanism by which the variance in traits and behaviors can be decomposed. Accordingly, genetic influences appear to have moderate to substantial effects on certain behaviors, personality and temperament characteristics, and disorders. Shared and nonshared environmental influences have also been found to be impor-tant sources of variation in behavior. Between 20% and 30% of the variation in personality, psychopathology, delinquency, and alcoholism appears to be environ-mentally influenced (Plomin, 1990).

More often than not, however, nonshared environmental influences appear to be more important than shared environmental influences. The importance of non-shared environmental influences in explaining variation in antisocial behavior was illustrated by Rowe (1986). In his study of 265 twin pairs, he discovered that shared environmental influences were not significantly related to delinquent behavior, but genes and nonshared environmental factors were (see Figure 4.2). Similarly, other studies have found that shared environmental influences comprise only 5% of the variance in personality (Loehlin & Nichols, 1976) and account for 0% to 10% of any behavioral outcome.

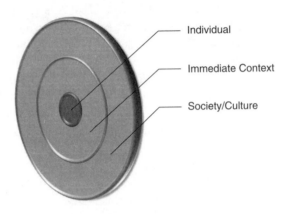

Individual

Immediate Context

Society/Culture

Figure 4.2   Hierarchical Relationships

BOX 4.2   The Continuing Saga of Stanley: Pre- and Perinatal Factors

Shaw (1930) did not have a comprehensive description of Stanley's biosocial/perinatal measures that may be related (positively or negatively) to future criminal offending. One reason for lacking such information is the problems in retroactively obtaining this type of data from hospitals, and so on. Another reason is that medical/perinatal measures and records before 1920 had nowhere near the technological sophistication as in the latter half of the century, let alone modern-day measures. Thus, the perinatal record of Stanley is lacking, by today's standards; however, we will examine what limited data were recorded.

First, there were some indicators of problems in Stanley's embryonic development/infancy that could have impaired his development. For example, at the time of conception, Stanley's father was a heavy drinker, which increases the likelihood that his mother was also a drinker or that those close to him generally engaged in unhealthy behaviors. Additionally, Stanley's natural mother was "sickly" (Shaw, 1930, p. 198) at the time of conception and during pregnancy. The effects of such behaviors and conditions can directly and/or indirectly affect an embryo or infant, via physiological, psychological, or social mechanisms (e.g., an infant may produce antagonism among his or her caretakers by being a "difficult" child as a result of such maladies).

Although Stanley's delivery was classified as "normal," his birth weight was six and a half pounds, which does not constitute low birth weight; however, this weight is not much higher than the acknowledged criteria (i.e., under 6 pounds). Furthermore, he had both chicken pox and measles before the age of 3, which may (or may not) have had a negative influence on Stanley's neuropsychological development. Numerous studies (Centers for Disease Control & Prevention, 2005) have shown that these types of illnesses at early ages can have a profound impact on a child's development, particularly before the age of 3. Such illnesses can affect an infant's development by having a negative impact on the individual's central and autonomic nervous systems, as well as the level of neurotransmitters that provide key information processing in the brain. Many studies and theoretical perspectives (for reviews, see Ellis & Walsh, 2000; Raine, 1993; Wilson & Herrnstein, 1985) have emphasized the importance of abnormal functioning of the nervous system and low levels of neurotransmitters (particularly serotonin) in determining the conditionability or learning ability of individuals. This would naturally affect a person's likelihood of engaging in antisocial behavior.

Thus, these early events in Stanley's development, ranging from his natural mother's "sickly" condition during pregnancy to his early experience with notable illnesses, suggest that he was at high risk for subnormal growth. Without sophisticated data, we can only speculate on the impact that these factors had on his development. However, when these problems are combined with the poor family environment and socioeconomic barriers that he experienced (these will be examined in subsequent chapters), it is likely that the interactions between the perinatal complications and his disadvantaged environment significantly contributed to his tendencies toward criminal activity.

Stanley's intelligence, as measured by IQ tests, was not measured empirically until he was 7 years old; therefore, this aspect of Stanley's development, as well as most of his early personality traits, will be discussed in Chapter 5. Still, it is interesting to note some early indicators of his personality, particularly those that may be largely attributable to Stanley's parents (likely via both their genetic traits and socialization [or lack thereof] of Stanley). For example, Stanley's father, a Polish immigrant, was an excessive drinker and often abusive of the other family members. Such behavior is consistent with a model of low self-control (e.g., impulsive activities that have negative long-term consequences, self-centeredness, short-tempered), which we will see is clearly evident in Stanley at a very early age. It is possible that his father's influence on Stanley's disposition was not entirely social, but partly genetic. However, like most examinations into such matters, it would be futile to try to determine to what extent each aspect influenced Stanley's development.

It is also interesting to note the juvenile court records of Stanley's siblings and half-siblings, because it suggests the influence of shared versus different biological parents. Stanley's biological mother was his father's second of three wives. His father had five children with his first wife, none of whom ever appeared in juvenile court. His father's third wife, Stanley's stepmother, brought into the marriage seven children from previous marriages, none of whom ever appeared in juvenile court. Stanley was raised in more or less the same environment as many of these stepbrothers and stepsisters, so it is surprising that none of the 12 children was brought to the court's attention.

It is just as interesting, if not more so, that all three children born to his father and Stanley's natural mother (the second wife) became chronic delinquents who appeared in juvenile court. Specifically, Stanley had an older brother who was committed to the Chicago Parental School for truancy, theft, and other offenses, and he also had a younger sister who was removed from the home due to chronic truancy and theft. Although Stanley's full and half-siblings were raised together in similar conditions, only the children born to his father's second wife (i.e., Stanley's biological mother) appeared to be disposed toward criminality. Although several explanations are possible, this pattern seems to suggest that Stanley and his full siblings likely inherited this predisposition from their mother, because the father's influence (genetically and sociologically) was shared by all of the children and thus cannot explain the extreme differences between Stanley's natural family and his half-siblings.

Conclusion

We chose to limit the debate that surrounds linking biological and genetic influences to criminal behavior for several reasons, but primarily because we have grown tired of defending an area of scientific research. Instead, we sought to minimally recognize the history of the issue and then to present the evidence. It is, after all, evidence that should guide science and not the desire to be politically or disciplinarily correct. If the evidence failed to reveal genetic influences on criminality, we would report that, but that is not the case.

Genes are always with us. They influence us in ways that are complex and sometimes indirect, but they are always with us. From our point of view, it is better to know how much, or how little, traits and behaviors are influenced by genetic and biological processes than to remain willfully ignorant of the facts. Only by recognizing genetic and biologically influenced proclivities, such as criminality, can we fully and completely understand complex human behaviors. Understanding these influences does not rule out or mitigate the influence of social processes—quite to the contrary, they highlight them. In the next few chapters, we show exactly why this is the case as we investigate healthy human brain development and what can happen when that development is compromised.

CHAPTER 5

Introduction to Brain Structure and Basic Functions—Part I

The Hindbrain, Midbrain, and Limbic Structures in the Development of Criminality

If the human mind were so simple that we could understand it, we would be so simple that we couldn't.

Emerson M. Pugh

The most amazing and complex thing known in our world is the human brain. Although the average adult brain weighs approximately 3lbs., this relatively small mass of squishy tissue is the source of every thought, emotion, decision, and action that is made by an individual. Traditionally, it was believed that by the time the brain had reached adult size (around age 10), it stopped growing and producing new cells. However, research in the past decade has demonstrated that the brain is constantly developing and making new cells (called "neurogenesis") even into old age (Gage, 2002; Gould, 1999; Ritter, 2002).

For many years, researchers believed that the only vital period of growth in the brain was in the first few years of life. It is true that the most significant and vital period of development occurs in the perinatal and early years. To illustrate, approximately 95% of a child's brain has structurally developed to adult size by age 6. In addition, most of the neurons we have were developed when we were still in the womb; actually, adults typically have fewer than they had before they were born because of the extraction of those that are unused in development. Although it is true that the brain develops in structural volume very little after age 5, key stages of growth in both structure and function occur throughout life, especially through age 25. Furthermore, neural paths are formed throughout the life span of normal individuals.

Given that the brain plays such a vital role in all cognitive functions, it follows that criminal activity is a result of the various processes going on in our heads. Whether the reason to commit an offense is to make money, to get revenge, to get a "rush," or just sheer stupidity, the brain always plays a central role. Therefore, any reasonable attempt to explain criminal behavior must incorporate an understanding of the brain, particularly the likely problems that can occur in its structural development and intricate processes.

Unfortunately, the amazing complexity of human cognition makes it particularly vulnerable to a myriad of developmental maladies that can result in mental deficits, which may predispose individuals to criminality. This chapter, as well as the following chapter, will present a basic overview of brain structure formation with a special emphasis on the differential functions of the various structures and lobes, with the current chapter focusing on the hindbrain, midbrain, and subcortical regions, and the following chapter focusing on the forebrain. Although this review is far from comprehensive, our goal is to discuss the relevant concepts and issues that most likely affect our cognitive configuration and functioning in terms of developing criminality. The reader should note that other considerations that we do not discuss may be important in the way the brain affects our behavior; however, because of space limitations, we have narrowed our discussion to the concepts and issues that have received the most attention and empirical support, or seem to be particularly worthy of more attention in the etiology of criminal offending.

Brain Development and Structure

The brain, which is composed of many regions and structures, is the most important bodily organ in the commission and inhibition of criminal behavior. This much we know. However, outside of this general statement, links between specific brain structures and particular types of behavior have not been well established. This is largely due to the fact that our understanding of the brain and its development is still rather primitive. The good news is that scientific knowledge on cognition is growing at an exponential rate. Because of this immense growth in information, a comprehensive description of brain development would take many volumes. Therefore, our review in this chapter (and the following chapter) will focus on basic essentials that are most relevant in understanding neurological influences in individuals' development toward criminality.

It should be noted that developmental differences may be related to brain *structure* and/or brain *function,* which may occur independently or simultaneously. In other words, a tomographical image of the brain structure of an individual may appear quite normal, whereas the actual functioning (internally, externally, or both) may be abnormal in that there may be structural maladies that do not allow healthy functioning of the brain. Given this distinction, we will first examine brain configuration and issues related to formative development. After identifying individual brain structures and their location, we will provide descriptions of the primary jobs that each of the structures is responsible for carrying out. Most importantly, we will discuss some of the observed links between these specific brain structures and criminality. Thus, the focus in this chapter is on hindbrain and subcortical structure and region-specific regulations, whereas the forebrain structure is the focus of the following chapter, and the specific mechanics of brain and nervous system functioning is the emphasis of the following chapters.

The reader should keep in mind that some of the current conclusions regarding links with criminal behavior are still somewhat preliminary and not yet well-established. Future research will ultimately determine which of these associations is valid in explaining our decisions to commit (or not commit) crime. Nevertheless, we provide the current state of understanding regarding brain development and criminality.

Hindbrain Structure and Functioning

The initial sequence of brain configuration is largely programmed by one's genetic makeup when in the womb. Soon after conception, the brain begins as a primordial tube-like structure that develops rather quickly into three distinct parts: hindbrain, midbrain, and forebrain. Also referred to as the brain stem region, the *hindbrain* forms as a continuation of the spinal cord and includes such structures as the medulla oblongata, cerebellum, raphe nucleus, and pons (see Figures 5.1 and 5.2).

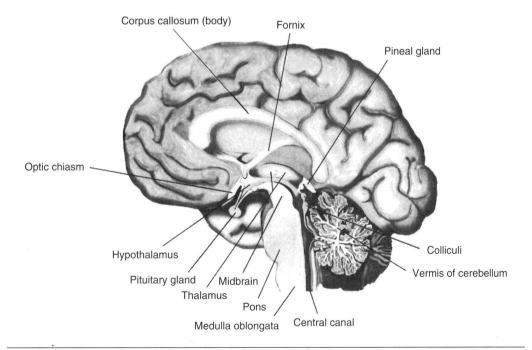

Figure 5.1   A Midsagittal View of the Human Brain. Here, major midline structures may be seen from the level of the hindbrain through the forebrain

This lower portion of the brain is the most primitive region; in fact, we inherited the brain stem from our reptilian ancestors. Although it has been altered in humans through evolution, the basic structure of the hindbrain is often referred to as the *r-complex* (as in reptilian) because of its developmental origins. This region is responsible for maintaining life without conscious thought. This may be why many lower species generally function the same when their forebrain is removed. They continue to breathe, eat, sleep, and mate much like before such removal took place. Because they never engaged in much problem solving or abstract thinking, their existence is largely unchanged despite this significant difference in brain structure. Still, it is important to understand the primary structures in the human hindbrain because if they are not functioning properly, that can seriously affect cognitive ability and resulting behavior.

The *medulla oblongata* contains tracts and reflex centers (part of reticular formation [see below]) that are largely responsible for basic bodily functions such as respiration (e.g., breathing); cardiovascular function (e.g., heart rate, blood pressure); and other essential processes (e.g., vomiting). The medulla is the lowest lying structure of the brain and can best be thought of, in terms of structure and functioning, as an enlarged extension of the spinal cord.

Key for our purposes, the medulla oblongata is an important "station" for the reticular formation—also called reticular activating system (RAS)—which is an organized network of nerve cell bodies that extends to other regions of the brain, including those in the midbrain and forebrain areas. The RAS is vitally important in controlling complex reflexes (e.g., sneezing) and motor activities, and most importantly, in aiding higher brain centers in determining levels of arousal. The importance of this last function of reticular formation will be discussed later, but the reader should note here that structural damage or abnormal functioning of the RAS in the medulla oblongata is a predicting factor in the development of disposition toward criminality.

The *cerebellum*, like the medulla, contains reflex centers for maintaining posture and advanced motor activities (e.g., muscle contractions, limb movements). Two important functions of the cerebellum are of particular interest to criminologists. The first involves aiding the higher brain centers in establishing effective spatial orientation, which we will see has important implications on the cognitive processes of an individual. The other key function of the cerebellum for our purposes is that it acts as a type of mediator or command center for a variety of sensory signals. More specifically, it integrates numerous forms of information from the eyes, ears, skin, and so on, and combines this knowledge with that of its spatial function and messages from the higher brain areas in order to produce the most effective motor response in a given situation. Studies have shown that the cerebellum coordinates learning and helps coordinate fine-tuning of social tasks, and that structural changes in this brain region peak at age 18.

Sometimes, our complex motor skills are primarily learned in other areas of the brain but then stored in the cerebellum. This makes it much easier for us to engage in complex physical tasks without having to learn them over and over again. Rather, we can devote more of our brain "energy" to other purposes once we have initially learned the motor skill. For instance, when initially learning to walk, ride a bike, or drive a car with a stick shift, we would be using the motor cortex region of the brain (which is located near the top of the cerebral cortex where the frontal and parietal lobes meet; see Chapter 6). However, retaining the ability to walk, ride a bike, or drive a manual transmission from that point would largely be a function of the cerebellum.

Animals that engage in complex motor activities that require the highest levels of equilibrium, balance, and spatial positioning—for example, birds that fly—have the largest cerebellums relative to size (Starr & Taggart, 1987). The malfunctioning of the cerebellum is perhaps best illustrated in humans when a large quantity of alcohol has been consumed. The effects of alcohol on the cerebellum are what cause the "drunken sailor" walk, often to the point of falling down. Other complications resulting from a poorly functioning cerebellum are dizziness/nausea (i.e., vertigo), slurred speech, loss of motor coordination, and tremors. The implications of structural differences in the cerebellum will become clear later when we discuss such links with criminality, particularly the differences between men and women in terms of brain functioning.

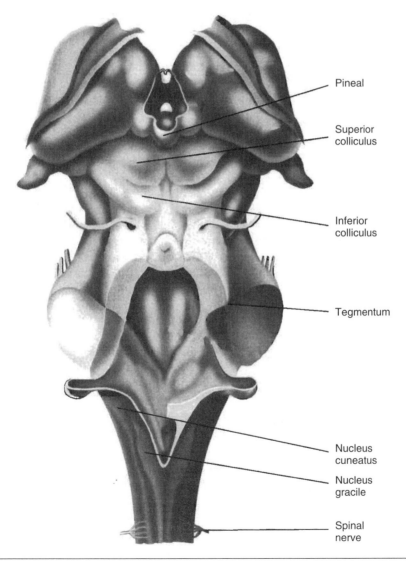

Pineal

Superior colliculus

Inferior colliculus

Tegmentum

Nucleus cuneatus

Nucleus gracile

Spinal nerve

Figure 5.2   The Human Brain Stem. Here, the major structures of the brain stem may be seen

As shown in Figure 5.2, the *reticular nuclei* is a portion of the brain stem that is home to neurotransmitter cell bodies (e.g., serotonin; see Chapter 7) that create and disperse such neurotransmitters to other parts of the brain. (This system consists of the *nucleus cuneatus* and *nucleus gracile,* as shown in Figure 5.2.) This section of the brain stem has been implicated in several clinical disorders. For example, this region has been found to be lacking in serotonin by as much as 40% in individuals who have been diagnosed with bipolar disorder, which may contribute to atrophy of neuronal and synaptic development.

Another structure of hindbrain is the *pons* (see Figure 5.1), which is largely a region through which nerve tracts pass on their way from one brain center to another. In fact, the word *pons* means "bridge." This is an appropriate name for this structure because of its primary function of connecting the rest of the hindbrain, particularly the cerebellum, to the higher brain centers such as the limbic system. One of the known features of the pons is that it acts as a key structure in our ability to experience dreams, which occur during rapid eye movement (REM) episodes of the sleeping state (Kantrowitz, 2002; Solms, 2004). Research has established that such phases of sleep are necessary for internalizing and interpreting memories in our brain. Recent studies have also found that inhibited or interrupted REM states can have a profound effect on behavior. For example, individuals who fail to experience a healthy level of REM sleep have been shown to be more irritable and aggressive, and they lack the ability to remember as compared to those who do not experience such sleeping states.

Although the pons has not been linked directly with criminality, its malfunction is likely to be an intervening element in brain processes that are commonly found in chronic offenders. For instance, if the stimuli normally processed in the medulla and cerebellum are not properly transferred to the mid- or forebrain regions, then sound cognitive decision making will be inhibited. Another possible scenario involves the lack of REM sleep in producing a disposition toward irritability and aggressiveness that has been observed in individuals who have an impaired pons. These types of scenarios, as well as other possible deficiencies, suggest that the pons and other areas of the hind region should be examined more by future criminological research.

Midbrain Structure and Functioning

The *midbrain* is an important area due to the convergence of sensory information in this region. Although the midbrain is much more important in controlling bodily responses in fish and amphibians (e.g., frogs can function normally without their forebrain as long as their midbrain is intact), it is still an important region in humans despite its relatively small size. The roof of the midbrain, called the *tectum* (meaning "roof" in Latin), integrates incoming visual, tactile, and auditory signals in order to coordinate reflex responses. The tectum contains nerve tracts that attach directly to the thalamus and ultimately link up to the cerebrum and other forebrain regions.

Also important in the midbrain is the reticular activating system (RAS), also called the reticular formation, which includes the *tegmentum* (meaning "cover" in Latin) and various nuclei (as shown in Figure 5.2) and *colliculi* (meaning "little hills" in Latin), as shown in Figures 5.1 and 5.2, which provide necessary communication paths between the hindbrain and forebrain areas. Although the RAS begins in the core of the medulla oblongata and stretches through the midbrain to the lower regions of the forebrain, the central core of the RAS is located in the midbrain. In ways that are not yet fully understood, the reticular formation works to sort out important stimuli from all input so that it may be forwarded to the higher brain centers that manage conscious thought processes. Studies suggest that this filtering function of the RAS is likely developed from both innate genetic wiring and learning, and its effectiveness can be seen in a mother who sleeps through loud noises but wakens upon hearing the faint cry of her infant (Audesirk & Audesirk, 1989).

Furthermore, the RAS serves as a type of toggle switch that controls which higher brain system—limbic system or cerebrum (higher brain)—is in charge given the current situation (both of these systems will be discussed below). This toggling of the RAS tends to occur when we are either emotionally charged or relaxed (Howard, 2006). When we are in a highly emotional situation, such as being in danger, the RAS tells our brain to shut down the higher brain (cerebrum) functioning while emphasizing the limbic system (emotional center). This fight-or-flight mode forces our brain to rely on instinct or previous experience in handling the situation. Such situations occur when we are being challenged by others or during scary events, such as encountering a bear when we are hiking in the woods. On the other hand, the RAS will tell our brain to relax the limbic system when we are relaxing in our home, which allows our higher-learning brain to take control of our functions. This is why constructive learning can take place only if an individual is in an environment that poses no danger or risk to the individual. Implications from this can be seen in the learning differentials between students in stable, safe schools as compared to those in schools that are riddled with gangs and crime. If students are always on guard against potential dangers, they will not learn as efficiently as those in safe environments.

Colliculi, which are responsible for reflexive responses to auditory and visual stimuli, are divided into two structures: inferior colliculus and superior colliculus (see Figure 5.2). The inferior colliculus is responsible for responding quickly to auditory stimuli. For example, if a sudden blast occurs, we will automatically jerk to look at it. However, this reflex can be controlled, particularly if we are expecting such a noise, such as when someone is hunting and he or she hears a crack of a twig. The superior colliculus is responsible for reaction to visual stimuli. When you see a movement in your peripheral vision, you will automatically look at it. Such quick and automatic response is generally important for survival given the need to see projectiles coming at one's body. This reflex is harder to control than auditory signals governed by the inferior colliculus, even when one is anticipating such visual stimuli. For example, planes that drop nuclear bombs tend to use heavy curtains to protect their crew from inevitably looking when the bomb goes off. All persons will look toward strong rays of light, even those that may damage their eyes. This reflex is a result of millions of years of evolution and, thus, is almost impossible to override even when one makes every conscious effort to do so.

After reviewing the brain stem region and midbrain, it is not surprising, given the limitations of their cognitive structure, that fish, amphibians, and reptiles are capable of little else than sleeping, eating, fighting, and reproducing. Although the reticular formation strongly links the hindbrain to other regions and allows for some level of arousal in this basic makeup, no advanced cognitive thought processes are possible without the more advanced regions (e.g., forebrain). Fortunately, our brain structures evolved considerably beyond this stage.

This is not to say that this region is not extremely important in terms of emotions and behavior that directly affect criminality. For example, recent brain imaging research has shown that modern drugs (e.g., selective serotonin reuptake inhibitors [SSRIs]) that are effective in curbing depression and other disorders work by affecting the functioning of the primitive hind regions of the brain (see Mayberg et al., 2005). Despite the primitive nature and limitations of the r-complex, the brain structures (e.g., ventral tegmental) and functioning in this region—particularly that of the RAS—have important implications for criminality that will be addressed later in this chapter. Nevertheless, the significance of the hindbrain and midbrain regions is often overshadowed by the more distinguishable region in humans: the subcortical region of the forebrain area.

Structures of the Subcortical (Limbic) Region

Covering the hindbrain and midbrain regions, the next area to develop is the *limbic system* (or leopard complex) that evolved during the emergence of new lifestyle characteristics, particularly those of early mammalian life forms (e.g., leopards) who spent more time involved in play, pair-bonding between sexual partners, and nurturing their young (Ellis & Walsh, 2000). Along with the brain stem, the limbic system (see Figure 5.3) helps regulate blood pressure, heart rate, blood sugar, and other important bodily functions. Importantly, this region of the brain, which is also called the paleomammalian system (*paleo* meaning "early") because of the evolutionary stage in which it emerged, largely coordinates nerve impulses to and from the skeletal muscle and internal organ activity involved in emotional expression (particularly the "social emotions" that will be discussed at length later).

Through a complex series of processes, these emotional impulses trigger limbic structures (e.g., hypothalamus) to release a variety of hormones that physiologically alter our bodies both structurally and functionally via chemical and electrical stimuli. Importantly, the limbic system also communicates with the frontal cortex and other higher regions, where the emotional signals and reason are integrated into purposeful planning and decision making. Thus, it is easy to understand how a breakdown in the functioning of the limbic system could have serious implications in terms of criminal behavior.

Accounting for approximately one fifth of brain volume, the limbic system consists of a diverse group of brain structures that play key roles in responsiveness and learning, which are essential in understanding the development of criminality. Although considered a portion of the forebrain, the limbic system lies below the relatively large cerebral cortex (also called the cerebrum) and is therefore considered part of the *subcortical* region.

The limbic system is responsible for a variety of functions, including regulating motivation, libido, bonding with others, appetite, sleep, and other activities. More

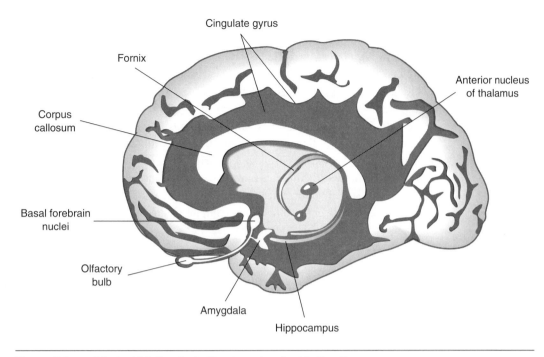

Figure 5.3   Principal Midline Brain Structures Involved in Emotions

importantly, this system sets the emotional state of the brain and remembers such emotional states. If a person has problems in the limbic system, he or she is more likely to be irritable, pessimistic, unmotivated, and isolated, as well as criminal. Although most brain studies (for a review, see Raine, 1993; Rowe, 2002) have implicated the frontal and temporal regions of the cerebrum as being the most vital areas for criminological research, we disagree. We believe most of the problems with individuals are due to problems in the limbic system structures and their interconnections, or lack thereof. The diverse group of structures that makes up the limbic system will now be reviewed.

Amygdala and Hippocampus

Found in the lower part of the limbic region (see Figure 5.3), the *amygdala* is an almond-shaped emotion and partial memory center, and the *hippocampus* is the primary memory center. These two brain formations are believed to be the most relevant portions of the brain underlying emotions and feeling states related to survival functions (e.g., fighting), as well as to social functions and responses (e.g., jealousy, anger). For instance, the amygdala has been found to be directly responsible for changes in violent or hostile activity, particularly when it is injured or altered (Blundell, 1975). Ironically, much has been discovered about the amygdala inhibiting aggression in animals, which is likely in humans as well (Mirsky & Siegel, 1994). The amygdala has been implicated in numerous clinical problems. Specifically, in bipolar disorder the amygdala appears to show a significant increase in neural transmissions toward emotional stimuli, and in many situations shows a reaction that goes beyond a typical response.

The amygdala has also received a lot of attention because it is the most seizure-prone structure in the brain. Modern medical procedures that have been developed to limit excessive epileptic seizures have, in turn, also led to procedures to manipulate the amygdala in order to reduce aggression in people, typically psychiatric patients. In fact, amygdalectomies—the severing of neural connections between amygdala and surrounding regions—have been used for some time in countries such as Japan and India to diminish aggressive and destructive behavior in both children and adults. Such attempts have shown mixed success, but the ethical problems in using such measures among convicts would generally preclude its use. Nevertheless, a relatively recent review of these studies (Raine, 1993) concluded that "amygdalectomy may be more effective than earlier studies indicate" (p. 124).

The amygdala is extremely important in integrating senses (such as combining what is heard with what is seen) and in forming memories by linking particular emotions with given inputs from the environment. This last function is especially important in the maintenance of social emotions (e.g., shame, pride) and moral reasoning that seem to play a significant role in dispositions toward criminality (Chandler & Moran, 1990; Tangney, 1995; see Chapter 8). It is notable that the brain structures that regulate the amygdala, such as the frontal lobe, are not completely developed in teenagers, which may explain why they seem to engage in impulsive behaviors without any constraint or consideration for long-term consequences of their actions.

BOX 5.1   Psychopathy, Amygdala Dysfunction, and Inability to Recognize Emotion

---

A revealing study that was published in the *Journal of Genetic Psychology* (Stevens, Charman, & Blair, 2001) examined the ability of children with behavioral and emotional difficulties, who had been divided according to their scores on a psychopathy screening device (see Frick & Hare, 2001), to recognize emotional facial expressions and vocal tones. The children with psychopathic tendencies and a group of comparison children were presented with two facial expression and two vocal tone subtests from the Diagnostic Analysis of Nonverbal Accuracy (Nowicki & Duke, 1994). These subtests measure the ability to accurately identify happy, sad, fearful, and angry facial expressions and vocal effects. The children with psychopathic tendencies showed impairments in the recognition of both fearful and sad facial expressions as well as a sad vocal tone. The results were interpreted by the authors as suggesting that the development of psychopathic tendencies may reflect early amygdala dysfunction.

Given the important role of the amygdala in the area of recognizing and responding to various emotions, it is not surprising that this study and others have consistently reported finding deficiencies in this brain structure among psychopaths. After all, one of the key characteristics of psychopaths is the inability to feel strong emotional bonds with others or to empathize with their victims. It is likely that this lack of emotion is also tied to their amazing ability to lie to others and treat others poorly without feeling pangs of conscience or guilt. So trauma or other negative influences in the early development of the amygdala (as well as other structures in the limbic system) can have profound effects on the development of psychopathic and antisocial tendencies.

Named for its resemblance to a seahorse, the hippocampus is another very important structure in the lower limbic region. Along with the frontal cortex and thalamus, it is one of the most important structures in the formation of long-term memory and is vital in the integration of certain types of information, such as associations between one thing and another. Failure to understand links between different occurrences (or the ability to remember those links) reduces the ability of individuals to anticipate and/or comprehend cause-effect relationships; criminals, particularly violent offenders, have been found to lack this ability (Larson, Lynch, Games, & Seubert, 1999). To clarify, if an individual cannot predict how his hitting a co-worker will likely result in loss of employment, then this obviously would predispose such an individual toward using violence in times of anger. Continuously communicating with the frontal cortex, a healthy functioning hippocampus is key in forming cognitive maps of such causal processes.

Besides being a key memory center, one of the responsibilities of the hippocampus is to maintain equilibrium among the flow of signals between neurons, which are communicating important signals to different regions of the brain. This function becomes particularly important during times of stress or arousal, which we will see is of particular interest in understanding criminality. Because the hippocampus is a primary memory structure and regulatory unit of the brain, it is easy to imagine that a damaged or malfunctioning hippocampus would produce various implications for predisposing one to developmental problems throughout life, such as learning disabilities, poor school/work performance, and so on.

Recent studies have shown that new cells are often produced in the hippocampus, as well as other areas of the brain (e.g., the olfactory bulb). However, when individuals experience a prolonged period of stress, it triggers a state of depression, which suppresses neurogenesis (i.e., origin of cells) in the hippocampus. This results in a shrinking of the hippocampus. Recently developed drugs attempt to compensate for this reduced rate of cell production, but their delayed rate of effect is understandable in the sense that it takes time to tell the hippocampus to produce new cells that lift the mood of individuals. Notably, physical exercise naturally increases the production of neurogenesis in the hippocampus, as does electroconvulsive therapy, otherwise known as "shock therapy," which is currently practiced by many respected institutions.

The results reported above are consistent with a recent study that further explored the effects of hippocampus size (Gilbertson et al., 2002). This study examined 40 twin pairs (80 identical twins), 40 who saw combat in Vietnam and their identical counterparts who did not see combat, and found that the size of the hippocampus predicted the vulnerability of certain individuals to posttraumatic stress disorder (PTSD). None of the "stay-at-home" twins had experienced PTSD, and of the combat veteran twin counterparts who were diagnosed with PTSD, there was a statistically significant likelihood that they had a smaller hippocampus than their counterparts. In the veterans who were affected, hippocampal volume was 10% smaller on average than that of others who had seen combat. This study actually showed that individuals with smaller hippocampal structures are more likely to suffer from PTSD and other anxiety or mood disorders.

Additionally, other studies using brain imaging have found that individuals with smaller hippocampus structures are more susceptible to clinical depression (Sheline,

Mittler, & Mintun, 2002). This problem has become a priority in mental health because of recent findings that show an actual shrinkage of the hippocampus in persons suffering from forms of dementia and Alzheimer's disease. However, preliminary studies also indicate that new medications may not only delay this reduction, but may actually reverse it in many cases (Underwood, 2002). Some experts currently believe that directly stimulating the hippocampal region may actually be a more efficient way of dealing with depression, as opposed to more indirect ways of manipulating neurotransmitters (e.g., serotonin) via current mainstream drugs (SSRIs).

One related area of research involves what causes the hippocampus to shrink. The best guess currently is the stress hormone cortisol and its chemical cousins or derivatives. *Cortisol* is key in priming the mind and body for stressful events, but studies have established that in frequently high levels, cortisol negatively affects the hippocampal structure and function, as well as other related areas of the brain. So one promising area of research involves medication and/or behavioral therapy that attempts to keep cortisol levels in check. We will see in following chapters that cortisol and other related hormones have implications for gender differences in cognition and even criminality, which are likely related to its influence on the hippocampus and related brain structures.

Not surprisingly, studies have shown that injury to or failure of the amygdala/hippocampal area has been linked to criminality, particularly when the injury was to the left hemispheric portions of these centers (for a summary, see Volavka, 1999). It is important to note that the amygdala and hippocampus are two of the most "plastic" structures of the brain, meaning that they change physiologically as a result of cues from environmental experiences. This, too, will become important later when we further discuss the behavioral inhibition system of individuals that suppresses irrational behaviors (similar to Freud's superego). For now, it is sufficient to realize that the amygdala/hippocampal area is continually being calibrated according to cumulative experiences and that the earlier these experiences occur, the more effect they seem to have for better or for worse (Walsh, 2002).

Thalamus, Hypothalamus, and Pituitary

Other important structures of the limbic region include the *thalamus,* the *hypothalamus,* and the *pituitary gland,* which all play key roles in the functioning of the nervous systems—both central and peripheral—for which the brain acts as command central (see Figure 5.4). The thalamus is a major coordinating center for sensory and motor signals. It serves as a relay station for sensory impulses (e.g., pain) from all over the body, sending them on to the higher regions in the cerebral cortex. The thalamus receives and passes on sensory impulses for all of our senses except for smell (which is unique in that it goes directly from the olfactory area in the lower frontal lobe to the hypothalamus). Because of this role in the relaying of most of our sensory information, the thalamus is very important in the formation of memory, which is basically the process of storing things that we see, hear, touch, and taste, so that we can use that information in a useful way, such as positive reinforcement or punishment for behavior. One example of the importance of the thalamus in feeling sensations of pleasure and pain is its strong relation to *septal nucleus* (i.e., septum), which sits adjacent to and just in front of the thalamus and is the center for sexual orgasm. Obviously, if the thalamus is not operating efficiently, our ability to sense and learn from our environment, as well as the capability to remember such experiences, will be seriously impaired.

The thalamus not only passes on this sensory information to the higher regions of the brain, but also plays an important part in sorting what is important from what is unimportant. One of the key areas to which the thalamus projects these signals is known as the "prefrontal" area of the cortex, which is the most anterior part of the frontal lobe. This prefrontal area is generally considered the brain region that is most centrally involved in abstract cognitive functions and higher intelligence, as well as behavioral inhibition and emotion regulation. Furthermore, the thalamus works in conjunction with another subcortical structure, the hippocampus, to assist the cerebrum in regulating individuals' level of cortical activity.

This level of activity can be measured, albeit not specifically, by an electroencephalograph (EEG, which will be discussed in more detail in a later section). Unfortunately, the EEG cannot distinguish the particular roles of the thalamus or hippocampus in the regulation of such activity. Nevertheless, the role of the thalamus in processing brain signals, especially those related to criminal behavior, is very important. Unfortunately, research has not explored the direct links between thalamus dysfunction and criminal activity.

Just below the thalamus sits the hypothalamus, which largely monitors body temperature and blood pressure, as well as hunger and other visceral activities. Along with

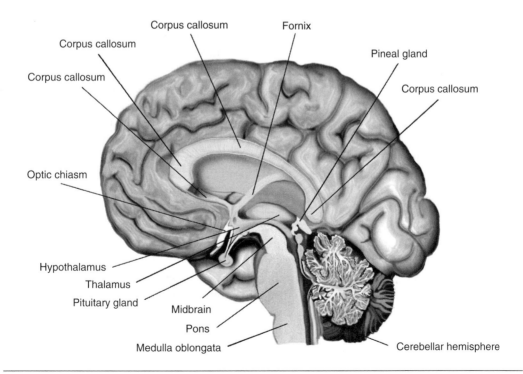

Figure 5.4   A View of the Human Brain Showing the Hindbrain and Forebrain Structures

the thalamus and hippocampus, the hypothalamus works with the frontal cortex in the formation of long-term memory. The hippocampus has close communication lines established with the hypothalamus, largely by way of a bundle of axons called the *fornix* (see Figure 5.4). It is likely that when there is a communication problem in the hippocampus-fornix-hypothalamus system, there are perceptual and consequential behavioral problems (Fishbein, 2001). Perhaps most importantly, the hypothalamus, along with the *pituitary gland* (see Figure 5.4), coordinates the *neuroendocrine system*. Together, the hypothalamus and pituitary form a partnership, often referred to as the H-P system, that determines the levels of various chemicals throughout the brain and body that largely regulate the way we perceive and behave in our environment.

The neuroendocrine system consists of the complex network of structures and processes whereby a variety of hormones are released internally into the bloodstream in order to influence the activities of tissues and organs. The hormones are released by various glandular structures (e.g., the thyroid and adrenal glands), with the "master gland" being the pituitary, which is suspended by a slender stalk that extends downward from the hypothalamus. It is interesting that the pituitary is relatively small in all humans (about the size of a green pea), given the pervasive role it plays in a variety of functions.

The pituitary has a posterior lobe and an anterior lobe. The posterior lobe is largely responsible for producing hormones that regulate kidney function through the production of antidiuretic hormone, which is not known to have links to criminality. On the other hand, the anterior pituitary produces a variety of hormones, including growth hormone, prolactin, and adrenecorticopic stimulating hormone (ACTH). Problems, including those of perception and behavior, tend to occur when there is an excess or deficiency of one of these hormones, especially ACTH (which will be discussed later in this book). It is obvious that there are many criminological implications regarding the pituitary in regulating various hormones that influence decision making and rational thought processes. We will be reviewing some of these effects below, as well as in the following chapter.

One of the most important roles the pituitary gland plays is in the realm of sleep. During sleep states, the pituitary releases growth hormone, which stimulates the production of various proteins that aid in helping to repair damaged tissues in the body. Also, this pituitary gland releases important sex hormones during puberty that help explain the intensity of teenagers' emotions and may be responsible for their erratic behavior. In conjunction with the hypothalamus, the pituitary works to regulate hormones that control human emotions, including aggression, that have vital implications for criminality. More discussion regarding such hormones will occur in future chapters.

The hypothalamus is, in a sense, a "brain of the brain" in that it sends electric and chemical signals that command the secretion of various hormones—such as stress and sex hormones—that set into motion an immense number of actions in various parts of the body. One well-known example is menstruation, which begins (obviously in females only) in the brain as a hormonal feedback loop between the hypothalamus and the pituitary gland (Halpern, 2000). The neuroendocrine system will be discussed in more detail in later chapters, as will the specific hormones that have been linked to criminality.

A part of the hypothalamus called the *supra chiasmatic nucleus* (SCN) interprets signals from the eyes to control falling asleep and awakening. The SCN is named for its location above (hence *supra*) the optic chiasm, which is shown in Figure 5.4. The SCN is composed of the cells in the front of the hypothalamus that are active in sleep but not in the waking period, and these frontal cells communicate to the back portions of the structure to tell what is going on; however, in some individuals, this communication is not efficient or is disturbed by abnormal biochemical signals. This results in sleeping and waking disorders that may have profound effects on individuals' behavior. Also, signals from the retina in our eye determine information that is relayed through the optic nerve, the optic chiasm, the SCN, and the rest of the hypothalamus. When the sun goes down each day, the SCN also communicates with the pineal gland (shown in Figure 5.4) to trigger the production of melatonin, a hormone that induces sleepiness. Interestingly, melatonin levels can be reduced at night if an individual stays in bright light; on the other hand, melatonin production can be triggered during the day if an individual is in darkness.

The hypothalamus has been found to have important effects on various correlates of criminality. For instance, the hypothalamus largely controls heart rate and other functions of the autonomic nervous system, which has been strongly linked to criminality (see future chapters). The hypothalamus is a vital component in the management of affect and emotion, which, of course, is essential in understanding situational behaviors (Fishbein, 2001). Studies have also shown that lesions in the hypothalamus caused by severe head blows from child abuse has been linked to the development of criminality, particularly violent offending, in later years (McCanne & Milner, 1991; for a discussion, see Raine, 1993).

Furthermore, the relative size and structure of the hypothalamus has been shown to vary between human males and females, as well as across rodent species, due to evolutionary adaptations (see Walsh, 2002). Regardless of size differences, the hypothalamus-pituitary connection is important in the production of reproductive hormones (e.g., androgens). Studies have clearly shown that when male hormones are produced, typical male behavior results, and when such androgens are removed, typical female behavior results (for a review, see Halpern, 2000). This link has important implications given the consistently strong finding that males tend to be much more aggressive and criminal than females (see following chapters). Thus, whether as dual control centers for the neuroendocrine system or as separate brain structures, the hypothalamus and the pituitary gland are certainly two of the most important structures in the development of criminality (see further discussion of the hypothalamic-pituitary-adrenal [HPA] axis). Studies have also linked the hypothalamus with headaches due to its part in regulating hormones, sleep, and hunger. For example, migraine headache symptoms are linked with nausea and vomiting, which are signals sent from the hypothalamus to the migraine generator of the brain, the upper brain stem. Research regarding headaches is largely unexplored but is quite worthy of further investigation by criminological researchers.

Another important factor related to the HPA system is the level of anxiety persons experience. The abnormalities that cause some people to have health and psychological problems are often due to a system that causes "overdrive" production of the fight-or-flight response, which results in such physiological responses as higher breathing and heart rates, as well as increases in blood pressure. Specifically, abnormalities in the hypothalamus can cause an excess in chemicals that stimulate the pituitary gland. This often results in overproduction of ACTH in the pituitary (see above), which tells the adrenal glands to kick in. In turn, the adrenal glands release the hormone *cortisol*, which acts to boost blood sugar to give the body more energy to deal with stress. There are important functions and reasons for the production of ACTH and cortisol, which are vital for normal functioning and adapting to stressful conditions. However, some individuals have physiological dispositions or environmental conditions that tell their nervous system to produce an excessive amount of these chemicals.

Problems with this system, such as excessive levels of stress because of abuse, can lead to difficulties in handling normal activities. Studies have shown that abnormal levels of cortisol are significantly linked to criminal activity (for a review, see Raine, 1993). Chronic levels of cortisol production, as well as other chemicals involved in this process, can actually lead to death because of the constant draw on the body from unrelieved stress. A healthy HPA system is required for healthy and normal functioning, but that system can be detrimental when one of its components, be it the hypothalamus, pituitary, or adrenal glands, is not functioning properly and gears our system into a constant state of arousal. This type of system is often seen in persons who were chronically abused or neglected in early years of development (Perry, 2001).

Other important brain structures located in or near the limbic region should be discussed. Although virtually no studies have identified these areas as important in the study of criminality, we believe their possible role should be considered more carefully. The first of these structures, the *pineal gland*, can be found on the back side of the limbic region, situated just behind the thalamus (almost like a stub tail; see previous figures). This cone-shaped structure has been considered a vestigial third eye in light of its important role in receiving nerve impulses from the eyes and its prominence in certain species that depend on extraordinary sight, such as birds. The pineal gland, like most other structures in the neuroendocrine system, largely functions according to signals it receives from the hypothalamus. As regulated by the SCN (see above), the pineal gland releases melatonin, which is a hormone that brings on sleep and drowsiness.

Although more important in lower species, the pineal gland still plays a role in reproductive physiology and, more uniquely, is responsible for regulating the circadian rhythms in humans through hormone secretion, particularly melatonin, which is secreted most at night and suppressed when light is detected. Circadian rhythms are those in which physiological events recur approximately every 24 hours, often even in the absence of environmental cues. In addition to hormonal secretion, these physiological effects include significant changes in basic metabolism, body temperature, heart rate, and blood pressure, as well as telling the body when to go to sleep and when to wake up.

Studies have shown that people are physiologically designed (although less so than most plants and animals) according to such a "biological clock," which is an internal time-measuring mechanism that has a biochemical basis. Environments that aren't congruent with such human biorhythms tend to cause mood disorders (see Nilsen, Hansen, & Olstad, 2004). For instance, the limited amounts of daylight in winter, particularly in areas far from the equator, cause what has been labeled *seasonal affective disorder*. This condition, even in relatively weak levels, has been shown to influence rates of depression, anxiety, and other clinical disorders that have been found to be correlated with criminal behavior (Ennis & McConville, 2004; Nilsen et al., 2004), and some of these links may be related to dopamine receptor genes.

An example is provided by Davies (1982), who found that assaults by prison inmates tend to be clustered at a certain time of day. Interestingly, that peak time is 11:00 to 11:30 a.m., which would correspond to the approximate midpoint of waking hours, as well as the time in which glucose levels likely hit their lowest point (Marks, 1976). A deficit of glucose (blood sugar, which can be seen as brain "fuel") not only limits concentration and sound decision making, but also causes irritability and aggression, especially in hypoglycemics. So, for a variety of reasons, it is important to monitor inmates' diets, which studies demonstrate can influence violent behavior in prisons (Brown, Esbensen, & Geis, 2006). Solutions include eating multiple meals throughout the day, rather than only two or three. Also, modern medicine has made significant progress in this area, particularly with drugs, such as the hormone glucagon, that stimulate the release of glucose. These are just two examples of possible links between circadian rhythms, glucose levels, and criminality, and they suggest that the pineal gland and related chemicals should be a target for future research.

Such research on the pineal gland and circadian rhythms seems even more relevant given that scientists have recently (February 2002) reported the discovery of new photoreceptor cells that actually reset the body's master biological clock (Berson, Dunn, & Takao, 2002). Until now, scientists have always assumed that rods or cones in our eyes were responsible for both vision and this "resynchronizing" of our circadian rhythms. However, by observing animals and humans who were blind and without rods or cones, scientists now realize that there are actually two different systems in the eye: one for vision via rods and cones, and another for setting the clock that involves these new cells communicating with the appropriate brain structures, such as the pineal gland. This breakthrough is currently changing scientific knowledge about how light is received and interpreted by our nervous systems, and further implicates the pineal gland and the body's biological clock as a potential source for affecting human behavior.

Additionally, it is also possible that the effects of the pineal gland and circadian rhythms may be more indirect, namely, through seasonal changes. To clarify, in some species of birds, the sex hormones are increased in the summer because of extended periods of light that is absorbed by the pineal gland. This increase in light tells the pineal gland to secrete less melatonin, which is secreted at night and, thus, suppressed by light. Without the hormone's inhibitory effects, the gonads of the birds increase in size, which then causes numerous behavioral changes (e.g., migrating, singing, courting) related to mating. This type of cycle based on extended hours of light is called *seasonal photoperiodicity* and increases the likelihood that successful reproduction in many bird species will take place at the most optimal time.

Perhaps this same type of cycle in humans is related to the disposition and incidence of criminality. For example, studies have shown that the incidence of most serious crimes increases dramatically in the summer and warmer months (see numerous years of data from the Department of Justice's *Uniform Crime Reports,* which is also provided on a state-by-state basis; e.g., see State of New Jersey, 2004) and studies have also found that criminality is associated with higher levels of sex hormones, such as testosterone (Archer, 1991; Booth & Osgood, 1993; Olweus, 1987) or those related to menstrual cycles (for a review, see Fishbein, 1992). It is possible that one of the reasons for the increase in crime in summer and/or warmer months is due to the extended periods of light that limit the amount of melatonin that the pineal gland secretes, thereby allowing for elevated levels of sex hormones, which have been clearly linked with criminal behavior. Although there are other established explanations for the increase in crime during the summer (e.g., more opportunities), this does not mean that the influence of circadian rhythms can be ruled out. The criminological literature is silent about this possibility and, thus, should be examined in future research.

Another limbic-related structure that has received virtually no attention in the criminological literature is the *cingulate gyrus* (see Figure 5.3). Sitting atop the limbic region and corpus callosum, but covered by the higher cortical regions, the cingulate gyrus is in a great position to act as the brain's "gearshift," allowing it to transfer from one thought to another. It receives signals primarily from the thalamus and the cerebral cortex, but from other areas, too. It has been linked to several clinical disorders, including obsessive-compulsive disorder, as well as to disorders related to the prefrontal cortex (see below), basal ganglia, amygdala, and other structures (Damasio, 1994; Diamond, Scheibel, & Elson, 1985; Eccles, 1989). The anterior portion of the cingulate gyrus is the most responsible region for relating to the prefrontal cortex and areas of the limbic system, and it has been linked to the rage responses of individuals (Guyton & Hall, 2006). When working properly, the cingulate gyrus works toward flexibility and shifting attention—in other words, adaptability. Consistently, it also helps postpartum women facilitate maternal care and play, and regulate audiovocal signals.

When it is not working, the cingulate region causes excessive worrying and argumentativeness, which is largely due to inflexibility and an inability to adjust to environmental factors (Guyton & Hall, 2006). It is not surprising that abnormalities in the cingulate gyrus result in behavioral problems such as obsessive-compulsive disorder and road rage, both of which deal with chronic fixation on a regular ordering of the world, which almost never happens in reality. Individuals with an abnormally functioning cingulate region respond to environmental stimuli in an exaggerated, often criminalistic way that does not correspond to a normal disposition. Again, this mostly goes back to the ability to be flexible, which problems in the cingulate gyrus hinder. This results in a person becoming argumentative and uncooperative in situations that can be resolved easily.

In fact, some studies using an imaging technique called single-photon emission computed tomography have shown that if the cingulate gyrus region is not functioning properly, individuals may not be able to successfully handle anxiety or stress. Furthermore, this structure is especially important for criminality, because it helps regulate emotional responses, especially those regarding aggression and pain. It has been theorized that individuals with a malfunctioning cingulate gyrus can actually get "stuck" on bad thoughts, and they can't move past them in a healthy fashion (Begley, 2001a).

Additional research has shown how a deficient cingulate gyrus can even make an individual believe that he or she is hearing voices when the sounds are actually produced in one's head (Begley, 2001b). On the other hand, in healthy individuals, this "reality-check" region is the structure that typically notifies us when we are dreaming. This structure examines the images we perceive and determines their authenticity. So, it is not surprising that when this structure is not working properly, an individual can believe that he or she is seeing or hearing someone who is really there. Furthermore, these images appear as real as the images you are seeing or hearing at this moment. Studies have shown that overactivity in this area is linked to chronic offending, particularly violent offenses, along with a diminished amount of activity in the prefrontal cortex and the left temporal lobe (see Begley, 2001b).

Studies examining sex variations in EEGs and regional cerebral blood flow have found that one of the most significant differences when individuals are posed with a problem to solve is that women had higher metabolism rates in the cingulate region than did men (Gur et al., 1995). Perhaps this is one step in understanding why women tend to make different (usually better) decisions when it comes to deviant behavior. Ultimately, we believe that the cingulate gyrus is a brain region that may be more involved in the development of criminality than would be suggested in the extant literature.

One mesolimbic structure that has been linked to deviant activity, particularly drug abuse and other compulsive behaviors (e.g., chronic gambling), is the *nucleus accumbens,* which is located in an area lateral to the septal region. This region is often referred to as the reward center of the brain, probably because this structure is strongly affected by the release of a neurotransmitter called dopamine, which communicates pleasure in the brain. The link between the nucleus accumbens, dopamine, and the frontal cortex of the brain is believed by many experts to be one of the key functioning systems in individuals' sensation-seeking drive (often referred to as the behavioral activating system), which we will discuss in detail in the next chapter. Researchers have linked poor teen motivation to an underdeveloped nucleus accumbens; specifically, teenagers had less activity in this region during a gambling game, which therefore has significant implications regarding motivations and rewards (Bjork et al., 2004).

In fact, results from brain imaging studies show that this is one of the key structures implicated in the addiction to smoking tobacco, which research has shown to be the most addictive drug (and certainly the most deadly) in modern society. The nicotine creates sensations of pleasure via the nucleus accumbens by telling it to release dopamine. Notably, the nucleus accumbens appears to be one of the primary structures involved in pleasure seeking and thus is implicated in risk-taking behavior. This has become one of the premier personality traits in the criminological research (see Gottfredson & Hirschi, 1990), so the implications of a deficient nucleus accumbens are obviously an important area for future research regarding personality traits and disorders.

The *anterior cingulate cortex* is also shown by recent research to be one of the primary portions of the brain that becomes activated when painful events occur

(Lieberman & Eisenberger, 2005). This research has not only implicated this region for developing bonds and closeness in primates, but has also been found to be key in creating feelings of depression and anxiety when individuals were rejected in social situations. Therefore, given the extensive research on the cingulate cortex in regard to anxiety, depression, and adaptability, this remains an important area for future criminological research.

Also, the *ventral striatum* (which is part of the ventral tegmental area) appears to be an important limbic-related structure in the behavior of individuals. The ventral striatum receives input that is important for regulating the emotional input of various limbic structures. This structure has been referred to as the "crossroads" for where the emotional activity of the brain connects with the motor activities of the cerebrum. For example, in the diagnosis of bipolar disorder, the ventral striatum appears to be defective in the sense that studies show that overactivity in this brain region is related with an enhanced likelihood of individuals to lack judgment in how impulsive behaviors (e.g., sexual impulsivity, overspending) will affect their lives.

This brain structure was implicated in a recent study that showed that actually earning money creates happier feelings than simply being given it, such as through inheritance (Pagnoni, Zink, Montague, & Berns, 2002). This study demonstrated that simply having money does not produce the same feelings of happiness as actually earning it. This implies that the ventral striatum is not only important in reinforcement activity, but it is particularly important in the rewarding of earned activity. Studies have clearly shown that chronic offenders tend to be more motivated to change when given positive reinforcement than when they are punished. Therefore, the ventral striatum may be considered a key area for future research in regard to the feelings of reinforcement that seem to be important in rehabilitative techniques that are emphasized in most correctional programs. In addition to these issues, studies have shown that clinical disorders (e.g., bipolar disorder) are correlated with a significant reduction in gray matter in the ventral striatum region of the brain. Thus, any clinical attempts to address various disorders should consider the physiology of the ventral striatum.

One region in the midbrain that is strongly linked to the limbic system (as well as the frontal cortex), known as the *ventral tegmental area* (VTA), has been shown in recent research to be an important portion of the brain for stimulating desire or interest (Guterl, 2002). Not surprisingly, this structure is a primary area for initiating dopamine production (see Chapter 6), which is largely responsible for feelings of pleasure in the brain. When this area of the brain was excited, mice ignored food and other objects in order to search for other forms of stimulation. This shows that this region of the brain may govern the search for knowledge and new experiences. Interestingly, the VTA provides an important communication function between the frontal lobes, the midbrain, and the limbic/mesolimbic system (to the nucleus accumbens), so a weakness in the VTA can be extremely important in the functioning of many regions of the brain.

The ventral tegmental area is highly activated in persons who are highly aroused, such as people who are looking at the love of their life. Recent studies using brain imaging showed that when passionate lovers were aroused, their ventral tegmental areas were highly active, as was an associated area near the midbrain called the *caudate nucleus* (see Figure 5.5). The caudate nucleus is a large C-shaped region near the center of the brain linked to, among other things, the addiction to nicotine, which is found in cigarettes and other forms of tobacco). Furthermore, brain imaging studies have demonstrated that persons with attention deficit hyperactivity disorder have significantly less volume in the caudate nucleus.

Obviously, an impact or trauma to the ventral tegmental or caudate nucleus can have significant effects on behavior, particularly regarding emotions or affective responses, with many of the effects in these two areas being related to their direct impact on the production of brain chemicals called dopamine and norepinephrine. These chemicals are called neurotransmitters, and they will be discussed in detail in the following chapter. For now, it is only important to know that such chemicals are largely responsible for producing feelings of pleasure; thus, if there is a problem with the structures that produce such chemicals and resultant feelings, then the result can have profound effects on an individual's behavior.

Strongly associated with the caudate nucleus, another important set of structures in the limbic region is the *basal ganglia* (see Figure 5.5; this chart actually makes illustrative connections with basal ganglia), which surrounds the limbic system and

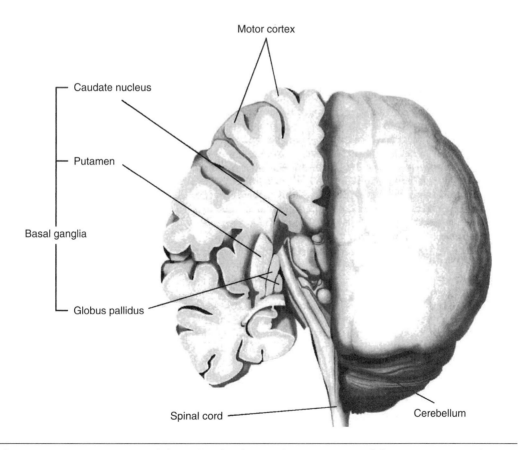

Figure 5.5   Motor System of the Brain. The three major components of the motor system—the motor cortex, basal ganglia, and cerebellum—may be seen

aids in the integration of thoughts, perceptions, and bodily movement. As shown in Figure 5.5, basal ganglia consists of the caudate, the putamen, and the globus pallidus (Beatty, 2001). Perhaps most important, the basal ganglia helps regulate the transition between emotional feelings, such as anxiety and pleasure (e.g., falling in love). For example, these structures have been implicated in the states of shock that people feel during or after traumatic events, in the sense that people do not respond or feel during this period; in fact, people tend to become immobile or frozen in terms of both actions and rational thought. The basal ganglia has also been implicated in the occurrence of panic attacks and prolonged cases of posttraumatic stress disorder, which reflects excessive activity in this structural system.

Interestingly, individuals with attention deficit disorder (ADD) are actually less likely to freeze during traumatic events, which brain-imaging studies suggest is due to an underactive basal ganglia, which in turn is likely due to significantly less brain volume in this structure (much like the caudate nucleus). On the other hand, it is believed that the low activity level in the basal ganglia is responsible for, using a noncriminological example, poor handwriting skills in ADD individuals because it requires a shift to fine motor activities, as opposed to print writing (a more smooth motor activity), for which those with ADD tend to perform much better. Studies have shown that medications that raise levels of dopamine (see following chapters) in the basal ganglia raise the activity in this structure, and thus persons with ADD are able to handwrite better, as well as perform better on other motor activities. Perhaps most importantly, recent studies have shown that the basal ganglia has profound effects on regulating (or not regulating) the anxiety levels in individuals, which are extremely important in the production and inhibition of criminality, and will be discussed at length in the following chapter.

Unfortunately, criminological research has not examined structural or functional problems with most of the brain regions discussed above, particularly those of the limbic system. However, it is very likely that trauma to or developmental problems in such structures and/or functions have significant influences on criminal tendencies. Obviously, one of our major recommendations in this chapter is to encourage much more research in these areas, because as it stands now, only indirect conclusions can be made.

BOX 5.2 The Continuing Saga of Stanley: Personality Dispositions

Stanley's early psychological development likely had a great impact on his offending career. Given the self-reported and officially documented information that we have of Stanley's personality in his early years (i.e., ages 6–18) we have fairly good insight into his psychological dispositions at various stages. This information reveals that whereas Stanley had a relatively average intelligence (he scored a 104 on the Stanford-Binet IQ test at age 7 [100 is average]), he scored relatively low on mathematics, which indicates that he may have had problems in linear thinking. Such an observation indicates a likely deficit in problem-solving ability or left-hemisphere functioning, which could have a strong impact on Stanley's ability to deal with conventional learning and/or and/or functioning. Individuals who have such deficiencies tend to be predisposed to deviant behavior (Coren, 1993); however, Stanley did score relatively high in history, which suggests a tendency toward humanities and a right-hemisphere emphasis in his brain orientation. Nevertheless, this would further predispose him to a more nonlinear, holistic train of thought, which would again reinforce his opposition to most conventional, scholastic activities.

Furthermore, Shaw (1930, p. 190) noted Stanley's early rise and persistence of a sense of injustice, which is evident throughout Stanley's narrative of his life. Furthermore, he was "hypercritical" of others and rarely, if ever, took the blame for his actions. Rather, Stanley usually placed the blame for his own behavior on an external source, which recent psychological studies show is quite common among offenders (for a review, see Walters, 2002). Showing signs indicative of a low-functioning autonomic nervous system (which would likely warrant a contemporary diagnosis of ADHD), Shaw reported that Stanley often showed an excessive interest in attention (i.e., stimulus hunger). Additionally, he often readily made friends, but such relationships quickly dissolved, which furthered his already strong feelings of isolation, suspiciousness of others, and self-pity.

Regardless of whether these personality/psychological traits were due to genetics, embryonic/delivery complications, or environmental factors, it is clear that Stanley developed the above attitudes and that these remained with him for some time. Although empirical studies (see text) suggest that it is likely that all of the influences listed above contributed to Stanley's acquisition of such personality traits, what is important for this section is that he did acquire the traits of an individual who exhibits low self-control (Gottfredson & Hirschi, 1990). This is seen in Stanley's dispositions toward feelings of

> never takes blame but readily blames others, readily makes friends and as easily breaks with them, . . . absorbed in his own ideas . . . and relatively immune to suggestions from others, resentment of correction and resistance to direction, tendency to escape from unpleasant situations, . . . speed of decision. (Shaw, 1930, pp. 190–191)

Such aspects exemplify an individual with a low level of self-control, which is consistent with numerous recent studies and theoretical models that would predict Stanley to become a serious, persistent offender.

In addition to clearly exhibiting signs of low self-control, Stanley reported experiencing feelings of excitement and euphoria when committing offenses. For example, Stanley claims that "I got the thrill of doing the stealing" (Shaw, 1930, p. 53). Even when Stanley was placed in a relatively good foster home that he described as "like a sweet dream . . . the luxury seemed to dazzle and blind me" (pp. 18–19), he soon felt as if

> there was something missing. . . . I longed to go back to my friends . . . and could play and romp and gamble and swear. . . . My adventurous spirit rebelled against this dry life, and it soon won out. . . . What's the use of having riches, if you can't enjoy life? (Shaw, 1930, p. 19)

This type of mentality was highlighted by Jack Katz (1988) in his book *Seductions of Crime*. Katz explains that much delinquency is due to the feelings of exhilaration and excitement produced during the commission of the crime. Stanley obviously got a "rush" or pleasurable feelings when he engaged in illegal activity. Such feelings are typical of delinquents, as Shaw points out in quotations from youths other than Stanley.

(Continued)

(Continued)

For example, one youth reported,

> When we were shoplifting we always made a game of it. For example, we might gamble on who could steal in the presence of a detective and then get away. We were always daring each other that way and thinking up new schemes. This was the best part of the game. (Shaw, 1930, p. 7)

This same youth reported taking hats from stores and explained, "It was the fun I wanted, not the hat" (Shaw, 1930, p. 7). Shaw also quotes another youth, who claimed, "The first time I ever stole anything . . . I just thought it was an interesting game. I thought this quite an adventure and enjoyed taking the fruit very much" (Shaw, 1930, p. 15). Another youth reported that "when I was eight years old I did my first job in the racket. This job was the biggest thrill I ever got in my life" (Shaw, 1930, p. 16).

Ultimately, Stanley appears representative of many other delinquents in having an attitude toward committing crime that sees such activity as being fun and pleasurable. How Stanley acquired such an attitude is unknown. However, this attitude is consistent with dispositions toward low self-control, and it is likely that such time-stable traits in Stanley enhanced the likelihood of his becoming a chronic offender.

Conclusion

This chapter discussed the various regions and structures of the hindbrain, midbrain, and limbic system, with an emphasis on those that are most relevant in the development of criminality. This chapter provided a basis for understanding primal functioning, so that the following chapter, which deals with the more advanced (human) portions of the brain, namely, the forebrain or cortical regions, will make more sense to readers. Still, the more primitive and subcortical regions of the brain that we examined in this chapter are often directly influential in terms of human decision making and behavior.

CHAPTER 6

Introduction to Brain Structure and Basic Functions—Part II

Forebrain Formation, Trauma, and Criminal Behavior

The greatest discovery of my generation is that man can alter his life simply by altering his attitude of mind.

William James (1842–1910)

This chapter will provide a follow-up to the previous chapter, in discussing the various brain structures that have been found to be affiliated with criminal offending. As was mentioned in the previous chapter, brain structure and brain function tend to overlap to some extent, but this chapter will focus on differences in brain structure, as opposed to those dealing with brain function, which will be dealt with in more detail in future chapters.

Forebrain: Cortical Region

Of all regions of the brain, the cerebral cortex (i.e., cerebrum) is the largest and most evolved, which is why it is often referred to as the neocortex or neomammalian compex (*neo* meaning new). The relative size of the human cerebrum is unique and extraordinarily large compared to that of all other animal species. It can be argued that it is this part of the brain that makes us human in the sense that it is the realm for our highest levels of reasoning and decision making, which is why the cerebrum is referred to as the "learning brain" (MacLean, 1990). Most (approximately 75%) of the cerebrum grows once the infant is outside the womb, which highlights the importance of postnatal care in ensuring healthy development. Furthermore, different regions of the cerebrum develop at varying rates and, in some ways, never stop developing. As will be discussed later in this chapter, studies have shown that the brain—particularly the regions of the cerebral cortex—continues to develop in many ways throughout life, largely due to the impact of environmental influences.

Lateralization and the Corpus Callosum

Like many other human organs that appear bilaterally symmetrical, the cerebrum is split into two halves—called hemispheres—each of which seems to be a virtual mirror image of the other in physical appearance. However, the differential functioning of each hemisphere is an important area of concern regarding the development of criminality. Specifically, researchers have found an association between criminality and persistent individual differences in the hemispheric emphasis in completing (or not completing) certain types of tasks, which will be explained further below.

The left and right hemispheres are connected by a thick band of up to 800 million neural fibers called the corpus callosum (see Figure 6.1). As the largest fiber track in the brain, the corpus callosum carries the messages needed to coordinate and integrate left- and right-brain functioning. By acting as a bridge for communication between the two hemispheres, the corpus callosum plays a vital role in cognitive functioning and human behavior, which is significantly affected when this band is altered, damaged, or severed.

Some scholars (e.g., Raine, 1993; Schalling, 1978) have suggested that psychopathic criminal behavior may represent a partial interhemispheric disconnection syndrome, but very few studies have examined such a direct relationship. Although one study (Raine, O'Brien, Smiley, Scerbo, & Chan, 1990) using dichotic listening methodology did not confirm this proposition, the lead author later concluded that this "hypothesis is an interesting one warranting closer scrutiny" (Raine, 1993, p. 121). Raine's reasoning is that because the corpus callosum is central to the transfer of information between hemispheres and it plays an important inhibitory function, damage to callosal fibers may cause functional predominance of one hemisphere over the other, as well as other types of dysfunction. Despite a lack of research on the direct relationship between the corpus callosum and criminal behavior, there has been substantial growth in studies that have examined potential *indirect* relationships between this structure and dispositions toward criminality.

Although the corpus callosum has been traditionally difficult to study because of its irregular shape, modern use of magnetic resonance imaging (MRI) has enabled its study in living people rather than relying on autopsies. There is now a voluminous research literature examining the issue of whether the corpus callosum differs in shape, size, or some other way across certain groups, most notably males

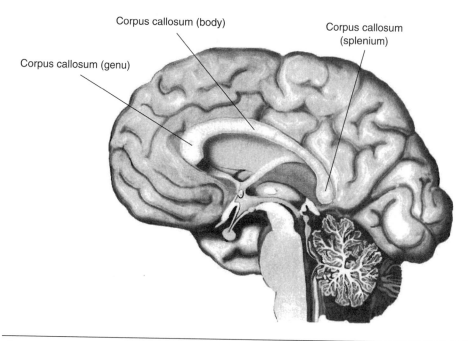

Corpus callosum (body)

Corpus callosum
(splenium)

Corpus callosum (genu)

Figure 6.1   The Commissures of the Neocortex. Two commissures connect the neocortical tissue of the right and left cerebral hemispheres. Of these, the corpus callosum is by far the largest; the anterior commissure contains many fewer fibers. In addition, other commissures connect nonneocortical structures, such as the hippocampal commissure linking the right and left hippocampus

and females (for reviews, see Bishop & Wahlsten, 1997; Holloway, 1998). This research on sex differences regarding the corpus callosum has shown that human females generally have a significantly larger (relative to brain weight) and more bulbous structure than males (Hines, 1990; Steinmetz, Staiger, Schlaug, Huang, & Jancke, 1995). In fact, although it is unethical to employ hormonal manipulation with humans, studies with other species (e.g., rats) have shown that when female hormones are administered to newborns, the corpus callosum grows to a larger size (Fitch & Denenberg, 1998). These researchers also found that when pregnant females were given hormones, the corpora callosa of their offspring were significantly different in size. It is likely that hormones play a key role in determining the size of the corpus callosum in humans as well (Halpern, 2000). Studies have shown that the corpus callosum is important in the acquisition of self-awareness and intelligence, and that this cable of nerves continues to develop significantly into an individual's later stages of growth, particularly through his or her teenage years and into his or her twenties.

One reason why the size of the corpus callosum is important is that a number of researchers have implicated this size difference as a primary explanation for why female humans appear to have better connectivity between their left and right hemispheres and have been found to transfer information at a higher rate compared to males (Innocenti, 1994; Jancke & Steinmetz, 1994). Many researchers believe that this enhanced transference of information between hemispheres is an important factor in the well-established sex differences in verbal ability, specifically that females are better than males in verbal fluency (Halpern, 2000). From a criminological standpoint, research has long shown that individuals with low verbal abilities are more likely to commit various types of offending (Farrington, 2005; Gibson, Piquero, & Tibbetts, 2001; Raine, 1993; Wilson & Herrnstein, 1985), not to mention the vast differences between men and women in deviant activity. The implications of such sex differences in laterality patterns will be discussed in more detail in Chapter 9. For now, it is important to acknowledge only that the size and function of the corpus callosum is of particular interest for understanding the development of criminality, especially in the context of gender differences and hemispheric specialization.

The Four Lobes of the Cerebral Cortex

Occipital Lobe

As shown in Figure 6.2, the cerebral cortex (as well as each hemisphere) can also be broken into four lobes or regions, each of which contains more specified areas and functions. The area at the lower back portion of the cerebral cortex, just above the cerebellum, is called the *occipital lobe.* The occipital lobe is primarily known as the home of the visual cortex, where sensory information from the eyes is processed and interpreted. Although this region is relatively less susceptible to trauma than other areas because of its location, damage to the occipital lobe can have profound implications. Such effects typically include visual impairments or blindness, but sometimes the trauma is related to clinical disorders and criminality.

For instance, trauma to the occipital lobe has been found to be linked to the occurrence of visual hallucinations and illusions. Obviously, such psychosis-type effects can produce maladaptive, irrational behavior, particularly if such damage is not properly diagnosed and treated. Thus, it is not surprising that Virkkunen, Nuutila, and Huusko (1976) found that open head injuries to the occipital cortex were most predictive of high crime rates among soldiers, as compared to injury in other regions of the cerebral cortex. In fact, damage to the occipital lobe was more than twice as likely among criminals (11%) as was damage to the frontal or parietal lobes (4%).

Perhaps these findings reflect the importance of the occipital lobe in functions such as reading and writing. Obviously, proper functioning of the visual cortex is a key element in written communication and processing. Given the consistent links shown between low verbal ability and criminal offending (Gibson et al., 2001), it is not surprising that occipital lobe damage has been implicated in the development of criminality. The occipital lobe is also a key region (along with the parietal and temporal lobes) in the formation and retention of short-term memory, which involves organizing and retaining what one sees and hears. It goes without saying that short-term memory is an essential element in everyday functioning; those with poor memory are likely to have serious problems in life and may be inclined to resort to criminality.

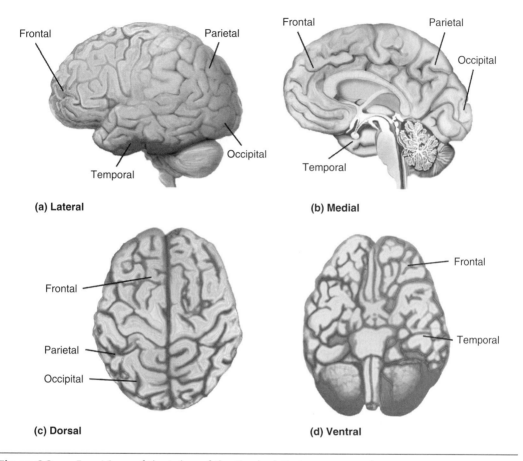

Figure 6.2   Four Views of the Lobes of the Cerebral Cortex

Other links between occipital lobe injuries and offending may be due to the problems related with hallucinations and other visual illusions. Studies have consistently linked such psychotic symptoms with deviant behavior (for a comprehensive review, see Raine, 1993). These are just some of the ways that damage to the occipital lobe can predispose individuals to criminal tendencies; future investigations must further specify the causal mechanisms involved in these links, as well as discover new ways in which the occipital lobe plays a role in criminality. Although some criminological studies have examined occipital lobe damage, virtually none of this research has been done recently, and it is apparent that more research is needed in this area.

Parietal Lobe

Another major area of the cerebral cortex is the *parietal lobe,* which is located in the central part of the cerebrum, near the back and top portion of the head (see Figure 6.2). Because of its close proximity to the primary motor cortex, the parietal lobe largely influences voluntary motor activities involving goal-directed movements and manipulation of objects. This area of the brain receives data from the skin and is the primary destination for signals of touch and sensation. Furthermore, the parietal lobe is known to be the area that is most responsible for integrating various messages from our different senses to create comprehensible representations of a single concept or memory.

As mentioned above, the parietal lobe works with the occipital lobe and the upper temporal lobe in the formation of short-term memory. Another very important cognitive function of the parietal lobe is recognizing what an object is and where an object (or our own body) is in space, otherwise known as spatial processing (Kandel, Schwartz, & Jessel, 1991). Given these roles of sensory integration and spatial relations/positioning, it is not surprising that abnormal activity in the parietal lobe has been linked to schizophrenia (Rowe, 2002), which often involves perceptions of hearing voices or seeing hallucinations. This function of spatial cognition will be discussed further in Chapter 8, when we discuss gender differences in cognition.

Injury to the parietal region is more likely to occur than damage to the occipital lobe because of its location. Some of the problems that have been observed when the parietal lobe is damaged include difficulty in naming objects, difficulty in distinguishing left from right, difficulty with drawing objects, and difficulty with doing math. Brain-imaging studies (for a review, see Sowell et al., 2003) have demonstrated that individuals diagnosed with attention deficit/hyperactivity disorder show a significantly low volume of gray matter in the parietal lobe. This obviously affects their ability to perceive and respond to their environment, particularly when it comes to learning and adapting to their environment. These types of activities are very important in determining success in school and employment. As such, if there is a problem in the functioning of the parietal lobe, it can have detrimental effects on basic skills and abilities.

Although damage to the parietal lobe may be linked to criminality due to the functions described above, the most direct ties to chronic offending have been demonstrated by studies showing *higher* levels of activity in this region. As reviewed by Raine (1989), there is a substantial amount of evidence that chronic offenders, who generally exhibit low levels of arousal (e.g., stimulus deprivation), tend to show *more* arousal when presented with certain types of stimuli, particularly that of increasing intensity and interest. To further clarify, studies (e.g., Forth & Hare, 1990) have found that chronic offenders actually show enhanced activity in the parietal lobe when presented with certain forms of stimuli, especially risky behaviors (e.g., gambling).

This phenomenon has been interpreted as a predisposition toward sensation seeking and is consistent with recently proposed theoretical frameworks (e.g., Gottfredson & Hirschi, 1990; Katz, 1988; Wilson & Herrnstein, 1985) that emphasize the seduction that crime can have on individuals who tend to be risk takers. The evidence regarding the hyperstimulation of the parietal lobe in offenders appears to provide a physiological reason for why certain individuals appear to be oriented toward such risky behavior, such as violence. Still, researchers are quick to point out that even with such physiological tendencies, adequate steps can be taken to steer such risk taking and sensation seeking toward more conventional activities, such as "risky business ventures, the armed forces, or motor racing rather than crime and violence" (Raine, 1993, pp. 179–180), whereas others have noted the appropriateness of law enforcement for such personalities (Arrigo & Shipley, 2004; Eysenck & Gudjonnson, 1989). Another perspective is to focus on enhanced parietal lobe functioning, which would suggest steering young antisocials toward activities that involve advanced spatial abilities, such as mechanics or artwork (Raine, 1993). Furthermore, the amplified activity of the parietal lobe in chronic offenders may also partially explain why reinforcements (i.e., rewards) used in correctional treatment settings tend to show more positive results than the use of punishments (i.e., anxiety), which would be unlikely to have much effect on participants with low arousability.

Temporal Lobe

As shown in Figure 6.2, the *temporal lobe* can be found just above the ear on each side of the head, so it is not surprising that one of its primary functions is hearing and auditory perception. In fact, the region most responsible for speech comprehension—called Wernicke's Area—can be found in the temporal lobe and is approximately the size of a poker chip in adults. It is to this area that auditory impulses are sent and processed for interpretation, often for storage as memory. Persons who sustain damage to the temporal lobe often experience difficulties in understanding spoken words, which is referred to as Wernicke's Aphasia. Thus, the temporal lobe plays a key role in determining an individual's aptitude regarding verbal communication.

Given the consistent findings linking poor verbal ability to criminality (for a review, see Gibson et al., 2001), it is easy to understand the importance of healthy temporal lobe functioning for our purposes. It is also interesting to note that trauma to a particular side of the head may have differential effects because for most people, or at least most right-handed individuals, the speech center is located in the left temporal lobe, as opposed to the right. This issue will be discussed further in Chapter 8, when we discuss the laterality, or the tendency for certain functions of the brain to be housed in either the left or right hemisphere.

Auditory processing and speech comprehension are among the many important functions of the temporal lobe that likely implicate it in the development of criminality. The temporal lobe is very important for its relations to the brain structures that are in its proximity, namely, those of the limbic system. For instance, one structure found in the temporal lobe, the *parahippocampal gyrus,* plays a large role in the integration of internal signals with sensory information from the external environment (e.g., auditory, visual). This structure is obviously important for maintaining a healthy equilibrium in brain functions and is key in the process of categorization of objects and memory acquisition. Perhaps this is why temporal lobe damage has been linked to an inability to identify and verbalize about objects, as well as to both short-term and long-term memory loss. Similar to these problems, one interesting manifestation of temporal lobe injury is experiencing great difficulty in recognizing faces, a phenomenon called *prosopagnosia.*

Most importantly, abnormal (usually reduced) activity in the temporal lobe region has been strongly linked to schizophrenia (Rowe, 2002), as well as criminal behavior (Raine, 1993; Raine, Buchsbaum, & LaCasse, 1997). A series of studies has found an even more consistent association between temporal lobe abnormalities and sex offending, such as incest and pedophilia (Hucker et al., 1986; Langevin, Wortzman, Dickey, Wright, & Handy, 1988; Wright, Nobrega, Langevin, & Wortzman, 1990). Unfortunately, theoretical reasons for why temporal lobe dysfunction is linked to criminality are much less agreed upon, but strong arguments have been made that it is likely due to failure in the functions of the temporal lobe described above (e.g., poor speech comprehension, reduced memory acquisition). But this does not logically explain the even stronger association with sex offending, so other hypotheses must be considered.

One of the likely possibilities is that temporal lobe dysfunction is strongly linked to sex offending (whereas frontal lobe dysfunction is not) because of its close working relationship with the structures of the limbic system. Many of these structures, such as the amygdala and pituitary (see above), are the primary centers for controlling our emotions and sexual drives. Consistent with this line of reasoning, research has shown that damage to the temporal lobe often significantly alters sexual drive and activity in humans (e.g., see Garnett, Nahmias, Wortzman, Langevin, & Dickey, 1988; Mosovich & Tallaferro, 1954; for a review, see Reiss, Miczek, & Roth, 1994). Relatedly, temporal lobe epilepsy has been shown to cause personality changes, particularly aggressive rages (Blumer & Benson, 1975; Raine, 1993).

Another area of disorders that directly involves the temporal lobe is that of seizures, typically experienced by epileptics. A seizure is a sudden electrical disturbance of brain function that often results in uncontrollable actions, which is typically accompanied by a loss of consciousness. These seizures are found most commonly in individuals at the extremes of life—young infants and toddlers or the elderly—and they are generally caused by anything that tends to irritate the brain. Such irritants can include brain abnormalities present at birth, fever, tumors, anoxia (i.e., lack of oxygen to the brain), infections, or adverse reactions to toxic chemicals and drugs. The recurrence of seizures is clinically referred to as epilepsy, which has traditionally been linked to criminality even by the earliest criminologists (see Lombroso, 1876).

Currently, an electroencephalograph (EEG) is often done to confirm the diagnosis of seizure and help to pinpoint possible lesions for surgical removal, as well as to classify the type of seizure (e.g., tonic-clonic [grand mal] vs. petit mal seizures) in order to determine which anticonvulsant/antiseizure drug to use in reducing the symptoms. For example, whereas grand mal/tonic-clonic seizures typically result in loss of consciousness followed by falling to the ground and rhythmic jerking as the body becomes stiff, petit mal seizures tend to involve a loss of consciousness but not falling to the ground; rather, the person becomes immobile for approximately 15 seconds and then continues activity as if there was no lapse. Other forms of epilepsy include juvenile myoclonic, which tends to run in families and causes a jerking of limbs without loss of consciousness, as well as temporal lobe epilepsy that tends to involve making strange faces, twitching, or muttering while being awake but not knowing what is going on around them.

In many individuals, the best alternative is a temporal lobectomy, which involves severing a specialized number of connectors between the temporal lobe and other regions of the brain (such as the limbic structures). Fortunately, such surgical procedures and/or antiseizure drugs are effective in at least reducing the frequency of seizures in the vast majority of individuals who undergo this form of treatment. On the other hand, many persons who suffer from seizures do not benefit from such medical treatment and are predisposed toward criminality. This may be due largely to the treatment's impact on the person's education and functioning, which would affect his or her abilities in school or at work.

Although it has not been directly shown, it is likely that the consistent findings regarding sex offenders and/or epileptics are largely due to problems involving the complex processes between the temporal lobe and the limbic system structures. This explanation is also supported by the fact that many researchers have noted the ambiguous nature of the results of brain studies, such as those using an EEG and certain forms of brain imaging. Specifically, given the imprecise nature of such instruments, what appears to be dysfunction in the temporal lobe region may be due mainly to abnormalities in proximate limbic structures, such as the amygdala. Because instruments like the EEG use measures only on the exterior of the skull, distinguishing which internal structures are responsible for results showing inactivity is virtually impossible. As more sophisticated technologies are incorporated into this area of research, more specified conceptualizations of the effects of lobe dysfunction can be developed, including functions that are done in conjunction with limbic structures, as well as those that are unique to the temporal complex. Currently, we can only say that temporal lobe dysfunction is consistently linked with criminality, particularly that which is sexual in nature.

Frontal Lobe

Located right behind one's forehead (see Figure 6.2), the anterior portion of the brain is the *frontal lobe,* with the most anterior part of this lobe called the *prefrontal cortex.* Being the last area of the brain to develop in terms of both evolutionary and personal growth, the frontal cortex is the largest and most distinguishing feature of the human brain, and it goes the furthest in setting us apart from other animals in terms of anatomical structure and cortical functions. Regarding its structural uniqueness, the prefrontal cortex makes up more than 30% of the human brain, which is relatively much more than that of any other species (Fuster, 1989; Walsh, 2002). The functional differences in humans, many of which are discussed below, are perhaps best demonstrated by studies in which the frontal cortex is removed from the brains of lower animals (e.g., reptiles) and their behavior continues virtually unchanged. The animals continue to eat, sleep, fight, and so on, largely because those functions do not necessarily involve higher reasoning.

To clarify, the frontal lobe in most other animals is relatively small and does little in determining behavior. On the other hand, the frontal cortex in the human brain largely represents humanity, in that it is most responsible for the very activities that make us so unique in abstract thought, intellect, and even personality. Interestingly, the paradox is that while being most responsible for our humanity, the frontal lobe is the most vulnerable to injury due to its location (Levin, Eisenberg, & Benton, 1991) and, ironically, is also the region of the brain most implicated in the development of criminality and other disorders (Kolb & Whishaw, 1990). Notably, the frontal region of the cortex, which governs rationality, stays underdeveloped throughout the teenage years in individuals, possibly limiting judgment skills. We will discuss the reasons for this in detail, but first we will review some of the specific functions of the frontal cortex.

Besides being very important in the formation of memories and some motor activities, this region is likely what most people think of when considering the brain because it represents the highest order of thought processes in human beings. These thought processes, often referred to as executive cognitive functions (ECFs), include problem solving, abstract reasoning, concentration, spontaneity, speech production, and direction of goal-oriented behaviors (Giancola, Martin, Moss, Pelham, & Tarter, 1996; Mirsky & Siegel, 1994). For example, the frontal lobe is responsible for our consciousness, or knowing who we are and what we are doing within our environment. It is interesting to note that the prefrontal area is the last portion of the brain to mature in human development (because it was the last portion added in evolution), which can be seen in children not being able to develop self-consciousness until at least 18 months of age (Lewis, 1992). The role of the frontal lobe in the development of self-consciousness has important criminological implications that will be discussed later (see Chapter 8), but this region of the brain has many other important functions.

One of these jobs is initiating activity in response to environmental stimuli. In other words, the frontal lobe is largely responsible for determining how well one can adapt to external obstacles, which is such a necessary part of success. Recently proposed models of criminality (e.g., Buss & Plomin, 1984; Gottfredson & Hirschi, 1990; Patterson, DeBaryshe, & Ramsey, 1989; Wilson & Herrnstein, 1985) have emphasized the inability of some individuals (often chronic offenders) to engage in efforts to improve their well-being, particularly if these attempts involve long-term exertion and go beyond their "here-and-now" orientation. Evidence has clearly shown that antisocial behavior may be characterized by cognitive difficulties in assessing potential consequences of behavior, as well as acting on such assessments (Newman, 1987; Newman, Kosson, & Patterson, 1992; Seguin, Pihl, Harden, Tremblay, & Boulerice, 1995; Shapiro, Quay, Hogan, & Schwartz, 1988; for more discussion, see Fishbein, 2001; Moffitt, 1993a). These traits are quite consistent with frontal lobe dysfunction, which studies (for a review, see Levin et al., 1991) have shown cause difficulties in both problem solving and ability to focus on tasks (i.e., *attending*), as well as an inability to plan a sequence of complex actions needed to complete multistep tasks (referred to as *sequencing*). For instance, prefrontal cortex dysfunction has been consistently linked to attention deficit hyperactivity disorder (Barkley, 1997). Furthermore, studies show that there is a 20% to 40% reduction in gray matter in the prefrontal cortex region of the brain in individuals diagnosed with bipolar disorder.

At the same time, these same individuals tend to be stubborn and inflexible toward their environment, regardless of the characteristics of the surroundings, to the point of making those around them become more hostile (Buss & Plomin, 1984; Moffitt, 1993b; Patterson et al., 1989). Experimental studies with animals, such as rats (Pallone & Hennessy, 1998), have demonstrated that regardless of whether the animals are peaceably or aggressively nurtured, those who had induced frontal lobe damage respond to other animals in a uniform way: They attack with vicious, lethal aggression when another animal is presented into their cage. Furthermore, the animals with frontal lobe damage exhibited a different form of killing that went beyond the utility of the act; for example, the animals often continued striking or biting the "victims" even after they were dead.

Although often not lethal or quite as violent, a relatively similar pattern is consistent with frontal lobe dysfunction in humans, which often results in loss of manners in interacting with others, high propensity toward violence, loss of flexibility in thinking, and severe mood changes. The neuropathology of the frontal lobes was examined in a recent study of more than 2,100 offenders, which found that those individuals who had committed the most serious, chronic pattern of violent offenses were those who had the greatest degree of problems in the frontal lobe region (Pallone & Hennessy, 1998). Specifically, the incidence of neuropathology among homicide offenders (94%) greatly exceeded the incidence in the general population (3%). The authors point out that this is an approximate 3,200% increase for violence among those who have neuropathological problems in the brain, particularly the frontal lobe region (Pallone & Hennessy, 1998). However, the causal mechanisms of such a profound effect between frontal brain damage and criminality is often not obvious.

One of the most promising links is that people with frontal lobe damage have been found to exhibit little facial expression (Kolb & Milner, 1981) or the ability to use external cues to guide behavior (called *associated learning*) (see Damasio, Tranel, & Damasio, 1990). This latter deficiency is consistent with criminological models that hypothesize that impaired ECFs reduce the ability to interpret social cues during interpersonal interactions, which may lead to misunderstandings or differential perceptions in social situations (Damasio, Grabowski, Frank, Galaburda, & Damasio, 1994; Giancola et al., 1996). Such interpretation problems are particularly problematic among individuals who have been consistently abused or grossly neglected in childhood, and therefore have developed a fast "trigger" for dealing with threats, even if they are false threats (this will be discussed at length in the next chapter). This issue of individuals eliciting negative responses from others around them is perhaps one of the more important in developmental theories of criminality and, therefore, is discussed in more detail in other chapters in this book.

Another job of the frontal lobe involves making decisions, often moral judgments, about what actions we choose in our daily lives. The healthy frontal cortex is constantly communicating with other regions of the brain, particularly the sensory and limbic systems, and is always receiving signals regarding such things as our emotional impulses. The frontal lobe is responsible for organizing and controlling these emotional drives in an adaptive manner, through rational decision-making processes.

So, it is not surprising that modern brain-scan studies on dreaming show that the frontal lobes become inactive while the limbic structures show a very high rate of activity during these dream periods of sleep (Nofzinger et al., 2004). When we dream, our rational frontal lobes are not working properly, so we are not able to realize that we often are experiencing something impossible or surreal, which is driven by our memory (hippocampus) and emotional (amygdala) centers. This is also a reason why our dreams don't seem to make sense; our linear thought processes are not functioning, so the story line of our dreams is often distorted or unrealistic. Interestingly, the same type of brain activity pattern (low frontal/high limbic) is seen during acute schizophrenic episodes, in which the individuals see visions or hear voices that appear as real as any actual reality. Again, our rationality is highly dependent on the functioning of our frontal lobe region.

Obviously, frontal lobe trauma is likely to affect one's ability to control irrational emotional impulses, and studies have linked such damage to impulsivity and feelings of indifference to consequences of behavior (Damasio, Tranel, & Damasio, 1990; Fishbein, 2001). Thus, it is not surprising that research has found that individuals who have frontal lobe injury frequently experience a change in their personalities, often becoming short-tempered and aggressive (Blumer & Benson, 1975; Raine, 1993; Volavka, 1999). In another light, this may be related to recent research that shows the effectiveness of cognitive-behavioral therapy (CBT) (see Van Voorhis et al., 1999), which research has shown is the most effective form of therapy for criminal offenders and various clinical disorders (e.g., depression), probably because it purposely engages the frontal region of the brain. For example, brain imaging studies have shown that CBT (Mayberg et al., 2005), which is essentially teaching individuals to think before they act, significantly affects the frontal lobe's functioning; thus, it actually does make individuals think before they act. Perhaps this is why such programs have been shown to be effective, particularly among teenagers, whose frontal lobes are still developing.

BOX 6.1   ADHD, Psychopathy, and the Young Brain

Recent brain imaging studies (Sowell et al., 2003) have also helped identify which regions of the brain are most implicated in attention deficit hyperactivity disorder (ADHD). The frontal lobe (along with limbic-related structures [caudate nucleus and basal ganglia]) is one of the areas that exhibits the most significant differences with regard to this disorder. Specifically, the right ventral dorsolateral (front side) area of the brain shows large decreases in gray matter for individuals with ADHD as compared to normally developed brains. This may explain the lack of planning or long-term consideration that is so common in persons diagnosed with ADHD. Notably, the same studies (Sowell et al., 2003) showed a volume deficiency in the posterior temporal lobe, which is strongly linked to the limbic system (see the discussions in the previous chapter regarding these regions). Along with other disorders related to criminality, it is clear that the structural development and functioning of the ADHD brain has an extremely important effect on the way we perceive and behave, particularly in relation to criminality. Unfortunately, the number of youths diagnosed with ADHD has increased exponentially in the past two decades (although many were improperly diagnosed), and the influence of such disorders on predicting criminality seems to be especially problematic among children in our society.

At the same time, you may have noticed that many of the descriptions of brain-functioning problems that were discussed above resemble the natural tendencies of young children and teenagers. Beyond clinical and neurological disorders, even among normally developing brains in this age group, there is good scientific reason for this seemingly erratic and irrational behavior. To clarify, individuals in their early teenage years experience alterations to their brain structure and processing that resemble many cognitive problems that are known to be predictive of offending, and are often associated with antisocial and psychopathic tendencies. Therefore, it should come as little surprise that teenagers are responsible for a very large percentage of crime in virtually all societies across time and place.

Specifically, the teenage brain involves a combination of factors in both structure and function that predispose them toward impulsive behavior and low self-control. For example, the pituitary gland (see above), which releases large amounts of sex hormones, is very active in teens, resulting in extremely large amounts of androgens in males and varying ratios of estrogen/progesterone in females. Studies have consistently shown that these drastic fluctuations in hormones, particularly increases in testosterone and progesterone, cause cognitive propensities toward violence (see Booth & Osgood, 1993; Walsh, 1995; for reviews, see Fishbein, 2001; Rowe, 2002; Walsh, 2002). Thus, some experts have noticed the similarities between the functioning of the youthful brain and the functioning of adult psychopaths, with the primary difference being that most people experience maturation of the cerebral cortex, which tends to inhibit such impulsive behaviors over time. Given that the most rational, inhibiting part of the cortex—the frontal lobe—does not fully develop until approximately the mid-20s, it is not surprising at all that teenagers behave irrationally and impulsively. So, to some extent, psychopathic behavior can be seen as manifestations of a brain that never structurally or functionally matured, at least in a normal and healthy way. This theory is consistent with that of Dr. Bruce Perry, whose theory of altered brain development we will examine in subsequent chapters.

In addition to not yet having acquired a fully developed frontal lobe, teenagers also rely more heavily on the amygdala (the emotion center of the brain) in making behavioral decisions than do adults. On the other hand, the frontal lobe of the brain, which governs rationality and inhibition, stays underdeveloped throughout the teenage years. Additionally, the cerebellum remains undeveloped until the end of the teenage years; although a "primitive" hindbrain structure, it is key in successfully performing social tasks and learning. This is further exaggerated by the underdevelopment of the corpus callosum, which helps connect the two hemispheres and allows for more efficient problem solving and self-awareness. As you have probably guessed, teenagers have a more primal functioning brain in the sense that they are directed more by their emotional center and hormones, and less so by the rational (frontal) portion of the brain. So, it is not surprising that persons in this age group comprise, by far, the largest group of offenders by rate. An examination of the arrest rate by age, in any year for any society, shows that the age-crime curve peaks at approximately age 17. This universal trend, especially to the extent that it exists across all cultures for all years, would only be likely if there was a physiological difference in teenagers throughout the world. This physiological explanation does, in fact, exist.

To expand on this important stage of development, modern studies by Jay Giedd and his colleagues at the National Institute of Mental Health using magnetic resonance imaging (MRI) have shed extensive light on brain development, especially during the teenage period (e.g., Giedd et al., 1999; also see Wallis, 2004, for a review of Giedd's research). The longitudinally administered MRI photos of twins have shown that, although many experts claim earlier cessation of growth, the brain continues to grow significantly until at least age 25. This obviously has huge implications for policy in the sense that previous implementations assumed the brain was configured much earlier in life (see Walsh, 2002). It is now obvious that the brain does not reach structural formation until the mid-20s, and further-more continues to be reconfigured throughout life, largely in attempts to adapt to the environment.

One of the most significant findings of Giedd's research is the realization that although the brain is set by a genotype to be built a certain way, subtle changes occur in the gray matter structure based on environmental differences and experi-ence. In Claudia Wallis's (2004) review of Giedd's research, she claims that the brain is the most notable organ for which experience becomes flesh. We not only agree, but believe that this is one of the most efficient and profound claims in this book. It sums up the ironic fact that the brain is "hard-wired" to be "soft-wired," in the sense that all normal developing brains are programmed to learn and adapt from their environment.

Giedd's studies have shown that in addition to the explosion of growth that occurs in the perinatal stage of brain development, there is a second stage of growth and weeding of neural paths that occurs in later childhood and teenage years. This involves not only the development of key synaptic paths, but also the pruning of neurons and pathways that are not being used. Thus, if certain brain mechanisms are not being used, they will be eliminated due to prioritization in the brain. This results in a significant amount of nerve cells and synaptic connec-tions being discarded in high amounts, which distinguishes this stage from the prior stage of growth in the perinatal stage. This stage of discarding neural paths is referred to as "neural Darwinism," in which the fittest synapses survive and the least used synapses die. Thus, the educational and life experiences during the teenage years are quite crucial in the configuration of the brain for determining the structure and function of cerebral quality for life. After all, if you don't use it, you lose it.

Explaining "Neural Darwinism": The Pruning of Neural Pathways

To elaborate, during the late childhood and early teenage years, the neurons grow in volume and a thickening of the gray matter occurs. At a certain point in the early to mid-teens, this gray matter starts to diminish because of the discarding of unused synaptic paths, which continues until an individual is in his or her mid-20s. During this mid-teenage period, there is extensive growth in white matter, which provides insulation and communication efficiency for the neural axons. This process functions under the old premise of "quality over quantity" in the sense that it makes the used neural paths more effective and quick, while getting rid of the paths that are not deemed as important (in that they are not being used). So, it is during the teens and early 20s that the brain becomes the efficient machine we use for the rest of our lives.

Examples of neural Darwinism have been documented by scientific research. Studies have shown that persons who depend on certain brain functions show not only improved function, but also enhancements in key structures. For example, individuals who depend heavily on recalling geographic patterns, such as cab drivers, show a significant amount of growth in areas that aid in memory of such patterns, such as the hippocampal region (Wallis, 2004). In addition, research has shown that persons who start learning how to play the piano develop a thickening of neurons in regions of the brain that govern finger movement and coordination. It is not just the higher brain areas that are affected by this prioritization. Studies have shown that one of the key areas for neural Darwinism is a hindbrain region, the cerebellum (see above), which is one of the essential brain regions for learning from experience.

Although the lower and hindbrain areas are influenced by the pruning process, it is still the higher brain regions that experience the most effects, particularly the frontal and prefrontal lobes that are most affected, probably because of the back-to-front development of the brain. Notably, these regions are primarily responsible for problem solving and higher brain functions. Thus, the frontal region of the cerebrum is altered the most due to experiences and learning in the teenage years.

So, although the impact of hormones on decision making and behavior is extremely important in the teenage years (see subsequent chapters), there is a lot more going on in this age period than just a surge of chemicals. It is now clear that significant structural and functional changes are occurring that go well beyond hormonal levels. Specifically, the most rational parts of the brain and communication abilities are simply not fully formed until the mid-20s.

It should be obvious that when surging hormones (e.g., testosterone, progesterone) are present in the absence of developed higher functions of rationality, teenagers are highly susceptible to engaging in behavior that does not make sense, and is often criminal. Furthermore, studies have shown for certain individuals experiencing early puberty that there are often large increases in developmental hormones long before the maturation of the frontal lobes takes place, which even further increases their risk for criminality. A good example is provided by studies (e.g., Moffitt, Caspi, Belsky, & Silva, 1992) that show that females who begin menstruation early are far more likely to engage in criminal behavior than their late-onset counterparts.

It is a dangerous combination when raging hormones are telling a teen to take risks and engage in adult-like behaviors, while the appropriate parts of the brain have not fully formed to tell the individual that what he or she is doing is irrational. Unfortunately, the hormonal surge of puberty and the development of the frontal lobes of the brain are not linked, and appear somewhat independent of each other. Perhaps it is not surprising that studies show teenagers tend to identify pictures of persons in fear as being angry, which is believed to be one of the reasons why they often misinterpret emotional cues and feel that people are angry at them when it is not true (for more discussion, see Wallis, 2004). Not surprisingly, teens are more likely to make risky decisions. For example, in an experimental driving simulation game, simulated drivers had to decide whether or not to run a yellow light

(Steinberg, 2004). In this study, teens made safe decisions when they were alone, but when they were with others, they made more risky decisions than did the adults when they were with others. This is not surprising, given that most delinquent offenses take place in groups of teens. Furthermore, adults tend to be able to make personal decisions, even in the presence of others, probably due to the further development of the higher brain areas.

Lobe Connections to Sensation Seeking

Returning to brain structure, the frontal lobe region is strongly linked to a structure called the *ventral tegmental area* (or VTA), which lies in the midbrain (the tegmentum region was shown in Figure 5.2). Recent research has shown that this region of the brain is responsible for our "seeking" drive, similar to Freud's idea of libido in the sense that it is believed to make us search for something unique (see Solms, 2004, for a review; for further discussion, see Guterl, 2002). As an example of this sensation seeking, when the ventral tegmental is stimulated in rats, they will run around and even ignore food in the search for other stimulating objects. This area appears to drive our determination toward something new, but whether it be a Freudian libido effect or a "Coolidge effect" (i.e., sexual desire in males increases with different partners), experts are not sure. Regardless of how the effect occurs, the ventral tegmental appears to be very important in the seeking of new experiences and feelings. Thus, it is likely that this region may differ in structure and/or function in chronic offenders as compared to nonoffenders because of the consistent finding that persistent offenders are more oriented toward risk taking, impulsiveness, and sensation seeking (for a review, see Pratt & Cullen, 2000), as well as applications for short attention spans in children diagnosed with attention deficit disorder. However, virtually no research has been directed toward examining this potential link, particularly for criminality.

The frontal region is also responsible for directing one's motor activity once a decision has been made, the primary motor cortex being located near the posterior portion of the frontal cortex, bordering the parietal lobe. This is why individuals with frontal lobe damage often have loss of simple or fine movements of some body parts, such as hands and fingers (Kuypers, 1981). Frontal lobe dysfunction has also been linked to fewer spoken words (Kolb & Milner, 1981), which is consistent with the finding mentioned above that frontal cortex dysfunction is related to fewer facial movements in social situations. Further, the center for speech production, Broca's area, is also located in the frontal cortex (see Figure 6.3), and damage to the frontal lobe has been consistently linked to an inability to express language (called Broca's aphasia). Given the consistent association between low verbal skills and criminality that has been demonstrated in the extant literature (for a review, see Gibson et al., 2001), this is another reason why the frontal cortex is so important in terms of deviant behavior. Sometimes, individuals with frontal lobe dysfunction do well on IQ tests despite their condition, probably because of traditional tests' emphasis on assessing convergent rather than divergent (e.g., problem solving) thinking abilities, with only the latter being significantly affected by the frontal lobe. Thus, it is important to keep this in mind when screening individuals for potential problems related to frontal lobe dysfunction, and it may be necessary to use more sophisticated instruments, such as brain imaging techniques.

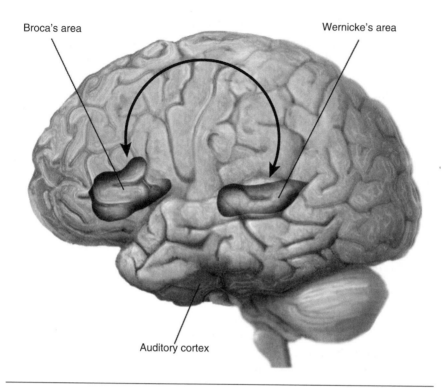

Broca's area

Wernicke's area

Auditory cortex

Figure 6.3   Broca's Area and Wernicke's Area in the Left Hemisphere

Structural and Functional Issues Regarding the Prefrontal Cortex

Of all the regions of the brain, dysfunction of the prefrontal cortex has been the most directly linked to aggressive behavior, as well as to personality changes toward impulsivity and irritability (Kandel & Freed, 1989; Volavka, 1999). Furthermore, brain imaging techniques, such as positron emission tomography (PET) and magnetic resonance imaging (MRI), have provided support for this position. Specifically, some studies show that brain activity (as measured by glucose metabolism) is significantly lower in individuals who are persistently aggressive (Goyer et al., 1994; Raine et al., 1997; Zametkin et al., 1990; for more details, see Fishbein, 2001; Rowe, 2002).

Structural differences in the prefrontal cortex, as measured by MRI, have been noted by Raine and his colleagues (1997). Specifically, the researchers found that antisocial individuals had significantly less (11% less) gray matter in the prefrontal area than did the controls, but there was no difference in the white matter (Raine, Lencz, Bihrle, LaCasse, & Colletti, 2000). To clarify, gray matter consists of the clusters of cell bodies and their nearby synaptic connections in the nervous system. For example, the surface layer of the cerebral cortex has a gray appearance because large numbers of cells are packed together. White matter, on the other hand, refers to axon tracts, the bundles of extensions that project from the cell bodies and send their output to other neurons; these axons are covered with a fatty sheath (called myelin) that gives them a whitish appearance (Halpern, 2000).

Beyond the structural aspects discussed above, there are also significant differences in the functioning of the prefrontal cortex in offenders. A study using PET showed that glucose utilization and blood flow measurements in the prefrontal cortex were abnormal in violent individuals, and that these abnormalities tended to be in the left portion of the cortex (Volkow & Tancredi, 1987). Furthermore, several studies by Adrian Raine and his colleagues (Raine et al., 1997; Raine, Meloy, et al., 1998; Raine, Phil, Stoddard, Bihrle, & Buchsbaum, 1998) have demonstrated reduced prefrontal glucose levels among murderers. Interestingly, some of Raine's studies have discovered that there are more abnormalities in the glucose utilization for murderers who had no history of child abuse or neglect, which suggests that the functional problems in some violent offenders are so influential that they do not require an environmental trigger. Some experts have claimed that this reflects a taxonomical path in which impulsive murderers (as opposed to premeditated, predatory murderers) are predisposed to commit such offenses due to abnormal neurobiology, namely a prefrontal cortical dysfunction (Volavka, 1999). Thus, both the structure and functioning of the prefrontal cortex have been found to be significantly different in individuals who consistently show aggressive behavior.

Recent research has also demonstrated that such structural differences are largely due to genetic differences. For example, using brain scans of twin pairs (monozygotic and dizygotic) and unrelated subjects, Thompson et al. (2001) found that the distribution of gray matter across the cortex is under significant genetic control, particularly the frontal cortex and the primary language areas such as Broca's and Wernicke's regions (see Figure 6.3; for more discussion, see Chapters 7 and 8). Furthermore, Thompson et al. found that the quantity of frontal gray matter was strongly related to individual differences in IQ. Thus, Thompson et al. (2001) concluded that the brain maps revealed "a strong relationship between genes, brain structure and behavior, suggesting that highly heritable aspects of brain structure may be fundamental in determining individual differences in cognition" (p. 1). Other brain scan studies have discovered similar genetic influence in the structure of several regions we discussed earlier in this chapter, such as the corpus callosum (Oppenheim, Skerry, Tramo, & Gazzaniga, 1989; Pfefferbaum, Sullivan, Swan, & Carmelli, 2000), as well as the overall volume of the brain itself (Tramo et al., 1998).

Studies have further implicated the right ventral prefrontal cortex (RVPC) in mediating the pain response from being rejected in social situations (Eisenberger, Lieberman, & Williams, 2003). This research has shown that feelings of pain from social rejection are quite similar to the feelings of physical pain, which the RVPC region also helps to inhibit. Therefore, trauma or abnormal functioning in this region would tend to exaggerate such feelings of pain, whether due to physical or social origin. So, such problems with functioning in this region are likely to produce problematic behavior, especially in terms of criminality.

Although the frontal lobe, particularly the prefrontal cortex, is particularly vulnerable to injury and the structure most often associated with developmental problems, it appears to be the most "plastic" area of the brain. This means that the synaptic paths of communication are relatively flexible in this region in that they are essentially in a dynamic state of change, ready for learning new ideas and behaviors. Even Thompson et al. (2001) and other brain scan researchers discussed above have noted the importance of environmental influences on brain structure and function that go beyond the genetic, heritable influences. The good news is that this means that, in many cases, these communication paths can be reconfigured significantly with the proper treatment. Ultimately, this gives a sort of physiological reason to have faith in correctional programs, particularly those that are based on cognitive-behavioral models of therapy (see Van Voorhis, Braswell, & Lester, 2000).

Furthermore, the findings of these studies on the frontal cortex are even more intriguing when we consider the results of a recent study by researchers at the University of Wisconsin's Lab for Affective Neuroscience (Jackson et al., 2003). The authors of this study were primarily concerned with identifying the areas of the brain that cause some individuals to be consistently optimistic, despite stressors that present themselves in life, compared to other individuals who tend to always be pessimistic and have consistent negative dispositions, regardless of how well their lives may be going. This study used advanced brain imaging technology to identify the specific area that serves as the center for positive and happy feelings. The researchers concluded that the brain region that was most responsible for optimistic and happy feelings was the left prefrontal cortex. The left frontal lobe is one of the most likely to suffer trauma because of its location; a majority of individuals are right-handed, so if a blow is struck to the head, it is most likely to hit the left frontal lobe. It is rather ironic that one of the most important regions of the brain with regard to both cognition and criminality is also likely the most vulnerable to damage because of its location.

Unfortunately, this is consistent with studies we discussed above that show that trauma to the left frontal area of the brain is most predictive of future criminal activity. It is quite likely that persons who experience such trauma become less happy (or more negative) with life, and this may help explain why such individuals are so much more likely to commit such deviant acts. Studies have shown that people who have strong activity in the left frontal region of the brain tend to be more optimistic and positive in their outlook, as well as to report feeling happy (Davidson, Shackman, & Maxwell, 2004); those who do not have this capacity will naturally be more predisposed to engage aggressively when interacting with others. Additionally, it may explain why individuals who do not have healthy left frontal functioning are more prone to have a negative attitude about society and life in general and are more apt to commit antisocial acts.

BOX 6.2   The Continuing Saga of Stanley: Early Child Rearing

As mentioned before, Stanley's treatment by his parents in his early years was miserable. Stanley himself claimed that "as far back as I can remember, my life was filled with sorrow and misery" (Shaw, 1930, p. 47). One important factor was that Stanley's natural mother was "sickly," and she died of tuberculosis when Stanley was 4 years old. Thus, it is not surprising when Stanley says,

> I never knew a real mother's affection. My father remarried when I was five years of age. The stepmother who was to take the place of my real mother was a rawboned woman, devoid of features as well as emotions. . . . To this day I wonder how my father could have picked out such a woman for a wife. (Shaw, 1930, pp. 47–48)

Needless to say, Stanley's relationships with maternal figures were grossly inadequate. Numerous theoretical frameworks and empirical studies (Gottfredson & Hirschi, 1990; Hall, 1954; Hirschi, 1969) have consistently shown that such substandard nurturing at young ages greatly increases the likelihood of faulty psychological and sociological development.

According to official documents, his stepmother was physically and emotionally abusive toward Stanley, as well as other children in the household. Stanley reported that his stepmother was

> a hell-cat full of venom and spite. The first time she struck me was when I was playing with the cat. . . . She beat me, striking me in the face and on the back with her hard and bony hand. . . . After many beatings, I became more and more afraid . . . I became unhappy. (Shaw, 1930, p. 49)

Such excessive beatings have been linked with future disciplinary problems in children (Straus, Gelles, & Steinmetz, 2006), as well as other developmental problems (e.g., neuroticism, depression, low self-esteem, etc.). Additionally, Stanley's father never seemed to notice his new wife's treatment of the children, which was consistent with his general attitude of indifference toward them. Stanley claimed, "My father gave me no comfort. He spent his time at work, at the saloon, and in bed. Never did he pet or cheer me" (Shaw, 1930, p. 49). Studies (Gottfredson & Hirschi, 1990; Hall, 1954; Straus et al., 2006) have consistently shown that such emotional neglect (not just physical abuse) by caregivers has profound implications for a child's development.

Unfortunately, according to Stanley, all his father cared about

> was his regular meals, a bed to sleep in, and his daily can of beer and whisky. His mind was like a motor, always on one course. He didn't think of his children as boys and girls to be loved. He thought of us as just "kids" who had to be provided for. . . . There his parental duties ended. Never did he show love or kindness. (Shaw, 1930, pp. 48–49)

Furthermore, his father was frequently drunk and often became abusive toward Stanley's stepmother in front of the children. Social learning models (Akers, 2000; Bandura, 1979) stress the profound influence of the modeling of violent behavior, especially when those observing such activity are young children.

Most surprisingly, Stanley reported that his stepmother actually encouraged him to go out and steal valuable items. Stanley elaborates on this point by describing incidents when he was 6 years old and he returned home with food and other items from boxcars he had broken into. His stepmother's typical reaction is shocking: "After we arrived home with our ill-gotten goods, my stepmother would meet us and pat me on the back and say that I was a good boy and that I would be rewarded" (Shaw, 1930, p. 53). Such positive reinforcement and encouragement from his stepmother was likely very damaging to Stanley's development and is a perfect example of what not to do according to most theoretical perspectives (Akers, 2000; Skinner, 1953; Sutherland, 1947) and empirical studies (for a review, see Akers, 2000).

This poor treatment of Stanley continued for several years, during which time he became a chronic (or, in Stanley's words, "professional" [Shaw, 1930, p. 64]) runaway to escape such conditions. Finally, after being picked up by police dozens of times, Stanley had committed enough delinquent acts to be placed in the Chicago Parental School at age 9. This started a series of intermittent placements in institutions (e.g., Chicago Detention Home, St. Charles Training School, Illinois State Reformatory, the House of Correction, etc.) and foster homes that largely became his new guardians. Stanley had no feeling of loss in being removed from his family. In fact, when he was released from the Parental School, Stanley said he felt that

> I was sorry when my stepmother came to the school to take me back home, or the place I wanted to stay away from. I had come to like the place [the School], at least, more than I did the hole to which I was returning. (Shaw, 1930, p. 201)

In a few weeks, Stanley was back in an institution because he kept running away and living on the streets.

It is also important to mention at this point that Stanley's neighborhood was one of the most disreputable areas of Chicago. This area was known locally as the "Back of the Yards," which is literally bordering the Union Stock Yards and the central manufacturing district in the years when Stanley was young. According to Shaw (1930), "It is one of the grimiest and most unattractive neighborhoods in the city . . . comprised largely of unskilled laborers. The air in the neighborhood is smoky and is always filled with a disagreeable odor" (p. 34). Such poverty and dilapidated conditions are likely to increase the desire of residents to move out of the neighborhood.

As an important case in point, we will see that Stanley eventually fulfills his dreams by moving out of a decrepit area. This high level of transiency into and out of this neighborhood (as well as the generation gap between foreign-born parents and their native-born children that was so prevalent in the early 1900s) was influential in breaking down any social organization that may have existed among the residents. Theoretical frameworks and empirical studies have consistently linked this type of social disorganization with higher delinquency rates in neighborhoods (Sampson & Groves, 1989; Shaw & McKay, 1942).

Several causal mechanisms have been identified for explaining why delinquency thrives in these neighborhoods with low social disorganization. As Shaw points out:

> In the light of the disorganized community situation back of the yards, the persistence of a high rate of delinquency is not at all surprising. With the marked changes in the composition, diffusion of divergent cultural standards, and the rapid disorganization of the alien culture, the continuity of community traditions and cultural institutions is broken. Thus the effectiveness of the community in the control and education of the child is greatly diminished. (Shaw, 1930, p. 37)

Furthermore, this breakdown in control allows for youths to be "educated" in an alternative and dangerous fashion: Children learn rules of the street from older children. This process whereby youths learn delinquent traditions from older youths on the street will be examined in detail in the next section of the Saga of Stanley.

Conclusion

This chapter discussed the various regions and structures of the brain, with an emphasis on those that are most relevant in the development of criminality. If one thing has been established clearly at this point, it is that many complex processes are occurring in our brain all the time, and that any type of damage or trauma to such brain structures can have a devastating impact on our perceptions and behavior, particularly in terms of criminal offending. Furthermore, even if the brain structure is adequate and healthy, many individuals experience problems with the way their brains function. Thus, the processes occurring in the brain are further complicated and affected by the various hormones, neurotransmitters, and other functional activities that are continuously altering the way we interpret and adapt to our world. Such issues and problems in brain functioning will be examined in the following chapter.

CHAPTER 7

Concepts and Issues in Neuropsychological Functioning

The human brain, then, is the most complicated organization of matter that we know.

Isaac Asimov

I n the previous chapter, we reviewed the basic structure of the brain and how the different areas of the brain are responsible for different actions. However, the actual processes by which the brain functions are a complex set of operations that involves electric signals that are communicated across neurons to various destinations. This communication largely depends on the healthy formation of synaptic paths (similar to telephone lines that carry brain messages), as well as sufficient levels of hormones and chemicals called *neurotransmitters* that physiologically send these electric messages across gaps between the neurons.

Everything we experience, even when we are in the womb, has an effect on how our brain responds. Recent evidence has shown that early formation of synaptic paths is crucial for the healthy development of all cognitive functions; for instance, if an infant does not sufficiently form these "lines of communication" in his or her brain by a certain stage in the first months of life, then basic skills (such as sight or verbal communication) can be lost permanently. In the meantime, new brain cells are constantly being developed, even into old age, but such alterations in the brain are largely contingent on what the individual has experienced in his or her environment. In this chapter, we will present the essential concepts and mechanisms involved in the functioning and responses of our brain and nervous system, particularly in light of external factors. Moreover, we will examine the importance that variations in these processes have on promoting or inhibiting the development of criminality.

Basic Structure and Functioning of Our Nervous Systems

The Nervous System

Similar to the brain, the human nervous system is involved in virtually every thought, action, and function that takes place in our body. There isn't a millisecond that transpires in which the nervous system is not working to continue our survival. In essence, the nervous system is a rapid transmission network that is constantly sending information (often commands) from one part of the body to another. Thus, it is obvious that the functioning of our nervous system is an important factor in the decisions we make and our consequent behavior.

The nervous system is actually split into specialized, albeit highly coordinated, parts. One of these is the *central nervous system* (CNS), which primarily consists of the brain and spinal cord (see Figure 7.1). The CNS is primarily responsible for coordinating muscles in our conscious, voluntary motor activities. We shall see that chronic violent offenders have slower and more abnormal brain wave patterns (for a review of applicable studies, see Raine, 1993).

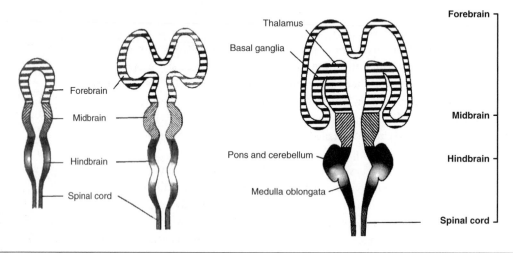

Figure 7.1 The Plan of the Developing Central Nervous System. The drawing in the lower center shows the outline of the neural tube early in development; three divisions may be seen in the area that will become the brain. In the upper left and upper right drawings, increased differentiation is apparent. Here, the major divisions of the central nervous system may be distinguished. This general organization persists in the adult human brain

The other portion, called the *peripheral nervous system* (PNS) consists of bundles of neurons and neuronal processes (i.e., ganglia and nerves) that essentially connect the rest of the body to the CNS (see Figure 7.2). Specifically, *afferent nerves* carry sensory input to the CNS, and *efferent nerves* carry messages from the CNS outward to various parts of the body. The PNS is further broken into the *somatic nervous system,* which is a series of efferent cranial nerves and spinal branches consisting of sensory and motor neurons leading to skeletal muscles, as well as the *autonomic nervous system* (ANS). As shown in Figure 7.2, this latter system includes nerves leading to the internal or "visceral" portion of the body and is responsible for a variety of functions, such as anxiety and involuntary motor activities that have extensive implications in the etiology of criminality. We shall see that chronic violent offenders have lower levels of ANS functioning, which has numerous implications regarding conditioning and inhibition in terms of criminal behavior.

Regulated primarily by the hypothalamus (see Figure 7.2), the ANS is further split into two subdivisions: sympathetic and parasympathetic. The *sympathetic* nervous system prepares the body for energetic or stressful activity, such as the fight-or-flight response, by acting on the internal organs. For instance, when a threat occurs, the sympathetic system restricts the activity of the digestive system while redirecting blood to other organs, such as the muscles and lungs, which are needed in such situations. Resulting physiological changes often can be seen or felt, including a faster heart rate, dilation of pupils, and the expansion of air capacity in the lungs. During these episodes, blood glucose levels rise and blood circulation gets much faster, which distributes oxygen and energy (in the form of glucose) throughout the body. On the other hand, the *parasympathetic* nervous system controls basic maintenance or "housekeeping" tasks in the body that can be carried out at a more leisurely pace. During such periods of rest, the digestive tract becomes more active and the heart rate slows.

Both divisions of the autonomic nervous system are activated involuntarily most of the time, and this activation generally is produced by nervous outputs from the hypothalamus. At all times, both types of autonomic nerves carry signals that bring about minor adjustments in our inner organs and processes. A good example is heart rate, which is constantly receiving signals from the sympathetic and parasympathetic signals, such that at any given moment, one's actual heart rate is the net outcome of these two sets of messages. However, sometimes, this equilibrium seems to go amiss. For example, an integrated model proposed by Venables (1988) attempts to synthesize the invariable findings of significantly lower heart rates in chronic offenders (for a review of this research, see Raine, 1993). Venables explains that these findings are consistent with a phenomenon known as *vagotonia,* which is a predominance of the parasympathetic autonomic processes over the sympathetic system. Vagotonia is thought to occur from overstimulation of the vagus nerve, which encourages the release of insulin from the pancreas and often leads to hypoglycemia, which is also linked to criminality (see Virkkunen, 1982). Because low heart rate is an indicator of parasympathetic tuning or vagotonia, this is a likely candidate for such consistent findings regarding heart rate.

This perspective is also linked to abnormally slow brain wave patterns seen in chronic offenders (for reviews, see Milstein, 1988; Venables & Raine, 1987), as

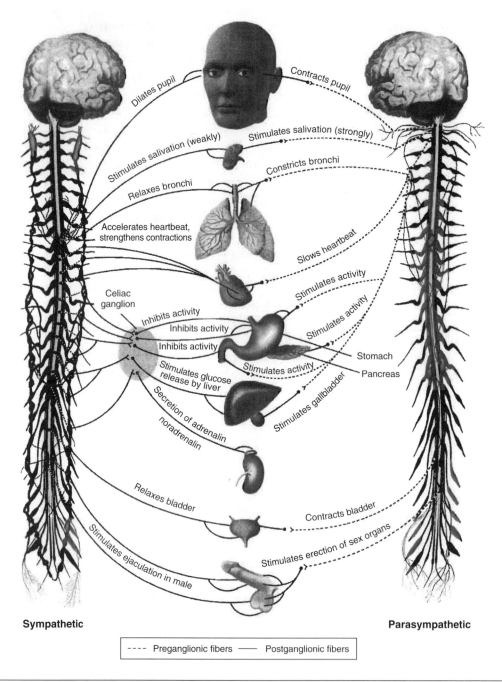

Sympathetic   **Parasympathetic**

---- Preganglionic fibers ——— Postganglionic fibers

Figure 7.2   The Peripheral Pathways of the Autonomic Nervous System. The sympathetic and parasympathetic branches of the autonomic nervous system often exert opposing effects on the organs that they innervate. All autonomic nerves synapse once at a collection of nerve cells called a ganglion before reaching bodily organs. The sympathetic ganglia are located close to the central nervous system, whereas the parasympathetic ganglia are found near the target organs

measured by an electroencephalograph (EEG), which is used to measure CNS functioning. Specifically, slow brain wave patterns found in offenders are more likely to be seen in individuals with vagotonia, as well as in individuals who show higher levels of sympathetic functioning. Because slow brain wave patterns are an index of cortical underarousal, this finding is consistent with those of other studies showing that vagotonia and other disorders are related to an unhealthy balance between the sympathetic and parasympathetic systems.

One neurological theory that is categorized as central nervous system but is directly related to nervous system functioning and gaining support in the literature is reward dominance theory (for a review and discussion, see Walsh, 2002). This perspective, which was originally formulated by Jeffrey Gray (1981, 1987) and further developed by others, such as Robert Levenson (see Levenson, 2003) and Richard Davidson (see Davidson, 2004), is often referred to as *BAS/BIS theory* because of its emphasis on the interaction between two essential function systems of the brain. The first of these systems is the *behavioral approach* (or *activation*) *system* (BAS), which can be thought of as the "go" system in the sense that it drives individuals to seek out rewards or satisfaction (e.g., happiness). The BAS is primarily based in the left frontal cortex (Davidson, 2004), but also includes other regions, especially mesolimbic/limbic structures such as the nucleus accumbens and ventral striatum. The nucleus accumbens and ventral striatum are key pleasure zones of the brain, largely due to the effects of dopamine, which is the brain chemical most involved in BAS functioning. We will discuss dopamine in detail later in this chapter, but for now it is important to know that it is the chemical that is released when we have pleasurable experiences or feel good.

Simply put, this perspective claims that our motivation and our sensation-seeking behavior are due to the interplay of the left frontal lobe, mesolimbic structures, and chemicals, most notably dopamine. The BAS creates the drive in us to seek out essentials of life, such as good food or a love interest. If we succeed, these structures feel the reward or pleasure from such acquisitions, and this reinforcement is an extremely powerful motivation for future pursuits. This drive can be quite beneficial and adaptive, in the sense that we often accomplish a lot and get much work done under the assumption that we will be rewarded for it (see Walsh, 2002).

Unfortunately, this system, if unchecked, creates an excessive and unhealthy drive to seek pleasurable sensation (some have called this the "craving brain") (Ruden, 1997), even if it means engaging in criminal activity, such as drug use or chronic gambling. Furthermore, some theorists (e.g., see Katz, 1988) have suggested that criminal behavior is intrinsically pleasurable due to the "rush" one gets from offending. Empirical studies have consistently found support for the proposition that offending is fun, and this motivates individuals to engage in impulsive, often criminal, activity (Nagin & Paternoster, 1993; Piquero & Tibbetts, 1996; Tibbetts, 1997). This rush can be a strong physiological motivation for reoffending, so it is important that the countering system—the BIS—be functioning properly.

Appropriately named, the *behavioral inhibition system* (BIS) is responsible for keeping our BAS in check by responding to cues of danger or punishment that may exist when considering whether to engage in risky, impulsive behavior. The BIS is primarily associated with limbic structures, such as the hippocampus (the memory center), as well as the inhibitory brain chemical serotonin (see below). Whereas BAS-related dopamine is a chemical that promotes goal-directed activities, BIS-related serotonin moderates or reduces such behavior. Also, limited research has suggested that the right prefrontal cortex may be involved in this system. The interaction between these structures and serotonin is believed to be the fundamental system for inhibiting our impulsive behaviors.

Most people respond well to both rewards and punishments/danger because we have proportional BAS/BIS functioning. Problems typically arise when there is an imbalance in the functioning of either one of these systems. The assumption that criminals have an imbalance in this ratio is the heart of reward dominance theory. For example, if the BAS functioning is low or the BIS level is too high, this can result in depression and anxiety disorders (e.g., obsessive-compulsive disorder). On the other hand, if the BAS is overactive or the BIS is underactive, the individual tends to be extremely extroverted and emotionally unstable, often to the point of sociopathy. Walsh (2002) described this situation as similar to a powerful runaway train (high BAS) with no brake (weak BIS), which, of course, is not a good combination for making decisions when criminalistic opportunities arise.

Studies have indirectly supported reward dominance theory. Specifically, criminals tend to be much more reward-oriented than noncriminals, but they are far less inhibited by punishments or danger (for a review, see Raine, 1993). This suggests that criminals tend to have systems in which BAS functioning is abnormally high and BIS functioning is significantly low. This is consistent with studies that show that serotonin levels are significantly lower in criminals (which will be discussed at length later in this chapter).

As you have probably guessed, reward dominance theory has many implications for autonomic nervous system functioning, largely because the BAS corresponds to the sympathetic branch (fight or flight) of the peripheral nervous system, whereas the BIS corresponds to the parasympathetic branch in that it helps restore equilibrium.

We will see later in this chapter that individual propensities in levels of ANS functioning have important implications for the development of criminality. However, it is important to realize that although traditionally, scientists believed that the autonomic nervous system was "self-regulated" (which is what *autonomic* means), it is now understood that biofeedback from the central nervous system, as well as the external environment, has a significant impact on the ANS. As will be explained below, recent research has also shown the impact of the environment and certain substances on variation in ANS functioning.

Neurons and Their Working Environment

All parts of the nervous system discussed in the previous section are made up of neurons. *Neurons* are individual nerve cells and the basic units of the nervous system (see Figure 7.3). Amazingly, each individual has billions of these cells working in unison, essentially acting as a complex communication network throughout the body. Although modern studies demonstrate that some new neurons develop into adulthood (Shonkoff & Phillips, 2000), the estimated 100 billion neurons with which we are born are the foundation of our brain's communication system. Furthermore, it is how these neurons are connected that determines our mental characteristics. Put simply, neurons receive signals from other neurons and then transmit these signals to adjacent neurons. There are three major categories of neurons—sensory neurons, interneurons, and motor neurons—that are largely analogous to the functions of the nervous system divisions.

Sensory neurons, generally considered part of the peripheral nervous system, serve as receptors or are activated by receptors to changes in the internal and/or external environment. The receptors detect touch, pressure, pain, muscle tension, chemical concentration, joint position, light, mechanical stimulus, and other information regarding bodily changes, including those in the environment. These sensory neurons send these signals to *interneurons,* which are generally considered part of the central nervous system. Interneurons are located in integrating centers (such as the spinal cord or brain), which interpret and synthesize these signals. Then, *motor neurons,* generally considered to be part of the peripheral nervous system, carry signals away from the integrating centers to the site of the receptors in order to respond to the detected change. Such processes are constantly being initiated and completed every millisecond at various places in our body. It is the speed and efficiency of this process that makes it so remarkable.

It should also be noted that other cells, called *glial cells* or glia (meaning "glue"), are nonnervous cells that actually make up most of the volume of the nervous system. Although glia are not believed to transmit signals as nerve cells do, they are believed to have important functions. Specifically, glia provide protection and nourishment for the surrounding neurons, and they produce sheaths containing neural pathways that can affect the speed with which messages can be sent. Also, research has found that glial cells have been known to "mop up" damaged or dead nerve cells so that the environment will be clean for processing signals. Thus, glial cells can be seen as similar to connective tissues and structures (e.g., ligaments) in other parts of the body in the sense that they play supportive, albeit essential, roles in nervous system functioning.

The input portion of a neuron is the *cell body,* which is usually clustered with cell bodies from other neurons in distinctive structures called *nuclei* (those in the spinal cord or brain) or *ganglia* (those in regions outside the CNS). As shown in Figure 7.3, each neuron cell body contains a *nucleus* that regulates the activities of the neuron, sort of like a "cell brain." Typically on the same end of the neuron as the cell body are branching structures or "processes" called *dendrites,* which receive signals from surrounding cells. These dendritic structures vary drastically in number and shape, showing that there is no such thing as a typical neuron. After receiving the signal, the dendrite sends the message down the branch to the cell body. It is then the job of the nucleus to interpret the signal(s) and integrate the often varied signals (e.g., excitatory vs. inhibitory) into a sort of "net" signal that takes all the signals into account so that it can be passed on in an efficient and effective manner.

Attached to the cell body of a neuron is a relatively lengthy cylindrical structure called the *axon* (see Figure 7.4). The axon is primarily responsible for transporting the signal created by the cell body. In carrying the signal from one end of the

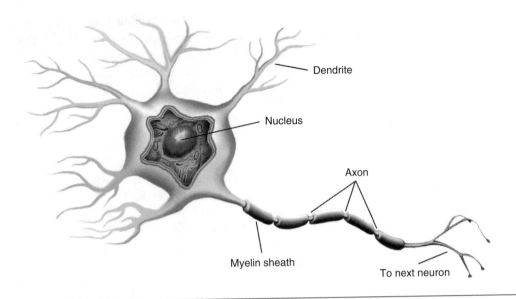

Dendrite

Nucleus

Axon

Myelin sheath

To next neuron

Figure 7.3   The Basic Components of a Neuron

neuron to the other, the axon, also known as the *conducting zone,* performs a vital task with regard to the speed and accuracy of the message. The way the axon relays this message is via membrane excitation; in other words, the signal is transmitted down the length of the cell as an electrochemical impulse.

As mentioned in the previous chapter, aiding this transmission are structures outside of the neurons that have important supportive roles. One of these structures is *myelin sheaths,* which are glial cells that have a plasma membrane, wrap around axons, and act as a sheath. These structures form along the axon, and in between are *nodes of Ranvier,* which are small gaps in which the axon is exposed to the surrounding fluid. Interestingly, these nodes have an enhanced amount of sodium for transferring the signal, which is much more efficient than the areas that have the myelin sheaths. Thus, the electric signal often seems to jump from node to node, which has been called *saltatory conduction.* Such transference of signals is often most efficient this way, and studies have shown that in even the most myelinated axons, a signal can travel 120 meters per second by jumping across sheaths from node to node.

Still, most transfer of signals remains via axons, in which an electric voltage potential (i.e., voltage differential) is created between the inside and outside of the cell body, as well as between regions in the neuron. Once a potential has reached a certain point in the cell body, the signal begins to flow through the axon via the raising and lowering of electrical voltage of a region of a cell as it passes through. This alteration of voltage is produced by a series of proteins, called *voltage gated ion channels* or "gates," that are embedded along the axon. When one of these gates opens, the ions carrying an electrical charge are emitted from the cell and flow outside. The voltage differential in that area increases and causes the adjacent gate to open and allow more ions out (see Figure 7.5). At the same time, the prior gate becomes inactive and closed in order to prevent backward transmission of the

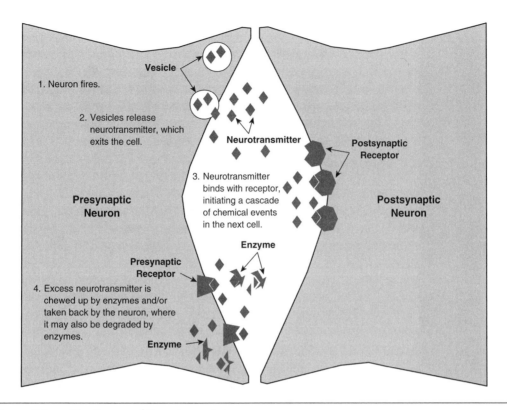

Figure 7.4   The Process of Neurotransmission

signal. During this closed, inactive phase, the steady voltage difference across the cell membrane is said to be at a "resting membrane potential." In this state, the neuron is polarized, and the inside is more negatively charged than the outside.

The specific ions that cause a change in this state are sodium ions and potassium ions (see Figure 7.5). The electric gradient depends largely on the unequal distribution of these two types of ions. When a change in the relative distribution between these two ions occurs, it results in a type of ripple effect similar to dominoes falling when lined up. These effects are known as "graded potentials," in which the electrical changes in a membrane vary in magnitude depending on the magnitude of the stimulus. If enough energy is detected, then a significant change in the voltage differential can occur in the cell and can initiate an "action potential." Such an occurrence will result in the alteration of the ionic distribution (specifically, positively charged sodium ions rush in), which will inevitably result in triggering a new one at an adjacent area along the membrane (positively charged sodium ions rush in to those sites). During an action potential, the regional membrane of a neuron is depolarized, meaning that the inside is more positive than the outside. Following the action potential, the membrane is repolarized, in which the resting conditions are returned to their original, polarized state.

By way of this elaborate system, the electrical signal moves incrementally down the axon, much like a boat going through a channel of locks (see Figure 7.6). Amazingly, it is estimated that action potentials can occur several hundred times a

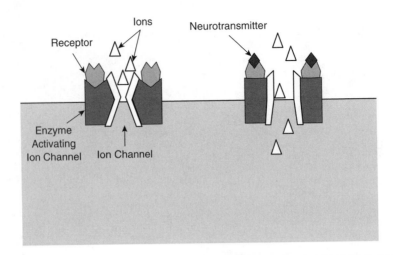

Figure 7.5   The Immediate Effects of Neurotransmission: Opening (or Closing) Ion Channels That Alter the Electrical Potential of the Postsynaptic Neuron

second in one neuron. Given that this process occurs literally millions of times every second in each individual, it is understandable that even the slightest complication in such transmission could lead to devastating results. Of course, this lends credence to arguments that diet and hormonal deficiencies, which are required for such processes to occur, may cause antisocial behaviors.

Assuming that the transference of the message is not significantly disturbed, this process continues to the point that the signal reaches the end of the axon, which, like the other end of the neuron, can consist of a number of branches. These branches of the axon have specialized endings, called *axon terminals* (see Figure 7.6), that make connections with other cells. These terminals are considered the output zones of the neuron, because this is where the signal is sent across gaps to tell other neurons or cells what to do. It is at this stage that many implications for criminality, as well as many psychological disorders, become apparent.

Synapses and Formation of Synaptic Paths

In order to transfer a signal from one neuron to another, the signal must be transported through the origin nerve cell and across the gap between the nerve cells, which is called a *synapse*. As the brain develops after birth, encoded lines of communication develop according to synaptic pathways that are created as we adapt to our environment. The development of synaptic pathways occurs at an extremely high rate during the early years of life, with the paths that we use often becoming strongly encoded (for better or for worse). On the other hand, the synaptic paths we do not use are weakened, or even discarded. It has been estimated that of the 1,000 trillion synapses that form by age 3, approximately half of them will be discarded by adolescence (Shore, 1997). The amazing, and quite adaptive, ability of

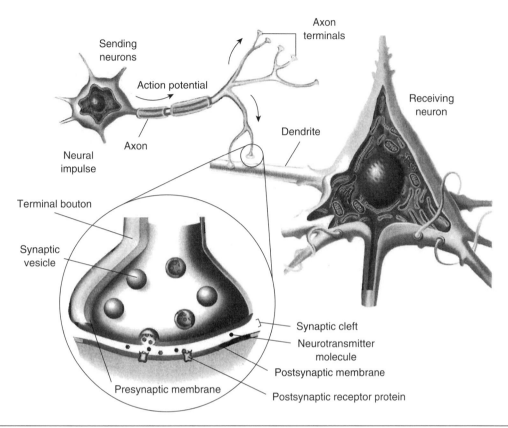

Figure 7.6   The Basic Structure of a Chemical Synapse. In this illustration, the major features of a chemical synapse are shown: (a) the axon terminal of the presynaptic ("sending") neuron, and (b) the postsynaptic membrane of the "receiving" neuron, and the space between them, which is called the *synaptic cleft*. Molecules of neurotransmitter substances communicate between the presynaptic and postsynaptic cells at the synapse

the brain to encode useful neural pathways and discard those it does not use is referred to as *plasticity*, and in many ways is very dependent on the environment. One of the key factors in understanding plasticity and the development of synaptic paths is the functioning of neurotransmitters.

In order to get the electric signal across the synaptic gaps between neurons, the messages must be sent chemically via neurotransmitters. *Neurotransmitters* are biological chemicals that carry the impulse from one neuron to another. Most synapses are *axodendritic* (i.e., axon to dendrite), which means that the axon terminal of one neuron synapses with the dendrite of another neuron. The neuron sending the message is said to be "presynaptic." The neuron receiving the message is called "postsynaptic." But the majority of the synapses that we will be discussing are electrical synapses called *axosomatic* (i.e., axon to cell body), which are commonly found in the brain and depend on neurotransmitters to transport the signal chemically across the synapse. Furthermore, sometimes numerous synapses among many axons will form along a dendritic spine and will be surrounded by a glial sheath.

When the voltage potential reaches the end of the axon terminal, packets of neurotransmitters are released into the synaptic region. More specifically, as the impulse reaches the axon terminal, calcium ion channels are opened in the cell membrane and a surplus of calcium pours into the axon terminal. Then, *synaptic vesicles* loaded with neurotransmitters (e.g., norepinephrine, dopamine, and so on), which are influenced by the incoming calcium, migrate toward the presynaptic receptors and fuse with them.

Following this fusion, neurotransmitters are spilled from the synaptic vesicles into a relatively small cove, called a synaptic cleft; this process is called *exocytosis*. Neurotransmitter molecules then bind to receptor proteins on the postsynaptic membrane and the ion channels open (Kapit & Elson, 2002). From there, the receiving membrane potential carries the signal through the adjacent cell in a similar way as described above. Finally, the neurotransmitters that were used to transport the signal are "mopped up" or taken back into the presynaptic neuron, usually by proteins or enzymes, and these neurochemicals are broken down or stored until needed again. Some inactivated portions of neurotransmitter fragments are taken up by the presynaptic membrane (i.e., endocytosis) or are resynthesized.

There are external ways to improve the ability of making the synaptic connections work better. For example, because the operation of synapses depends on calcium ions, some experts have suggested the intake of calpain, which is a compound derived from calcium. Calpain serves as a type of cleanser that dissolves protein buildup at synapses, which act to mop up excess and waste at the gaps between neurons (see Howard, 2006). Research has shown that consuming dairy and vegetables can increase the level of calpain in one's system. On the other hand, too little calcium results in a buildup of protein in synapses, which results in a loss of mental performance. Furthermore, research has shown that this lack of calcium results in a slowing of the electric signal due to its failure to "jump," or relay via saltatory conduction. However, if there is too much calcium in one's diet, the excess calpain actually interferes with neural transmissions. As always, the suggestion is to follow a moderate diet with a healthy dose of all of the food groups. This is one of the reasons why certain diets have been found to cause differential behaviors and attitudes in prison inmates (see discussion in Brown, Esbensen, & Geis, 2006).

Synaptic pathways, or lines of communication in the nervous system, are often hardwired by biology, but virtually all of them must be established through social experiences; for example, an individual experiences a traumatic event that he or she cannot seem to forget. This is the result of the formation of synaptic pathways and is a manifestation of evolutionary development. Our survival, as individuals and collectively as a species, largely depends on remembering dangerous things that have happened to us in the past and imprinting those conditions in our brain so that we will make better and safer decisions in the future. When we experience a traumatic or anxiety-producing event, our nervous systems go into high gear and rapidly fire up neurons to alert the body to enter fight-or-flight mode. The paths that the neural signals take generate a pattern that is likely to be retained for a long time. If similar conditions present themselves in the future, then they can trigger the same brain patterns and behaviors.

Although such a mechanism is beneficial and needed for survival, it is easy to see how such imprinting of synaptic paths can lead to clinical problems, such as anxiety disorders. For instance, in posttraumatic stress disorder, an individual's fight-or-flight mode and related memories may be triggered by situations that remind him or her of past traumatic events, even when no danger is currently present. Despite the potential problems with the overactivation of such patterns, there is no doubt that the formation of synaptic paths is a vital component for all of our thoughts and behaviors.

Although synaptic paths are anticipated innately from the time we are conceived, research has shown that if certain communication lines are not used by a certain age, then these lines will be closed off. This can be seen in the early stages of development of infants who do not receive adequate interaction with others. Case studies in the psychological literature have established that individuals who do not have interaction with others until later years may never develop the ability to speak or understand language, as exhibited by children who were locked away from social interaction (Greenough, Black, & Wallace, 1987; Perry & Pollard, 1997).

One good example of this phenomenon is seen in the severely neglected children who were adopted from Romanian orphanages in the early 1990s. Many of these children were so deprived of stimuli as infants that they had lost the ability to form language or engage in healthy social interaction. Not only can this severe neglect be observed via behavior, but researchers using brain scans have clearly demonstrated that the brains of sensory-deprived 3-year-olds are significantly smaller than those of their normal counterparts (Perry & Pollard, 1997).

Another example of the "use it or lose it" principle in terms of synaptic pathways would occur if infants are blindfolded at birth for a few months. As demonstrated by studies with young rats (Heynen et al., 2003), such children would never develop the ability to see when the blindfold is removed because the synaptic paths that must be cultivated in that formative period were not encouraged and thus would never be able to develop. This is largely due to the fact that virtually all neurons originate in the central part of the brain and then migrate outward into the outer parts of the cerebrum and other structures, and much of this neuronal migration takes place in the first months or years of life. However, if something (such as early head trauma) retards this process of migration, then the development of the brain will not reach its potential and, if severe, may result in the brain being significantly smaller and lacking in the higher brain regions.

As exhibited by these studies, there is a biological "window" in which these synaptic paths must be formed. If these communication paths in the brain and body are not allowed to develop, then they are forever lost. Such information regarding the importance of early development and interaction with others demands the implementation of policies to ensure that not only infants and toddlers, but also embryos and fetuses, are given the attention and nurturing that they require for adequate maturation. These early social experiences are necessary, and most infants do receive an adequate amount of interaction with others. Unfortunately, the same cannot be said about adequate levels of healthy biochemical functioning. Specifically, many individuals do not have sufficient levels and/or function of neurotransmitters in the development of synaptic pathways.

Many different types of neurotransmitters exist that allow for the transmission of these **electrochemical** signals. These chemicals vary quite drastically, which is essential because within each synapse, there are hundreds of receptors (typically dendrites) that are waiting for the proper chemical to be exuded for them to receive. Whereas some neurotransmitters are excitatory (e.g., acetylcholine [Ach], norepinephrine), others are inhibitory (e.g., gamma aminobutyrate [GABA], serotonin). Neurotransmitters fall under a larger category of chemicals called *ligands*, which are "informational substances." This category of ligands also includes steroids and peptides. The informational substances move from axon to dendritic receptors in a "lock-and-key" manner, such that one type of receptor will accept a particular substance and no other. For example, dopamine (a neurotransmitter) will fit only in a receptor for this type of neurotransmitter. Because it is likely that the most important reason that people behave the way they do is dependent on their level and functioning of neurotransmitters, we are going to spend a long time discussing their content and consequences.

Neurotransmitters

Everyone has approximately the same amount of neurons. It is the neurons' ability to function that makes up our individual personalities and intelligence. Most of our 100 billion neurons are each adjacent to approximately hundreds of other neurons, and the communication among these neurons depends on the levels and functioning of neurotransmitters. Neurotransmitters function as carriers of electric messages from neuron to neuron. The circuits of a single neuron can be compatible with up to at least five types of neurotransmitters; this becomes complex because the transmitters come in various forms (e.g., weak, medium, and strong). Thus, the state of a neuron can range in thousands of ways, given the type and form of the various transmitters.

New synaptic paths are formed as a result of experience and learning, which depends on a given level of neurotransmitters. In fact, learning has been considered a "pattern of connectivity" between neurons (Black, 1991), which neurotransmitters facilitate. Neurotransmitters can be categorized into two groups according to effect: excitation and inhibition. Thus, these chemicals have been described as the "alphabet of personality" (Howard, 2006), because they allow for manifestation of neural input and output.

Neurotransmitters are responsible for virtually every human function, ranging from the regulation of thinking to sleeping to crying to laughing. Certain enzymes (e.g., monoamine oxidase) are active in the functioning of neurotransmitters by "mopping up" or breaking down neurotransmitters in a metabolic process, which can determine the extent to which the neurotransmitters are active in your system. Given the difficulty in directly measuring levels of neurotransmitters, often the presence or absence of these enzymes is used to measure the level of neurotransmitter activity (see below). There are many important neurotransmitters, but only the most essential for the examination of criminality will be reviewed here.

GABA

Gamma aminobutyric acid (GABA) is an inhibiting neurotransmitter. Low levels of GABA have been found to be associated with aggression and violence, whereas high levels of GABA have been associated with passive behavior. One of the primary functions of GABA is to filter out "noise" in the brain while directing the activity of the nervous system involved in senses, such as hearing and vision, as well as cognitive skills (e.g., memory). Low levels of GABA allow neurons to fire randomly, making incoming signals incomprehensible and unable to be interpreted. For example, alcohol mimics the effects of GABA, in the sense that we are not able to interpret what is going on around us.

Prolonged use of alcohol tends to decrease natural production of this neurotransmitter, which would eventually be a factor in the presence of withdrawal symptoms, as well as chronic problems in understanding one's environment. Also, barbiturates produce the same effects on the mind and body as GABA. Addicts of depressants typically show symptoms of having serious problems in interpreting the environmental cues in reality.

Recent studies have examined the positive effects of GABA on aging brains (Leventhal, Wang, Pu, Zhou, & Ma, 2003). It was previously believed that aging brains simply lost cells and were deteriorating. Today, we know that although this does occur to some extent, such deterioration can be slowed or even prevented. The more we know about the aspects of the brain that deteriorate, the more we can do to prevent such degeneration.

Recent studies using monkeys have shown that synthetically providing higher levels of GABA helps in aiding vision and thinking processes even into older age, which is likely due to the ability of GABA to reduce the amount of random activity in the electric level of neuronal activity (Leventhal, Wang, Pu, Zhou, & Ma, 2003; Wang, Fujita, Tamura, & Murayama, 2002). These studies showed that giving the monkeys GABA provided the aging monkeys the brain power of their youth, at least regarding most sensory mechanisms, such as vision, hearing, and memory. Similar effects have been seen on aging human adults who are given drugs that increase GABA, such as benzodiazepines (e.g., Valium). This seems counterintuitive in the sense that an individual can improve mental aptitude through the use of depressants or tranquilizers, but it is true. Thus, the levels of GABA are not only important from a criminological perspective, but also from a humanitarian and social perspective as well.

Recent media attention has been focused on the "date rape drug," or gamma hydroxybutyrate (GHB), which is a type of depressant that resembles an extreme form of GABA. This drug has been used by predatory males who mix this drug in the drinks of unsuspecting women. The women then pass out, allowing the men to take advantage of them. This shows how powerful the effect of this neurotransmitter can be. Regarding its relation to criminality, studies (for reviews, see Franklin, 1987; Howard, 2002) have shown that individuals who watched violence experienced a significant drop in GABA. This study also supports the idea that social and environmental variables can influence physiological factors.

Acetylcholine

Another inhibiting neurotransmitter is *acetylcholine* (Ach), which is a product of metabolized fat in our diet (Howard, 2002). This transmitter is necessary for activating REM sleep (see Chapter 6), which is essential for our body and mind to grow and process information. Drugs such as muscarine mimic the effects of acetylcholine, whereas drugs such as atropine and scopolamine block acetylcholine receptors. Acetylcholine is important in helping to translate messages, but studies have shown that stress causes an abnormal version of Ach to be produced that doesn't provide the same type of neuronal signaling. Brain scans of mice that were exposed to high levels of stress showed a significantly higher level of Ach than did the brain scans of mice that did not experience such stress (Meshorer & Soreq, 2006).

Serotonin

Serotonin is also an inhibitory neurotransmitter that has been found to constrict blood vessels and contract smooth muscles, while also being associated with mood and anxiety (Howard, 2006; Soubrie, 1986). Serotonin is more widely distributed relative to other neurotransmitters in that it travels to many different structures of the brain (for a detailed description of how serotonin functions and is metabolized, see Volavka, 1999). Low levels of serotonin have been linked with a variety of deviant behaviors and clinical disorders, including suicide, schizophrenia, and alcoholism (for a review, see Volavka, 1999). Low levels have also been associated with depression and an inability of the reticular activating system (see Chapter 6) to function properly. Some drugs, such as lysergic acid diethylamide, or LSD, mimic the effects of serotonin. Also notable, many prescribed antidepressants, known as SSRIs (selective serotonin reuptake inhibitors), block the reuptake channels of serotonin.

Of all the neurotransmitters, low levels of serotonin have been most consistently linked with criminality (for reviews, see Fishbein, 2001; Raine, 1993; Volavka, 1999). Low levels of serotonin have been linked with more violent forms of suicide (such as using a gun vs. pills); in addition, more compelling evidence has been observed by studies that have found that juvenile and adult offenders have significantly lower levels of serotonin (Coccaro, Bergeman, & McClearn, 1993; Scerbo & Raine, 1992; Virkkunen & Linnoila, 1990). It is important to note that in many of these studies, particularly those that measure levels in cerebrospinal fluid (CSF), serotonin is referred to as 5-HT (meaning 5-hydroxytryptamine), which refers to the way it is formed in the body. Specifically, the amino acid tryptophan, which is an essential amino acid key in many physiological functions such as sleeping, goes through a decarboxylation and hydroxylation in producing serotonin. In synthesizing serotonin, a required component in its hydroxylation is tryptophan hydroxylase (TPH), which has been mapped to the short arm of chromosome 11 (Nielsen et al., 1994; Volavka, 1999) and has been found to be much more common in males. Generally, studies suggest that reduced CSF levels of 5-HIAA (5-hydroxyindoleacetic acid, a serotonin metabolite) indicate a reduction in central serotonergic activity.

Also, the reuptake of serotonin requires a carrier of plasma membrane (5HTT), the transporter of 5-HT (serotonin). The gene for this transporter has been mapped to chromosome 17, and thus, serotonin activity and synthesis are largely controlled by one's genotype (Collier et al., 1996; Volavka, 1999). Although the information discussed here seems rather technical, it is important for readers to become familiar with the terms and substances related to the production and reuptake of serotonin, particularly the derivatives and supporting substances that are used to measure serotonin levels in the body. Without such a working knowledge of these terms and processes, reading studies examining this neurotransmitter are akin to a foreign language.

Studies have consistently found strong links between low levels of CSF 5-HIAA with both violence and suicide, and such dispositions toward aggression were typically found throughout the life course (Asberg, Traskman, & Thoren, 1976; Brown, Goodwin, Ballenger, Goyer, & Major, 1979; Mann, 1998; Volavka, 1995). Similarly, individuals with the TPH genotype tend to have personality disorders and behavioral problems, especially those related to impulsivity and aggressiveness (New et al., 1998). The low-activity 5-HTT genotype and other indicators of abnormal serotonergic activity have been linked to alcoholism, particularly the Type 2 version, which is considered the more serious form of alcoholism (Hallikainen et al., 1999; LeMarquand, Pihl, & Benkelfat, 1994; Virkkunen & Linnoila, 1990). Interestingly, Type 2 alcoholism—commonly referred to as *early-onset alcoholism*—is found much more commonly in males, is believed to be primarily due to genetic inheritance, and is strongly linked to violent behaviors starting early in life (Volavka, 1999). So, there appears to be a consistent trivariate association between low serotonin activity/levels, alcoholism, and violent behavior, with abnormal genotype being the most likely cause of this complex relationship. Still, the environment plays an important role. For example, a recent study of primates revealed that CSF 5-HIAA concentrations were affected by how they were raised; monkeys who were raised by their mothers showed levels of CSF 5-HIAA that were significantly different from the levels of monkeys who were raised by their peers.

The predominant theme in most recent studies on serotonin levels is that low levels of this neurotransmitter result in failure of individuals to inhibit their behavior, causing them to act impulsively and without restraint. This model is consistent with control models of criminality (e.g., Gottfredson & Hirschi, 1990; Hirschi, 1969) that assume that humans are naturally aggressive and risk taking, and without mechanisms to restrain their innate tendencies, they will engage in spontaneous, selfish activities. Thus, the best conclusion that can be made at this point is that low levels of serotonin in individuals are not conducive to the development of social or self-control in these individuals. It is not surprising that such propensities are exacerbated by indulgence of depressants, such as alcohol, which go even further toward predisposing one toward aggression and violence (Coccaro & Murphy, 1990; Linnoila et al., 1994).

One recent study by Donald Dutton (2002) examined the levels of various neurotransmitters just after "abandonment homicide" by males who had recently murdered their wives after being left by them. He found that during the period of attachment dysfunction, the offender had significantly low levels of serotonin. Dutton concluded that such offenders experience a trauma, and that this, along with other biological changes (e.g., frontal cortex; see Chapter 6), can contribute to the offense, particularly when the offender had experienced a traumatic childhood that was related to abandonment.

Another area of research regarding serotonin is that involving clinical disorders. As mentioned above, serotonin levels appear to have an important role in depression. A recent study by researchers in Great Britain, New Zealand, and the United States (Caspi et al., 2003) showed that a particular gene affects individuals' serotonin levels, especially when people had the "short" version of this gene. One sign of significant progress is that researchers have traced many of the problems with serotonin production to chromosome 17, which is responsible for the primary serotonin transporter 5-HT (a metabolite called 5-hydroxytryptamine). Specifically, the researchers in the international study tracked 800 young adults over a 5-year span and found that 33% of the subjects with at least one "short" type (a less efficient producer of serotonin as opposed to the "long," more efficient type) of the serotonin transporter gene became depressed after stressful life episodes, which would include events such as losing a job or the death of a loved one. Furthermore, individuals with two copies of the "short" form of the gene (we receive two copies, one from each parent) showed even more susceptibility to depression. On the other hand, only about 17% of individuals with the "long" type of this gene became depressed under the same circumstances.

As we discussed previously in this section, modern medical research has developed excellent pharmaceutical drugs to deal with clinical depression (namely SSRIs) that allow serotonin to remain in the system on a more normal basis. Obviously, healthy levels of serotonin are required for finding happiness and pleasure in life, which is acquired by SSRIs' role in sending electrical signals from neuron to neuron. One anomaly that has baffled researchers for a while is that SSRIs typically take several weeks to become effective in changing the mood of the person taking the drugs. Given that the drugs produce a fast increase in serotonin, a major question is why it takes so long for the person to feel significant improvement in mood (Volavka, 1999).

Fortunately, research appears to have answered that question. Specifically, studies suggest that a complex series of events occurs after the healthy levels of serotonin are reached, which include the hippocampal structure of the brain (see Chapter 6). A chemical referred to as brain-deprived neurotrophic factor (BDNF) that enables the hippocampal neurons to grow and form new connections with other regions of the brain takes time to change, and this may largely explain the delay in the administration of such drugs. It also shows the complexity that exists in creating drugs or other antidotes that alter brain function; a direct change to one component affects many related regions and processes.

BOX 7.1 Association of Serotonin With Psychopathology

A recent study by Retz, Retz-Junginger, Supprian, Thome, and Rosler (2004) examined the link between a certain form (i.e., polymorphism) of the serotonin transporter promoter gene and violence, particularly with antisocial personality disorders and childhood psychopathology/ADHD. They examined 153 males and found that, indeed, there was a significant association between serotonergic dysfunction and violent behavior, and that nonviolent offenders (who also had been diagnosed with other psychological disorders) did not have this type of genetic disposition. Thus, the authors concluded that there appeared to be categorical differences between violent and nonviolent offenders, and that a significant factor in this variation had to do with the type of genetic code for serotonin activity.

This finding is highly consistent with previous studies regarding the link between low serotonin levels and criminal offending, but the direct link to psychopathology is the important contribution of this study. Perhaps the most profound of the authors' conclusions is that "this study provides a rationale for further investigation of the genetic basis for violent behavior, as well as for potential therapeutic effects of drugs that interact with the serotonergic system" (Retz et al., 2004, p. 423). Thus, it appears that some of the most recent research on gene types that affect serotonin activity suggests that there is a biological basis for the link between serotonin activity and criminality. Not only does this study support the other studies we examined in this chapter, but it also supports the basic theme of the book: specifically, that some individuals have a biological propensity toward criminality. And much of this may be explained by the level of serotonin production in individuals, which largely depends on their genetic makeup.

It is interesting to note that recent studies have shown that serotonin levels can be significantly affected by various environmental factors, such as the weather and seasons. For example, serotonin levels go down markedly during winter and rise again in the spring. This may be one of the reasons why some violent crimes, such as robbery and murder, tend to peak in the winter months. Although not yet confirmed by medical research, such low levels of serotonin are likely the reason for seasonal affective disorder (SAD), which is the clinical depression that strikes individuals in the fall and winter seasons. Regardless of whether serotonin levels are responsible for these cycles, it is relatively clear that low levels of serotonin are linked to criminal activity. Although criminological studies are mixed on whether depression causes or inhibits criminal behavior, it is clear that the severe alterations in brain chemistry that occur in depression are linked to the development of criminality.

Dopamine

Dopamine is an excitatory neurotransmitter that has been linked to the punishment/reward systems of the brain, which are tied to the regulation of mood. A person's state of arousal is generally increased due to dopamine activity, which can enhance problem solving, directed thinking, and attention span. Perhaps this is why studies have shown that physical exercise, a known dopamine producer, enhances mental performance and focused behavior. Thus, it makes sense that although dopamine originates in the brain stem, its paths of distribution are concentrated primarily in the frontal lobes of the brain, which are responsible for our higher reasoning activities.

In addition, dopamine often produces a "high" feeling when we experience pleasurable things, such as good food or sex. Again, an increased amount of dopamine is one of the primary reasons why we feel good after a hard run or workout, as well as why depression is found more often in people who do not routinely exercise.

Furthermore, amphetamine drugs tend to block natural dopamine reuptake channels, which extend this "high" feeling; however, prolonged use of such amphetamines (e.g., cocaine) can result in the inability to produce dopamine from naturally pleasant activities. For example, sometimes the only way a cocaine addict can get the "high" feeling is through increased dosages of the drug. This results in a vicious feedback loop that makes the addict desire the drug all the more.

Overproduction of dopamine has been linked with aggression and violence (Fishbein, 2001; Gabel, Stadler, Bjorn, & Shindledecker, 1995). In fact, even in animals, dopamine metabolism has been shown to increase aggressive behaviors (Cases et al., 1995). Furthermore, high dopamine levels have been linked to psychotic disorders, such as schizophrenia, in which dopamine surges out of control and disrupts normal cell communication. Traditional antipsychotic drugs have completely blocked the absorption of dopamine in mesolimbic pathways, but at the same time, this leads to blocking parts of the brain from receiving dopamine, which results in their inability to remember or feel pleasure from everyday joys.

New antipsychotic drugs (called "atypicals") are more like smart bombs in the sense that they have shown more success in binding less strongly to receptors. Thus, this results in blocking enough dopamine to ease symptoms while still allowing connections elsewhere, so that these drugs can allow individuals with forms of psychosis to hold jobs and have meaningful experiences with their families. Additionally, researchers have learned ways to use embryonic stem cells to relieve symptoms of Parkinson's disease in rats, demonstrating that cells can be turned into neurons that make dopamine, and researchers are hoping to show the same results in humans. Therefore, regulation of dopamine is an extremely important, cutting-edge area of current research. The implications of such research will likely have a profound effect on the criminality of individuals.

Although some studies show negligible effects of dopamine on human aggression (Scerbo & Raine, 1992; for a review, see Raine, 1993), there are also some empirical studies that show a significant effect for higher antisocial tendencies; thus, this neurotransmitter appears to be an important factor in predisposing individuals toward criminality (Gabel et al., 1995; Tiihonen et al., 1995). Specifically, lower and higher dopamine metabolic activity appears to be linked with aggression and antisocial tendencies. It is likely that there is a curvilinear relationship between dopamine levels and criminal activity, such that persons who have abnormally high and low levels of this neurotransmitter are more likely to commit criminal acts. This hypothesis has not been explored by research, but we feel that this is the current conclusion that can be made regarding abnormal levels of dopamine.

Norepinephrine

Norepinephrine (also called noradrenaline or *adrenaline*) serves to fix information into long-term memory through new synaptic formation. Norepinephrine is an excitatory chemical that is quite similar to dopamine (actually, it is a derivative due to a conversion process), but it is distributed throughout the brain in a unique fashion. Specifically, the distribution pathways of norepinephrine are more concentrated in the cerebellum and hindbrain regions, but can be found in the region between the brain stem and the cortex. Some of the primary structures in this region are those of the limbic system, such as the amygdala, which are most responsible for our emotions. Like dopamine, amphetamine drugs block the reuptake of norepinephrine, so people remain high because this chemical is not removed from the brain. This makes sense when one considers the normal function of this neurotransmitter, which is essentially to produce such excited feelings as to save one's life, which we will now discuss.

The release of norepinephrine is often the result of sympathetic arousal in a type of fight-or-flight experience, which is why we remember episodes of fright or anger so well. Thus, this neurotransmitter is important in the formation of synaptic paths, particularly those that are likely to remain in an individual's memory for a long period of time. A number of studies (for reviews, see Magnusson, 1988; Raine, 1993) found an association between high levels of norepinephrine and aggression, whereas other studies have not supported this relationship (e.g., Linnoila et al., 1983).

Additional studies have shown that plasma levels of epinephrine and norepinephrine were related to hostile behavior (Gerra et al., 1997). One important study revealed a positive relationship between high levels of norepinephrine and aggression (Dutton, 2002). Dutton found that males who murdered their wives exhibited high levels of this neurotransmitter at the approximate time of the act. Also, a review by Volavka (1999) concluded that higher levels of norepinephrine/noradrenergic activity were related to hostile or aggressive behavior in individuals, albeit indirectly, such as through plasma levels as in the Gerra et al. study described above. Also, a growth hormone response to an adrenergic receptor has been linked to irritability (Coccaro et al., 1991). Further evidence of this relationship has been observed in the effectiveness of drugs that block adrenergic activity being given to patients with disorders related to aggressive activity (Citrome & Volavka, 1997); namely, they seem to work.

A recent review of empirical studies concluded that "the majority of studies indicate that higher levels of norepinephrine are associated with aggression and violence" (Fishbein, 2001, p. 39), although other reviews conclude that low levels of CSF norepinephrine are predictive of criminality (Raine, 1993). As with the effects seen for dopamine, it is likely that the effects of norepinephrine are curvilinear, meaning that both very high *and* very low levels are linked to criminal behavior. Although this conclusion is tentative given the current state of research, this type of relationship would make sense because that is the case with most chemicals or neurotransmitters. Specifically, it is likely that too much is bad, as is too little. The same can be said for most behaviors or substances, so it makes sense to form this conclusion until further research is completed.

Finally, recent studies have shown that physical exercise actually increases levels of dopamine, serotonin, and norepinephrine (Carmichael, 2007). According to Carmichael, studies show that levels of dopamine, serotonin, and norepinephrine are all elevated after a bout of exercise. So, having a workout will help with focus and calming down, not to mention feeling better; as some researchers have claimed, exercise can be like "taking a little bit of Prozac and a little bit of Ritalin" (Carmichael, 2007, p. 43). This conclusion makes sense because short-term increases in each of these neurotransmitters are likely to lower the disposition of individuals to commit crime, as long as they don't produce levels that are excessively high.

Monoamine Oxidase

Monoamine oxidase (MAO) is an enzyme that helps regulate the levels of neurotransmitters, including norepinephrine, dopamine, and serotonin. The amounts of this enzyme are often used as a proxy measure of the levels/functioning of these neurotransmitters, especially norepinephrine. MAO helps "mop up" used transmitter molecules from the nervous system. It should be noted that antidepressant drugs are often designed to shut down monoamine oxidase enzymes so that they do not mop up neurotransmitters that may be needed in abnormally functioning systems.

Because MAO activity is particularly high in brain regions involved in higher thought processes (e.g., the frontal lobes) and emotional states (e.g., limbic structures), it is not surprising that abnormalities in MAO levels have been linked to criminality. For instance, low MAO levels result in excessive levels of dopamine and norepinephrine, which are linked to aggression and violent behaviors (Fishbein, 2001; Rowe, 2002). Additional studies have linked variations in MAO levels to sensation seeking (Hsu, Powell, Sims, & Breakefield, 1989) and psychopathic tendencies (Lidberg, Modin, Oreland, Tuck, & Gillner, 1985). Low levels of MAO activity have been found in violent offenders (Volavka, 1999).

As these studies have shown, abnormally high or low levels of MAO have been linked to aggression and criminality. Most recently, a study (Caspi et al., 2002) showed that low levels of one type of MAO—the A type (MAO-A), which is believed to be genetically determined—interacted with physical abuse in children to strongly predict who would become violent later in life. The genotype for the A type (as well as the B type) of MAO is located at the X chromosome. The authors of this study concluded that the combination of low MAO-A genotype and maltreatment predicted future violent behavior as much as high cholesterol predicts heart disease!

Not only is this a demonstration of how important healthy regulation of neurotransmitters is to inhibiting criminality, but this study also showed the vital importance of the interaction between physiological factors and the environment. Similar findings for both MAO-A and MAO-B are reviewed by Volavka (1999) and are likely to relate to lower activity in the platelets of violent offenders (Belfrage, Lidberg, & Oreland, 1992). Studies have demonstrated that mutations on the MAO-A gene and animals completely lacking the gene overwhelmingly led to aggressive behavior (Brunner, Nelen, Breakefield, Ropers, & van Oost, 1993; Cases et al., 1995). Notably, the MAO-A genotype has been found to be more common in human males than human females. The conclusion that can be made at this point is that low levels of MAO activity (probably due to genotype) in individuals are strongly and consistently related to impulsive aggression, especially when coupled with environmental problems such as abuse and maltreatment.

Nervous System Functioning and Criminality

Numerous studies have linked abnormal functioning of the nervous system to criminal behavior. This section will provide a very concise review of this literature, which includes the studies of various portions of the nervous system. We shall see that individuals with low functioning of the CNS and ANS are predisposed to criminality, largely because of their lack of conditioning or feelings of anxiety.

Regarding the CNS, which is responsible for voluntary motor activities, studies using electroencephalograms (EEGs) have consistently shown that chronic violent offenders (i.e., psychopaths) have slower and more abnormal brain wave patterns than do normal individuals (for a review, see Raine, 1993). In fact, chronic offenders often show categorically different brain wave patterns. For example, the types of brain wave patterns that are observed from an EEG are classified as (from slowest to fastest): delta, theta, alpha, and beta. Many studies (as reviewed by Raine, 1993) have found that the brain wave patterns of chronic offenders tend to have far higher delta (slow) activity than those of normal individuals. This low level of CNS functioning is consistent with a low level of ANS functioning, which we will now discuss.

Regarding the ANS, which is responsible for involuntary motor activities, studies have consistently shown that chronic violent offenders have significantly (up to 10 beats) lower heart rates than nonoffenders, as well as lower skin conductance rates (for a review, see Raine, 1993). This lower level of ANS functioning is vital in terms of conditioning; after all, individuals who have a low propensity to feel anxiety are not likely to be deterred by the anticipation of punishment. These individuals tend to have a lower base rate of ANS functioning, and even when confronted with potential punishment or other noxious stimuli, they tend not to show much anxiety compared to normal individuals. Thus, it is not surprising that many chronic offenders have neurological disorders, such as ADHD.

A current method for dealing with some of these deficiencies in ANS functioning is to provide the individual with stimulants (e.g., Ritalin and others) that bring the ANS functioning to normal levels. By stimulating the ANS functioning level, it brings the anxiety levels into a normal zone so that the individual can learn through discipline. Despite the high rate of misdiagnosis for ADHD, if it is properly diagnosed, medication for this neurological disorder can do much to prevent criminal activity among youths, in addition to aiding their educational pursuits. Unfortunately, in current times, ADHD tends to be diagnosed in many children who are simply being children, and they are given drugs, such as Ritalin, that tend to turn them into zombies because the stimulants increase their normal level of ANS functioning to a level in which they no longer seek out normal levels of stimuli. Outside of this problematic consequence, the pharmacological effects that some modern drugs have had are indeed useful in helping individuals avoid criminal trajectories.

Hormones and Their Effect on Physiology and Behavior

Like neurotransmitters, hormones are important in the communication systems of our body. *Hormones* (from the Greek word "hormon," meaning to set into motion) are biochemicals that are secreted into the bloodstream in order to direct the activities of various tissues and organs. A good example to which all adults can relate is the drastic changes that took place throughout each of us when we went through puberty. Virtually all of the noticeable changes were caused by an increased level of hormonal secretion, consisting primarily of testosterone in males or estrogen and progesterone in females (see Chapter 8).

What distinguishes hormones from neurotransmitters is that hormones are relatively slower in their sending of a signal, which is largely due to their targeting cells that are often not in close proximity to the source of the secretion. (It should be noted that a small, albeit important, portion of neurotransmitters, often called neurohormones [e.g., dopamine], are transported via the bloodstream to nonadjacent targets.) Another distinguishing feature is that hormones are secreted by endocrine glands located throughout the body such as the gender-specific structures (e.g., ovaries, testes), the pancreas, and the pituitary gland. Furthermore, hormones are not generally associated with electrochemical events, as are neurotransmitters. In other words, neurotransmitters are chemicals that help send electric signals, whereas hormones send nonelectric signals; they are messages in their own sense. Whereas nerve cells are more precise and efficient in sending signals, hormonal secretions are sent indiscriminately through the bloodstream and generally involve exposing millions of cells to the signal.

Hormones, such as testosterone and estrogen, carry chemical signals to the body as they are released from certain glands and structures. Some studies have shown that a relatively excessive amount of testosterone in the body is consistently linked to criminal or aggressive behavior, with most studies showing a moderate relationship. For example, a key study showed that high levels of testosterone predicted higher levels of criminality (Booth & Osgood, 1993). However, the authors noted that this finding was conditioned by social factors. Other studies (see Walsh, 1995) showed that there is a linear increase in deviance/criminality across chromosomal mutations in degree of testosterone production (see Figure 7.7). In other words, the more testosterone an individual has, the more likely he will be disposed to commit crime.

On the other side of the coin, studies have also shown that hormonal changes in females can cause criminal behavior. Specifically, a high proportion of the women in prison for violent crimes committed their crimes during their premenstrual cycle (PMS), at which time women experience a high level of hormones that make them more "male-like" during that time, due to relatively low levels of estrogen as compared to progesterone (for a review, see Brown et al., 2006). Such findings indicate that the more "male-like" the female hormonal makeup, the more they offend. Thus, this is a strong statement for the effect of hormones.

If anyone doubts the impact of hormones on behavior, one should examine the scientific literature regarding performance on intelligence tests at different times of day. For virtually all individuals, persons perform better on spatial and mathematical tests early in the day, when each individual has relatively higher levels of testosterone and other male hormones in his or her body; on the other hand, virtually all individuals perform better on verbal tasks in the afternoon or evening when they have relatively higher levels of estrogen or other female hormones in their system (Howard, 2006). Furthermore, studies have shown that individuals who are given shots of androgens (male hormones) before math tests tend to do significantly

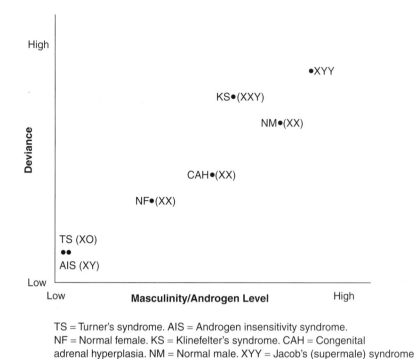

Figure 7.7   Hypothetical Scattergram Relating Masculinity/Androgen Level
(Designated by Karyotype) to Deviance

better on spatial and mathematics tests than they would do otherwise; scientific
studies show the same is true for persons who are given shots of female hormones
prior to verbal/reading tests (Halpern, 2000).

It is important to realize that this process of differential levels of hormones
begins at a very early age, specifically at about the fifth week of life in the womb after
conception. It is at that time that the Y chromosome of the male tells the developing fetus that it is a male and to stimulate production of higher levels of testosterone.
So, even during the first few months of gestation, the genes on the Y chromosome
significantly alter the course of genital, and thus hormonal, development.

This level of testosterone not only alters the genitals of the fetus/embryo
through gestation, but the changes in the genital area later produce profound
increases in testosterone in the teenage and early adult years. Not only does this
produce physical differences, but it also results in huge personality and behavioral
alterations. High levels of testosterone and other androgens tend to "masculinize"
the brain toward risk-taking behavior, whereas lower levels that are typically found
in females tend to result in the default feminine model. These high levels of testosterone result in numerous consequences, such as lowered sensitivity to pain,
enhanced seeking of sensory stimulation, and a right-hemisphere shift of dominance in the brain, which has been linked to higher levels of spatial aptitude, but
lower levels of verbal reasoning and empathy. This has profound implications for
criminal activity and has been found to be more likely in males than females.

Other levels of hormones have been found to be important in predicting criminality. For example, low levels of cortisol have been consistently linked to chronic offending (for a review, see Raine, 1993). This likely has to do with the lack of anxiety or low functioning autonomic nervous system (i.e., anxiety) in habitual offenders. Specifically, as mentioned in Chapter 4, cortisol is involved in the hypothalamus-pituitary-adrenal (HPA) arousal system of the ANS. Indeed, studies have consistently shown low levels of cortisol in chronic violent offenders, aggressive or highly impulsive children, and adolescents who have been diagnosed with conduct disorders (studies are reviewed by Raine, 1993). Furthermore, there is some evidence that testosterone and/or alcohol interacts with cortisol, and that such interactions may actually influence individuals with *increased* levels of cortisol, not low levels reported by most studies (Buydens-Branchey & Branchey, 1992; Dabbs, Jurkovic, & Frady, 1991). So, once again, we see a type of curvilinear effect regarding cortisol levels; specifically, both high and low levels of this hormone have been linked to criminal offending, and it appears to depend on the individual and his or her physiological makeup. Thus, like the other hormones and neurotransmitters, far more empirical research is required to understand the various hormonal and chemical interactions that occur among individuals in producing criminality.

Ultimately, hormones have a profound effect on how individuals think about and perceive their environment. Furthermore, the release and effects of such hormones and other chemicals appear to have profoundly different influences across individuals, especially in terms of such factors as hypoglycemia (i.e., low blood sugar levels), which has been linked to chronic violent offending, and diets that consist of high levels of simple carbohydrates (i.e., sugars) (for a thorough review, see Raine, 1993). It should be apparent that all criminal behavior, whether it is something we do or don't do, comes down to cognitive decisions in our 3-lb. brain. So, it should not be surprising that hormones, as one of the many factors in our cognitive processes, play a highly active role in this decision-making process.

Integrating Concepts of Physiology and Environment

There are numerous examples of how the nervous system functioning is dependent upon environmental factors. This section will provide several examples of how basic brain and nervous system development and functioning can lead to propensities toward criminality. We will start with an example of the early effects of the environment on physiological development.

As noted above, the most important period of time in the formation of neural migration and generation of synaptic paths is in the first years of life (i.e., from conception to approximately age 5). For example, the brain reaches 90% of adult size by age 3, despite the fact that at this time the rest of the body is less than 20% its eventual adult size. This shows the importance of early brain development. One notable area of concern is that of infants who have suffered trauma from caregivers. Thus, we will devote this section to integrating the concepts we have discussed in this and the previous chapter that show the impact that such detrimental environmental aspects can have on the structure and functioning of the brain.

Recent research on physiological reactions of severely neglected and/or abused (hereafter deprived) children show that they readily adapt a fear response. This fear response is the result of a very elaborate network of neural systems that the human brain has evolved to deal with threats. However, the human brain did not evolve under the abnormal conditions of constant stress that deprived children tend to experience, and individuals who experience such early, consistent stress develop differently from normal children.

There are a number of observable differences in the structural and functioning brains of deprived children as compared to normal children. The nature of brain formation follows that of evolutionary appearance in the sense that in human beings, the first part to form in our development is the brain stem, which is responsible for our most essential activities, such as breathing (see Chapter 5). The next level of formation is our midbrain, followed by our limbic system, which consists of our primary emotional regulatory structures (amygdala) and our memory center (hippocampus).

These structures play a key role in the body's arousal system in the sense that they affect the central (voluntary) and autonomic (involuntary) nervous systems. Stress hormones (e.g., cortisol) and stress-related neurotransmitters (e.g., norepinephrine), which deprived children produce much of, tend to target the hippocampus and amygdala and alter their synaptic formation and dendritic structure. Specifically, repeated stress in early formative years appears to retard the development of neurons in a particular section of the hippocampus, while causing atrophy in the dendrites of regions of this structure and others (for more details, see Perry, 2000). Such neuropsychological differences are most likely due to observed dysfunctions in learning and memory that are consistent with stress-related syndromes, such as battered women's syndrome and posttraumatic stress disorder.

Regarding the amygdala, which is largely responsible for regulating an individual's emotions in the sense that it receives messages from the brain stem, the body, and the higher brain, this structure must orchestrate responses to this plethora of information by sending messages to several brain areas. Like animals, humans store perceptual information in this brain structure that can be crucial in recalling stress and anxiety, primarily regarding emotional memory. The amygdala is perhaps most important in remembering anxiety and stress, and it becomes one of the most common areas (along with the hippocampus) found by brain imaging studies to be linked with abnormalities in ANS and CNS functioning. Such functioning has been found to be significantly different between deprived and normally reared children (Perry, 2000). This is consistent with other studies that have implicated the amygdala/hippocampal region in criminal behavior (Raine, 1993; Yeudall, Fromm-Auch, & Davies, 1982).

The final, yet most important, area of the brain to develop is the cerebral cortex. The interaction that the cortex has with the lower structures of the brain is vital and has a great impact on the quality and nature of the thought processes that occur in the higher brain. After all, the cortex provides the subjective interpretation for any emotion or memory that is provided by the amygdala or hippocampus. In fact, it is largely due to interpretation of messages from the lower brain area by the cortex that leads to given feelings and reactions by individuals that result in criminality. Although not based on young children, studies have clearly shown significant functional differences in the cerebral cortex (namely the left side) of criminal individuals versus those who are not chronically criminal (for a review, see Raine, 1993, pp. 150–153; Raine et al., 1998).

Another portion of the limbic system that is found to be different in young children who are abused or neglected is the hypothalamic-pituitary-adrenal (HPA) axis or system. In humans and many animals, the HPA axis serves an important function in initiating and regulating the stress response, which involves various neurophysiological and neurochemical responses to threats in the environment. However, excessive use of this system, such as when a child is constantly being threatened or deprived, often results in alterations or damage to this system. One common type of change is that certain brain structures may become "worn out," particularly those in the HPA axis and other limbic structures. For example, Teicher, Ito, Glod, Schiffer, and Gelbard (1994) and Perry (2000) have found that abused children tend to have a much higher incidence of hippocampal abnormalities, which obviously has profound consequences for the individuals' memory, cognition, and arousal.

Additionally, the neurochemical systems often become damaged from such chronic threats and maltreatment. Specifically, studies have shown that levels of dopamine and norepinephrine become irregular, which results in a variety of negative manifestations including sleep deprivation, impulsiveness, failure to concentrate, and loss of fine motor control (Perry, 1994, 2000). In light of these symptoms, it is not surprising that traumatized children are much more likely to exhibit hyperactivity, behavioral impulsivity, anxiety, hypertension, and sleep disorders (DeBellis, 1997; Raine, 1993).

The leading explanation for this phenomenon is that children who are constantly exposed to threats from the environment experience "use-dependent" organization of neural pathways that reflects an ability to adapt to a world characterized by chaos, fear, and unpredictability. One consequence of this organization is the excessive triggering of the HPA system stress response involving constant neurophysiological reactions called "hyperarousal" (Perry, 1994). In this condition, the individual's stress response is always going, with virtually no down time (Perry, 2000). Such individuals tend to have a short temper and react aggressively toward even benign stimuli. Eventually, the child becomes abnormally sensitized (or in some cases excessively desensitized) to the stress-related systems because of the repetitive reexperiencing of the trauma, resulting in dysregulation of many brain functions in various regions from the brain stem to the cortex (Perry, 2000).

Unfortunately, once these neural patterns are formed, it can be difficult to alter them. After all, not only has the brain changed in order to fit its environment, but for survival reasons, the brain is programmed to especially remember traumatic events to make sure we don't forget what caused such stress and danger. Although other memories and episodes are retained, the ones that pose a danger or cause us pain make a much more pronounced impression on the brain (Perry, 2000; Teicher et al., 1994). The neural pathways that are linked with traumatic events are much more easily triggered, likely because of the necessity of our ancestors to recall what would eat them. This evolutionary adaptation, which has aided humans for centuries and continues to do so, becomes quite problematic when it involves a child who lives in an abusive home and is constantly threatened every day.

It is likely that all readers can relate to feeling very threatened at some point, when you felt your fight-or-flight response to stress or danger kick in. Perhaps it was before or during a presentation in front of a large group of people. Perhaps you were in a heated argument or even a physical confrontation with someone. Perhaps you were caught doing something that you shouldn't have, such as seeing a police car when you are going faster than the speed limit. Remember the rush of adrenaline you felt, and how you could feel your heart beating very fast. Perhaps you experienced a loss of coordination or were shaking. Perhaps you spoke much faster than normal, or couldn't speak at all. Now imagine being a young child who feels this way every single day.

After months and sometimes years of such stress response, it is understandable how the body eventually loses its ability to adequately respond to cues in the environment. Many times, the body will overreact to harmless stimuli, and other times, it will not react when real dangers present themselves. There is some evidence that individuals will overreact to some cues as a method of controlling the situation (Perry, 1994). On the other hand, other individuals appear to be nonreactive or numb in the face of threatening environments, which is likely a form of dissociation (i.e., the "surrender" response) (see Perry, 2000). This makes it very difficult for chronically abused and neglected children to function normally and adequately in conventional society.

It is apparent that both structural and functional differences exist between children who are adequately socialized and those who are not. However, there exists a complementary area of explanation that emphasizes communication skills among individuals. Specifically, social-emotional communication is very central to the necessary processes that exist in human groups, which include the capacity to appreciate and understand others' signals, as well as to express intent and meaning to others (Perry, 2000). After thousands of generations, the human brain has developed a physiological tendency for "social" perception and communication, including both verbal and nonverbal messages, as well as affectual bonds (Rowe, 1992). All functions, including eye contact, cooing, smiling, and so on, are translated by sensory organs into interpretable patterns of neural activity, which is then processed and organized by cortical brain structures, particularly the prefrontal cortex. Over many thousands of years, evolution selected persons to perceive (both verbally and nonverbally) when conditions were safe and when they were dangerous.

At the same time, a capacity among humans evolved that allows individuals to match multiple sources of stimuli, and thereby detect deceit. When tone of voice or bodily movements do not match words from an individual, the normally developed human brain has evolved to become alert and to take notice. Unfortunately, this type of reaction is put in "hyperdrive" when individuals are exposed to a consistent state of stress, because persons who are deprived are never given the chance for their systems to calm down and are constantly in stress. Interestingly, such consistent states of stress can begin in the womb. A recent study from London's Imperial

College (Glover & O'Connor, 2002) found that women who had high levels of anxiety during pregnancy were twice as likely to give birth to a hyperactive child. The authors of the study claimed that this was likely due to the high levels of cortisol—a stress hormone—that the mother had in her system that directly affected the fetus. It is clear that such prenatal factors can have a profound effect that can last a lifetime.

Many of these types of individuals constantly perceive everyone as a threat, rather than discriminating between persons who mean well and others who do not. They have lived so long with constant stress that their nervous systems no longer function properly. Perhaps this is why such individuals are much better at easily lying without detection or pass lie detector instruments without blinking an eye. Likely, it is because such persons have been raised without the normal socializing controls, both internal and external, that would explain their deceit and unresponsiveness to society. To these individuals, it is merely a natural response (or adaptation) to deceive others in their environment in order to gain resources in the inconsistent environment that has presented itself. Such low levels of anxiety, typically due to low autonomic nervous system functioning, have long been observed in psychopaths and chronic offenders (Wilson & Herrnstein, 1985).

The human brain evolves and develops from the bottom up, or from lower areas to higher areas. Thus, earlier stages of development are more linked with lower areas of the brain (e.g., brain stem, hindbrain). The more advanced issues of brain development are related to the areas that develop in later stages (e.g., limbic system, cortex). Although most individuals experience brain development through these various stages, the point at which they exhibit abnormality in formation plays a key part in the etiology of an individual's brain structure. If individuals have a difficult time modulating the more primitive brain stem (mediated state of arousal), the child will seem to constantly kick, scream, and hit (Perry, 2000). On the other hand, if problems are encountered at progressive stages, subsequent antisocial tendencies will often become obvious by the child's negative reaction toward caregivers (Buss & Plomin, 1984; Patterson, DeBaryshe, & Ramsey, 1989).

Studies have shown that children who are found in a stressful environment tend to have high levels of stress hormones that produce "neuron death," which is related to delays in their cognitive and motor development, as well as their social skills (Gunnar, 1996). This directly affects higher brain development. Specifically, primates raised in isolation had significantly altered brain structures and functioning, which resulted in a lack of ability to organize emotional behavior in response to situations. In other words, brain development is based on a "use-dependent" system, meaning that the growth and function of neural pathways that are constantly being developed (more so at young ages) are determined by experiences and stimuli. Essentially, the brain is made to be quite malleable so that it can adapt to one's environment and whatever conditions and culture in which the individual is raised.

Significant differences have been observed in the actual functioning of areas described above, such as the limbic system and cerebral cortex; namely, the brain cells do not communicate well because the neural paths are abnormally formed. Brain scans have shown that the electric signals are radically altered by such structural deficiencies, as well as irregular levels of neurotransmitters. Such problems have profound effects on individuals' nervous systems and ultimately affect the way people behave in and learn (or not) from their environment. Another example is demonstrated by recent studies by the National Institutes of Health that have found that animals who experience painful trauma that mimics that of infants causes them to become more sensitive to pain as they grow older. The reason for this is believed to be that the pain causes the developing nervous system of the young infants to grow more nerve cells that carry more signal potentials of sensation to pain to the brain.

Regardless of the exact reasons for particular physiological abnormalities, it is clear that children who experience a lack of adequate bonding or socialization exhibit significant dysfunctions regarding their brain formation and/or functioning, particularly the higher brain. The relationship between criminality and childhood abuse and neglect is one of the most consistently supported findings in the literature (for a review, see Heck & Walsh, 2000). Such problems are likely the result of weak development in brain configuration that is linked with inadequate formation of self-consciousness and social emotions, such as shame, guilt, embarrassment, pride, empathy, and possibly self-control. These emotions start to develop at approximately 18 months of age, which is the time that self-consciousness starts to develop (see Lewis, 1992; Tibbetts, 2003).

Without a healthy level of knowledge in social interaction and regulation of behaviors by these self-conscious emotions, an individual is likely to breach many social mores and norms, which will result in their being ostracized by conventional peers and authority. Naturally, this will result in their predisposition to hang out with others who have been ostracized, namely others who have a propensity toward rule violation (for a similar perspective, see Becker, 1963). Thus, a failure to develop adequate social skills will lead to a "birds of a feather flock together" phenomenon in which children who are deprived will have a propensity to depend on one another for companionship. This will lead to a vicious feedback effect in which the negative influence of their friends will encourage the criminal activity of the deprived individual who has been selected to associate with this group, and this very activity will lead to further segregation from conventional society (see Thornberry, 1987, 1997).

BOX 7.2   The Continuing Saga of Stanley: Effects of Peer Groups

In the previous entry concerning Stanley, we examined the familial and neighborhood environment in his early years. It was concluded that Stanley was raised in a state of disorganization and lack of control. In the absence of such social controls, children will tend to seek out alternative normative systems, which make them particularly vulnerable to adopting delinquent traditions and values provided by older youths on the streets. Shaw (1930) explains that in socially disorganized neighborhoods such as Stanley's, "contact between the young child and the older delinquent is almost inevitable. . . . Delinquency has become a more or less permanent aspect of the social life among boys in the area" (p. 36). It is during this "inevitable" contact that the "permanent" delinquent traditions are passed.

(Continued)

(Continued)

Additionally, Shaw (1930) explains that because of the

> definite break between the foreign-born parents and their native-born children . . . the relation between the child and parent assumes the character of an emotional conflict, which definitely complicates the problem of parental control and greatly interferes with the incorporation of the child into the social milieu of his parents. (p. 35)

The result is that such youths, who are figuratively isolated from their parents, will bond together against the adult authorities. Furthermore, these unsupervised peer groups will be free to engage in deviant activities, often in defiance of the traditional social controls. Such reaction formations against conventional society are a likely source for street gangs and other types of delinquent peer groups (Cohen, 1955). We will see that Stanley's experience fits this model very well.

Both traditional and recent studies support the extensiveness and importance of peers in the occurrence of delinquent activity. Contemporary statistics from the federal department of the Office of Juvenile Justice and Delinquency Prevention (OJJDP) (Snyder & Sickmund, 2006) reveal that whereas the majority of adult crimes tend to be done by lone offenders, most delinquent offenses occur in groups. However, this would not surprise Shaw or Stanley. Shaw reported statistics in 1930 from 6,000 cases brought before the Juvenile Court of Cook County. Of these cases, more than 90% involved two or more boys.

Additionally, Shaw (1930) also reported numerous anecdotes in which children reported the impact that their peers (usually older youths) had in encouraging their delinquency. For example, one youth stated,

> When I started to play in the alleys around my home I first heard about a bunch of older boys called the "Pirates." My oldest brother was in this gang and so I went around with them, . . . When I started to hang out with the Pirates I first learned about robbin. (p. 10)

This same youth continued: "The guys stuck together and helped each other out of trouble. . . . They were always planning new crimes and new ways to get by without being caught. Everyone hated the police and looked upon them as enemies" (p. 11). The reinforcement and encouragement that the young boys received from older youths, albeit often superficial, was a very powerful source of esteem for children who were not receiving it elsewhere. Shaw (1930) quotes one youth explaining that "I felt like a 'big shot' after that night and the big guys said I could go with them every time they went robbin" (p. 17).

No case provides a better example of the influence of peers than that of Stanley. After numerous beatings by his stepmother, Stanley started hanging out on the streets in order to avoid being at home. As Stanley explains,

> The life in the streets and alleys became fascinating and enticing. I had two close companions that I looked up to with childish admiration and awe. One was William, my stepbrother. The other one was Tony, a dear friend of my stepbrother. They were close friends, four years older than me and well versed in the art of stealing. (Shaw, 1930, p. 50)

Stanley obviously was influenced by the older delinquents in his neighborhood, which was largely due to the isolation he felt from his parents.

Stanley mentions the direct encouragement he received from these older youths:

> *Tony liked his whiskey and . . . he would dare me to drink and I would, although it burned my throat. I was what they call "game" and I just swallowed it without a word, to maintain that high distinction which I was openly proud of. (Shaw, 1930, p. 51)*

Besides stealing and drinking, Tony and his sisters exposed Stanley to many other deviant behaviors: "At first I was too young to know what it all meant, but I soon learned and developed many sex habits, like masturbation and playing with girls" (Shaw, 1930, p. 51). Stanley summarizes his feelings of committing crime with his older brother when he says, "How I loved to do these things! It was an honor to do such things with William. . . . I was ready to do anything William said, not because of fear, but because he was my companion" (p. 52). It is obvious that Stanley was profoundly influenced by the older youths to whom he was exposed. These older delinquents "educated" Stanley in how and why he should commit crime and reinforced such behavior by encouraging him afterward, which is consistent with dominant theoretical perspectives of crime (e.g., differential association theory [Sutherland, 1947]; differential reinforcement theory [Akers, 2000]).

Although we have discussed only the disadvantageous aspects of peers in influencing criminal behavior, peers are actually an inhibiting factor for many individuals. In a future chapter, we will see that Stanley will meet a new group of friends that helps lead him away from his life of crime and poverty.

Conclusion

This chapter discussed the functioning of the brain and related nervous systems. Specifically, we discussed the way that our nervous systems work and the various chemicals that influence such functioning. We explored the existing scientific literature findings regarding the levels of autonomic and central nervous system functioning, as well as the existing conclusions regarding the levels of neurotransmitters and hormones that are predictive of criminality. Ultimately, this chapter has revealed the way the brain works and functions differently for chronic offenders as compared to normal, nonoffending individuals.

CHAPTER 8

Gender Differences in Brain Processes and Laterality

There's a scene in the film Annie Hall *where Woody Allen tells his psychiatrist that he and Annie have sex "hardly ever, maybe three times a week," and she tells her shrink that they do it "constantly, I'd say three times a week."*

New Zealand Listener, 28i–3ii, 1995

The most consistent finding in the criminological literature is that males are significantly more violent and aggressive than females. This has been found to be true in virtually all societies, across time and place (Blumstein, Cohen, Roth, & Visher, 1986; Stark, 2002; Volavka, 1995, 1999). In fact, the predominance of males in offending, especially violent acts, is so prevalent that it appears to be the closest thing we have to a "law" in criminological discipline.

Male offenders commit the vast majority of murders, robberies, and burglaries throughout the world. In the United States, approximately 85% of arrests are of male suspects, particularly for the serious violent offenses, such as murder and armed robbery (e.g., see U.S. Department of Justice, 2005). Furthermore, studies have shown that the gender difference in physical aggression is evident even before the preschool years (Tremblay, 2006), and it is fully expressed by puberty (Volavka, 1995, 1999). Recent studies show men even dream about physical violence more than women, and this difference is generally true across all cultures that have been studied (Domhoff, 2003). It is likely that this consistent sex difference in aggression is partly due to societal causes (e.g., child-rearing practices), but the extant evidence, as well as the observed universal pattern, indicates that most of the discrepancy is of biological origin.

This biological difference is now accepted in most scientific fields, particularly medicine and related physiological disciplines. For instance, the editor of the *Journal of the American Medical Association* (*JAMA*) has instituted a policy whereby all research studies published in *JAMA* are required to perform and report gender-specific results, unless the topic is a disease that affects only one sex. This was a significant step considering that traditional medical research even up to the 1990s, like most traditional criminological studies and theorizing, excluded women largely due to the belief that women were, for the most part, the same as men (except for reproductive organs). The medical field now appears to explicitly reject a unisex model, as do many experts who specialize in social psychological aspects related to gender. Scientific journals in criminology and other social sciences would be wise to consider such a policy on gender-specific analyses, given the profound differences in physiology and cognitive functioning between males and females.

As an example of how such sex differences of biological origin can affect social behavior, researchers have pointed to the propensity for males to develop Type 2 alcoholism, which is largely inherited (Volavka, 1999). Furthermore, the genotypes associated with violent behavior discussed in previous chapters (e.g., TPH and MAO-A) are almost exclusively found in males. Additionally, it goes without saying that excessively high levels of testosterone are far more common in young males than in young females. Still, when high levels of testosterone are found in females, it is generally in their teenage years or in periods of their premenstrual cycle, which is the time that females peak in offending, particularly for interpersonal violence (Dabbs & Hargrove, 1997).

However, some researchers have clearly stated that attempts to develop theoretical frameworks for why men differ from women in propensities toward offending are a waste of time (Smith & Paternoster, 1987). Their argument is that the causal processes involved in promoting or inhibiting criminality are the same across gender, but simply vary as a matter of degree and not of substantive difference. They go so far as to say that scientific examinations of differences between male and female offending are the "Dark Ages" of empirical research (Smith & Paternoster, 1987).

In light of recent studies (for a review, see Halpern, 2000; also see Tibbetts, 2002; Tibbetts & Herz, 1996), we strongly disagree with this position. Rather, we believe that there are fundamental differences between males and females in regard to socialization factors and, more importantly, the way their brains generally function, and that these dissimilarities largely contribute to the extensive gender disparities seen in criminal offending. Specifically, the evidence suggests that females are more strongly influenced by their internal mechanisms, such as moral beliefs and shame, than are males (Tibbetts, 1997, 2003; Tibbetts & Herz, 1996). In addition, females simply have different cognitive styles of thinking as compared to males. Furthermore, these differences that have been observed between males and females are caused by both biological and environmental differences.

In this chapter, we will present evidence that there are significant physiological differences in the way the male and female brains develop. Many of these gender-specific variations are structural. For example, whereas men have an average of approximately 100 grams more brain matter than women, as well as more brain cells, women tend to have more efficiency in the communication among their brain cells and neural activity, likely due to more dendritic connections. Another important example of gender differences in brain structure is the limbic system (see Chapter 5). Specifically, females have larger deep limbic structures (e.g., amygdala) than do males, which may partially explain why women tend to be more in touch with their feelings and typically show stronger propensities to bond with others (and perhaps the higher likelihood to become depressed and attempt suicide, which is three times more likely than for males). Some of these formative differences are evident very early on, even in the first trimester of pregnancy, whereas others develop later in life (e.g., adolescence).

Of course, not all gender differences in the brain are structural; in fact, most of the disparities appear to be functional in nature. Specifically, many of the gender differences in cognitive processing appear to be related to variations in *laterality*, or preferences toward having certain functions (e.g., verbal abilities) primarily controlled in a particular hemisphere of the brain. There is considerable evidence that many of the differences between males and females in laterality are due to hormones and their effects. Such variations in lateralization go a long way toward accounting for such gender disparities in criminal offending. Thus, both structural and functional differences will be reviewed and applied toward an understanding of criminality, particularly in the sense that these brain differences affect how males and females respond and adapt to their environment.

Gender Differences in Hemispheric Lateralization

Although all embryos begin their development in the same way, sometime near the fifth week approximately half of the embryos will be signaled (by a Y chromosome) to grow testes, which will profoundly affect the levels of androgens to be produced in an individual. This one factor present (or not) at 5 weeks will significantly determine abilities on certain cognitive tasks throughout life. The newly forming brain, as well as the differentiation of the sexually specific genitals, depend on the type and quantity of the various sex hormones that are provided.

As shown in previous chapters, the brain visually appears to be bilaterally symmetrical, with the two halves each called a hemisphere (like a globe of the earth). The two halves are connected by a thick band of neural fibers, called the corpus callosum (see prior chapters and Figure 8.1). This band of fibers allows the hemispheres to communicate effectively with each other. It is now well established that individuals tend to be oriented to one hemisphere, with males tending to being more unihemispheric than females (Howard, 2006), perhaps due to the significantly larger corpus callosum in females (see below). Some experts have gone so far as to conclude that what people believe to be the unconscious or subconscious mind, which relates to Freudian psychological theory, is actually signals from the other, nondominant hemisphere in most individuals. Specifically, it is believed that signals from the nondominant hemisphere of the brain may be so subtle, albeit present, that it drives individuals to acknowledge or act on those signals. For most individuals, the nondominant hemisphere is the right hemisphere, which is usually the nonverbal, emotionally driven portion of our brain. (For strong left-sided individuals, this would be their left hemisphere.)

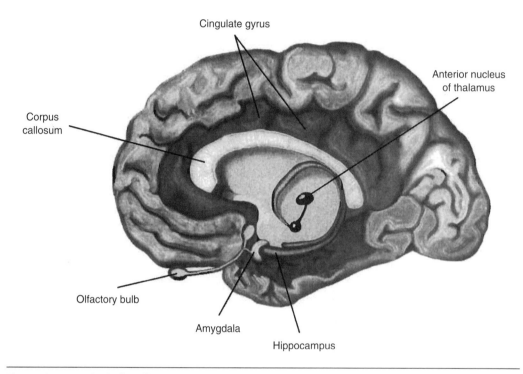

Figure 8.1   Principal Midline Brain Structures Involved in Emotions

The left hemisphere of the cerebral cortex receives sensory information from the right half of the body, whereas the right hemisphere receives sensory information from the left side of the individual. This is called *contralateral* control, which means "opposite-side" control. Although these two halves of the brain are visually mirror images of each other, decades of research shows that the two hemispheres are neither functionally nor structurally symmetrical. Modern research has established that different parts of the brain, and often only in one hemisphere, are more specialized for certain cognitive functions.

There is now a voluminous research literature examining the issue of whether the corpus callosum differs between males and females (for reviews, see Bishop & Wahlsten, 1997; Holloway, 1998). This research on sex differences regarding the corpus callosum has shown that human females generally have a significantly larger (relative to brain weight) and more bulbous structure than males (Hines, 1990; Steinmetz, Staiger, Schlaug, Huang, & Jancke, 1995). Studies with other species (e.g., rats) have shown that when female hormones are administered to newborns, the corpus callosum grows to a larger size (Fitch & Denenberg, 1998). These researchers also found that when pregnant females were given hormones, the corpora callosa of their offspring were significantly different in size, depending on which hormones were given.

It is likely that hormones play a key role in determining the size of the corpus callosum in humans as well. Studies have shown that the corpus callosum is important in the acquisition of self-awareness and intelligence, and that this cable of nerves continues to develop significantly into an individual's later stages of growth, such as into their teenage years and 20s (for a review, see Halpern, 2000).

One reason why the size of the corpus callosum is important is that a number of researchers have implicated this size difference as a primary explanation for why female humans appear to have better connectivity between their left and right hemispheres and have been found to transfer information at a higher rate compared to males (Innocenti, 1994; Jancke & Steinmetz, 1994). Specifically, males usually have the language functions housed in the left hemisphere (left-handed males typically have language skills housed in the right hemisphere), whereas females use both hemispheres for language skills. Many researchers believe that this enhanced transference of information between hemispheres is an important factor in the well-established sex differences in verbal ability, specifically, that females are better than males in verbal fluency (Halpern, 2000). Studies have consistently shown that females perform better on verbal tasks and affective memory (Caplan, Crawford, Hyde, & Richardson, 1997; McGivern et al., 1997; Seidlitz & Diener, 1998).

This may be one of the primary reasons that some educational systems divide mathematics classes into male-only and female-only courses. Specifically, recent reports show that at least six states (New York, Ohio, Oregon, Pennsylvania, South Carolina, and Texas) prescribe all public schools to separate arithmetic classes by sex. Furthermore, the number of public school districts offering single-sex classes such as these has increased from 4 to 140 in the past 8 years ("Single-Sex Classes Increasing," October 5, 2004). The advocates of these programs claim that separating students by sex in these classes improves learning by improving the self-esteem of females and easing peer pressure that may occur. This approach has been challenged by organizations such as the American Civil Liberties Union. But it remains a fairly common practice because of established correlations shown by observations and scientific studies that males are innately better at mathematics. An inevitable question is why segregated classes are not also created for language courses, in which females hold an advantage. This question remains unanswered and, for the most part, unacknowledged. Perhaps if this policy was implemented in such school districts, the American Civil Liberties Union would not have a problem with such segregated courses.

From a criminological standpoint, research has long shown that individuals with low verbal abilities are more likely to commit various types of offending (Farrington, 1987a; Gibson, Piquero, & Tibbetts, 2001; Raine, 1993; Wilson & Herrnstein, 1985), not to mention the vast differences between men and women in deviant activity. For most individuals who tend to be right-sided (e.g., right-handed), the language areas of the brain are found in the left hemisphere, which tends to be responsible for linear and logical thought processes. On the other hand, the right hemisphere is more responsible for nonlinear or perceptual processing in most individuals (Banich & Heller, 1998). Some individuals who are left-sided (e.g., left-handed) tend to have diminished likelihood of these specializations, but still these persons show specialization in various regions of the brain. Notably, males are far more likely to be left-sided and therefore tend to have more right-hemisphere orientation in thinking (see Coren, 1992; Halpern, 2000).

Due to its importance, we will now go more in depth regarding the language regions of the brain. Because it is consistently supported, one good example of regional and hemispheric specialization is Wernicke's area (see Figure 8.2), which is found in the left half of the brain in virtually everyone. This area is primarily responsible for comprehension of speech, whereas Broca's area (also in the left hemisphere temporal lobe for most people [see Figure 8.2]) is primarily responsible for speech production.

As discussed in Chapter 5, various regions of the brain have specific responsibilities and activities, particularly the left and right hemispheres. Not only have studies shown that each side of the brain controls different functions, but an extensive amount of research has shown that this is likely due to a difference in the relative levels of hormones during the pre- and perinatal stages of fetal development. Although certain regions of the brain, such as the frontal lobes (see Chapter 6), aren't fully developed until much later in life, it is likely that vital differences between boys and girls are established quite early, even before they are born.

There is a relatively large difference between the hormones that are present for male fetuses as compared to female fetuses, particularly during the times that human brain development undergoes extreme change. For example, during the

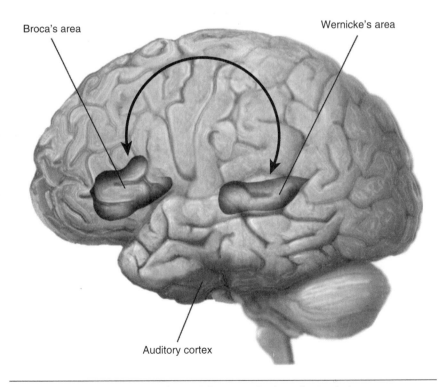

Figure 8.2   Broca's Area and Wernicke's Area in the Left Hemisphere

34- to 41-week period in the gestational age of a fetus, which is when the brain is in a vital period of formation, levels of male hormones (such as testosterone) are generally 10 times higher in male than in female fetuses (Swaab, Zhou, Fodor, & Hofman, 1997). It is believed that during this period, the essential sexual-specific structure of a fetal brain takes place. Functional asymmetry—the specialization of each hemisphere for certain types of cognitive processes—begins before birth and is mostly complete by age 5 (Halpern, 2000; Martin, 1998). To clarify, studies suggest that much of the extent to which human individuals think like males or females takes place at this early point of life (i.e., the first 5 years, and primarily before birth).

But what constitutes thinking like a male or female? Some sociologists believe such a question is ridiculous, because they believe that the differences in cognitive abilities and behaviors between sexes are due to socialization and cultural differences. We take a strong stance against such a proposition. Rather, we believe that the evidence strongly supports a physiological difference between boys and girls, as well as men and women, in their dispositions to think in certain ways (with some ways being linked to criminality). We also believe that most of the source of this disposition goes back to differences in their cognitive structure and function, which are mostly established during prenatal and early development.

For example, meta-analyses examining hundreds of studies have shown that even from very young ages, males exhibit much more aptitude on mental rotation tasks (Collins & Kimura, 1997; Silverman, Phillips, & Silverman, 1996), whereas females are much better at remembering where things are located and memory of emotional events (for an excellent review, see Caplan et al., 1997; Halpern, 2000; Seidlitz & Diener, 1998). Many experts have proposed that this is a holdover of evolutionary adaptations of our ancestors in which the more successful male hunters were better at navigating the correct route home (by rotating the path taken to find prey), whereas the more successful female gatherers excelled in remembering where plentiful food sources were located and for recalling episodic events that produced negative emotions (e.g., shame, embarrassment, fear, etc.). Such differences are likely to have a strong influence on how modern-day males and females perform on certain tasks.

Another functional difference that has been found between males and females is found in the hindbrain region, specifically the cerebellum. As you may recall from Chapter 5, the cerebellum is largely responsible for integrating numerous forms of information from the various senses and combines this knowledge with that of its spatial function and messages from the higher brain areas in order to respond most effectively in a given situation. One notable study (Gur et al., 1995) demonstrated that males have more metabolism in the cerebellum than do females, which may partially explain why males are better at spatial intelligence tests. Perhaps this is a result of higher levels of androgens that program the brain to think more "male-like," which is believed to be an evolutionary holdover of hunters finding their way back home after hunting game in distant places, as discussed above.

Another example is the tendency for males to do better at mathematical/ quantitative functions, whereas females appear to have more natural ability at verbal skills. Specifically, males are nearly twice as likely as women to score more than 700 (out of 800) on the SAT math test, which is used for college admissions. Males are also four times more likely to become engineers, which rely heavily on natural aptitude in spatial/quantitative functions. On the other hand, females tend to score higher than males on the verbal portion of the SAT and are more likely to enter professions that emphasize verbal skills (e.g., speech pathology) than are men.

Many critics have claimed that traditional educational systems have "tracked" males and females differently, in that males were expected to excel in and encouraged to pursue areas involving math and spatial analysis, whereas females are encouraged to pursue areas of verbal communication. However, perhaps the most comprehensive review of all studies in differential cognitive abilities between males and females (Halpern, 2000) concludes, against a noted bias before examining the empirical research, that these dispositions toward such tasks are evident in very young male and female children. This conclusion was made based on studies performed on subjects before any bias of the educational system takes place. Some of this can be seen in any preschool class during free play. Boys are more likely to play independently with blocks or other mechanical activities, whereas girls are more likely to play in groups with less mechanical toys. These particular sex differences in cognitive functioning, especially the latter finding, will be discussed below with regard to why females tend to be less antisocial than males.

It is not just in humans that such gender dispositions toward activities are found. A study by Alexander and Hines (2002) found that male monkeys chose to play with a ball and car over other available toys, whereas the female monkeys chose to play with a doll and a pot. The researchers had also designated gender-neutral toys (a picture book and a stuffed dog), which were chosen equally by both genders. Thus, the conclusion was that designated "male-like" toys were chosen significantly more often by males, and the designated "female-like" toys were chosen significantly more often by the females, with the neutral toys being chosen equally. Perhaps human children are not as removed in their choice of toys and play activities from our closest primates. Furthermore, these findings suggest that sex hormones or related factors may program our brains toward a particular perspective or different style of thinking, to the extent that we seek out varying types of activities, perhaps in line with our given aptitude toward different tasks.

Regardless of theory and function, research has shown that there are structural differences between the sexes at puberty. For example, the sexually dimorphic nucleus (SDN) of the preoptic area (POA) becomes so much larger in male brains than in female brains that the difference in size is obvious even to the naked eye (Halpern, 2000; Lund, Rhees, Setchell, & Lephart, 2001). Consistent with such findings, LeVay (1991) recently reported that the POA in homosexual males is significantly smaller than in heterosexual males.

Another important difference between the structure of male and female brains is that found in the frontal and temporal lobes, as well as the limbic system. As discussed in Chapter 6, these areas of the brain have been identified as perhaps the most important in terms of criminality. A recent study by Gur and his colleagues (Gur, Gunning-Dixon, Bilker, & Gur, 2002) examined magnetic resonance imaging (MRI) of these areas for 57 men and 59 women, in which an automated tissue segmentation procedure was used to obtain separate measurements for gray and white matter. After controlling for cranial volume, women were found to have larger orbital frontal cortices—an area that modulates emotional behavior—than men, resulting in a highly significant difference in the ratio of orbital gray matter to amygdala volume (Gur et al., 2002). Gur and his colleagues concluded that this larger volume of cortex devoted to emotional modulation may relate to behavioral evidence for sex differences in emotional processing. As noted by Gur and his colleagues, this finding was consistent with studies that have shown sex differences in perception, experience, and expression, most notably in greater male aggression.

Regarding brain function, and consistent with this last structural difference reported by Gur et al. (2002), was a recent study that appeared in the *Proceedings of the National Academy of Sciences* (Canli, Desmond, Zhao, & Gabrieli, 2002). This study, which also used MRIs to image male and female brains, found that women's brains are wired to both feel and remember emotional experiences more than men's brains. In this study, Turhan Canli and colleagues examined the MRIs when subjects were asked to recognize approximately 100 highly evocative pictures a few weeks after seeing them. The women's recall rate was significantly higher than the men's rate. The MRIs showed that women's neural activity when presented with the emotional scenes was actually much more intense and active than the men's responses. The authors concluded that women's brains are simply better organized and built for receiving, experiencing, and recalling emotions (Canli et al., 2002). Additional studies have found that women perform better in emotion recognition tasks (e.g., Seidlitz & Diener, 1998).

Furthermore, studies have shown that there are significant differences between male and female brains in regard to the cingulate gyrus (see Chapter 7), which is very important in regulating aggression and emotions. The cingulate gyrus is part of the limbic system of the brain, which largely produces our response mechanisms toward external stimuli (i.e., emotional response). Studies have found that female brains have a larger cingulate gyrus than do male brains, which is one possible reason why women exhibit more emotions, and retain in memory more emotional events, than do men. Significant structural differences have also been found in the hypothalamus, with some subregions of this structure showing large gender variation (see Figure 8.3). Specifically, LeVay (1991) reported the interstitial nucleus of the anterior hypothalamus as being twice as large for males as compared to females and homosexual males. Another study by Swaab and Fliers (1985) found the preoptic area of the hypothalamus to be an average of 2.5 times larger in males than in females. Notably, it is believed that high levels of androgens, such as testosterone, are key in creating these structural differences between men and women. In reviewing these studies, Walsh (1995) concluded that the differences in hormonal and neural differences, as well as the resulting structural variations, observed between males and females have profound implications for resulting sexual and social behavior, particularly criminality.

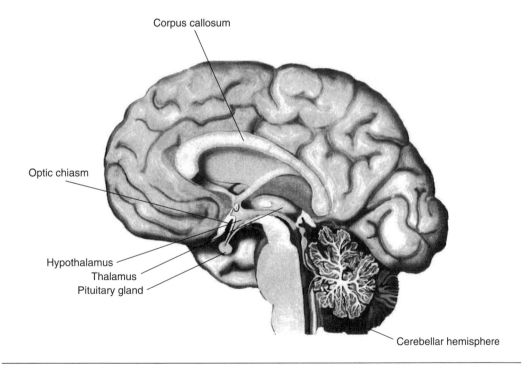

Figure 8.3   A View of the Human Brain Showing the Hindbrain and Forebrain Structures

Thus, recent studies have consistently shown that there are significant structural and functional differences in male and female brains that explain, among other things, why women are much better at feeling and remembering emotions than are men (Canli et al., 2002; Gur et al., 2002; Halpern, 2000). Such differences are believed to have profound effects on the development of criminality and will be discussed in depth later in this chapter. Studies have shown that there are other significant differences across sexes regarding brain function. For example, studies by Shaywitz et al. (1995) using magnetic resonance imaging showed that males were lateralized to the left hemisphere (frontal gyrus region) on phonological tasks, but females showed more general activation involving both hemispheres. Furthermore, a study by Hines, Chiu, McAdams, Bentler, and Lipcamon (1992) showed that more brain activity in a subregion (i.e., splenium) of the corpus callosum, due to its larger size, was linked to higher verbal fluency ability in females.

The Influence of Androgens (Male Hormones)

Do levels of androgens directly cause these changes in cognitive functioning? A growing consensus of theoretical and empirical evidence suggests that the answer is yes (see Halpern, 2000; Walsh, 1995, 2002). Obviously, the environment also contributes to such differences in cognition; however, the support for hormonal influence is overwhelmingly convincing. For instance, studies by evolutionary theorists (for a review, see Howard, 2006, pp. 232–234) show that even women show significantly better scores on mental rotation tests during menstruation, when their levels of androgens are relatively high (because their estrogen levels are relatively low). Furthermore, males who have relatively high estrogen levels (compared to other men) tend to score significantly worse on mental rotation tests. On the other hand, studies show that higher levels of estrogen in women (and men) are linked with better remembering of the relative location of objects than are lower levels of estrogen, which are linked to the evolutionary holdover of "gathering" (see above).

Observed examples can be seen in the differential hemispheric emphasis in functioning between males and females on various tasks, such as verbal skills (see Halpern, 2000, Chapter 5). More specifically, females are less lateralized than males in the sense that males have a strong concentration of cognitive functions (e.g., verbal skills) in a particular hemisphere, whereas cognitive functions in females are more bilaterally dispersed in both hemispheres. This presents a special vulnerability for the male brain because if some trauma occurs in that hemisphere, there is no "backup"; perhaps this is why studies consistently find that males are more susceptible to language disorders, such as dyslexia and aphasia.

Furthermore, women appear to be more oriented toward verbal/language use, whereas men tend to use more nonverbal reasoning. The classic example is the preferred method of directions: males tend to prefer nonverbal maps (applying the use of mental rotation), whereas females tend to prefer the directions written out in words. But why would the average woman be so predisposed toward verbal skills? What would make this adaptation advantageous from an evolutionary perspective?

The stance taken here is that women's natural abilities in language are related to other factors that are vital in child rearing. Obviously, the effective use of language is extremely important in the care and teaching of children, and we propose that this is one of the primary reasons why women have adapted such aptitudes via evolution. This disposition for higher verbal abilities may also account for the consistent association observed between low verbal IQ and delinquency (see Gibson et al., 2001; McGloin & Pratt, 2003). After all, much of the observed relationship between low verbal IQ among males is a likely explanation for why they may be more likely than females to commit delinquent and criminal offending. Specifically, if someone cannot communicate well with others, either verbally or in writing, it is likely that he or she will not be successful in any employment role.

This is consistent with other skills or tendencies that women seem to acquire as compared to men. As mentioned above, a recent study demonstrated that women are better at recognizing and recalling emotional events and that their neural responses (as measured by MRIs) to emotional scenes were much more active than men's (Canli et al., 2002). The authors concluded that a woman's brain is better organized to perceive emotions, and to effectively code that into memory. Perhaps the most convincing studies are those that have shown that women who receive androgen shots over time develop "male-like" thinking patterns in their MRI results, and the opposite pattern is found for males who receive female hormones (Raine, 1993; Walsh, 1995).

Evolutionary theorists have also cited studies that show that females are more sensitive to odors than males, which they claim is a result of natural selection for mothers who must be alert to olfactory indicators of infant distress. Again, researchers believe that this ability to detect odors is linked with higher estrogen levels (Howard, 2006). Additional findings have shown that women are better at nonautomatized behaviors such as listening and counseling, are more nurturing, and are more comfortable in close physical proximity to others of the same sex (who may be important in helping care for offspring) (Halpern, 2000; Howard, 2006, pp. 239–243).

Also, oxytocin levels rise in women when they give birth and/or breastfeed. This hormone is also believed to be related to a mother's amazing skill at picking out her infant's cry in another room when it is crying along with dozens of other infants. Such skills are conducive to child rearing and reflect the idea that women are "hardwired" to be more attentive to others, most importantly their children. Recent studies with rats have shown that mothers are less susceptible to stress than rats who have never given birth (Kinsley et al., 1999), and the mother rats have sharper memories. Experts claim that hormonal changes, especially surges of oxytocin and estrogen, cause significant alterations in the rats' brains after motherhood. Specifically, the mothers' brains develop more elaborate communication systems as the neural connections become more dense and the glial cells increase in number. Furthermore, neurons grow by the hundreds in the hippocampus region of adult female rats that care for rat pups (interestingly, male rats that care for pups show no such neural increases). Notably, the changes in hormone levels between rats and humans during pregnancy are quite similar, as are brain scans of activity patterns in pregnant subjects of both species (Carmichael, 2003).

Most of these differences are theorized as manifestations of evolutionary development that required females to be nurturing caretakers, and thus the bonding hormones of oxytocin and related chemicals were chosen through natural selection for survival. On the other hand, males are hardwired to be more aggressive and risk taking, and studies have consistently shown that high levels of testosterone are linked with violent behavior (Booth & Osgood, 1993). Such dispositions toward aggressive behavior had some evolutionary advantages (e.g., hunting, defending) while simultaneously reducing the skills desired for the effective hands-on caring of children.

Interestingly, and very importantly, this is not just a male versus female type of perspective. Recent studies have shown that after marriage, as well as after having children, males experience a significant drop in their level of testosterone production (Gray, Kahlenberg, Barrett, Lipson, & Ellison, 2002). This is believed to have the important result of raising the effect of oxytocin in the male system, which makes them more nurturing and caring for their family. Of course, males with very high levels of testosterone are probably less likely to experience such effects, but that is a proposition that has not been addressed by empirical research and is obviously an important question for future studies. Still, it is important to understand that although sociologists have long considered marriage/family to be an important control factor in maturing out of criminality (Matza, 1964; Sampson & Laub, 1993, 1994), there is a very important biological component in this life change. Specifically, the "great socializer" of marriage/children is at least partially due to hormonal changes that occur after such life events.

In addition to the "female-like" hormonal changes in men, further complicating (or perhaps clarifying) the issue of male/female hormones and criminality is the issue of degrees of male and female. Specifically, this involves the issue of "intersexuals" or hermaphrodites, who are individuals who fall somewhere between male and female, either genetically or in terms of hormone levels. There are many forms of this in-between status, with no less than 30 being recognized by science. This particular issue was addressed by Anthony Walsh (1995), and he reported that the extent to which the chromosomal makeup or hormonal type was more male-like (i.e., androgen producing), the more likely that form of mutation was to result in criminal activity.

For example, a person who had the chromosomal mutation of XXY (Klinefelter's syndrome) or Turner's syndrome (which is generally XO, indicating the absence of a second sex chromosome), was not nearly as disposed to criminality as a person who had the chromosomal mutation of XYY, which results in a significantly enhanced production of testosterone, the primary male androgen. In fact, Walsh concludes that there is a linear progression toward criminality as the genetic structure becomes more male-like (i.e., higher levels of testosterone). Studies have consistently shown that although there is a continuum between male and female, the impact that this has on criminality is the extent to which one falls on the continuum toward "maleness," and thus the increased chance one has of becoming criminal. Thus, the conclusion that can be made is that although some exceptions exist to our discussion of the male-female dichotomy in cognition and criminality, the overall conclusions are valid to the extent that the exceptions tend to represent the sex group that is relatively closer on the hormonal/chromosomal continuum category than the one further away.

Continuing on from our prior discussion, androgens and oxytocin are not the only hormones that make a difference when it comes to behavior. In fact, it is likely that all hormones make a difference to some extent, even hormones that do not appear to have a direct effect on criminality. For example, a recent study (Wolf, Schommer, Hellhammer, McEwen, & Kirschbaum, 2001) showed that young women are better able to cope with stress than young men. Given a word-recall memory test after experimentally being exposed to stress, women did much better than men on the examination. The authors concluded that women are better able to cope with stress likely due to their higher levels of estradiol, which is the principal estrogen hormone produced by women's ovaries. (On a side note, this estrogen level decreases radically during a woman's menstrual cycle, which may help explain why stress and criminal activity goes up during this phase.) Estradiol/estrogen appears to be a type of "antistress" hormone, which is found in high levels in women, but not in men.

In addition, it is not only structure and hormones—and consequent behavior—that are different between male and female brains. Another area that has been implicated is neurotransmitters, which send electric signals to different regions of the brain and body as messages of what is happening and what the body should do (see Chapter 7). Not only do males and females differ somewhat in levels of particular neurotransmitters, but the interactions with neurotransmitters differ significantly between men and women. For example, a recent study using brain scans (Reneman et al., 2001) showed that females were more susceptible to brain damage from the use of Ecstasy (methylenedioxymethamphetamine), which is an increasingly popular party drug, than were males. Interestingly, this study examined only those subjects who had taken fewer than 50 tablets of the drug, so it did not involve addicts, and it makes the findings even more important in the sense that there are far more social users than chronic addicts. The researchers of this study concluded that the brains of females who had used Ecstasy had significantly weaker concentrations of a neurotransmitter, specifically serotonin (see Chapter 7), than did women who had never used Ecstasy, implying that the female users had lost a significant number of brain cells. Importantly, this difference was not found in male subjects. Therefore, the conclusion made by the authors of the study was that females are more at risk for brain damage when they use recreational drugs similar to Ecstasy, which is a type of stimulant that induces feelings of energy and sexual arousal.

A Developmental Theory for Gender Differences in Criminality

Now that we have discussed the various physiological differences between males and females regarding the way they think and process information, it is important to discuss how this results in the wide disparity between the sexes in criminality. The integrated model presented in this book goes a long way toward explaining this universal pattern. A brief explanation of how this model—including physiological differences, social control, and self-conscious emotions—can be applied to the differential criminal activities between males and females will now be provided. One can look upon this section as an example of how our model of the development of criminality can be applied to observed differences in deviant behavior.

Biochemical and physiological differences between men and women, starting in the womb and continuing through adulthood, have an evolutionary basis, for they once were adaptations to the environment and they allowed for better chances of success in survival and reproduction. From the social control perspective, these biological differences help explain why females seem to develop stronger social bonds, such as attachments to others and involvement in social activities. One of the important consequences of such differential development is the tendency toward feelings of empathy, for which females appear to have a stronger disposition than males (Tibbetts, 2002). Even studies that have tested subjects on observing eye-facial expressions show that women do significantly better than men on accurately interpreting what the emotional expression actually was in the picture (Baron-Cohen, 2003). The importance of having mothers develop tendencies toward strong emotional bonds, interpretation of expression, and empathy cannot be understated. If there was a society in which mothers (or even most fathers) did not have such tendencies, the society likely would not exist for long because most of the offspring would die. Knowing what others (especially infants and young children) need or are communicating in verbal and nonverbal ways is a vital component of survival and success.

One recent review of the literature regarding sex differences in feelings of empathy concludes that females are simply programmed to be natural empathizers, whereas men are more programmed to be systemizers (Baron-Cohen, 2004). A case in point is that males are much more likely to be autistic, a disorder that in extreme forms is the absence of virtually all empathy. In fact, autism is seen by some experts as being an extreme form of the male brain; consistently, many severely autistic individuals excel in areas of spatial and quantitative abilities. For example, the character played by Dustin Hoffman in the Oscar-winning movie *Rain Man* was based on an actual case of severe autism, in that the person had almost no empathic skills but was a genius when it came to counting or quantifying tasks. Many autistic individuals, who are four times more likely to be male than female, are quite effective at such mathematical activities, but have severe deficiencies when it comes to emotional understanding or social skills. This is not to say that women do not have such tendencies; in fact, when slightly autistic women were analyzed, they outperformed normal men on systemizing tasks (Baron-Cohen, 2004). Thus, it is not a clear-cut sex difference, but rather a matter of degree in which men can think more like women and vice versa. Whether it is hormones or sociological factors, it remains important to understand what causes males to think differently from females, especially with regard to the ability to empathize with one's victims or potential victims.

A recent meta-analysis of the effects of empathy on antisocial behavior demonstrated its strong inhibitory effects on crime (Jolliffe & Farrington, 2004). Although this study did not examine the sex differences between levels of empathy, one recent study by Tibbetts (2002) confirms that differential levels of empathy largely explain the discrepancy in criminal offending between males and females. Specifically, once levels of empathy were accounted for, females were just as likely to commit a variety of criminal offenses. It was the high levels of empathy that appear to account for a significantly lower level of criminal activity. Thus, both experts and the available empirical evidence point to an important link between the lower levels of empathy and criminality, both of which are typical among males as compared to females. Importantly, preliminary studies indicate that individuals can be trained to develop a better sense of emotional interpretation. Specifically, Baron-Cohen and his colleagues found that when individuals were exposed and tested with distinct facial expression over a three-month period they showed significant progress in being able to interpret them (Baron-Cohen, 2004).

Building empathy and interpretation of emotional cues of others is not the only area of affect that is important in understanding or curbing sex differences in criminal offending. Studies show that males tend to be much more competitive and crave status significantly more than do females in virtually all species, including human beings. Documentation from empirical research of early development shows that boys are much more assertive than girls, even at very early ages of 13 to 24 months (Tremblay, 2006) (see Figure 8.4). This competitive aggressiveness is consistent throughout all age groups. In schoolyard play, boys tend to establish dominance hierarchies and maintain such systems throughout all forms of play, whereas females tend to engage in more cooperative, egalitarian play groups.

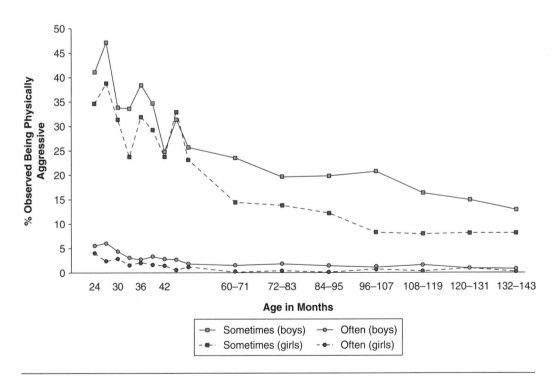

Figure 8.4   Frequencies of Hitting, Biting, and Kicking at Ages 2 to 12 Years

Recent research has shown that such differences in sex-specific group dynamics persist into adulthood. Specifically, studies show that men are likely to bond with one another, but only in the sense of forming alliances with fellow competitors (Campbell, 2002). Such dynamics among males have been found consistently throughout the animal kingdom, with males cooperating with each other only to the extent that it furthers their status and well-being in the group.

Like other animals, studies have shown that human males experience a surge of androgens (e.g., testosterone) when preparing for a challenge, whether it be a physical confrontation or a big presentation at work. Increased levels of such hormones boost performance in the sense of increasing body mass and aggressiveness. Studies show that the levels of these hormones peak during the event or contest, and afterward the level increases or decreases based on whether the individual wins or loses the challenge. Again, this is consistent with other species of animals, such as monkeys and apes, in which the winning male takes control of the group (increasing his testosterone level) and the losing male is forced to become submissive (thereby lowering his testosterone level). Evolutionary theorists believe this is an adaptation in the sense that individuals are physiologically encouraged or discouraged to pursue future challenges in their survival. After all, an individual who wins a contest has a high likelihood of winning the following confrontation, whereas an individual who loses a duel is quite likely to lose the next one (Walsh, 2002).

But why do males challenge one another for status more than females? From an evolutionary standpoint, males have much more to gain from competition and jockeying for higher status than do females, although many sociologists will disagree with such a proposition. Specifically, a female can't drastically spread her genes by gaining mating ability with numerous males; however, a male can monopolize, or at least gain greater accessibility for, the reproduction of his genes if he has higher status in his group. Although this proposition is more relevant in other animal species, many evolutionary theorists have linked this tendency in males to humans as well. They claim that numerous eons of evolution still manifest in modern-day humanity and group dynamics. After all, modern man can't simply defy the influence of millions of years of evolution.

On the other hand, success has become an intrinsic reward, which is evidenced in the statistics that show that the most successful Americans have a relatively low average number of children, often falling below the replacement value of 2.1 per family. Still, studies show that the most financially successful males are more desirable to females than are other males, even after controlling for age and physical attractiveness (Howard, 2006; Walsh, 2002).

Males who fail to achieve social success are much more likely to suffer ill effects. For example, males of low socioeconomic status are much more likely to experience depression, high blood pressure, criminality, heart ailments, and so on. Perhaps some of this relationship between low social status and problems is due to self-selection. Specifically, some individuals are predetermined to be more criminal and therefore more likely to be of lower socioeconomic status and more likely to suffer from illnesses. Such individuals tend to be more risk taking and selfish by nature. One recent theory of criminality that emphasizes individuals' levels of self-control appears to have touched upon this tendency toward self-selection.

Even the theory of low self-control (see Gottfredson & Hirschi, 1990) is easily applied to these evolutionary adaptations in the sense that males are more likely to exhibit risk-taking, aggressive behaviors than are females because they are biologically disposed toward such tendencies, which were required for survival. Even now, such tendencies are often required for success, as can be seen in the importance of risk taking and aggressiveness in the business world. It appears that the most successful "hunters" in modern-day society, such as the highest paid CEOs of top companies, tend to exhibit very high levels of aggressiveness and risk taking.

However, the tendencies of those with low self-control often are not directed in a beneficial fashion. Rather, they can manifest in quite deviant, or even felonious ways. The difference in how such tendencies toward low self-control are directed is often a result of opportunity, as was explicitly described by the theory's proponents (Gottfredson & Hirschi, 1990), as well as the ability of individuals to learn from informal social sanctions in their development. Many individuals, especially those with low levels of self-control, have a very difficult time learning from experience. Much of this learning requires a certain propensity to experience self-conscious emotions, such as shame, guilt, embarrassment, and so on. If individuals do not have adequate propensities to feel such emotions, then there is a high likelihood that they will not be conditioned to know what is right or wrong.

Regarding self-conscious emotions, there is a growing consensus (see Grasmick, Bursik, & Arneklev, 1993; Tangney & Fischer, 1995; Tibbetts, 2003; Tibbetts & Herz, 1996; Whitley, Nelson, & Jones, 1999) that women have much higher levels of inhibitory social emotions than males. Specifically, significant sex differences have long been found in levels of self-conscious emotions, with women generally scoring higher on measures of shame, guilt, and empathy (e.g., see Tangney & Fischer, 1995; Tibbetts, 2002) and males (and offenders) scoring higher on pride (Daniels & Tibbetts, 2005; Tangney & Fischer, 1995; Tibbetts, 2003).

Furthermore, numerous studies have demonstrated the pronounced inhibitory effects on deviant behaviors that internal factors such as anticipated shame or guilt tend to have for women; such factors are not as strong in men, if they have any effect at all. This conclusion is consistent with findings reported in many studies of criminal offending (e.g., Hagan, Simpson, & Gillis, 1987; Liu & Kaplan, 1996; Smith & Paternoster, 1987; Tibbetts, 2002; Tibbetts & Herz, 1996) that show that women are far less likely to offend and that much of this difference appears to be due to high levels of internal constraints, particularly shame, moral beliefs, and empathy, that act to inhibit offending behavior.

The extent to which males and females show differences regarding many emotional traits has resulted in most researchers, even some sociologists, concluding that the propensities appear to have some biological origin. Closely related to the research regarding emotions, a growing amount of evidence shows that women are more religious than men . . . everywhere! For example, a recent study by Stark (2002) examined the religiosity of men and women in 57 countries around the world and found that women were significantly more religious in all but one; however, even in the one country (Brazil) in which the difference wasn't significant, women were still more religious than men. Notably, this study looked at predominantly Christian countries, but it explicitly examined eight non-Christian countries to capture Asian and Islamic religions. The trend held in every country and for various measures. Somewhat regrettably, Stark (2002) concluded that there is likely a biological influence that is driving this universal difference; however, as a true sociologist, he held out hope that "if nothing else, this article may prompt creative efforts to salvage the socialization explanation" (p. 495). It is our position that the socialization explanation does not need to be "salvaged"; rather, we believe that Stark was correct in his conclusion that there is a biological tendency for women to be more religious than men, but that the sociological factors also contribute to the discrepancy in a variety of ways (e.g., gender roles, differential familial discipline).

One recent review of the literature (Pinker, 2002) has concluded that Stark was right in that there does appear to be a strong genetic link for religiosity, but the choice of religion (e.g., Catholic vs. Muslim) is almost entirely dependent on cultural factors. After all, if you were to ask virtually all persons in the world with which religious denomination/affiliation they identify, it is almost perfectly correlated with their parents' religious affiliation. Still, this conclusion goes a long way toward implicating genetics and inheritance for how religious an individual will be, regardless of the religion that a person's culture chooses for him or her. Furthermore, it is clear that regardless of the culture or the religion chosen, females typically will be more dedicated to the chosen religion than will the average males in the same culture. And this, of course, has a significant impact on the difference in level of criminal activity between males and females across the board. It is also notable that Pinker's review of the literature also claims that genetics and inheritance are determinants of aggression and criminal behavior in general, as they are for other personality traits (e.g., shyness) and mental disorders (e.g., schizophrenia, depression, obsessive-compulsive disorder), especially when coupled with negative developmental factors, such as abusive or neglectful parenting.

It appears that such gender differences in emotional traits are even further increased by the disposition of males toward feelings of pride, which is positively related to offending (Tibbetts, 2003). Such feelings of pride (particularly the "alpha" form that focuses on self as opposed to behavior) are likely to be found in persons who are less bonded to others and more self-centered, which may be linked to low self-control in such individuals. Thus, not only are inhibitory traits (e.g., shame, empathy, and religiosity) lower in males, but the emotions that are found to encourage criminal activity—namely, pride and low self-control—are found at higher levels in males. Therefore, it appears that males have the worst of both worlds when it comes to emotional dispositions.

As we mentioned earlier in this chapter, much of the extant evidence suggests that the gender differences in emotional traits and dispositions are likely due to structural and functional differences in the brain. These differences are later influenced by varied child-rearing practices and other forms of socialization that increase the development of gender roles that become internalized by boys and girls (for a review, see Lewis, 1992). For example, parents tend to verbally evaluate their young boys in global ways (e.g., "You are a good boy") when they succeed, whereas they tend to evaluate their young girls in act-specific ways when they succeed (e.g., "You did a good job"). In contrast, parents tend to verbally evaluate their young boys in act-specific ways (e.g., "That was a really hard job") when they don't succeed, whereas they tend to evaluate their young girls more globally when they don't succeed at a task.

BOX 8.1   The Continuing Saga of Stanley: School Influences

Stanley did not go to the same type of school as most children his age. His schooling was done on the streets and in various incarcerative institutions. In fact, Chapter 6 of *The Jack-Roller* is titled "Getting Educated," which was written while he was incarcerated and, thus, indicates the nature in which Stanley was "educated." However, Stanley did complete accredited schooling while institutionalized. The formal school education of Stanley, as we know it, is almost nonexistent.

There is some evidence that Stanley did read a lot, which explains his ability to communicate such an articulate review of his life. For example, Stanley wrote that during his time at the Reformatory in Pontiac, Illinois, "You get books twice a week and some magazines. The books and magazines are what saved my life down there" (Shaw, 1930, p. 205). Also, Shaw noted that Stanley claimed that his primary diversions from the monotony of incarceration were "reading and dreaming. . . . Every night after I went to bed I would read awhile by the light that trickled dimly in" (p. 154).

The application of Stanley's educational experience is not intuitive to the issues explored in this book. Nevertheless, it is beneficial to acknowledge that Stanley did complete an eighth-grade program at St. Charles (Shaw, 1930, p. 105) and later worked on completing a high school education (Shaw, 1930, p. 178), thereby allowing him to obtain employment later in life that could turn around his position in life. More specifically, Stanley and Shaw both attribute much of Stanley's turnaround to his employment in positions to which he was well suited, which we will examine in the next section. The fact that he completed a high school equivalency program is one testament to his desire to change his life.

Conclusion

Despite the consistency and importance of the findings showing gender differences in offending, few efforts have been made to further specify the causes for why women are more inhibited than males. Thus, this section has attempted to shed some light on this issue. Specifically, structural differences in the brain begin occurring early in the womb and continue throughout life. Higher or lower levels of male androgens (e.g., testosterone), as well as varying levels of female hormones (e.g., estrogen), appear to have profound effects on the cognitive functioning and temperaments of girls and boys, as well as women and men. Furthermore, the varying levels and effects of self-conscious emotions, as well as other aspects of cognitive functioning, between males and females appear to be linked to physiological differences between the two sexes.

Such differences in brain functioning cause women to be more oriented toward social bonds and nurturing attitudes, whereas men are disposed toward aggressiveness and risk taking. These tendencies are reflected in the development of varying levels of social emotions. Because of their inherent focus on the internal self in regard to their social environment, self-conscious emotions seem likely candidates to manifest the evolutionary and social-psychological differences between men and women in their cognitive abilities and their ways of dealing with the everyday world.

It is possible that the rational propositions and numerous empirical studies discussed in this chapter are not enough to convince some readers that there are important physiological and sociological factors that go a long way toward understanding why males and females think differently and, thus, act accordingly (i.e., criminal or not, perhaps respectively). If that is the case, perhaps they will appreciate the findings of a recent study that shows that women are much happier than men, across time and place. According to the Pew Research Center for People and the Press (2003), throughout the world, in both rich and poor nations, women are happier with their lives than are men. This study was based on a survey of more than 38,000 people in no less than 44 countries, and it supported previous findings from other, similarly conducted studies. In virtually every country, women reported being happier than their male counterparts, which may go a long way toward explaining why men commit a much larger percentage of crimes. So, regardless of one's beliefs on the universally held question of why males commit more crimes than females, he or she can always fall back on the consistent finding that males are more dissatisfied with life. Or, is it that females are just so satisfied that they do not see the need to offend? Even when considering the same finding, it appears to be a matter of perspective. Still, we suggest that all readers consider the scientific evidence on all cognitive sex differences, and then make their conclusion.

CHAPTER 9

Individuals and Their Social World

The art of living lies less in eliminating our troubles than in growing with them.

Bernard M. Baruch

If you can find a path with no obstacles, it probably doesn't lead anywhere.

Frank A. Clark

Human behavior is multidimensional. As we have shown thus far, biological and genetic influences are important factors to consider in human development. But development occurs within an environmental context replete with pushes and pulls, with risk and protective factors. It is clear that even biologically similar individuals, such as identical twins, are not identical in every measurable characteristic. Moreover, genetic influence is not constant over time and sometimes relies on environmental input. For these reasons, and more, environment can serve as an important, indeed, a critical source of variation in the development of serious antisocial behavior. In this chapter, we examine the limitations of biological influences, the important functions of environmental stimuli, and how individuals act in concert with their environment.

There Is Variation Left Unexplained by Genetic Influences

Perhaps the most telling evidence of the limitations of biological influences comes from twin and adoption studies. Although this body of literature has revealed the importance of genes to development, it has simultaneously shown that genetic factors alone are not sufficient causes for the complexity of human behavior. If a person's genetic makeup predetermines his or her behavior, then no differences between monozygotic twins would be observed for that behavior. Concordance rates would be equal to one, with the measured behavior either evident or absent in both members of twin pairs (Rowe, 1983). Instead, the myriad of sometimes startling similarities often reported is coupled with undeniable key differences in behavioral patterns. These differences are thus highlighted by the lack of perfect concordance between genetically identical twins, suggesting that factors in addition to genetics must influence individual differences.

Behavioral, temperamental, and cognitive differences between persons who are genetically identical reveal the inadequacy of relying solely upon biology as the sole cause of these individual characteristics (Plomin, 1990; Reiss, Neiderhiser, Hetherington, & Plomin, 2000). Even for behaviors that have proven to be largely driven by genetics, variation in those behaviors across individuals still remains. Recall, for example, that behavioral genetics findings show that up to 70% of the variation in aggressive behavior can be attributed to heritability (Cadoret, Leve, & Devor, 1997). A corresponding genetic effect has also been found for criminal behavior (Rowe, 1983), antisocial behavior (Lyons et al., 1995; Reiss et al., 2000), and aggression (Loeber & Hay, 1997; Miles & Carey, 1997), and for the stability of each across the life course (Olweus, 1979; Reiss et al., 2000). Although genetics explains a large proportion of the variation in behaviors, a third of the variation remains unexplained. Clearly, between-individual differences in aggression and criminality cannot be completely attributed to genetic differences alone; rather, factors in a person's environment also contribute to these differences.

The Nature of Genetic Influences Changes

A second characteristic of genetic influences also limits its explanatory power. Heritability estimates and the influence of genetically based characteristics change over a person's life course and also vary according to the environment in which they are studied (Onalaja & Claudio, 2000; Plomin, 1990). Heritability fluctuates over time, being a strong influence on particular behaviors at particular developmental stages. One of the most well-researched areas for which heritability has been found to differ across age is IQ. Heritability estimates for IQ increase from about 15% during infancy to about 40% during childhood to more than 90% in adulthood (Plomin, 1990). Similar findings have also been reported in research on the heritability of depression (Orvaschel, 1990). Although genetic factors appear to be the primary influences on adolescent-onset depression, environmental factors—particularly familial factors—are largely responsible for depression that first occurs during childhood.

A similar pattern of age-differentiated heritability estimates also occurs for delinquency and criminality. Although both are influenced by genetics, heritability estimates for adult criminality are stronger than those for juvenile delinquency. In fact, numerous studies have found only a moderate genetic effect for delinquency, and instead have found that environmental variables exhibit stronger effects on juvenile offending (DiLalla & Gottesman, 1989). Examining studies that calculated concordance rates for identical and fraternal twins' criminal records, DiLalla and Gottesman (1989) found that an average of 87% of identical twins and 72% of fraternal twins were concordant for delinquency. When comparing these results to averages calculated for similar adult studies, the concordance rates drop to 51% for identical and 22% for fraternal twins. Traits and behaviors that are related to delinquency and criminality, such as antisocial personality and aggression, are also increasingly influenced by genetics as a person moves from adolescence into adulthood (Lyons et al., 1995; Miles & Carey, 1997).

The effects of genes can also change over the life course, thus producing continuity and change throughout development. Genetic factors may be responsible for change in behaviors over time just as they may alternately influence stability (Reiss et al., 2000). Either way, genetics may influence behavior differently at different ages, with a particular genetic factor being related to early childhood delinquency but a different genetic factor being related to crimes committed during late adolescence and adulthood.

If genetic factors are related to delinquent and criminal behavior over time and in the same degree, then estimates of heritability should remain relatively stable (Plomin, 1990). It is possible, however, that the exact genetic factors producing stability in heritability estimates are not themselves the same. Instead, salient genetic effects may differ across developmental periods; thus, the gene or genes that influence behavior at one time may produce different outcomes, or may not produce any measurable effect at a later time (Plomin, 1990; Reiss et al., 2000). The differential expression and activation of genes is produced by biological processes and environmental stimuli that switch genes on and off (Reiss et al., 2000). Any between-individual differences, then, in genetic composition will ultimately produce differences in the way in which individuals respond to changes in their environment. As environmental triggers change across developmental periods, the influence, type, and amount of genetic factors affecting behavior will also be altered.

Heritability Estimates Differ Across Environments and Populations

Not only can the influence of biological factors change over time, it can also vary according to the environment and the population in which the factors are studied. Heritability estimates provide an estimate of the amount of variation of a trait that can be attributed to genetic influences *for a given population* (Plomin, 1990). These estimates can be affected by a range of factors specific to a particular population such as sample size, gender, location of the population, and the outcome variable of interest. It is important to remember that heritability estimates do not tell us what percentage of crime, for instance, is directly related to genetics. Rather, an estimate would be calculated for a particular sample to tell us the proportion of the variation in crime found in a specific sample that is associated with genes.

Two factors are especially notable when examining heritability estimates. First, heterogeneity of the environment will affect the amount of variation that can be linked to differences in the environment, and, subsequently to the amount that can be linked to genes (Walsh, 2002). If the population that is being studied shows little variability in its environment, then the estimate of heritability for a given trait will be higher than that for populations that have variability in their environment (Walsh, 2002). Consider a study of criminality among a population of middle-class, suburban college graduates. Assume that there is little variability within the environment for those studied and a moderate amount of variability in their criminal behaviors. To what can we attribute the variation in offending? After all, environmental influences are substantially similar under these conditions. Factors that do not vary across individuals cannot explain differences between individuals. In this situation, because the range of environmental factors is similar for everyone, heritability estimates will be stronger.

The second aspect of the environment that has been found to be systematically related to estimates of heritability is that the influence of genes is stronger in some environments and weaker in others. Estimates of genetic influences sometimes differ across environments, with disadvantageous environments limiting genetic expression and more advantageous environments allowing greater genetic expression (Walsh, 2002). Some environments may be so noxious, harmful, or bleak that they overwhelm genetic predispositions. Conversely, enriched environments allow for the expression of genetically endowed traits and characteristics. Again turning to studies of IQ, analysis of twin data has shown that heritability estimates for IQ (Fishbein, 1990) and for criminality (Christiansen, 1977) are greater for twins who are raised in more advantageous environments. That is, a greater proportion of the variation in IQ and offending for twins in stimulating environments is related to heritable traits as compared to the proportion for twins reared in cognitively deficient environments.

Along with being dependent upon the environment in which it is studied, heritability estimates will also differ based upon the population being studied and the outcome variable of interest. Characteristics of population members such as age, gender, and period of development may all affect heritability estimates. As previously noted, intra-individual changes associated with age and development may create differences in the types, number, and strength of genes that are expressed. Relatedly, developmental changes experienced by a population may serve to change the estimates of heritability, not because of gene activation or deactivation, but because of changes in behavior that are associated with development.

To illustrate this point, let us revisit the finding that heritability estimates for delinquency are typically lower than estimates for involvement in serious crime. For juveniles, involvement in delinquency has been found to be so common that not engaging in some degree of misbehavior is anomalous (Moffitt, 1993a). Most adolescent misbehavior, we note, is relatively nonserious, involving no loss of property and no loss of life. It is, for lack of a better word, developmentally normal.

Some individuals, however, showed serious behavioral problems as young children and escalated their misbehavior, and the seriousness of their misbehavior, upon reaching adolescence. And while "normal" youths desisted in their youthful displays of misbehavior, the early-onset youths continued to offend. In essence, those with a strong predisposition to criminality remain involved in crime and other antisocial activities well into adulthood (Rowe, 2002). When a behavior is relatively rare, such as serious criminal conduct, estimates of heritability increase, reflecting the increased influence of genetics (Rowe, 2002).

Brain Plasticity Is Environmentally Influenced

A key way in which the environment affects development is through its influence on brain activity. Until recently, it was generally believed that humans were born with all of their necessary brain structures formed and that a person's individual brain structure was determined by genetics. Although genes do program for biological structures so that an infant is born hardwired for cognitive functioning, these structures are not fully developed (Greenough, Black, & Wallace, 1987). In fact, the development of connections between nerves in the brain is somewhat dependent on an individual's experiences in his or her environment (Clark & Grunstein, 2000). As such, enriched environments can activate brain mechanisms that allow for the acquisition of memories, a process that involves the development of neural pathways to process the information (Clark & Grunstein, 2000).

Findings from both animal as well as human studies have shown that brain activity spurred by experiences can increase the activity of genetically driven mechanisms that may ultimately affect behavioral change. In studies conducted on rats, for example, it was found that housing young pups in enriched environments created changes in overall brain weight—an increase between 7% and 10% after 60 days—and increases in the number of synapses located in the brain (Kolb & Whishaw, 1998). Conversely, rats exposed to visually depriving environments created impairments in visual discrimination tasks (Greenough et al., 1987). In extreme cases, unstimulated synaptic connections "die off," leaving a person, or a rat pup, less likely to be able to benefit from future experience (Greenough et al., 1987).

In total, these findings highlight the interconnections between experience and gene expression. Taken together, these findings also highlight the fact that biological and environmental influences coexist and are mutually dependent. An observed phenotype owes its genesis to both biological processes and environmental triggers. As discussed in the previous chapters on biology, genes alone do not cause individual behavior per se. Rather, genetic influences predispose an individual toward particular outcomes, yet the environment must provide an adequate arena in which these genetic predispositions can become behavioral realities. Environmental triggers are sometimes necessary to activate genetic expression; thus, the presence or absence of such triggers can help to determine which genes will be expressed as well as when the expression will occur. For example, a person who is genetically susceptible to alcoholism will not become an alcoholic if he or she is not provided with and does not partake of alcohol. In other words, without consumption of alcohol, the gene(s) influencing alcoholism may remain dormant, only to be fully realized with the stimulus of the environmental trigger (McGue, 1997).

Humans Are Not Blank Slates,
Nor Are They Fully Developed at Birth

We cannot rely solely on biological or environmental influences to understand serious criminal behavior. In each respective area of research, left unexplained is the variability in behavior evident in persons who are genetically identical or who are exposed to the same environmental stimuli but who show manifestly different behavioral patterns. In light of these empirical findings, researchers began to recognize the joint contributions that biology and socialization influences have on criminality.

Humans are not born as blank slates, with their characteristics and their actions summarily determined by their environment; nor are they born biologically destined to become serious, chronic offenders. Instead, biology sets the stage for development by influencing the nature and strength of within-individual traits and by placing limits on the influence that environmental variables may exert. In this way, although the environment plays an integral role in development, its effects are conditioned by biological factors. In other words, a person's biological makeup may produce certain individual characteristics that influence his or her susceptibility to environmental influences and to social interactions.

Individual differences at birth have been linked to a lifetime of problematic behavior. This relationship becomes clear upon examining biologically based characteristics present during infancy and how they relate to human development over time. For example, infants are hardwired for certain cognitive functions and behaviors. These cognitive abilities and behaviors influence the way they perceive environmental information and the manner in which this information is processed and interpreted. This is part of the reason that very young children do not experience or respond in the same way to common environmental stimuli. Although some environmental stimuli may evoke predictable responses among many, differential response patterns do exist, and thus the total effect of an extra-person variable will vary from person to person. Evidence of such difference includes the resiliency of some youths who are raised in harmful or risky environments but manage to nonetheless maintain prosocial behavior and otherwise escape the snare of their negative, criminogenic environments.

In another fashion, a person's genetic structure may place him or her at an increased risk for harm from environmental factors. Notably, when some individuals are exposed to negative environmental forces, they may be harmed whereas others may be essentially unaffected. One such example pertinent to life course criminology concerns the effects of exposure to lead.

Antisocial behavior, learning disabilities, attention deficit hyperactivity disorder, and criminal involvement each have been found to be related to high levels of lead in individuals (Masters, 1999). One study of youths in Cincinnati found exposure to lead to be positively and linearly related to the number of delinquent acts the 195 juveniles reported (Dietrich, Ris, Succop, Berger, & Bornschein, 2001). Yet there is variability in how lead affects individuals (Onalaja & Claudio, 2000). The most severe effects of lead absorption are experienced by those who have a genotype that retains lead more easily (Masters, 1999; Onalaja & Claudio, 2000). For these individuals, lead and other neurotoxins are more likely to stay in their body and thus to do damage to the brain and central nervous system. Resiliency to lead exposure, however, has been linked to genotypes that can successfully process out, rather than to absorb into the body, these types of neurotoxins (Onalaja & Claudio, 2000). In this way, individual genes structure the level of risk experienced by individuals who share similar environmental factors.

BOX 9.1   The Cincinnati Lead Study

The Cincinnati Lead Study (CLS) is an ongoing, prospective study of individuals born in lead-infested parts of Cincinnati's inner city. The study, directed by Kim Dietrich, is now in its 27th year and has produced some important findings linking lead ingestion in childhood to a range of problematic outcomes in adulthood. Along with Doug Ris, Richard Hornung, Bruce Lanphear, Kim Cecil, and an array of other scholars, Dietrich's work has empirically demonstrated a link between childhood lead ingestion and low IQ, juvenile delinquency, deficits in executive functioning, and adult criminal behavior.

Using functional magnetic resonance imaging, Dietrich's research team has shown how lead ingestion in early and late childhood (around 5 to 6 years of age) is associated with language deficits and other executive function deficits. Individuals with relatively greater blood lead levels had reduced activation of the left frontal cortex, which houses Wernicke's area, and greater activation in the right temporal cortex in the area that houses Broca's area. These findings are consistent with damage to the structures of the brain responsible for the generation of language with contralateral reorganization (offset activation in Broca's area). A follow-up volumetric MRI study revealed further that childhood blood lead levels were significantly correlated with reduced brain volume in adulthood. Specifically, significant reductions in gray matter in the prefrontal cortex and the anterior cingulate cortex were detected. These regions are responsible for rational decision making and other executive functions.

Dietrich's lifelong work has shown how an environmental toxin influences the neurological and behavioral development of exposed children. Exposure to lead, and the deleterious, lifelong consequences associated with lead ingestion, are fully preventable. For our purposes, Dietrich's work highlights the connection between a potent environmental risk factor, brain development, and the development of criminality.

Not only can genes influence the way a person responds to his or her environment, they also may determine the presence of particular individual-level traits that themselves influence development. Previous chapters identified many traits that are heavily influenced by genetics. Many of these traits are related directly or indirectly to involvement in antisocial and aggressive behavior. For example, a person's genetic makeup will determine the functioning of his or her neurotransmitter synthesis. Even minute differences in serotonin and dopamine production can create observable behavioral differences across persons. By kindergarten, these and other substantive differences in adjustment and cognitive functioning can be detected. Over time, these differences accumulate and interact to engender variation in language acquisition, self-regulation, autonomy, cognitive styles, and memory. Those individuals with deficiencies in some or all of these areas are at risk for experiencing school failure, peer rejection, psychological distress, and an inability to inhibit aggression—all of which are interrelated with antisocial behavior (Revelle, 1995).

The Correlation and Interaction Between Genes and the Environment

Gene-Environment Correlations

The correlation between a person's genes and his or her environment indicates that neither is haphazardly distributed—that is, people with particular traits are more likely to be found in certain environments. In other words, certain environments will be easy to navigate and succeed in for some genotypes, whereas others will be less accommodating. For example, if you wanted to identify a group of impulsive individuals who have difficulty in delaying gratification, you would be more successful searching among gamblers at a casino then among attendees at an all-day seminar on investing for the future. The highly heritable trait of impulsivity would be correlated accordingly with environments that do not require individual restraint and concentration over a long period of time. These types of patterns are referred to as "Gene × Environment Correlations." We outline three types below.

Active Gene-Environment Correlation. This type of gene-environment correlation occurs when a person selects to attend an environment that allows for the expression of his or her traits. When individuals are free to choose the type of environment they desire, we often find that those environments are compatible with individuals' genetic predispositions. As previously mentioned, our genes will influence the ways in which environmental stimuli are interpreted and subsequently structured according to their importance. Instead of choosing environments in which it is difficult to successfully operate, individuals tend to choose to maximize the potential of being successful by selecting to participate in environments and situations that allow, encourage, and reward their genetically based traits.

This process of self-selection occurs in a variety of arenas across a person's life. The delinquent adolescent may seek out other youths involved in delinquency, and antisocial adults may choose as their romantic partners those who share their antisocial traits. The chosen peer group or romantic partner serves to reinforce and accommodate the traits of the individual. With regard to peer group formation, researchers have shown that youths selectively affiliate with friends whose involvement in antisocial behavior matches their own (Caspi & Moffitt, 1995). Given the mutual acceptance of deviant behavior among members, the group provides an arena in which continued involvement in such behavior is facilitated (Keenan, Loeber, Zhang, Stouthamer-Loeber, & Van Kammen, 1995).

A similar process, referred to as assortative mating, occurs when persons choose romantic partners. Individuals tend to select mates with similar physical attributes, similar personalities, and similar IQs (Caspi & Herbener, 1990). Assortative mating also reinforces individual differences. In a study of marriage and its contribution to continuity and change in personality over time, it was found that people tend to select marriage partners who are similar to themselves, and by doing so, they increase the likelihood of their own individual personalities remaining stable (Caspi & Herbener, 1990). In light of this finding, assortative mating is a mechanism of self-selection that allows for the expression of genetically based characteristics.

Purposefully choosing supportive environments that allow for individual characteristics to be realized is not the only way in which a person's genetic predispositions are related to the world around him or her. Another active gene-environment correlation occurs when we structure our environment by selectively attending to cues in the environment. As we move from day to day, we are bombarded with countless stimuli and a constant stream of information for possible consideration. We are not able to decipher the purpose and meaning of every cue to which we are exposed. Instead, we pay attention to the elements of any situation that we consider to be most relevant.

This decision is not always a conscious one; rather, our brain perceives, filters, and reacts to environmental stimuli in a way that corresponds with our cognitive frameworks and our past experiences. Upon exposure to a given stimulus, the brain first perceives the stimulus and then uses past experiences to integrate the perceived event with previous stimulus-response sequences (Clark & Grunstein, 2000). Once integrated, a response to the stimulus can be made that is rooted in the individual's own cognitive and behavioral patterns. In addition to operating within the context of past experience, this process is also governed by the way the brain synthesizes information, communicates this information to the body, and leads a response to the information (Clark & Grunstein, 2000). Accordingly, two people who face identical environmental challenges will not invariably evince the same behavioral response.

It is apparent that the reality of an individual's experience will differ from another's according to, at least in part, differences evident in each person's cognitive and perceptual processes. Similar to how our genetic predispositions influence our selection of similarly situated friends, genetic predispositions also affect the brain's consumption of information and the ability of a person to respond effectively. In other words, cues in the environment that are in concordance with and reinforce individual characteristics will be most salient, whereas stimuli that challenge these characteristics and necessitate a response outside of the person's behavioral repertoire more than likely will be ignored.

Because individual attributes are related to the interpretation of environment, persons with aggressive dispositions may be more likely to perceive their environment and the actions of others as threatening than will those who are less attuned to hostile cues (Rintoul et al., 1998). Furthermore, the response will be constrained to the rules and schemas acquired in prior social interaction; thus, they may be limited in their ability to respond in a prosocial manner (Dodge, 1990). Aggressive, antisocial responses will typically carry with them a host of negative consequences that can further ensure the continued use of such responses. Those who are capable of interpreting their environment correctly will be more likely to use a range of behavioral responses. Being able to make sound decisions and plan ahead are two genetically influenced mechanisms through which a positive life pathway may be sustained (Clausen, 1991).

Passive Gene-Environment Correlation. It is possible for measures of the environment to be correlated with genetic factors without a person overtly selecting a specific environment. A common example of this passive gene-environment correlation is found when, for instance, an athletically gifted child is raised by parents in a household where access to athletic equipment and instruction is readily available. In this situation, the child's athletic ability is attributable to being born with the genetic capability to become an athlete and to having parents, themselves most likely athletic, who provided the tools to develop this capability.

A passive gene-environment correlation is unlike the active gene-environment correlation in that the individual does not seek out but rather is exposed to an environment conducive to successful participation in athletics. It is also important to remember that the child is not exposed to this environment purely by chance; rather, athletic parents are more likely to both have children who are athletic and provide reinforcement for involvement in athletics. Because genes for parent and child are related to each other and to the environment, special care should be given when trying to delineate the specific nature and influence of genetic and environmental influences.

Evocative Gene-Environment Correlation. The relationship between environment, genes, and behavior is further complicated when we understand that genetically influenced traits can elicit differential responses from the environment. An evocative gene-environment correlation is perhaps easiest to understand by considering parental responses to their children. A child who has a difficult temperament may not receive as much warmth and affection from a parent as would a child with a more agreeable nature. An unpleasant disposition, then, can effectively evoke a parenting style that is not used in interactions with a child's siblings.

Because children raised in the same family do not experience the same environment, environmental measures for one child cannot be extrapolated unequivocally for another (see Harris, 1995). Twin studies have provided evidence that the family environment is indeed experienced differently across siblings. When assessing parental acceptance-rejection, monozygotic twins have been found to have higher correlations than dizygotic twins, suggesting not only that there is variation in experience but also that genetic factors influence the way in which the familial environment is perceived (Rowe, 1981). Research on siblings and families has supported this conclusion (Pike, McGuire, Hetherington, Reiss, & Plomin, 1996; Reiss et al., 2000).

We can provide one other illustration of an evocative gene-environment correlation. Consider a highly antisocial child who is impulsive and temperamental, and who is placed in a regular school classroom. It is very likely that this child's behaviors will interfere with the teacher's desire to maintain an orderly classroom. The more the child misbehaves, the more the teacher escalates the penalties associated with the misbehavior. In this case, the child's behavior can be thought of as provoking a response from the environment.

Gene-Environment Interaction. Gene-environment correlations focus attention on how genetically endowed traits are more or less likely to be expressed in certain environments and, more importantly, how these environments function to make the traits more, or less, stable over time. Genes and environment may also interact with each other, however, to produce effects on behavior. A person may be born with a genetic predisposition toward problematic behavior, but without the presence of environmental stimuli, this predisposition may not be realized. Accordingly, disadvantaged environments may not have the sufficient protective capability to quell individual proclivities, thus allowing them to be expressed. Individuals who have a criminal disposition may also be more sensitive to adverse conditions. Environmental factors, however, do not always bring out the worst in people. In fact, the same individual in an enriched environment may not express these traits.

Either way, when an environment produces different responses across genotypes, a gene-environment interaction occurs. The co-occurrence of genetic predispositions and certain environmental conditions has effects on behavior that would not occur had only one of these factors been present. This relationship is central to the very nature of interactions in that the effect of two elements on behavior is greater than the main effect each produces. Merely considering the independent effects of genetics and the environment is, as a result, masking what may be a significant combined influence.

To address this problem, researchers have employed twin, adoption, and family studies that consider similarities in outcomes across different levels of genetic relatedness and environmental or familial environment. Taken as a whole, this extensive body of research has shown that both genetic and environmental factors are influential, and that the two indeed often interrelate in complex ways. In fact, the nature, power, and consequence of the relationships fluctuate across developmental periods. In what specific ways do these factors then affect a person in terms of his or her participation in problematic behavior? As you will read, there is strong evidence to suggest that early biological and genetic characteristics of a person exposed to a host of disadvantageous influences will, in part, place him or her on a pathway characterized by difficulty.

Developmental Risk Factors

Pre- and Perinatal Factors and the Environment

This interplay between the individual and the environment is influential throughout a person's life, from conception until death. Although it may seem as though infants are incapable of actively interacting with their environment, they act on their environment as much as their environment influences them. Anyone who has been around a "fussy" baby can attest that an infant can have a significant effect on a household! To understand this interactive process, one must consider the importance of biological factors and biologically driven characteristics within a person's environmental context. This consideration, however, should begin at conception. Although the fetus at this stage of development plays a relatively passive role, its environment plays a critical role. For a fetus, the environment consists of the mother's womb; thus, any factor that changes this physical environment or otherwise affects the fetus via this environment may also alter its developmental course.

Although it may be hard to imagine, prenatal and perinatal factors can have long-lasting and far-reaching effects on an individual's development.

Genetically identical (monozygotic) twins may have noticeable physical and behavioral differences that may be related to their prenatal experience. These influences can include the seemingly innocuous timing of when the egg splits to form two zygotes to the more foreboding transference of umbilical substances from one twin to the other. These differences can cause identical twins to be different in noticeable ways and, sadly, can also lead to serious complications.

These effects do not necessarily cause an individual to act in a particular manner; rather, experiences during the gestational period and immediately following birth may place an individual at an increased risk of having a variety of problems in his or her life. Again, it is the environment that will provide for the expression or the suppression of these biological risk factors. In this way, pre- and perinatal events interact with environmental facets to produce effects that are greater in magnitude and scope than either creates when experienced alone.

Effects of Alcohol and Drugs on Fetal Development

It has long been recognized that the gestational period provides a fetus the time and opportunity to grow and develop so that at birth, it has the capacity and foundation to begin its life outside of the mother's womb. Unfortunately, this period is often marked by less than optimal conditions for both the mother and the fetus. Because the foundations for brain development and functioning begin at this time, disruption to the fetus and the womb may negatively affect cognitive functioning, behavior, and temperament. After birth, these biological traits will be carried into interactions with the environment

One such prenatal factor associated with problematic cognitive and neurochemical functioning is in utero exposure to alcohol, drugs, and tobacco. When pregnant, and especially through the first 8 weeks, the consumption of chemicals and exposure to other teratogens is generally not recommended as the fetus receives nutrients from the mother's blood through the placenta. It is during this period when the central nervous system and other organs develop and cell differentiation begins, making the fetus particularly susceptible to the chemicals' negative effects (Karr-Morse & Wiley, 1997). Generally, such exposure has been implicated in a wide range of neurological harms.

Many women are not aware of their pregnancy during the most crucial periods of fetal development. Consider first that alcohol is a commonly used drug by women in their childbearing years—more than 60% of women in this category report using alcohol at least occasionally (Stratton, Howe, & Battaglia, 1996). Second, alcohol can damage developing neural cells as early as the eleventh day following conception (Karr-Morse & Wiley, 1997). Sadly, it has also been found that alcohol can cause damage to organs and connective tissue, weakened cognitive development, deficits in motor skills, attention difficulties, and problems with behavioral regulation (Karr-Morse & Wiley, 1997).

Women who consume alcohol during pregnancy are also at an increased risk for delivering a low birth weight infant (Day et al., 2002). The size deficit at birth for babies born to mothers who drank heavily while pregnant has been shown to remain through age 14 (Day et al., 2002). In more extreme cases, an infant may be born with fetal alcohol syndrome, which is characterized by facial malformations, small head circumference, social deficits, and damage to the central nervous system (Karr-Morse & Wiley, 1997). The severity of and the exact form of damage that alcohol can have on the development of the fetus depends on the developmental stage in which it is ingested and the quantity that is ingested.

At any rate, if damage to the developing fetus does occur, it is likely that the effects from such damage will be varied, pervasive, and long lasting. Persons exposed to alcohol in their mother's womb often begin their lives with an increased risk for future aggression and other behavioral problems (Sood et al., 2001). Although alcohol exposure itself is not considered a direct cause of later antisocial behavior, it does cause an increased risk for evidencing attention and memory problems, delays in reaching developmental milestones such as language acquisition, and learning difficulties—all implicated in violent and severe problematic behavior. Similar negative outcomes have been associated with mothers who consume cocaine (Delaney-Black et al., 2000) and heroin or are exposed to lead. More recently, research on rats and their offspring found that babies born to mothers exposed to a chemical in marijuana displayed short-term hyperactivity and long-term memory problems (Mereu et al., 2003). Exposure to drugs in utero can initiate a process that places a person at an increased risk for negative life experiences and childhood traits that are themselves related to disorders in adulthood.

Prenatal Exposure to Nicotine

Similar to the negative effects that exposure to alcohol and other chemicals can have on a developing fetus, maternal nicotine use has also been found to cause harm. Smoking serves to reduce the level of blood flow to the fetus, causing damage to the placenta and effectively restricting the amount of growth hormones and nutrients received. In part, this reduction in flow to the placenta can lead to low birth weight, miscarriage, premature birth, and lung problems for the infant (Faden & Graubard, 2000). Recent evidence from a study that followed women during pregnancy and birth suggests that infants born to women who smoke tend to be smaller overall and smaller in terms of both length and head size than infants whose mothers refrained from smoking during pregnancy (Faden & Graubard, 2000).

In addition to observable physical differences, cognitive impairment and behavioral problems have also been linked to prenatal exposure to nicotine. During childhood, persons whose mothers smoked while pregnant have, on average, lower IQs (Fried, Watkinson, & Gray, 1998), more trouble self-regulating their behavior, greater attention problems, and greater involvement in hyperactive behaviors (Day et al., 2002). This increased risk applies to conduct disorders in children as they reach adolescence (Fergusson, Woodward, & Horwood, 1998) and even to arrest for violent crimes during early adulthood (Brennan, Grekin, & Mednick, 1999).

Exposure alone to these harmful chemicals and drugs may cause serious problems for the developing fetus. It is possible for the infant to develop normally if he or she receives proper care, attention, nutrition, and nurturing. Environments for these infants, however, tend to be less than optimal, usually being characterized by uncertainty, insufficient attention, and even worse, neglect and abuse (Tibbetts & Piquero, 1999).

This interactive effect is quite marked for nicotine exposure—infants whose mothers smoked during pregnancy are more likely to participate in violent, recidivistic, and late-onset offending when other psychosocial risk factors are also present. Although nicotine exposure alone is related to an increase in offending, when the individual is raised in a single-parent family, born to a teenage mother who did not want to be pregnant, and lags in motor development, the risk of recidivistic violent offending increases dramatically (Rasanen et al., 1999). Others have found an interactive effect of maternal smoking and having a parent absent to be predictive of early-onset offending (Gibson & Tibbetts, 2000). It appears, then, that the double dose of exposure to nicotine and other drugs and chemicals in utero and being raised in a disadvantaged environment is especially likely to place a person on a life course that is characterized by early and serious violent behaviors.

Prenatal Care

Because so much of an infant's future depends on its safe and healthy prenatal experience, it is imperative that women take proper care of themselves and seek the care of a physician. As previously mentioned, proper care is especially important during the first 8 weeks of the pregnancy when the major body systems are developing. Recent figures from the National Center for Health Statistics show that in 2000, 82.3% of all live births were to mothers who began prenatal care during the first trimester. Although this statistic reflects a gradual increase in the past 10 years in the percentage of women who receive early prenatal care, more than 15% of women were not under the care of a physician prior to giving birth.

In addition to monitoring the general progress of the pregnancy, a doctor can provide information that will aid the mother in having a problem-free pregnancy and ultimately a healthy baby. Part of this care entails providing information regarding physical and psychological health for both the mother and the infant. It is essential that a pregnant woman consume enough nutrients to provide the necessary fuel for the fetus to develop optimally. Malnutrition may inhibit the growth, development, and metabolism of the central nervous system in offspring (Wachs, 2000). Mothers who do not consume enough amino acids or proteins may limit their, and subsequently their child's, ability to produce and synthesize the neurotransmitters serotonin, dopamine, and norepinephrine (Wachs, 2000). Because deficiencies in vitamins and minerals (e.g., iron, vitamin C, and riboflavin) also play a key role in neurotransmitter synthesis and regulation, their intake during pregnancy is required for the most favorable prenatal development. Recall from Chapter 8 that research has linked abnormal levels of neurotransmitters to aggression, violence, and criminal offending.

So far, we have discussed the relationship between the woman's physical health and that of her offspring. This discussion can be expanded to include psychological well-being. Briefly, the experience of stress and other negative emotions can affect the aforementioned systems of the fetus. Just as leading a stressful life takes a toll on our bodies—think of the high-powered executive who works 80 hours a week and also has high blood pressure—it can also affect the well-being of the fetus. Maternal stress may actually be experienced by the fetus as conditions in the uterus and in the bloodstream change according to stress levels. In an even more striking example of the ways in which the fetus may be affected, when the mother experiences stress, it may even activate in the fetus the "C-fos" gene that is thought to contribute to the development of neural connections that do not fire normally (Kaufer, Friedman, Seidman, & Soreq, 1998). It has been proposed that activation of this gene may lead some to be hypersensitive to stress in their lives and unable to appropriately match their behavior or emotion to what the situation may normally elicit (Fishbein, 2001). Clearly, the tenuous environment of the womb can do much for fetal development, but good or bad, these effects will be played out over the life course.

Perinatal and Early Infancy Events

Birth holds its own set of potential complications, the effects of which may unfold in various domains. Although not exhaustive, such problems can include premature birth, prolapse of the umbilical cord, oxygen deprivation, and breech birth, to name a few. It is believed that such trauma can cause damage to the brain of the fetus. Specifically, damage to the brain may be an antecedent to the development of neuropsychological deficits that make it difficult for an individual to be socialized (Piquero & Tibbetts, 1999).

When birth complications are coupled with other psychosocial risk factors such as family discord, maternal rejection, and disadvantaged family environment, an individual is more likely to offend. One study found that perinatal risk factors and living in a disadvantaged environment interacted to increase the violent offending as an adult (Piquero & Tibbetts, 1999). Raine, Brennan, and Mednick (1997), in a study of violent offending by males aged 34, found that early maternal rejection interacted with birth complications to predict early-onset, serious, violent offending. This interaction was not found to be predictive of nonviolent or late-onset offending (Raine et al., 1997).

Along with experiencing actual trauma during birth, babies who are born with minor physical abnormalities (MPAs) may also be at increased risk for being impulsive and engaging in delinquency and crime. MPAs are thought to result when abnormalities occur in the development of brain structures. Many studies have shown a link between antisocial behavior in juveniles and adults and the presence of MPAs (Raine, 2002). These MPAs have the most impact on antisocial behavior when they occur in tandem with family adversity. This body of research also suggests that the co-occurrence of MPAs and family adversity does not increase the likelihood of all antisocial behavior. Rather, individuals are particularly likely to engage in violent behavior.

Sometimes, there are no observable complications with the birthing process, yet problems associated with the characteristics of the birth can place a child at risk. Low birth weight, for example, is a substantive risk factor for a range of cognitive problems. Low birth weight results from either slow growth in the womb or from being born too early. Infants born at a low weight are vulnerable to developing a range of health problems as they grow (Faden & Graubard, 2000). They may also fare more poorly in their mental development than their normal-weight peers. A recent study conducted in England has reported that 16-year-olds who were low in weight (less than 3.3 lbs.) when they were born received lower grades on a standard exam given to all secondary education students (Faden & Graubard, 2000). The effect of birth weight on offending is not direct; rather, when low birth weight infants are raised in inadequate social environments (Tibbets & Piquero, 1999), in families marked by instability (Kandel, Brennan, & Mednick, 1990), or in low socioeconomic status families (Ross, Lipper, & Auld, 1990), they are more likely to engage in offending and other behavioral problems.

It is likely that babies who experience complications associated with birth are more likely to be born to mothers who are not equipped to care for them. This interaction increases the likelihood that the children will suffer from certain neuropsychological deficits. These deficits may hinder their general intellectual ability and the development of self-regulation. These children need high levels of parental supervision, support, and understanding. As such, parents who themselves have cognitive impairments or who do not have the necessary available resources to meet their child's needs are likely to provide environments that exacerbate their child's problems. Poor parenting in its extreme may take the forms of neglect and abuse. These practices and their ensuing effects on a child's behavior are discussed later in the chapter.

Biosocial Issues in Development

As you can surmise from the discussion on pre- and perinatal factors, the early beginnings of a person's life may foretell the type of future that he or she is likely to face. Because of the gross increase in brain development during this time, any harm or other noxious environmental stimuli that infants experience may limit their cognitive ability, shape their cognitive processes, and influence their behavior negatively. The extent to which these and other individual-based characteristics will influence problematic behaviors depends on factors outside of the person.

In recent years, widespread attention has been given to a set of behavioral disorders that is increasingly evident in children and adolescents. As a group, the disorders are characterized by attentional problems, learning disabilities, and cognitive deficits. Three of these disorders, attention deficit disorder/attention deficit hyperactivity disorder, oppositional defiant disorder, and conduct disorder, are especially relevant to the study of the etiology of delinquent offending.

Attention Deficit Disorder/Attention Deficit Hyperactivity Disorder

Persons diagnosed with attention deficit disorder/attention deficit hyperactivity disorder (ADD/ADHD) typically fare poorly at problem solving, planning, tasks that require attention, and self-regulation (Karr-Morse & Wiley, 1997).

These difficulties clearly inhibit the ability to succeed in school both academically and socially (Barkley, 1998). Research in this area has provided affirmative support for the existence of a relationship between ADD/ADHD and delinquency. On a descriptive level, estimates of ADD/ADHD among adult inmates (approximately 25%) are higher than estimates derived for youths in the general population (range from 3% to 12%). In a synthesis of the existing empirical examinations of the relationship between ADD/ADHD and offending, Pratt, Cullen, Blevins, Daigle, and Unnever (2002) found that ADD/ADHD has a significant effect ($M_z = .155$) on crime and delinquency.

Other research has aimed to identify the environmental factors that appear to be the most harmful for persons suffering from ADD/ADHD. Although ADD/ADHD is caused by genes, the severity of the disorder and its effects vary in different environmental contexts. Even in the best environment, the symptoms associated with ADD/ADHD are difficult to address in constructive ways. In an environment that is lacking in resources, structure, or understanding, the individual may experience unnecessary developmental disadvantages (Moffitt, 1990).

Moffitt (1990) reports that during childhood, youths comorbid in ADD/ADHD and delinquency were more likely to suffer from significant deficits in their motor skills and to have greater family adversity. Ultimately, these cognitive deficits retarded their verbal abilities and limited their success in school. In turn, at age 11, a significant interactive effect between ADD/ADHD and verbal ability was positively related to involvement in antisocial behavior. Others have also reported a similar pathway linking cognitive and academic failure to later problems in adjustment (Campbell, Shaw, & Gilliom, 2000).

Oppositional Defiant Disorder and Conduct Disorder

Two other behavioral disorders that place individuals at risk for engaging in serious adult crime are oppositional defiant disorder (ODD) and conduct disorder (CD). These disorders are similar to ADD/ADHD except that they are characterized by more extreme resistance to discipline, more severe aggression, and more troubled relationships (Karr-Morse & Wiley, 1997). ODD is typically diagnosed earlier in life than CD and is less serious in terms of the antisocial behaviors it includes.

Whereas a person with ODD may be stubborn, dishonest, and prone to disobeying directives, CD sufferers participate in a range of more serious antisocial behaviors, including acts that cause physical harm to others and otherwise adversely affect their family environment, their peer relations, as well as their experience in school. These problems are exacerbated when ADD/ADHD co-occurs with conduct disorders, a phenomenon that all too frequently arises (Biederman, Newcorn, & Sprich, 1991). Individuals with this comorbidity are more likely than those with either disorder to display the most serious problems—involvement in serious, violent offending—and to have problems associated with the disorders for a longer period of time (Campbell et al., 2000).

Having ODD or CD results in an interpersonal style that alienates the individual from his or her family and peers. Much like parents of children with ADD/ADHD, parents whose children have either of these behavioral disorders are likely to have difficulty implementing effective parenting strategies. Parents not possessing the faculties that would allow them to monitor, supervise, and discipline their children can reinforce, rather than deter, harmful externalizing behaviors. It is also possible that the parents have similar dispositional characteristics given that the child inherits genes from his or her parents. It is unlikely that parents who have difficulties controlling their own behavior and/or have aggressive tendencies will be conscientious enough to discipline their child through the use of behavioral contingencies.

Other evidence also suggests the presence of a relationship between ODD and CD and environmental measures. Specifically, individuals with these disorders are prone to self-select delinquent partners (Quinton, Pickles, Maughan, & Rutter, 1993). Even when prosocial partners and peers are accessible, it is likely that ODD and CD youths will fail to use these social resources (Elmen & Offer, 1993). Aggressive and abrasive behaviors in childhood usually lead to rejection by nondeviant peers, further reinforcing antisocial dispositions.

Activity of Nervous System: Sensation Seeking

Recall from Chapter 4 that individual responses to environmental stimuli are dependent on a person's genetically influenced characteristics and his or her prior experiences. When exposed to novel and stressful situations, physiological structures are activated to initiate the fight-or-flight process (Gray, 1994). For this process to begin, the cortex filters potential incoming environmental stimuli, references relevant past events, and analyzes the current situation within its context. After the situation is assessed and an outcome behavior selected, a sense of fear is generated in the amygdala and the autonomic nervous system becomes fully active. Stress hormones are released by the neuroendocrine system that further enable physiological processes (e.g., increases in blood pressure, oxygen levels, and heart rate) required to confront and respond to the stressor. In choosing the behavioral response, the one that is likely to have the greatest benefit and the least cost will be given preference.

When this stress-response sequence is enacted at levels that correspond to the seriousness of the situational context, a person will typically learn to associate the outcome and the stressor in the future. In this way, a person becomes conditioned; future considerations of similar stimuli will include these attending consequences. Should the costs of choosing a behavior outweigh the perceived benefits, a conditioned person will be deterred. For others, they may not experience the same level of arousal in response to stimuli, and as a result may not fear or consider the possible negative results.

The low activity level of the central and autonomic nervous systems has clear implications for criminal behavior. If the fight-or-flight response is not activated—if the person does not truly fear—then a mechanism to deter involvement in crime is unlikely to be found (see Raine, 1993, for a discussion on fear and antisocial behavior). Not only would this dysfunction limit the activation of this response system, it may also "push" a person into selecting environments that will provide the external stimulation that he or she lacks internally. Personality and temperament research has linked lower stress-related cortisol levels to extroverted and uninhibited individuals (Kagan, Reznick, & Snidman, 1987). Aggression and antisocial behaviors provide a source of external stimulation to those without adequate levels of internal arousal. Individuals are more likely to engage in antisocial acts they find pleasurable when internal arousal is low. Consequences of behavior are given little consideration because low physiological arousal limits one's ability to plan and to empathize (Hastings, Zahn-Waxler, Robinson, Usher, & Bridges, 2000). In the end, the need for stimulation and the inability to restrain impulsive urges typically win.

Research using both behavioral as well as psychophysiological measures has found evidence to support this link. Children who display behaviors indicative of sensation seeking and fearlessness at age 3 were found by Raine, Reynolds, Venables, Mednick, and Farrington (1998) to be more aggressive than other children at age 11. A relationship between resting heart rate and violence has also been found to be significant for predicting adult male offenders (Farrington, 1987b). Of course, we must also consider the role of arousal in different environmental contexts. The structure and functioning of the ANS system is, in part, a function of heritability; however, environmental factors can place a person at an increased risk of engaging in antisocial behaviors associated with ANS functioning. Such has been the case in the Cambridge Youth Study, in which the risk of violent offending in adulthood was greatest for boys who had low resting heart rates, large families, and poor relationships with their parents (Farrington, 1997).

Deficits in Neuropsychological Functioning

Damage to the physical structure of the brain can limit the way in which it will be able to communicate to other parts of the body. Interaction between the external environment and the internal person can also be compromised should the brain experience damage. If executive functioning is impaired to the extent that a person neither perceives nor analyzes the outside world as others do, he or she may not be able to engage in complex reasoning and decision making. It is quite likely that the inability to integrate current stimuli, past experiences, and perceived outcomes into a thoughtful assessment of possible responses will generate unpredictable, maladaptive reactions.

The prefrontal cortex is primarily in charge of the executive functions, which, in addition to planning and problem solving, also include regulating emotion. Difficulties in these tasks are indicative of developmental disruptions that increase an individual's vulnerability to the forces of the environment. Unfortunately, these disruptions are strongly related to antisocial and aggressive behavior as well. Thus, deficits in neuropsychological development place a person on a path where misbehavior and negative consequences are more likely.

It is instructive that disruption in cognitive functioning has been included in theoretical propositions regarding the development of offending. Indeed, neuropsychological deficits are identified by Moffitt (1993a) in her developmental typology of offending as being key antecedents in the etiology of life course-persistent delinquency. These deficits can be the result of any prenatal event or environmental influence that causes augmentations in the development or function of the brain via the initial harm to the prefrontal cortex. Nonetheless, Moffitt (1993a) and others view the impulsiveness and the disregard for planning that characterizes most serious offenders as being at least in part driven by impairment in the prefrontal cortex.

Effects of neuropsychological deficits may manifest in a variety of ways. Individuals with deficits in cognitive ability and self-control have problems performing well in school. They are also likely to have poor parental and peer relationships. Persons with problematic cognitive functioning often perceive the world to be hostile, and they behave in ways that alienate those around them, often leading to their peers rejecting them and their parents being either overly hostile or indifferent (Moffitt, 1990; Rubin, LeMare, Lollis, Asher, & Coie, 1990). The most detrimental effects will be experienced by those individuals who, in addition to cognitive impairment, are exposed to a disadvantaged environment. Using low birth weight as a proxy measure of neuropsychological deficits, Tibbetts and Piquero (1999) found a significant interaction between disadvantaged environment and low birth weight to be predictive of early-onset offending. Additional implications of neuropsychological deficits for relationships and behavior are discussed later in the chapter.

Individuals in Their Environment

Much of what we have discussed in this chapter in terms of biosocial influences on behavior may, in one way or another, influence the way a person acts and reacts in any given environment. How these influences affect a person across his or her life is discussed in detail in the following chapters. As a prelude to this discussion, and to provide a synthesis of the information in this chapter, the ways in which two specific domains of youths' lives are structured by biosocial variables are discussed.

Participation in Peer Networks

Perhaps the most salient social group to which individuals belong during childhood and adolescence is the peer group. Individual differences exist in the preference for group membership. For the most part, individuals are more likely to prefer to associate with others with whom they have something in common. Commonalities might include the ability to play a musical instrument, the enjoyment of sports, and even shared behavioral patterns. Because individuals in a peer group share much in common, the group becomes an important source of attachment, esteem, stimulation, emotional security, and self-evaluation.

Peer group formation is, to some degree, socially structured. Individuals select friends from an available pool of potential friends, especially early in life. Children placed in day care or those in first grade have a limited supply of potential friends from which to choose. Even so, a desire to be part of a peer group may not be matched by a group of friends who covet your friendship. Instead, many children and teens are rejected by potential peer groups.

Individuals who suffer from ADD/ADHD, conduct disorder, or an affective disorder may be particularly susceptible to deviant peer influences, and they are more likely to be rejected from prosocial peer groups. As we have recently discussed, these individuals are likely to possess a disposition that is characterized by aggression, externalizing behaviors, an inability to inhibit behavior, and a lack of empathy. Persons with these problems are most likely going to act in ways that alienate those around them, thus limiting their ability to develop or sustain friendships and increasing their vulnerability to stress. Youths who exhibit problematic behaviors when interacting with their peers also show biases in the processing of social information (Dodge, 1986). Their cognitive functioning is characterized by inflexibility and immaturity when employing problem-solving or moral reasoning strategies (Ollendick, Weist, Borden, & Greene, 1992). Such individuals are likely to perform poorly in school and select to drop out, further severing their connections to prosocial groups and further locking them on an antisocial pathway (Ollendick et al., 1992).

Individuals and the Family Environment

The increased importance of the peer group to youths does not preclude the family as an important socializing agent. Much like the interactive nature of a person and his or her peer environment, the family unit interacts with its members by simultaneously responding to and influencing each constituent member. In this way, the characteristics of the parents influence their behavior toward family members as well as the genetic potentials of their biological children. Children, too, influence the behaviors of their parents.

It is first important to recognize that the family creates an environment where constant interaction occurs among its members. Because of this interaction, a person's experience in the family may differ sharply from the experience of a relative. In fact, each person has a niche in the family that is dependent on his or her and other family members' individual traits and interactional styles. Families, as others have stated, form a "total family system," where roles are acquired, reinforced, and expected. As such, one child may perceive a happy home environment in which equality, fairness, and generosity abound, whereas another child may feel isolated, discriminated against, and unsafe.

These unique experiences, or microenvironments, are influential in the development of serious misbehavior. For a person whose temperament can best be characterized as difficult, effective parenting may not exist—that is, even the best parenting styles may have little effect. Because the temperament of a child is influenced by the genes of the parents, it is likely that a child with a difficult, impulsive, or aggressive temperament also has parents with the same characteristics (Collins, Maccoby, Steinberg, Hetherington, & Bornstein, 2000). Unable to effectively manage their problem child, the parents may use hostility, criticism, and indifference as parenting tools (Collins et al., 2000). This child, much like the one experiencing peer rejection, will find his or her already unpleasant and ineffectual interaction style reinforced by the authoritarian style of parenting (Rubin et al., 1990). In these families, an aura of distrust and a pattern of aggressiveness are clearly visible.

Other factors also influence family functioning, including access to resources such as health care and education. As we stated earlier, individuals who suffer from neuropsychological deficits are more likely to be raised in disadvantaged environments. Environments deficient in support and nurturance, and consequently replete with stress and anxiety, tend to encourage antisocial behaviors in general, and biologically disposing tendencies toward aggression, drug use, and other problem behaviors more specifically.

Physical abuse and serious neglect are also important environmental stimuli. Some parents are so poorly equipped to respond effectively to a child that is acting out that they bring physical harm to their child (Caspi, Bem, & Elder, 1989). Research has shown that children who are prone to exhibit irritability and distress are also at an increased risk of evoking an abusive response from their parents (Collins et al., 2000). Physical abuse suffered as a child can have lasting detrimental effects on both the relationship between the parent and child and the development of the child (Karr-Morse & Wiley, 1997). Abuse can result in permanent damage to the prefrontal cortex of the brain (Rowe, 2002). It also can lead to learning difficulties because the neural structures may experience trauma (Raine et al., 1997). The empirically supported relationship between head trauma and/or experience of prior victimization and antisocial behavior is not merely coincidental (Karr-Morse & Wiley, 1997).

Parents who select the opposite extreme and instead ignore or neglect their child can also do serious damage. A child who does not have the sense of security that a parent can provide or the warmth of attachment to an adult who loves him or her will likely have difficulty securing such bonds with others during his or her lifetime (Karr-Morse & Wiley, 1997). This lack of attachment can have serious neurophysiological consequences.

BOX 9.2   The Continuing Saga of Stanley: Work Influences

Stanley started working when he was 12 years old. We will see that his early work record was unstable and included a wide variety of positions. According to Shaw (1930), such a pattern "indicates clearly the absence of a definite vocational interest and suggests the great difficulties that he encountered in making satisfactory adjustment to other persons" (p. 29). These problems, as well as other work-related troubles, simply represent behavioral manifestations of Stanley's attitudes and personality traits, which will be discussed below during our review of Stanley's work record.

Stanley started work at age 12 as an errand boy for a business in Chicago's central business district, "the Loop." He claimed he was laid off because he showed up late for work several times and "the boss got cocky with me" (Shaw, 1930, p. 30). This was the beginning of (according to official records) no less than 32 jobs that Stanley had between ages 12 and 20, which ranged from farm worker to machine operator in a factory to laboratory assistant in a hospital. The highlights of his work record will now be discussed.

Before discussing some of Stanley's key positions as an employee, it is worthwhile to review some reasons for why his status as an employee was terminated numerous times. Stanley's reason for leaving or being fired from his jobs were varied; it is interesting to note several categories that were reported (Shaw, 1930, pp. 30–31). These categories include Stanley leaving or being fired from jobs because (a) he was not treated with respect by the boss or his coworkers, several of which he ended up assaulting; (b) he distracted his coworkers, such as "playing around with the girls"; (c) he refused to work at numerous jobs because he perceived them to be "monotonous" or "too dirty"; (d) he showed up late or "refused to obey a supervisor"; (e) he left the city or ran away from the area; (f) he smoked on the job; (g) he claimed at one job that "above all things I hated to have a girl give me orders" (p. 176); and finally, our favorite, (h) he "didn't like inside work during the spring of the year."

Although virtually all of Stanley's jobs were short lived, and his reasons for leaving were rather consistent (typically a conflict with a coworker or the boss, often perceived as a issue of respect by Stanley), there were a few notable episodes in Stanley's career that seemed to have a profound impact on him, for good or bad. The early jobs that Stanley had were minuscule and really did not have much impact on his development, other than as a representation of his incompetence at that time. However, as time went on, several episodes did occur that were vital in the ultimate development of Stanley and his criminal career.

One of the primary transitions occurred when Stanley got a job working as a laboratory assistant in a hospital (which, chronologically, was his 17th position of 32). Stanley was assigned to take care of experimental animals and feed them. This appears to be the first time that Stanley perceived that he was actually doing something that he really liked and was appreciated by the staff. As Stanley explains,

> No more was work monotonous. . . . I got along with them nicely. . . . I wanted to be refined and know how to act when in contact with people who were intelligent. . . . They considered me as one of them, and that made me take stock in myself. (Shaw, 1930, p. 177)

This revelation by Stanley is of utmost importance because he realized that he was a significant force in the world, and he also realized he had something to lose. The commitment to conformity Stanley felt in this job had a profound impact on his development that would stay with him for a long time.

Stanley reveals his personal investment in this job and the feelings about himself that this position gave him. For example, he claimed that "I looked back at my foolishness and compared the fun I was having now. It was different. It filled me with new life. It made me feel like somebody" (Shaw, 1930, p. 178). It was during this time that Stanley fell in love with one of the girls at the hospital. As he explains, "She swept me off my feet the first time I saw her, and I began to dream dreams of future happiness. Dreams I had not dreamed before. So I began to take note of my personal appearance" (Shaw, 1930, p. 178).

Along with his appearance, Stanley seemed to take note of other aspects of his personality and self. As he reported,

> I had a good job, good clothes, and I was going to school. My sister told me that I had changed, and that she thought that I would get somewhere in life. The gang I had associated with looked upon me with more respect, and I realized and knew what it was to feel independent and able to take care of oneself. (p. 179)

(Continued)

(Continued)

Stanley worked at the hospital for some time, and during this time he felt "I could look anyone in the eye squarely without cringing" (Shaw, 1930, p. 179). Even though Stanley worked at the hospital for only half a year, it obviously made an impression in his life.

Such traditionally intermittent employment and the lack of commitment to any one job was a manifestation of Stanley's low level of self-control and lack of a "stake in conformity" that are so important in the socialization of individuals. Despite his relatively stable time as an employee at the hospital, Stanley proceeded to take on (and lose) numerous other employment positions. However, it is likely that Stanley never forgot the formative experience he had at the hospital. We will see that his experience in a similar form of employment (combined with other factors) will play a key role in his conformity.

CHAPTER 10

Prepubescence

Infancy and Childhood

In short, the habits we form from childhood make no small difference, but rather they make all the difference.

Aristotle (384–322 BC)

C riminology is blessed—some say cursed—with a wealth of theories. We have social structural theories, social process theories, social learning theories, and social situational theories. We have theories that link peers to crime, poverty to crime, and racism to crime. Crime is the product of differential association, symbolic interaction, stress and strain, blocked opportunities, anomie, opportunity, gangs, guns, and drugs. The list of possible causal factors is lengthy and growing. Like we said, criminology is rich in complicated, fancy, and incredibly complex theories. Unfortunately, all theories are not equally valid, and criminologists have a bad habit of failing to falsify most theories.

Take those traditional criminological theories that identify adolescence as the time period for the onset of criminal behavior. Most theories make the assumption that because crime rates and violence increase during adolescence, that criminal motivation must also develop during adolescence. Thus, the picture that has emerged from traditional criminological theories has been that criminal behavior starts somewhere between the ages of 12 and 18. Unfortunately, such theories are wrong, or at least mostly wrong. As the previous chapter made clear, the roots of crime stretch far back in time. At birth, it appears, certain individuals are more likely than others to engage in crime and violence in the future.

That the roots of crime can be traced back so far in time comes as a surprise to many. After all, how could an infant, who cannot yet walk or talk, engage in criminal or intentionally destructive behaviors? Moreover, given the amount of change that children undergo during this time period, wouldn't you expect serious misbehavior to be fleeting, or subject to substantial change? And if crime begins early in life, what does that mean for theories that identify deviant peers, poverty, and other "causes" that occur later in life? Are they relevant?

The answers to these questions are complicated; however, one of the great discoveries of the past century is that infants manifest measurable individual differences, and that these differences remain relatively stable across broad periods of individual development (Campbell, 1995). These differences, in turn, are related to future disobedient and criminal behavior. Although the processes that link differences between infants and children to future violence remain to be discovered and elucidated, the fact that individuals differ early in life is set in stone. Nothing, it seems, destroys fancy theories faster than stubborn facts.

In this chapter, we examine the research on human development and aggression in infancy and childhood. Our guess is that the vast majority of criminologists are unfamiliar with this literature and evidence. Even so, to understand serious, chronic, and violent behavior that so captures our attention, we must first understand how individuals develop across time. As the research will show, criminology can no longer ignore the developing years of infancy and childhood—a time when human growth and development are of critical importance.

What Do We Mean by Problem Behavior in Infancy and Childhood?

Infants and very young children are capable of a range of undifferentiated and ungeneralized behaviors. Prior to achieving directed mobility (crawling and walking), young children can cry, scream, thrash their arms and legs, grab and pull on objects with their fingers, and smile and coo (that sweet little sound they make around their caregivers). Yet their behaviors are not organized (goal driven), nor are they specific to varying contexts. Infants will cry on an airplane or cry in their crib. They do not yet realize that behaviors are sometimes context specific—that is, parents expect them to cry at home, but beleaguered parents would prefer they not cry on the airplane! Crying and thrashing about, although sometimes taxing on parents and those around them, are normal, age-appropriate behaviors for infants.

Young children also exhibit a range of behaviors, some troubling, some not. They can crawl and bump into objects, put their fingers into light sockets, scream loud enough to wake the dead, and bounce when happy or exhilarated. These behaviors are also normal and age appropriate.

Two points come from this discussion. First, infants and very young children have not yet learned to generalize their behavior from one setting to the next. They do not understand that the rules that govern social interactions vary across place and time. Generalization, however, is a key developmental goal largely because it shows that the child is learning both self-regulation and recognition of the social cues that differentiate appropriate from inappropriate behavior. Second, simply because a behavior is rude, disgusting, or inconsiderate (terms we typically reserve for the behavior of older people) does not necessarily mean it rates as "troublesome." Indeed, the majority of infants and very young people exhibit age-appropriate behaviors that are considered delinquent and even criminal later in life.

So, what do we consider to be "troublesome" behavior? Generally, scholars define early troublesome behavior as a constellation of age-inappropriate behaviors that persist across time and context and that interfere with the healthy development of the child. Temper tantrums, for example, are somewhat common very early in life. Children will yell, scream, cry, and toss themselves wildly on the ground to achieve some desired status or goal. This form of behavior, however, typically disappears by the time a child reaches school. Now, picture a 5- or 6-year-old engaging in this behavior at school in front of his or her peers and the teacher. Also imagine if this same child also steals from playmates, regularly disrupts class, lies, cheats, and destroys property. Clearly, the *pattern* of misbehavior is harmful to the child and others. And if this pattern of behavior persists across time and contexts, then the healthy development of the child is likely to be put at risk.

When childhood misbehavior reaches a certain level, we will often classify the child as "behaviorally disordered." For childhood behavior to be considered a disorder, certain criteria have to be met. We draw on the criteria outlined by Campbell (1995)

- A pattern or constellation of symptoms is present.
- A pattern of symptoms with at least short-term stability is present.
- A cluster of symptoms that is evident in several settings with people other than the parent is present.
- The symptoms are relatively severe.
- The symptoms interfere with the child's ability to negotiate developmental challenges. (p. 117)

Notice again that Campbell's criteria preclude the transient or temporary problems that sometimes occur when young children experience novel situations (movement into day care, divorce, etc.). For Campbell, and most scholars, early behaviors can be considered threatening only if they become a pattern of age-inappropriate misconduct that occurs over time and across settings. To think about this issue differently, compare two children: The first child misbehaves only at home, typically by throwing a temper tantrum when his parents do not give him what he wants. At preschool, however, the child does not throw temper tantrums, nor does he display any other misbehavior. The second child, however, throws temper tantrums at home, at school, at church, and out in public. He lies and steals, and finds it very difficult to socially integrate with other same-age, same-sex children. On one hand, notice how the behavior of the first child is isolated to home and is relatively restricted in range. On the other hand, notice how undifferentiated the behavior of the second child is, as well as its versatility. The second child likely meets the clinical criteria for being labeled as having a behavioral disorder.

So, when we talk about early problem behaviors, we must realize that assessments are made on different criteria, such as the age of the child, the range of misbehaviors in which the child engages, and the number of settings in which the child misbehaves. Children who engage in age-inappropriate behaviors, display substantial versatility in their misbehavior, and misbehave across a large number of settings are considered to be exhibiting "troublesome" behavior. If the misbehavior does not recede or terminate, and instead continues as the child ages, then the child may be labeled as having a behavioral disorder. Either way, early misbehavior has strong implications for the life course of the child and, as we will see shortly, predicts a host of negative adult outcomes.

The Prevalence and Frequency of Problem Behavior in Infancy and Early Childhood

Data from various cultures and time periods converge to show that the majority of children will demonstrate mild and transient age-inappropriate behavioral problems. For the majority of these children, their difficult behavior will dissipate or become extinguished prior to entrance into school. Other children, however, show signs of more serious problems. According to Campbell (1995), roughly 10% to 15% of preschool children can be expected to demonstrate mild to moderate forms of behavioral disorders. She notes that a study done in London found that 15% of the sample were classified as having minor problems, whereas 7% were classified as having moderate to severe behavioral problems (see Richman, Stevenson, & Graham, 1982). In a study of rural Pennsylvania 3-year-olds, Cornely and Bromet (1986) found that slightly more than 11% of youth met the cutoff for serious behavioral problems. Similar results were found in research by Newth and Corbett (1993) and by Stallard (1993). More recently, data from the Duniden study found that about 10% of 3-year-olds were rated as uncontrollable—impulsive, emotionally unstable, irritable, and restless (Moffitt, Caspi, Rutter, & Silva, 2001).

Finally, two studies examined data from very young children. First, Mathiesen and Sanson (2000) examined parent reports of their child's behavior at 18 months and 30 months. They found that more than 50% of Norwegian mothers reported moderate problems with their very young child(ren). These problems included age-inappropriate soiling, sleeping, overactivity, restlessness, concentration, attention seeking, discipline, and temper (p. 20). Thus, as we would expect, early problem behaviors (18 months) are quite normal and to be expected, showing that certain problems tend to dissipate over time. Second, in a study of 511 parental reports of 17-month-old children, Tremblay and his colleagues (1999) found that more than 50% of 17-month-olds take things from others, whereas 40% will push others to get what they want. However, around 20% were reported as having kicked, bitten, or physically attacked another. Fewer still were classified by their mothers as bullies (7.6%) or as cruel (3.3%). The prevalence of misconduct was significantly increased if the child had a brother or sister.

What do we make of these data so far? First, early problem behaviors are typically developmentally appropriate. Many very young children will engage in taxing and stupefying behaviors—much to the chagrin of their parent(s). Second, as infancy moves into toddlerhood, certain behavior problems become less prevalent unless there is a sibling in the home, in which case prevalence rates can be expected to remain relatively higher. Typically, less than 15% of preschool children can be expected to show high rates of hard-to-manage behaviors. Third, the prevalence rates decline substantially if we are interested in only those youth who show very high rates of problem behavior. Steiner and Dunne (1997) note that only 1.5% to 3.4% of children are diagnosed with conduct disorder. Other data indicate that conduct disorder is prevalent in 5% of 10-year-olds, and that oppositional defiant disorder is prevalent in 10% of children under the age of 12. When we include attention deficit hyperactivity disorder, we find that only 2% to 5% of children eventually qualify for the label. Clearly, the prevalence of misbehavior decreases as youths age, but for certain youths, the frequency with which they engage in problematic behavior continues unabated.

Studies on the frequency of early misbehavior are in short supply. However, a study by Willoughby, Kupersmidt, and Bryant (2001) stands out. These researchers contacted a random sample of child care centers across North Carolina. From these centers, they collected teacher and parent reports of children between the ages of 2 and 5. The thrust of their study focused on the frequency of misbehavior, not just the prevalence. More than 400 children were included in the study.

Willoughby and his colleagues found that 60% of the study children did not exhibit daily any of the 12 measured misbehaviors. Forty percent of the preschoolers exhibited at least one form of misbehavior daily, such as hitting, kicking, punching, or stealing. More importantly, about 10% of the sample demonstrated very high levels of misbehavior each day. This group engaged in six or more misbehaviors per day!

These results correspond largely to those from our own analysis of data from the National Survey of Children (NSC). The NSC collected data from parents and teachers on a representative sample of 1,423 children ages 7–11 in the first wave. We used five measures to examine the distribution of problem behaviors generally, and by age and sex: First, we look at a teacher report on the frequency of child fighting, bullying, and teasing. Afterwards, we present data on average levels of "overall" misbehavior by age and then examine the average level of bullying by age and sex.

The teacher measure of how frequently the child bullies and teases indicates that 58% of the youths never engage in this behavior—at least in front of teachers (see Figure 10.1).

When we examine the parental measure of destroying property, we find that most youths (87%) never destroy property (see Figure 10.2).

Again, these data conform to the general findings of Willoughby et al. (2001): Most youths never engage in serious misbehavior. However, a minority of youths engage in a broad range of problem behaviors as young children. Their misbehavior is not only serious, but frequent and pervasive.

The age-graded nature of misbehavior is shown in Figures 10.3 through 10.6. Overall levels of misbehavior appear to decline quickly after age 8 and continue to do so through age 11 (see Figure 10.3). Sex differences are also readily apparent (see Figure 10.4).

Figure 10.5 depicts the age-graded nature of a single misbehavior, bullying. The pattern is fairly clear: Bullying declines monotonically across time (at least through the ages from 7 to 11). Moreover, sex differences are again apparent: a greater proportion of males bully than do females (see Figure 10.6).

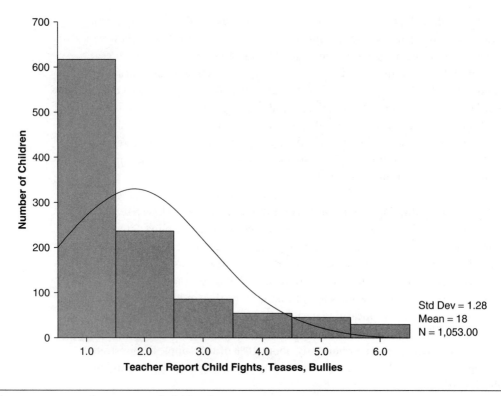

Figure 10.1 Teacher Reports of Child Fighting, Teasing, and Bullying

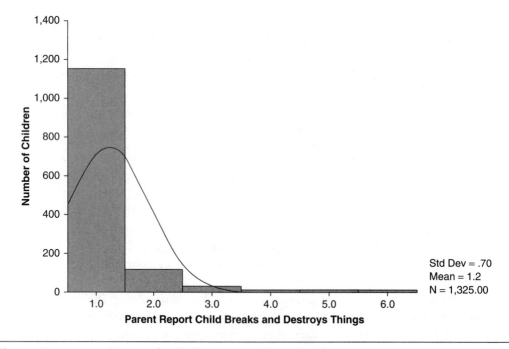

Figure 10.2 Parent Reports of Child Breaking and Destroying Things

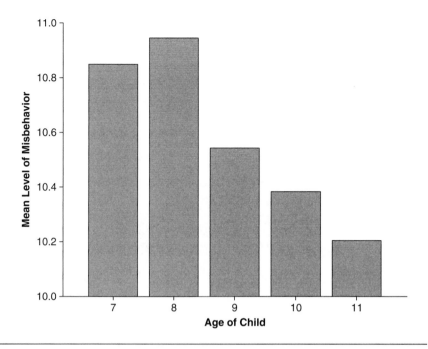

Figure 10.3   Mean Level of Child Misbehavior by Age

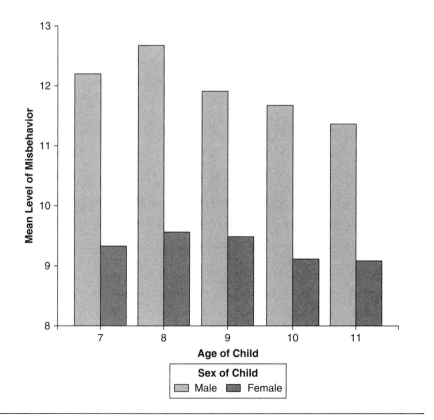

Figure 10.4   Mean Level of Child Misbehavior by Sex and Age

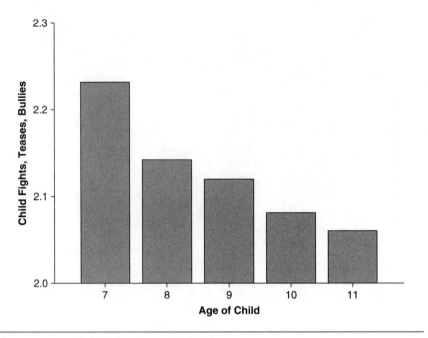

Figure 10.5   Child Fights, Teases, Bullies by Age

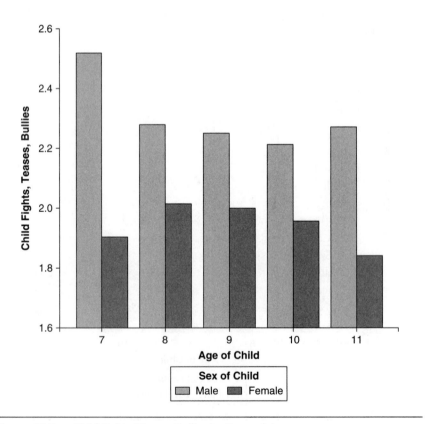

Figure 10.6   Child Fights, Teases, Bullies by Sex and Age

Overall, the picture that emerges from the NCS data corresponds with findings from other studies. Few children show very high levels of problem behaviors. Those children who do engage in misbehavior typically engage in a broad range of imprudent and taxing behaviors.

Continuity in Problem Behaviors Over Time

In Chapter 2, we discussed the difficult issue of stability in human behavior, and in Chapter 3, we discussed the various mechanisms that promote continuity in antisocial tendencies. These chapters focused largely on studies of adults and adolescents, where criminology has more information and more studies. In this section, we briefly discuss those studies that focus on young children. If there is reason to be concerned about troublesome behaviors of young children, it can be found in the studies that show relatively high rates of behavioral continuity over long periods of time.

Infants and young children possess a range of traits that make them more or less difficult to manage. Some infants, for example, are very difficult to please; they tend to cry a lot and to react with emotional outbursts to novel situations. They are also difficult to soothe, as efforts to comfort them are likely to be met with ear-piercing shrieks and tears. In short, difficult-to-manage infants create immeasurable stress and strain in the best and most consistent caregivers.

Unfortunately, many of these children will continue to exhibit their difficult and challenging traits over time. The fussy and irritable infant will often become a rambunctious toddler who then becomes a hyperactive, inattentive, and overtly threatening child. Left unchanged, these children will often develop into criminally active adults (Sampson & Laub, 1993). Of course, the period from infancy through childhood is one of rapid physical, emotional, and psychological change. Children rapidly increase in height, and their thinking slowly becomes more organized and sophisticated. Many children who show early signs of problem behavior do not continue to do so as they age and mature. Even so, given the host of biological and social changes that occur during this period, certain children show very high degrees of continuity in their behavior.

Studies show that 1- to 2-year levels of behavioral stability are rather high, typically above 0.80 (Pearson's correlation) (Achenbach, Edelbrock, & Howell, 1987; Campbell, 1995; Campbell, Breaux, Ewing, & Szumowski, 1984; Campbell, March, Pierce, Ewing, & Szumowski, 1991; Campbell, Pierce, March, Ewing, & Szumowski, 1994; Egeland, Kalkoske, Gottesman, & Erickson, 1990). Other studies also show that behavioral continuity remains strong even when measured across longer periods of time, between 3 and 7 years (Campbell & Ewing, 1990; Egeland et al., 1990; Fischer, Rolf, Hasazi, & Cummings, 1984; Richman et al., 1982). In one study, for example, Richman et al. (1982) followed a representative sample of London 3-year-olds. Using parent and teacher reports of the child's behavior, Richman found that the top 14% of the sample met the criteria for a behavioral disorder. Sixty-three percent of this group had persistent behavioral problems at age 4, and 62% were persistent at age 8, five years later. Children in this group were described as hyperactive, attention seeking, and lacking in concentration and self-discipline.

Other studies converge on the Richman findings. Egeland et al. (1990) studied a group of high-risk infants up to third grade. From infancy to first grade, 33% of the children in the sample remained classified as difficult. The percentage edged upward by second grade, when 47% were classified as persistent. Finally, in a study of Norwegian families, Mathieson and Sanson (2000) measured the behavioral difficulties of children at 18 months and then again at 30 months old. The correlation between the first and second measurement waves was 0.53, fairly strong by social science standards. Further analysis revealed that 37% of the 18-month-olds identified as high risk remained within the high-risk group at 30 months old.

Continuity in problem behavior has also been found when the length of the study period is expanded into adolescence. Investigators from the Dunedin, New Zealand, epidemiological study followed a representative birth cohort of children from age 3 onward, measured every 2 years (McGee, Partridge, Williams, & Silva, 1991). About 2% of the overall sample at age 3 were identified as difficult to manage, overactive, and inattentive by objective evaluators. At ages 11 and 15, 50% of the initially difficult 3-year-olds met the criteria for disorders specified in the *Diagnostic and Statistical Manual of Mental Disorders,* primarily attention deficit disorder (ADD). Similar levels of continuity were found in studies conducted by Campbell and her colleagues. Campbell and her research team studied two cohorts of "hard to manage" children who were 3 and 4 years of age. In the first cohort, parents identified problems with "inattention, overactivity, and discipline problems" (Campbell, 1995, p. 120). Researchers then followed up on the sample at ages 4, 6, 9, and 13. Campbell (1995) notes that at age 6, 50% of the children initially rated as very difficult at age 3 met the criteria for ADD. Teacher reports also confirmed that these children were more hyperactive and less controlled in the classroom. Again, at age 9, 48% of the group (initial 3-year-olds) met the diagnostic criteria for ADD, conduct disorder (CD), or oppositional defiant disorder (ODD), compared to only 16% of controls. Of those children who did not meet the diagnostic criteria at age 9 but who had shown consistently high levels of problem behaviors, many showed serious learning problems (Campbell, 1995). Finally, at age 13, children previously identified as having serious behavioral problems continued to manifest chronic signs of behavioral maladaptation. They were less socially competent, more aggressive, and more hyperactive. Very similar patterns were also detected for a separate sample of 4-year-olds who were followed up at ages 5 and 6. Children who scored above the 95th percentile on a measure of problem behaviors at age 4 were found to be highly likely to continue to be identified as difficult and troublesome. Forty-two percent of this group continued to score above the 95th percentile at age 5, and by age 6, more than 67% of the group met the diagnostic criteria of ODD and ADD. Only 18% of the controls met these criteria.

It is fairly safe to say that very early behavioral problems show a modest to high degree of continuity over time. Infants and children identified as particularly hard to manage are at an elevated risk of incurring a disorder later in life, especially those disorders related to activity level (ADD/ADHD), learning (LD), or behavioral disregulation (CD, ODD). In turn, early behavioral problems generate other types of risk factors, primarily peer rejection and school failure, that typically occur very early in the life course. These children, who are often hyperactive and who violate frequently rules for social interaction, are easily identified through the use of mother reports, teacher reports, and reports from students in the same classroom. Their disruptive behavior, more importantly, is likely to continue if left unchecked.

And continue it can. Olson, Bates, Sandy, and Lanthier (2000) studied 116 families over a 17-year period. Children were first assessed by their mothers at 6 months of age. Mothers reported on their child's negative emotionality and resistance to control. Children were assessed again at 13 and 24 months, at ages 7, 8, and 10, and again at 17 years. The researchers also used teacher reports of adolescent behavior, as well as adolescent self-reports of delinquent involvement. Their findings are startling: First, maternal reports of early behavioral problems (6 months, 13 months, and 24 months) were modestly correlated with maternal reports of aggression and hyperactivity between the ages of 7 and 10. These same reports, however, were largely uncorrelated with teacher reports of child problem behavior at the same age. Second, "toddlers who were perceived by mothers as highly unresponsive to them at ages 13 and 24 months received relatively high parent and self-ratings of externalizing problems late in adolescence" (p. 126). Third, infants rated as difficult to manage were also significantly more likely to be rated as hyperactive and aggressive at age 17. Finally, children who were rated as troublesome or difficult at age 2 were significantly more likely to rate themselves as inattentive at age 17. In short, Olson and her colleagues detected modest but substantial levels of stability beginning at age 6 months and extending to age 17—a period of 16½ years!

The consequences associated with long-term continuity in maladaptive behaviors are multifaceted and serious. A Finnish study conducted on 369 children—173 girls and 196 boys—measured them at the ages of 8, 14, 27, and 36. The researchers collected teacher and peer reports when appropriate, and self-reports. To help present the results, we have duplicated one of the figures used by Kokko and Pulkkinen (2000). Figure 10.7 tells part of the story of how early aggression increases the risk for social failures across the life course. From left to right, aggression measured at age 8 strongly predicted school maladjustment at age 14. In turn, school maladjustment at age 14 was substantively associated with reduced occupational alternatives at age 27 ($b = -.43$) and strongly increased problem drinking at age 27 ($b = .49$). These three measures each predicted variation in long-term unemployment between the ages of 27 and 36.

Childhood aggression sets off a chain reaction of consequences that extends across broad swaths of the life span. Aggressive children often become troubled and sometimes dangerous adolescents, who then become pathological adults. Along the way, they are very likely to fail in their education (Brook & Newcomb, 1995; Caspi, Wright, Moffitt, & Silva, 1998), suffer from serious relationship problems, be arrested and jailed (Sampson & Laub, 1993), experience mental disorders, or die a premature death because of poor health or a risky lifestyle. As if that were not enough, all of these "failures" tend to be interrelated. For example, failing out of school strongly reduces future occupational achievement, as will a criminal conviction or serving time in jail. The point is, continuity in problem behaviors located in infancy and childhood may stretch deep into the future and bring with it unwanted and deleterious consequences. For these reasons alone, serious and chronic behavioral problems demonstrated by very young children cannot and should not be ignored. If anything, early behavioral problems should serve as a large neon billboard that boldly displays things to come.

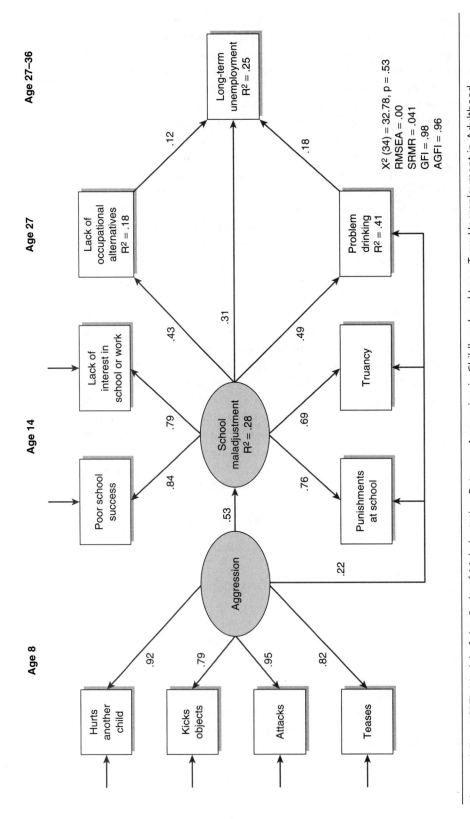

Figure 10.7 LISREL Model of the Cycle of Maladaptation Between Aggression in Childhood and Long-Term Unemployment in Adulthood

SOURCE: Figure from Kokko, K., & Pulkkinen, L. (2000). Aggression in childhood and long-term unemployment in adulthood: A cycle of maladaptation and some protective factors. *Developmental Psychology, 36(4)*, 463–472. Used with permission of the author.

BOX 10.1   Special Insert: Parenting and Aggressive Behavior

Parents are part of the "usual suspects" when it comes to causes of crime and delinquency. Any time a child or adolescent misbehaves, it is not unusual for someone to suspect that the parents erred in their responsibilities. Indeed, conventional wisdom identifies any number of parenting-related problems as the "cause" of youthful conduct problems. Parents can discipline their child too much (abuse) or too little (neglect). They can spend too much time with them (overbearing) or too little through divorce. They can supervise too much (overcontrolling) or turn a blind eye to the behaviors and whereabouts of their child (liberal parenting). The list of faults attributed to parents is long and wide.

To criminologists, it is almost an article of faith that parents influence the behavioral development of their children. Social learning theorists argue that parents model behaviors that are then mimicked, practiced, and used by their children. Social control theorists argue that parents have to set limits for their children, monitor and supervise their kids, and discipline them when they engage in wayward behavior. Strain theorists also argue that parents cause their children to behave poorly. Abusive and neglectful parents, for example, create strain and anger in their kids, who then turn their frustrations toward others. Of course, these theories are more complicated than we are making them, but the general thrust of each perspective is easily identified in the literature.

With so much attention paid to parents, it comes as a shock to many that numerous scholars now take a very critical view of the evidence relating youthful misconduct to parental socializing techniques or even to divorce. Some now openly question whether or not parents matter (Cohen, 1999; Harris, 1998; Pinker, 2002; Rowe, 1994). Perhaps the most recognized voice in this debate comes from Judith Rich Harris (1995, 1998). Her work has been the subject of numerous commentaries and debates, with some scholars being harshly critical. Nonetheless, her work is also important because it represents a serious challenge to those who locate the causes of youthful adjustment problems with parents. If her hypotheses, drawn from a larger theory, are correct, then much of the literature on the effects of parenting will be called into question.

Harris, and others, draws heavily on the work of behavioral genetics (BG). The field of BG has recently blossomed, and there are now hundreds of BG studies from which to draw data. BG is concerned with understanding how much of any given trait, such as hyperactivity or impulsiveness, is genetically influenced, and how much of the trait is environmentally influenced. Scholars in this area are quick to note, however, that families represent a "shared" environmental influence—that is, everybody within the family is exposed to the same environment. Other environmental influences, such as friends or teachers, those sources not shared by everyone in the family, are classified as "nonshared" environmental influences.

The problems with studying families, according to Harris, are twofold: First, most studies examine only one parent, usually the mother, and one child. Researchers then generalize their findings from that relationship to every other relationship in the household. Second, and perhaps more important, Harris correctly notes that almost all studies of parenting effects fail to take into account the shared genetic similarities between parents and their offspring. The evidence from BG studies, she tells us, clearly documents genetic influences on a wide range of human traits and characteristics (Plomin, 1990). According to Harris, once genetic similarity is accounted for, the association between parenting behaviors and child personality features should disappear.

(Continued)

(Continued)

So, do parents matter? And if they do matter, then how? Answers to those questions are still being sought; however, here is what is known. Children brought up in the same household often turn out very different from one another. These differences are important because they underscore one of Harris's assertions: Individuals exposed to the same environment often interpret it and respond to it very differently. This is certainly true in families. When all children and parents within a household are surveyed, clear differences between children emerge in their interpretations of their relationships with each of their parents. Parents, after all, do have favorites.

Variability within families must be contrasted with the numerous findings that show that criminal behavior is often highly concentrated in certain families. According to data from Farrington's longitudinal study of English males, 90% of all serious delinquents come from only 10% of all households. Likewise, knowing how criminally involved a youth's parents have been is a substantive predictor of that youth's future behavior. Similar levels of familial concentration have also been found for depression, anxiety, schizophrenia, ADHD, drug abuse, and alcoholism. Clearly, as we have documented elsewhere, genes play a central role in these problems. Genes, of course, are passed down from parent to child.

Studies that examine these characteristics generally find that genes are responsible for most of the variation in problem behaviors and traits—anywhere from 50% to 90%. After genes, the most influential effects are generated by nonshared sources of variation, predominantly peers. Finally, shared environmental influences, typically measured as parenting behaviors, are sometimes found to be influential, but most often not. When parenting effects are found to be influential, the size of the effect is usually small.

Does this mean that parents are unimportant in affecting their children's behavior? No, but the thrust of these findings does suggest that the ways that parents matter are likely more complex than we have realized. Parents can help to make their kids happy, or they can make them miserable. They make decisions over where their children live and consequently what schools they attend and to which types of friends they are exposed. Even so, this body of research does highlight and underscore the limits of parents to affect the traits of their children. Good parents can produce dangerous sociopaths through no fault of their own, while even the worst parent can produce a child that grows up to be a genius. Charlie Chaplin, the great star of silent films, was the unwanted son of a prostitute and an alcoholic father.

Boys and Girls

One of the more interesting issues embedded in the study of young children involves gender differences in behaviors. Data garnered from adolescents and adults tell us that there are substantial gender differences in participation in delinquency and crime, especially violent crime. Young men, it appears, exert a heavy toll on society. If we trace these differences back in time, however, several important findings emerge.

First, studies are mixed in terms of gender differences measured in infancy and very early childhood, up to age 5. Some studies show that boys are more likely to be rated as overactive, difficult to manage, and disobedient (Crowther, Bond, & Rolf, 1981; Henry, Moffitt, Robins, Earls, & Silva, 1993; Moffitt, 1990; Moffitt et al.,

2001; Willoughby et al., 2001), whereas other studies show no significant differences (Campbell & Breaux, 1983; Olson et al., 2000; Richman et al., 1982).

Second, although the evidence is mixed on gender differences early in life, there is considerable evidence of gender differences in misbehavior for school-age children (Achenbach, Howell, Quay, & Conners, 1991; Moffitt et al., 2001). Boys are far more likely to act out, engage in physical fights, and hurt or injure other children than are girls. This does not mean that girls are problem free. They are significantly more likely to experience "internalizing," as opposed to "externalizing," disorders, including depression, anxiety, and anorexia. Moreover, girls are significantly more likely to engage in indirect aggression. Indirect aggression involves the use of rumors or gossip designed intentionally to bring harm to another person. In one study of children born in Canada, researchers found that aggressive girls were almost five times more likely to engage in indirect aggression than were nonaggressive girls, and they were 16% more likely to use indirect aggression compared to highly aggressive boys (Pepler & Sedighdeilami, 1998).

Third, gender differences found in school-age children continue into adolescence and adulthood, only to become more marked and disparate. Males, the studies tell us, are more likely to show high levels of continuity in misbehavior over time (Tremblay et al., 1991). In the study of London 3-year-olds, for example, Richman et al. (1982) found that 73% of the boys continued to engage in problematic behavior through age 8, compared to 48% of the girls. For reasons unknown, girls do not engage in problem behaviors at the same levels as males, nor are they as likely to continue to act out if they do so early in life.

A Contemporary Understanding of Initial Differences

If the science of human development has revealed anything in the past 25 years, it is that infants and young children do not come into this world as empty vessels waiting to be filled with knowledge (Pinker, 2002). In many ways, they are already "wired" to behave in certain ways, acquire social knowledge, and acquire a language. This is why infants can vary tremendously in terms of temperament, with some infants being rather easy to soothe and care for, and others being unpleasant to be around (Kagan, 2003). As we have seen, these temperamental differences are related to a host of later life problems, especially as they relate to behavioral regulation. And as the previous chapter showed, there are factors that create these differences *before* the child is born.

Individual differences result from three processes: First, each person receives somewhat different DNA from their parents (monozygotic twins excluded). Second, during the process of cellular division, DNA is copied by RNA. However, only some of the original DNA is used in the process. Third, factors contained within the social environment interact with genes, and this interaction is encoded in our genetic makeup. Obviously, much of this process occurs when the child is still in the womb.

The processes that create differences between humans, in everything from eye color to behavior, begin at conception. As the process unfolds over the course of the pregnancy, the developing child begins to attain information about its environment. Modern studies, for instance, tell us that at a certain point in development, the child can hear sounds located outside the womb and will respond physically to the voice of the mother and father.

Fetal development thus takes on special meaning in understanding why human infants differ so dramatically. Nowhere are these differences more pronounced than in the development of the child's nervous system and brain. Indeed, a host of factors have been identified that influence the healthy development of a fetus's central nervous system (CNS). Mothers who live stress-filled lives expose their fetus to increased levels of stress hormones; those who smoke heavily introduce into their womb dozens of carcinogens; those who take drugs introduce potentially devastating teratogenic effects. All of these factors, unfortunately, tend to co-occur. Pregnant women who smoke also tend to live stress-filled lives, and they are at higher risk for using other drugs, especially alcohol. These combined effects take their toll on the developing nervous system and brain of the fetus, and, under certain circumstances, can permanently impair the child's growth. For example, a mother who uses cocaine (benzoylmethylecgonine) substantially increases the likelihood that blood flow from the placenta will be reduced, which, in turn, decreases nutrient intake and reduces fetal growth. The ingestion of cocaine also increases blood pressure, alters monoamines in the brain of the fetus, and impairs neuronal development (Volpe, 1992). In more extreme cases, these factors can lead to mental retardation, serious birth defects, and the death of the fetus.

The interlocking nature of these risk factors also tends to produce other risk factors related to birth complications. Obstetrical complications are significantly more elevated in drug-using mothers, but can also be prevalent in the general population. Certain complications, namely fetal hypoxia, preeclampsia, induced labor, and umbilical cord prolapse, pose substantially increased risks to CNS development. A series of studies indicates that obstetrical complications elevate the risk of future brain impairment, which, in turn, increases the risks for aggression and violence (Buka, Tsuang, & Lipsitt, 1993; O'Dwyer, 1997; Piquero & Tibbetts, 1999; Raine, Brennan, & Mednick, 1997). In one such study, Canadian researchers followed 849 boys from kindergarten through the age of 17. They gathered information on a range of obstetric complications and overall family adversity. Their findings revealed that birth complications, but especially preeclampsia, were associated with early aggressive behavior (measured at age 6) and later violent behavior (measured at age 17) (Arseneault, Tremblay, Boulerice, & Saucier, 2002). Especially revealing, however, these researchers detected important interaction effects that placed infants born to poor families at an increased risk of birth complications and later violent behavior (see also Piquero & Tibbetts, 1999; Raine et al., 1997).

Initial temperamental differences, which reflect CNS functioning, are thus strongly influenced by factors that occur before birth. The same system that links the developing fetus to the environment and allows it to differentiate the sound of a parent's voice out of a range of voices is the same process that places the fetus at risk for CNS and brain damage. These initial differences in CNS activity and brain development are largely what make infants dissimilar at birth. And as Pinker (2002) notes, this is the same evolutionary system that has allowed newborn infants the ability to operate on their environment.

Conventional wisdom once held that newborn infants were unable to act intentionally on their environment. Their cries, stares, and gazes were thought to be the work of mere reflexes. Conventional wisdom has changed. New studies have shown that newborn infants are remarkably capable of operating on their environment, of manipulating their environment to their advantage (Gopnik, Meltzoff, & Kuhl, 1999; Karr-Morse & Wiley, 1997). Indeed, infants are far more aware of their environment than anyone ever realized. Studies indicate that soon after birth, infants know the differences between things and people, that they prefer the sound of their parents' voices over any other voices, that they prefer the softness of cloth to the coarseness of a rag, and that they can mimic behaviors (Gopnik et al., 1999). In one famous study, researchers studied newborn infants, some only minutes old, by, of all things, sticking out their tongues at them (Meltzoff & Moore, 1977, 1983)! In response, Meltzoff found that infants will mimic the behavior by sticking out their tongues. Although this may sound less than impressive, it raises important questions. For example, how does an infant, who has never seen itself, know where its tongue is? And why should an infant be able to mimic social behavior? On closer inspection, and with additional evidence, it appears that newborns are, as Gopnik and her colleagues say, "computational machines." At birth, they are already processing environmental inputs and expressing their desires to be fed, cleaned, and held. Scientists, moreover, are still discovering the sophisticated nature of human infants.

Again, the point of this section is to draw attention to the factors that create initial differences between individuals and our contemporary understanding of infancy. These differences, as we've stated, are present at birth and likely extend to the developmental sequences found in the womb. Moreover, numerous other factors influence the development of the prenatal and perinatal CNS and brain. To the extent that these factors—be they genes or environmental toxins—interfere with, harm, retard, or damage the CNS or brain, they will affect the future behavior and socialization of the child. This is part of the reason that many scientists now give greater weight to understanding the effects of a child's temperament on family functioning (Harris, 1998). Given that infants seem to possess at least the rudimentary elements of a personality, and that they can engage in goal-directed behaviors, it is reasonable to assume that their temperaments will affect those around them (Brody, Stoneman, & Burke, 1988).

Development Across Childhood

The term *development* implies change from one point in time to another in some state, behavior, or trait. Applied to humans, we often talk of the development of social networks, or the development of cognition, or the development of gross motor skills. It is even "en vogue" for criminologists to discuss and research "developmental precursors" to later crime and violence. Although much is now being written about development and criminal behavior, there is little awareness of what is truly "developmental" about human development.

When we discuss human development, we are referring to the complex mix of human systems that converge to produce behavior. Humans are remarkably adaptive and show a unique genius in finding solutions to problems that are life-threatening.

We have created societies and governments that can aid in the dispersion of limited social resources, we have created medicines that vanquish illness and disease, and we have developed technologies that have elevated the quality of life for millions of humans across the globe. Add to this amazing array of achievements music and art and literature, and you can begin to see that we not only adapt to our environment, we exercise creative control over it. The point is, humans have evolved to the point where they can, for the most part, impose substantial predictability on their environment. Human beings are truly *homo sapiens* (thinking man).

Predictability emerges after rudimentary pattern recognition skills are acquired and exercised successfully. This process allows us to move from helplessness to self-sufficiency, from impulsiveness to self-control, and from social incompetence to social competence. These pattern recognition skills allow us to experience our environments through various systems. Cognitively, we accept social stimuli in the form of vision, tactile sensation, smell, and auditory signals. These various social stimuli are channeled to our brains where important information is encoded, stored, or retrieved as necessary. Depending on our cognitive abilities, we can think in the abstract, imagine the future, and plan and organize our lives. We can also understand cause and effect, as well as discern very small differences in meaning across similar situations. Our cognitive system thus attempts to make sense out of social input by recognizing patterns in our social world, encoding those patterns, drawing on them when necessary through memory, and adjusting stored patterns when new information is incorporated.

Relatedly, we also feel the various social stimuli that constantly bombard us. Music can bring us to tears or reduce us to anger. Words, spoken harshly by a friend, produce sensations of hurt and pain, whereas the sight of the sun beaming brightly on a warm day can make us feel alive and vibrant. Our emotions are closely tied to our cognitive abilities to understand subtle differences in the meaning of words, the tone in which they are said, and the manner in which they were delivered. Emotions also provide us with a way to understand our world and events that transpire within our environment. Thus, our emotional system connects us affectively to the world around us so that we not only cognitively experience an event, we give that event meaning by attaching emotions to it.

Emotions and complex cognitive interpretations influence our physiological system. The sight of a small child running into the pathway of an oncoming car generates feelings of distress that, depending on our individual differences, send some toward the child in a state of panic while others stand by frozen from fear. Visual images, say, of someone burning a flag, can generate anger, which elevates heart rate and increases blood flow and oxygenation. Certain sounds, namely, music or spoken words, can cause us to reflect on painful situations, which slows our metabolism and increases the production of serotonin in the brain, which, in turn, causes depression.

These systems are interlinked; growth in one system naturally influences growth in another. Thus, we become more cognitively advanced and more emotionally aware with age. Indeed, as we age, we are exposed to increasing amounts of social information. All the sights, sounds, actions, and reactions are processed through these systems, which ultimately draw out and record patterns. These patterns come in many forms; some are auditory, such as recognizing the sound of an alarm and making the mental connection between hearing the sound and understanding something is awry, whereas others are visual or somatosensory. Over time, we expand our pattern recognition abilities and thus develop an understanding, emotional and cognitive, of the world around us (Gopnik et al., 1999). Once we reach a level of awareness, we can then understand how our behaviors, our thoughts, and our feelings operate on our social environment. Of course, there is a wide range of variation in individuals' abilities to recognize social patterns; interpret those patterns correctly; store those patterns; and, especially, understand how their conduct affects others and their environment. The source of these differences is largely genetic and may be closely tied to IQ, mainly because individuals with low IQs have difficulty in recognizing patterns, making sense of them, and storing them for later use.

Increasing recognition of social patterns typically comes along with age and exposure to varied environments and thus represents one of the truly developmental aspects to human evolution. Embedded in the process of pattern recognition are two important concepts that also aid in the study of human development. The first is that of *context sensitivity*. Infants and very young children do not recognize the social differences that accompany varied contexts. Taking an infant into Kmart is, at least to the infant, much the same as going to a restaurant. Because they have not yet reached a level of cognitive sophistication, they do not recognize that behavioral expectations vary by context. As they age and as their brains mature, they begin to realize that behavior in one context is not appropriate in another. They will also recognize that other behaviors are no longer appropriate in any context, such as throwing a temper tantrum or playing with matches.

Context sensitivity occurs gradually over time but has an onset very early in life, typically within the first years of life. Sophistication in context sensitivity can continue to occur over long periods of the life course. Applied to the study of misconduct, recall that conduct-disordered children do not adequately recognize or respond to the behavioral expectations that vary across social domains. When they interact in certain social domains, especially school, that make outright demands on their behavior, conflict often emerges because youths with CD do not restrict their behavior to accommodate those demands. In environments where the rules for conduct are less well defined, such as on playgrounds or in the company of peers, CD youths will often not recognize the sometimes subtle behavioral expectations. In essence, they violate the informal rules for conduct that are present in most contexts.

Context sensitivity necessarily incorporates several features of human development: (a) an awareness that behavioral expectations vary by place and time, (b) an awareness that conduct can lead to conflict within the environment when behavioral expectations are not recognized or respected, and (c) an awareness that behavioral and emotional control is necessary to successfully navigate sometimes competing expectations and motivations. These three factors require advanced, but normative, cognitive functioning as they tie together processes of experience, memory, recall, and internalized regulation. Notably, these are qualities of the human brain that emerge rapidly over time but that are largely undifferentiated early in life.

The second guiding principle in studying human development is that of *self-organization*. Recall that we stated earlier that the brain is self-organizing—that is, *over time,* the various parts of the brain become organized into a single, integrated collective. Part of this process is due to the constant interaction between the brain, nervous system, and environmental stimuli. The constant interaction between environment and the brain helps to propel the brain into increased levels of efficiency and complexity. Thus, humans represent a "living system" that is "capable of responding and adapting to the environment" (Siegel, 1999, p. 215).

Viewed from the framework of self-organization, the growth that occurs from infancy through adulthood can be seen as a "movement from simplicity to complexity" (Siegel, 1999, p. 217). As children mature, they gain greater neuromuscular control, allowing them to gain mobility, and they accumulate experiences whereby patterns emerge and are reinforced. For example, toddlers gain coordinated muscle action that allows them to move from room to room, often in search of their favorite toy. As their capacity for recall also emerges, they remember where their favorite toy is typically located and the path necessary to take through their home in order to locate their toy. Movement is coupled to motivation. When they find their toy, their efforts at pattern recognition and prediction are confirmed and reinforced.

Yet what happens if the toy has been removed from its typical resting place? The pattern has been upset, thereby reducing the predictability of the environment. From the position of self-organization, one of two things is likely to happen: First, youths easily frustrated may react by crying or demanding the attention and assistance of their caregiver. Also, if they are not "object permeable," they may not cognitively understand that their toy exists elsewhere and has not simply disappeared. Either way, they have yet to gain sufficient cognitive complexity to realize that patterns are not perfect, that there is variability in outcomes over repeated attempts. Second, a youth may realize that the toy is not in its place but also realize that it may be elsewhere, such as hidden under the bed. This second child shows greater adaptability because he or she is able to respond to subtle differences found within overall general patterns. If the child seeks out and locates the toy hidden under the bed, his or her ingenuity and adaptive response pattern is reinforced (Siegel, 1999).

Complex systems thus propel humans toward maximum self-organization through a process that links biological development to environmental stimuli. This process also creates stability in behavioral response patterns over time, or as Siegel (1999) notes, "Stability of the system is achieved by the movement toward maximizing complexity" (p. 219). As experience increases and patterns are detected, successful adaptive strategies are employed that create increased behavioral flexibility to environmental demands. This, in essence, is maturation.

Stability in behavioral response patterns, as we have seen, can be adaptive (typically prosocial) or maladaptive (antisocial). Viewed from the lens of self-organization, antisocial behavior represents less-than-optimal behavioral and emotional responses to normative environmental challenges. In the example of the child who is frustrated over not being able to locate his toy, his response, crying, may provoke the caregiver to provide him with the object of desire. However, that process can also (a) establish future expectations that rely solely on the intervention of the caregiver, (b) link temperamental and ultimately inappropriate reactions to goal achievement, and (c) reduce the likelihood that other adaptive response patterns are envisioned and selected in the future (looking elsewhere for the toy).

The previous discussion sets the stage for understanding what is truly "developmental" about human development. The processes of self-organization and context sensitivity incorporate the various systems that compose humans. In the next section, we analyze the fundamental aspects of human development as they relate to these interrelated systems.

Physical Growth

The most obvious form of early development is physiological. From infancy through preadolescence, tremendous physiological growth occurs. During this time period, for example, individuals will grow more than 5 ft. on average and increase their weight by an average of 100 lbs. This growth is fueled by increased cellular metabolism, which requires sustained nutritional intake. With increased metabolism comes increased bone density, strengthening of the heart muscle, an expansion in the volume of the lungs, and increased nervous system activity. The rate of growth, especially during the first 3 years of life, is significant and remains unmatched until the onset of puberty. It has been estimated that if the rate of physical growth seen in childhood extended across adolescence, we would weigh more than 11,000 lbs. in adulthood.

Other forms of maturation are also clearly evident. Soon after birth, the uncoordinated actions of the legs and arms give way to advances in gross and fine motor skills that allow youths to crawl and eventually walk and run. The same processes allow youths to manipulate their digits with increased efficiency and precision, allowing them to clutch and grab hold of objects. It is interesting to note that aggression, in the form of hitting, stealing, biting, and slapping, increases precipitously at the time when a child gains mobility and coordinated muscle action. Mobility, coupled with fine motor skills, brings children into contact with others, and with valued objects. Thus, much of the misbehavior of young children may emerge out of increased contact with other children and with objects of their desire (Hay, Castle, & Davies, 2000; Tremblay, Pihl, Vitaro, & Dobkin, 1994).

Brain Development in Context

Outside of physical development, the real growth occurs hidden away from casual observation in the networks of synapses that fill the brain of the young child. At birth, the infant brain has just about all the neurons it will ever have, and that number will remain relatively steady until old age begins to reduce it. However, the construction of neural pathways that link axon to dendrite and that make the transfer of neurotransmitters possible increases markedly. Modern science, with its complicated imaging systems, now tells us that brain cells are "spontaneously firing, sending off bursts of electricity and trying to signal one another" even during "early embryonic development" (Gopnick et al., 1999, p. 184).

At no other point in time will growth in the brain equal the growth witnessed during the first 3 years of life. The expansion of neural pathways occurs at a rate unsurpassed even in adult brains. Although the brain of the young child is only one fourth the size of an adult brain, by age 2, it reaches metabolic rates on par with those of adults. Moreover, Gopnick and her coauthors (1999) tell us that "by age three the little child's brain is actually twice as active as an adult brain. This bristling activity remains at twice the level of an adult until the child reaches the age of nine or ten" (p. 186).

The growth in the wiring of the young brain appears even more pronounced when we consider that an adult brain has about 100 billion nerve cells, or "about the same number as stars in the Milky Way" (Gopnick et al., 1999, p. 183). If that is not enough to highlight the rapid growth in a child's brain, consider too that it takes about a "quadrillion connections—that's 1,000 trillion—to wire an adult brain" (Gopnick et al., 1999, p. 182). These connections, as we have noted before, are "activity dependent," that is, they depend on environmental stimulation to act as the impetus for growth in synaptic structures. The brain of the young child is thus bombarded with information that the brain attempts to make sense of—that is, to elucidate patterns. This information comes from internal states, such as being hungry or sick, as well as the external environment.

Recall, too, that the brain develops in a manner from least complex to most complex. Although we have covered the development of the brain in Chapters 5 and 6, it is important to note again that the areas of the brain responsible for self-regulation do not mature until around 25 years of age. The orbitalfrontal cortex, which is dually wired to the limbic system and the cortex, has a unique ability to regulate sympathetic and parasympathetic nervous system responses. In essence, the ability to control emotional states, and to respond to environmental stress and strains, emerges only after the orbitalfrontal cortex becomes sufficiently "wired." Of course, anything that interferes with the development of neuronal structures in the cortex, such as ingestion of neurotoxins, may retard further growth, thus allowing the limbic system greater overall influence on behavior.

Genes and the proteins they code for control the ontogenic development of the brain. It is estimated that 60% of our genes work to code for the brain, which should tell us something of its importance. Brain tissue is valuable material, evolutionarily speaking, and it forms at a great metabolic cost. Eventually, the frontal cortex of the brain will contain more than 60,000 miles of synapses, but before that degree of development is achieved, the young brain will have interacted with its environment for at least 25 years. These interactions are important for most children, but we are now only beginning to understand the physical and chemical reasons why early interactions with caregivers influence behavioral development.

Some of the most fascinating research in this area comes from studies into institutionalized children from other countries. For example, January 1990 saw the overthrow and eventual execution of Nicolae Ceausescu and his family. Ceausescu, the communist dictator of Romania, mandated that every woman under 45 years of age produce at least five children. Those who refused were imprisoned and contraception was made illegal. If a family could not support their offspring, they could turn them over to the state. The state, in turn, placed children in orphanages—many of which did not have running water or other basic necessities. Estimates indicate that more than 100,000 children lived in Romanian orphanages (Wilson, 2003). To say that the environments of these orphanages were neglectful would be an understatement; they were horrible places where young children suffered from a lack of human attention, a lack of love, and a lack of basic provisions, such as food. Eighty-five percent of the children were placed in orphanages in the first month of their life (O'Conner, Rutter, Beckett, Keaveney, & Kreppner, 2000). Infants spent up to 20 hours per day in their cribs, largely because caregiver ratios were 10:1 for infants and 20:1 for children more than 3 years of age (Ames & Carter, 1992; Chugani et al., 2001).

After the overthrow of the government in 1989, Romania allowed the world to look inside its once closed society. Much of the world was shocked to see infants and young children locked away in deplorable conditions. According to Federici (1998):

> The level of dirt, infection and contagion is overwhelming. Urine and feces typically line the institution floors. Viruses such as Hepatitis B and C, HIV, meningitis, and some instances of encephalitis and cyto-megalovirus . . . run rampant. . . . Abuse is common, with emotional deprivation being at the top of the list. . . . Children are bathed only once a week in mass groups with unsanitized water. There is virtually no heating or ventilation and most children are crowded together, with five to a bed. Babies are often left in cribs for days or weeks at a time, wrapped very tightly in blankets so they do not crawl or get out and injure themselves. The only term I can think of to adequately describe what I saw is "warehousing." Many of these children are so bored and isolated that they engage in repetitive self-stimulation or self-mutilation. (p. 70)

At the time, most of the orphaned children showed signs of severe neglect, including rocking back and forth, staring at the movements of their own hands, and even banging their heads against walls and other solid objects. Empirical examinations found that almost every child had severely delayed fine and gross motor skills, had delayed language development, and had delayed social-behavioral development (Glennen, 2002; Wilson, 2003). Almost 60% of children scored below the 5th percentile in weight at the time they were adopted (Ames, 1997); almost half were low birth weight infants (Johnson & Dole, 1999). Further research found that orphaned children lost 1 month of growth for every 3 months they spent in the orphanage. According to Glennen's review (2002) of institutionally raised youths, at the time of adoption children were usually 2 standard deviations below normal on height, weight, and head circumference.

Physical delays in development were not the only problems orphaned children developed. The most common problem, and one of the most striking, was a delay in language processing. Research by Gindis (1999) found that 60% of youths 24 to 30 months of age did not speak; by 1 year, 14% uttered two-word statements; by age 3 to 4, "the children were described as having limited vocabulary, receptive language delays, and unintelligible speech" (Glennen, 2002, p. 336). Three problems likely caused these delays in language acquisition: First, caregivers rarely spoke directly to the young children. When they did, it was in the form of a short command (e.g., "quit," "don't," or "be quiet"). Second, the overall environment offered little in the way of auditory, visual, or tactile stimulation. There were no televisions or any other sources from which language could be acquired. Finally, because children were separated by age, young children were not exposed to older youths and the language they had acquired.

Citizens from mainly Western countries adopted thousands of orphaned youths. This situation provided for a natural experiment. For the first time, large numbers of youths who had suffered from severe environmental deprivation could be studied and their progress tracked. These studies generally arrived at the same conclusions: First, the effects of severe environmental deprivation appear to depend, in part, on the length of time deprivation was experienced. Infants adopted prior to spending 6–8 months in the orphanage generally had better outcomes over time. Those who spent more than 8 months, especially those who spent more than a year in the orphanage, were generally those who had the most serious developmental problems later in life. According to Glennen (2002), 90% of youths adopted after the age of 12 months continued to show developmental problems. In contrast, children adopted before 6 months of age developed normally.

Second, and relatedly, not all children suffered developmental delays, even if they spent much of their childhood institutionalized. Rutter, Kreppner, and O'Connor (2001) found, for example, that at age 6, more than 60% of adopted youths (adopted prior to 6 months of age) developed normally and did not suffer any cognitive or behavior deficits. For youths adopted after age 2, 25% went on to develop within normal parameters. Again, we see individual variation to severe environmental stress: Some children who faced prolonged exposure to a neglectful, abusive environment went on to demonstrate remarkable developmental resilience.

Third, most youths who lived for a prolonged period of time in these environments suffered from a range of delays. Federici (1998) notes that most of the problems were "characterized by poor growth, regressive or absent language, problems with attention/concentration, self-stimulatory behavior, and deficient memory" (Wilson, 2003, p. 480). Other studies have found that these youths continue to show medical problems, behavioral problems, and limited cognitive growth to adolescence (Fisher, Ames, Chisholm, & Savoie, 1997; Marcovitch et al., 1997). They also have a difficult time bonding to their adoptive parents and appear indiscriminately friendly toward other adults.

Researchers suspected that early deprivation somehow influenced brain and endocrine functioning in these children. Lack of human contact produces stress, which in turn creates a physiological response. Stress is modulated by the hypothalamic-pituitary-adrenocortical (HPA) system. When stress is experienced, the hypothalamus will release corticotrophin releasing factor (CRF), which will enter the pituitary. The pituitary will then secrete adrenocorticotropich hormone into the blood, where it will trigger in the adrenal glands the release of stress hormones called glucocorticoids (cortisol and corticosterone). Cortisol levels can be detected through saliva and vary throughout the day. High levels of cortisol eventually feed back to the hypothalamus. When enough cortisol has built up, the hypothalamus will stop its release of CRF, which ends the stress response.

The HPA system usually functions to increase one's survival, but scientists have found that prolonged exposure to stress, and more importantly, to the hormonal by-products of stress, can have very negative effects on the developing brain. Cortisol, for example, is deeply implicated in learning, memory, and other cognitive functions. Under normal circumstances, such as when a physical threat is present, high levels of cortisol impair these functions so that the sympathetic nervous system can reflexively react to the threat. However, when the stress response stays on, the hormone remains present in the blood and interferes with cognitive processing.

Prolonged stress is also associated with major depression and psychopathology in animals and adults (Kaufman, Plotsky, Nemeroff, & Charney, 2000). Social deprivation, which likely causes an abundance of stress, has been shown to increase adrenocortical and noradrenergic responses, as well as reduce serotonin 5-hydroxyindoleacetic acid in animal models (Chugani et al., 2001). Prolonged exposure to glucocorticoids, the chemical by-products of stress, has been linked to damage to the limbic system of the brain (McEwen, 2000; Sapolsky, 2000), dendritic remodeling, and neurogenesis in the hippocampus (Chugani et al., 2001).

In a direct test of the effects of early social deprivation, Chugani and his colleagues (2001) used positron emission tomography (PET) to examine the brains of 10 Romanian children. They compared their results to the brain scans of 17 normal adults and seven other children. The Romanian orphans scored significantly below average across a range of neuropsychological measures, including low IQ (mean = 81.4), low receptive language, and low impulse control. They also scored in the clinical range on total behavioral problems, thought problems, and attention problems.

PET scans revealed decreased glucose metabolism bilaterally in the prefrontal cortex, the amygdala, and the hippocampus. As we mentioned before, the cortex and the limbic system are intricately wired together and work in a symbiotic fashion. Thus, it seems likely that structural deficiencies in the brains of Romanian orphans, most likely caused by prolonged exposure to stress and stress by-products, is responsible for the observable behavioral, emotional, and neurological problems exhibited by many of the young children. We note, however, that some of the children remained resilient to even the most extreme deprivation, which hints to genetic differences between children that insulate some youths from the deleterious effects of early social deprivation.

Of course, most children are not exposed to such brutal conditions. Instead, they develop in environments where their needs are met, they are showered with love and affection, and their safety is assured. If early social deprivation can cause structural and functional deficits in the child's developing brain, can social enrichment protect against risk, or even help build a healthy brain? The answer appears to be yes to both questions, but only to a degree.

Early attachment to consistent caregivers has been linked to a wide range of prosocial and adaptive behaviors. Historically, these findings have been interpreted from a psychosocial perspective—that is, early attachments influence the psychological and social functioning of the child. Modern science has helped to better specify the mechanisms that translate early emotional attachments to social adjustment. It appears that the love that caregivers feel toward their offspring has a biochemical basis. Moreover, the experience of receiving human love, in the form of physical holding, touch, and verbal soothing, stimulates and adjusts the neuro-chemistry of the growing child.

Although still tentative and in need of further study, two hormones, oxytocin (OT) and arginine vasopressin (AVP), have been found to be related to social bonding. Most of this evidence comes from studies of other mammals. In general, these studies find that as OT and AVP increase, they produce more positive social interactions, aid in the creation of social bonds, create selective parent-infant attachments, and reduce the intensity and duration of stress (Wismer-Fries, Ziegler, Kurian, Jacoris, & Pollak, 2005). In humans, studies have found that increased OT and AVP produce feelings of social trust. And in one of the more important studies, again using an experimental group of Romanian children, Wismer-Fries and her colleagues found that OT levels in youths from normal families were significantly higher than those in children who had experienced prolonged deprivation in early childhood. More importantly, after about a half-hour of physical interaction with their mothers, normal children experienced a marked increase in OT levels. Children with histories of significant neglect did not.

Social attachments likely have a biological underpinning. Assuming that OT and AVP can mitigate the effects of stress and can aid in the creation of attachments, it appears reasonable to assume that quality caregiving matters because it helps the brain to develop normally. Once more, however, even Wismer-Fries and her colleagues note that important individual differences remain. For genetic reasons, some children simply do not require as much adult interaction for bonds to develop, and they appear resistant to even the most severe environmental stressors.

Brain development in infancy and childhood remains unparalleled throughout the life span. At no other time in life will the brain undergo such rapid growth, nor will the brain be able to absorb the volume of information presented to the child early in life. Although much of this growth is directed by genes, the process of growth and differentiation can be influenced by a range of environmental variables, including prenatal drug exposure, lead, and social deprivation.

Language Development

Key to healthy development is the acquisition of language and symbolic thought. Why? On one hand, language allows for communication—the expression of wants and desires, emotions, and ideas. It allows two parties to verbally negotiate a situation, it allows for instruction and further learning, and it allows a parent to apply verbal limits to a child's behavior. In short, the acquisition of language allows the child to interact with the rest of the world.

Symbolic thought, on the other hand, coincides closely with the acquisition of language, largely because words are nothing more than symbolic representations for actions, feelings, and things. Take, for example, the letter "W." The letter W represents a certain sound, but it clearly does not take on a physical form (you have never seen the letter W cross the street in front of you). Similarly, numbers (1, 2, 3 . . .) are merely cognitive symbols representing some level of quantification. Like the letter W, the number 2 does not really exist (you cannot shake the hand of number 2).

Symbolic thought thus allows for cognitive abstractions, which gives children the ability to quantify objects, categorize sets of related objects, and react appropriately to complex social cues. This is especially important as children begin to act with intention on those around them. That is, as youths mature cognitively, they become more aware of how to accurately judge the intentions of others, as well as their emotional state. They begin to detect and understand subtle differences in facial expressions or the tone of a voice, and they begin to ascribe meaning to gestures, winks, and glances. These changes set the stage for youths to mature socially and to acquire increased information of substantially greater complexity. They also allow youths to better negotiate the complex social terrain found in schools, neighborhoods, and intimate social relationships. Language allows understanding, allows for planning, and multiplies the ways that people can solve problems.

It is the acquisition of language that sets children along a pathway toward or away from serious misbehavior. Indeed, the term *infancy* was taken from the Greek language and means "one without speech." For many years, scientists believed that language had to be taught to young children, much like they have to be taught to ride a bike when they get older. Many of our sociologically trained friends continue to point to language as being produced by the environment. And they continue to point out the fact that biology cannot tell us why some children speak Mandarin and others speak English.

Yet new insights into language acquisition have challenged these common assumptions. Today, many scholars openly call into question whether language is socially learned, or if language (any language) is simply acquired. Data from cognitive scientists now point out that the *capacity* for language is inherited, much like you inherit the genetic code to grow taller, gain weight, or lose your hair. As Pinker (2002) notes, barring serious defect or injury, all humans have the capacity for language. Language is what separates us from other species, and it is one of the most fundamental developmental goals for all children regardless of the culture in which they live. Indeed, so strong is the propensity for language that some twins, triplets, and quads will actually *develop* their own language. This process, known as "idiolalia," is largely spontaneous and thus has not been learned. Idiolalia allows twins, triplets, and quads the ability to communicate with each other, but to their parents and others their incomprehensible sounds have no meaning. They will lose this language once their primary language is acquired, and they will have no memories of once speaking this "foreign" language.

Infants and young children are preprogrammed to acquire a language, as their brains appear to organize over time in a way that makes verbal communication and mental abstractionism feasible. Further evidence shows that young children can acquire more than one language, and even have the capacity to develop specialized dialects and accents. More importantly, bilingual children are more likely to speak fluently the language of the dominant culture than they are the language found in their own home (Harris, 1998)! In all cases, however, the capacity to acquire a new language diminishes with age. As individuals mature, their ability to "learn" a new language deteriorates substantially. By the time a person has reached adulthood, learning a new language will take significant effort, and learning proper intonation, emphasis, and accent will likely never happen. The acquisition of language is thus heavily age graded.

The ability to acquire a new language may be age graded, but numerous similarities between languages make their acquisition easier for young children. For example, any language is composed of a set of rules. These rules govern the meaning of words (semantic rules), the construction of sentences (syntactic rules), and the sounds of words (phonological rules). Combined, these rules create patterns that can be understood and deciphered by young children once their brains have matured sufficiently. Interestingly, more than 70% of the world's languages share these rules (such as noun-verb agreement). That is, although they may sound different and employ different words for similar objects, the structure of many languages is similar. This similarity is likely what makes acquisition easier for young children.

But if the capacity for language acquisition is inherited, does this mean that environment does not matter? Of course not. Environment does partly determine which language and which dialect within a language a child will acquire. Environment is also the source of various forms of cognitive stimulation that will expand a child's vocabulary. On the extreme end, studies of severely environmentally deprived children have also revealed that there is a sensitive period for language development. By age 3 or 4, a child must be exposed to a language to effectively acquire it and be able to employ it. If they go without sufficient environmental exposure, the region of the brain responsible for language becomes closed off as plasticity is lost and lateralization inhibited (Karr-Morse & Wiley, 1997).

If all is in order, however, the coos of an infant will give way to utterances, typically of nouns, and then give way to simple statements (see Figure 10.8). All the while, children are gaining considerable knowledge about their surrounding world through the cumulative addition of words that are used to express feelings and ideas, and to label objects. But even here, children do not appear to simply add words to their vocabulary in a simple additive arrangement—that is, one word at a time. Research into vocabulary growth reveals instead that children's vocabularies grow at a compounding rate over time. Far from a straight line increase, a child's vocabulary grows by leaps and bounds through adolescence. At any one time, children may be "cognitively mapping" 1,600 words, acquiring an average of 3,000 new words each year.

Vocabulary growth, however, differs significantly from child to child. A high-achieving third-grade student, for example, can outperform a low-achieving 12th-grade student on vocabulary tests! Yet intervention efforts designed to expand a child's vocabulary have proven largely ineffective. In one such intervention, researchers Betty Hart and Todd Risley (1995) placed a group of children from a low-income, predominantly African American school into a vocabulary-intensive environment. At one level, as Hart and Risley note, the children seemed to learn new words and seemed to be able to employ those words accurately. However, Hart and Risley then compared their intervention children with children from a laboratory school. These were primarily children of college professors at the University of Kansas. The differences were startling: The professors' children spoke twice as much, asked more questions, and had significantly larger vocabularies. The intervention program, moreover, proved to produce only short-term results that could not be sustained over time. In the end, disadvantaged youths continued to fare worse than other youths. This led Hart and Risley to conclude that "by the age of 4, when the children had become competent users of the syntax and pragmatic

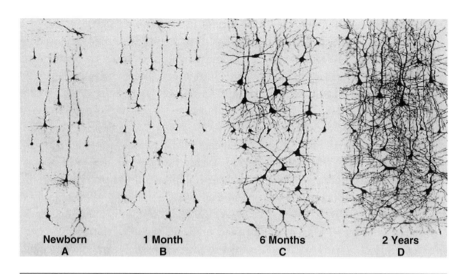

Newborn   1 Month   6 Months   2 Years
   A   B   C   D

Figure 10.8   Neocortical Growth Over the First 2 Years of Life

functions of their language, patterns of vocabulary growth were already established and *intractable*" (p. 16, emphasis added).

Years later, Hart and Risley again undertook a study of vocabulary growth. This time, they collected data on 42 families of mixed economic backgrounds. The research began when the children were between the ages of 7 and 9 months. Each month, Hart and Risley videotaped the casual interactions between parents and their children, and then they transcribed every word into a larger database. They followed each family for almost 3 years. Their results are presented in Table 10.1.

First, Hart and Risley (1995) note that between 86% and 98% of a child's vocabulary was shared by the parent. This finding strongly hints at the likelihood that parents are a substantial source of words and meanings. Second, as seen in Table 10.1,

Table 10.1   Averages for Measures of Parent and Child Language and Test Scores

	13 Professional		23 Working-Class		6 Welfare	
Measures & Scores	*Parent*	*Child*	*Parent*	*Child*	*Parent*	*Child*
IQ score at age 3	117	—	107	—	79	—
Recorded vocabulary size	2,176	1,116	1,498	749	974	525
Average utterances per hour	487	310	301	223	176	168
Average different words per hour	382	297	251	216	167	149

SOURCE: From Hart, B., & Risley, T. (1995). *Meaningful differences in everyday experiences of young american children* (pp. 176 and 234). Baltimore, MD: Paul H. Brookes Publishing Co., Inc. Reprinted by permission.

NOTE: Parent utterances and differeont words were averaged over 13–36 months of child age. Child utterances and different words were averaged for the four observations when the children were 33–36 months old.

children were much more like their parents in terms of total vocabulary size, average utterances per hour, and the number of different words they employed per hour. Yet these similarities also reveal substantial differences by social class: Professional parents averaged 2,176 words in their vocabulary compared to 1,498 words for working-class parents and only 974 words for parents on welfare. Similar patterns were also detected in average utterances per hour and in the number of different words used each hour.

Vocabulary growth also differed significantly by parental grouping. Hart and Risley estimate that over a 4-year period, a child brought up in a "professional" home would "accumulate experience with 45 million words, an average child in a working-class family 26 million words, and an average child in a welfare family 13 million words" (Hart & Risley, 2003, p. 9). More importantly, these differences, measured as early as 3 years of age, strongly predicted school performance at age 9 or 10. Children exposed to various words and their associated "symbolic thoughts" were substantially more likely to excel in school.

The acquisition of language thus varies across children, with those youths who gain greater language skills and vocabulary sizes typically faring better later in life. Yet differences between youths in vocabulary size and rate of growth are only part of the story told by Hart and Risley's data. When they examined the emotional content of the language to which children were exposed, they found very large differences between parents on welfare and middle-class and professional families. Hart and Risley (1995) counted the number of positive affirmations (I love you, you are great) and the number of prohibitions (don't do that, stop it, you are bad) stated by parents during each videotaped session. Children residing with professional parents were exposed to

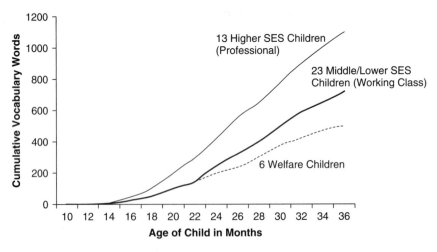

Figure 10.9   The Founders' Network

SOURCE: From Hart, B., & Risley, T. (1995). *Meaningful differences in everyday experiences of young american children* (pp. 176 and 234). Baltimore, MD: Paul H. Brookes Publishing Co., Inc. Reprinted by permission.

32 affirmations and 5 prohibitions per hour; children in working-class families were exposed to 12 affirmations and 7 prohibitions per hour; children in welfare families were exposed to 5 affirmations and 11 prohibitions per hour (the pattern of more positive affirmations and fewer prohibitions found in middle- and upper-class homes was reversed in welfare families)! Extrapolated over the course of a year, kids in upper-income families receive about 166,000 encouragements and 26,000 prohibitive statements. This is compared to welfare families, where children receive 26,000 encouragements and 57,000 discouragements!

These differences may translate into differences in behaviors. Silva (1987) estimates that language problems affect between 3% and 15% of the general population. These percentages are substantively different for children who display behavioral problems, however. Benasich, Curtiss, and Tallal (1993) found that language problems affected between 24% and 65% of children with obvious behavioral problems. Further estimates indicate that between 60% and 80% of all young children who display language deficits also display high levels of aggression (Brinton & Fujiki, 1993; Dionne, Tremblay, Boivin, Laplante, & Perusse, 2003). More importantly, language delays in infancy and early childhood appear to place children on trajectories toward aggression and later criminal behavior (Dionne et al., 2003; Stattin & Klackenberg-Larsson, 1993). Using a sample of 562 19-month-old twins, Dionne and her colleagues (2003) found that language delays *precede* the onset of aggression, and that aggression and expressive vocabulary were highly heritable. Physical aggression was 59% heritable in the sample of monozygotic twins, and vocabulary was 85% heritable.

The picture that emerges is one of cumulative disadvantage beginning very early in life. Differences in infancy carry forward in time to predispose certain youths to both aggression and language difficulties. By age 3, children differ markedly in their language skills and vocabulary sizes. These differences grow at a compounding rate over time so that by the time a child reaches fourth grade, his or her performance in school is easily predicted. Moreover, the negative and hostile communication patterns that comprise so many delinquent and conduct-disordered youths are shared by their parents, who offer only limited verbal praise and heavy doses of criticism. Taken in combination, youths from disadvantaged backgrounds appear to accumulate substantial delays in language that often co-occur with physical aggression. These early differences thus place children on pathways toward school failure and future violence, which may further mortgage their future (Sampson & Laub, 1993).

Social Development

The acquisition of language opens the door to further learning, but it also leads to increased social interactions. Humans are, by nature, social animals. And similar to our penchant to acquire language, we also seem preprogrammed to desire interactions with others. Of course, our first interactions are with our caregivers, usually our parents. These interactions encompass most of the first few years of life until we enter preschool or elementary school. At that time, our interactions blossom in number and diversify in quality as we are thrust into settings where other children and adults compete for our attention.

Social relationships are the glue of any society. They are the mechanisms through which information is passed, emotions are expressed, and cultural values are sustained. But on a smaller scale, social relationships form the bedrock of our experiences—experiences that ultimately influence the quality of our lives. It is in these relationships where individual differences in temperament, intelligence, language skills, and behavior coalesce into observable patterns of interaction. In these relationships, we are both passive recipient, influenced by the traits, behaviors, and beliefs of others, and active participant. We affect those around us as much as we are affected by them. And at their best, social relationships represent systems of exchange whereby benefits are bestowed and advantages realized. At their worst, however, social relationships represent another domain where individuals fail, bringing harm to themselves and to others.

Failure in social relationships is where our interests lie, if for only one reason: Childhood relationship problems represent one of the strongest and most enduring predictors of future problems across the life course. For instance, in one of the most extensive studies to date, Cairns and Cairns (1994) found that youths with serious relationship problems in the fourth grade were significantly more likely to drop out of school, use drugs during high school, and engage in aggressive behaviors later in life. Findings such as these have led some scholars to argue that childhood relationship problems serve as a forecast of the bad things yet to come (Bagwell, Coie, Terry, & Lochman, 2000; Coie, Terry, Lenox, Lochman, & Hyman, 1995).

What is it about problems in early social relationships that could be so foreshadowing? We offer three reasons why early social problems are telling. First, most conflict and aggression involve confrontation between two or more people. A child who disobeys his or her parents' commands generates stress and anger; a toddler who strikes another creates pain and resentment. Second, certain individuals possess traits that make conflict and aggression more likely. These traits, such as insensitivity to others, lack of empathy, selfishness, and impulsivity, are played out within social relationships. More importantly, many children do not possess these traits, and they find those who do difficult to associate with. This situation leads to certain youths being rejected from prosocial playgroups. Finally, failed relationships generate a range of consequences. As we have already pointed out, aggressive children are highly likely to be rejected by prosocial peers, but they are also likely to draw the ire of their teachers and to be labeled and stigmatized. Behavior has consequences, and these consequences begin to accumulate as soon as children enter into social relationships.

Young children are remarkably capable of expressing what they want from friends and playmates, and they actively select others to join their playgroups based on those characteristics (Coie et al., 1995). In other words, children are sophisticated actors within didactic and multichild relationships. These preferences hinge on many factors, such as age and gender, but some of these factors are also behavioral. Typical toddlers desire playmates who are trustworthy, fun, and accepting. And they exclude from consideration children who are temperamentally difficult or who violate playgroup norms. This is not to say that young children automatically exclude others who are aggressive. Even here, children ascribe different meanings to aggressive acts. Some aggressive acts are viewed as less blameworthy, especially when the aggression was used in an instrumental way (to get a toy, for example) (Hay, Zahn-Waxler, Cummings, & Iannotti, 1992). However, some aggressive acts are viewed by children as dangerous and unwanted. Typically, these acts involve the use of "dysregulated" aggression (Cummings, Iannotti, & Zahn-Waxler, 1989), or acts that involve the use of proactive aggression without thought of the feelings and reactions of others in the playgroup (Hay et al., 2000). As Hay and his colleagues found in their study of British 18- to 30-month-olds, very young children are capable of evaluating the intentions of others, and they base their behavioral responses on those intentions.

Children who use physical aggression without thought of the harm it brings to others show substantial degrees of stability in their behavior over time (Shaw, Gilliom, Ingoldsby, & Nagin, 2003). Physical aggression drops between the time children gain mobility until the time they enter school, but a small percentage of children, between 5% and 6%, continue to show dysregulated aggression (Shaw et al., 2003). These children are of special concern, primarily because they show high degrees of interactional continuity over time. These youths are also the ones most likely to suffer from a large range of problems throughout their time in school, including peer rejection, school failure, expulsion, and delinquency (Tremblay, Masse, Pagani, & Vitaro, 1996).

Physically aggressive children upset many of the social situations they enter. In a preschool, physically aggressive children are cause for concern because of the harm they can visit on other children. In elementary school, physical aggression interrupts the classroom environment. As a result, it also appears to jeopardize the education of youth, and it appears to create conditions within the environment where aggressive youths become more likely to associate with other physically aggressive children. The result is not difficult to imagine: Aggression becomes interwoven in the daily fabric of their lives. Physically aggressive children act on impulse, they show little remorse for their actions, and they consistently interpret the actions of others as hostile. Moreover, they also show little empathy and care for others, and what empathy they may have dwindles with every successful act of aggression (Hastings, Zahn-Waxler, Robinson, Usher, & Bridges, 2000; Kestenbaum, Farber, & Sroufe, 1989; see also Tremblay et al., 1994).

Such traits and experiences are not conducive to getting along well with others; learning; or acquiring the skills necessary for various life course transitions, such as getting a job or going to college. Unfortunately, without intervention, physically aggressive youths are likely to continue to act in ways that mortgage their future and that bring harm to the lives of others. Their physical aggression compounds their relationship problems and creates further learning deficiencies. With the onset of puberty, physically aggressive youths, especially boys, will undergo profound physical and social changes that have the potential to create serious harm—for themselves and for others. We examine these changes in the next chapter on adolescence.

BOX 10.2 The Continuing Saga of Stanley: A Good Ending

Shaw (1930) carefully followed Stanley's progress over his later teenage and young adulthood years. And what progress it was. Stanley reported that he had developed a strong and solid emotional relationship with Mrs. Smith, with whom Stanley had been placed as a guardian. Stanley said that Mrs. Smith was "a very kind and good woman with a pleasing personality and intelligent. At that time I did not realize how much her sympathy and advice would determine my whole life in the future" (p. 169). Stanley not only felt a bond with Mrs. Smith, but also with her children. For example, Stanley reported that "Her son was of my age, and I was fond of him from the start. . . . He was not the tough-guy type. . . . He was a gentleman, well-bred and refined" (p. 169).

Mrs. Smith's home and daughters also impressed Stanley.

> *They seemed to accept me and not look down on me. The home throughout was modestly furnished and had an atmosphere of warmth and kindness. . . . They took me at my face value and treated me as if I were an honest young man. (Shaw, 1930, p. 169)*

Thus, Stanley had found a home that he had never had, and this aspect of his life seemed to make a significant difference in his desire to commit criminal activity. Even when times were tough for Stanley, Mrs. Smith

> *stood erect and very calmly and seriously informed me that I was as good as anybody. . . . It impressed upon my mind that there were really some good people on this earth, and life was worth living with a kind woman like this. (Shaw, 1930, p. 172)*

As time went on, Shaw encouraged Stanley to take on a position in sales, which seemed suited for Stanley in terms of its autonomy and lack of supervision. Stanley took a job as a salesman, and in his own words, "Salesmanship is hard work, but I've learned to like it. It pays well and it puts a fellow on his mettle" (Shaw, 1930, p. 182). It appears that Stanley learned to respect work and conformity.

Whether it was himself, his family, his friends, his parents, his environment, or other players, we don't know. It seems that Stanley's transition to become a conventional citizen was rather amazing given his likely trajectory toward a life of crime. The fact that Stanley, given his early offending, did not end up becoming a chronic offender is atypical. Furthermore, it is pleasantly surprising that Stanley did not end up as one of the serious offenders that we had to worry about. Nevertheless, it is true—Stanley made it out of the prototype. Why did this occur?

The answer is that Stanley had the fortunate opportunity that most individuals who are predisposed to become chronic offenders do not. That is, Stanley was eventually taken in by a family who loved him, and he acquired a job that fulfilled him and met his expenses. Additionally, Stanley realized that he had an investment in conventional society; specifically, Stanley had a lovely wife and child and a job that he liked. These factors made Stanley committed to a crime-free life.

CHAPTER 11

Postpubescence

Adolescence and Adulthood

It is a youthful failing to be unable to control one's impulses.

Seneca (5 BC–65 AD)

What a mistake to suppose that the passions are strongest in youth! The passions are not stronger, but the control over them is weaker! They are more easily excited, they are more violent and apparent; but they have less energy, less durability, less intense and concentrated power than in the maturer life.

Edward Bulwer-Lytton (1803–1873)

According to Steinberg and Lerner (2004), two of the most respected scholars of adolescence in the United States, the study of youth has undergone three important phases. These phases, as we will see, have influenced strongly the study of delinquency and misbehavior. The first phase, which Steinberg and Lerner argue began in the early 20th century, was replete with grandiose theoretical models that sought to explain various aspects of juvenile behavior. These theories, note Steinberg and Lerner, were largely devoid of empirical confirmation. Instead, they sought to describe aspects of juvenile behavior, including the formation of youth gangs and the development of delinquent conduct.

Gains have been made, however. The second phase of study began in the 1970s and has continued through today. Again according to Steinberg and Lerner (2004), this phase was concerned with hypothesis testing; the collection and analysis of data; and the introduction of rational, empirical analyses into the formation of social policies that affected youths. It is likely not surprising that this phase also paralleled the advent of the self-report methodologies and the collection of longitudinal data.

The number of empirical studies into youthful misconduct exploded from the mid-1970s through today. In short, criminology evolved from a field where investigators sought to describe youths through narratives and field observations, to a discipline dominated by a concern for data and statistical analyses. With the widespread use of computers, file-sharing protocols, and standardized statistical programs, criminology moved from a discipline of "storytelling" to one of complex hypothesis testing.

This change, although undoubtedly important, has yet to fully transform the study of adolescence and crime. Why? Primarily because the hypotheses being empirically evaluated tend to be drawn from sociological theories that have their roots in the "grand" theories of the turn of the 20th century. Even today, criminology remains wed to the theoretical triad of strain theory, social control theory, and social learning theory—all of which identify adolescence as the time when misbehavior begins. Clearly, as the previous chapters have shown, we have been misled by the age-crime curve.

Yet all is not lost, as Steinberg and Lerner tell us that the study of youth is now entering a third phase—a phase we embrace and one that is demonstrated throughout this book. This phase emphasizes the developmental nature of juvenile problem behavior; it links preexisting traits to pivotal transitional events and periods that occur during adolescence; and it links the various biological, psychological, and sociological systems that influence the healthy development of youth. In short, this phase of study examines the dynamic unfolding of lives over time with an eye toward understanding the "complete" individual—that is, his or her prior behavioral patterns, traits and personality characteristics, and cognitive processes.

What Is Adolescence and Why Did We Include Adulthood?

Contemporary views of adolescence typically define it as a "transitional period" between childhood and adulthood. This image implies that there is an end to childhood, a start to adolescence, an end, and a moment where one evolves into an adult. On closer inspection, however, defining "adolescence" and identifying it as a unique period of development inevitably draws out the serious difficulties we have with providing a clear definition.

Most people believe that adolescence is defined by age, so youths between the ages of 13 and 19 qualify as adolescents. Others take a legal view, noting that the law prohibits certain types of behaviors based solely on the age of the individual. Still others view adolescence as an amorphous descriptive label that signifies an important intermediate period of development. At one level, all of these conceptions of adolescence are correct, or they at least have a ring of truth to them. Yet we must keep in mind that "adolescence" is a uniquely Western social creation. Many other societies do not recognize a "transitionary" period between childhood and adulthood. Instead, they tend to establish "rites of passage" that clearly articulate the requirements to transition between childhood and adulthood.

For various reasons, primarily having to do with keeping youths in school and out of formal work arrangements, Western societies developed, crafted, and tailored the concept of adolescence to further broader social goals. Thus, Western definitions of adolescence usually hinge on a socially constructed understanding of the intersection between age, age-specific legal arrangements, and social mores that direct or limit participation in social institutions. Notice, however, that the identification of adolescence as a unique period of human development was not grounded in any sound scientific reason to recognize adolescence as a period of human transition. As a period of development, adolescence exists for no other reason than we have structured our society in ways that reflect differential age expectations.

To be clear, we do believe that the study of youths is important; however, we must also recognize that the conception of adolescence as a unique period within the lifespan has led to some rather erroneous claims about the nature of crime. For example, it was once taken as an article of faith that adolescence is a period of "storm and stress," where conflict with parents arises naturally and where the onset of puberty makes youths mindless, emotional bots that overreact to every situation. Most youths, we have found, manage adolescence with skill; indeed, many even anticipate the changes they are about to experience and plan accordingly. Only about 25% of adolescents appear at risk for psychosocial problems (Carnegie Corporation of New York, 1995).

Our preoccupation with adolescence has also had the unintended consequence of separating a limited range of years within the lifespan from the years that preceded them and the years that follow them. For decades, criminologists never studied infants or children under the assumption that serious misbehavior is the domain of teenagers. Our inability to adequately define adolescence apart from the structure of our society has led some researchers to now argue for a period of "extended adolescence," or a period where the onset of traditional adult roles is even further delayed. Many individuals who have graduated from college, for example, now elect to live at home with their parents instead of starting a career of their own. Because they have delayed accepting adult responsibilities, should we consider them adolescents too? If so, we are likely to find that many people in their late 20s should be classified as adolescents.

What is it, then, that differentiates early development from later development? Our answer: sexual maturation. It is the ability to procreate that truly distinguishes individuals, and it is the ability to procreate that has historically served as the point of demarcation between childhood and adulthood. Once sexual maturation has occurred, the vast majority of individuals are capable of entering into traditionally adult arrangements. They can produce children and thus create a family kinship network, they can engage in self-sustaining employment activities, and they can navigate the complexities of economic and social interactions. Of course, in our society we do not view this as "optimal" development, but that does not deny the fact that for the numerous generations that have come before us, this developmental sequence was *normal and expected*. Teenage parenthood was at one time in our evolutionary past normative, if not necessary. Throughout our history, youths have worked in dangerous jobs and engaged in wars and battles—killing and being killed. Only recently have we sought to curtail their behaviors in these areas.

The differences between adolescence and adulthood thus become less clear once we realize that our social arrangements and labels are the product of historical forces that created these labels. More importantly, scientifically it becomes virtually impossible to make a clear case that adolescence exists in nature. There simply is no hard and fast set of rules that determines when one reaches adolescence or when one reaches adulthood. The only natural distinction occurs between those capable of sexual reproduction and those still too early in their development to reproduce. Other distinctions are largely artificial.

This is not to say that this period in the lifespan is unimportant, or that experiences that occur during this period are trivial—clearly, they are not. We draw out this point to show that human development occurs both independently of social and historical contexts, and in interaction with social and historical forces. Modern Western youths lead qualitatively different lives today than they did in 400 AD, or during the 1200s, or during the Industrial Revolution, but that should not be taken as evidence that the underlying nature of human development has changed all that much, as the quote from Seneca (shown above) so elegantly highlights. If we choose to, we could easily do away with the term *adolescence* and merely recognize childhood as a period prior to sexual maturity, and adulthood as a period after sexual maturity.

However, in an important evolutionary adaptation, *Homo sapiens* learned that a buffer period immediately following the point of sexual maturation aided individual adaptation and thereby benefited society. This buffer period between the point of sexual maturation and actually forming an extended family allowed humans time to master certain developmental tasks and to experience a range of new social behaviors. In a review of these tasks, Kipke and other scientists tell us that adolescence allows youths time to

- acquire new skills;
- continue brain growth, including continued myelination;
- develop abstract reasoning;
- learn how to navigate complex social arrangements and intimate relationships;
- develop autonomy and independence.

Today, we use adolescence as an extended "training period" where youths are subject to continued education and are allowed, if not encouraged, to experience a range of social contexts (sports, dating, work). Our early ancestors, namely *Homo erectus,* appear to have entirely skipped adolescence (Dean et al., 2001).

Sexual Maturation and Human Development

Nowhere is the guiding hand of evolution as visible as it is with sexual maturation. The biological processes that turn children into sexually motivated adolescents and adults is the *single most uniform experience* known to humans and other animal species. It is a process that is genetically controlled and yet, at least in the margins, environmentally influenced. It turns frail boys into muscular, sexually motivated men, and it transforms young girls into sexually desirable and sexually assertive women. If sexual reproduction is evolution's way of propagating the species, the processes underlying sexual maturation are its way of changing youths into adults.

Sexual maturation begins when the hypothalamus, along with the pituitary gland, secretes sex-specific gonadotropin-releasing hormones. The hypothalamus and pituitary gland are part of the endocrine system, which controls the rate of production and the rate of delivery of hormones throughout the body. Through a complex feedback loop, the endocrine system is always working to regulate the level and distribution of hormones, yet when puberty begins, the endocrine system floods the body with estrogen (in women) and testosterone (in males).

Until recently, however, scientists did not know what triggered puberty. We have known for some time that the average age of onset of puberty, at least in developed countries, has occurred earlier and earlier in the life span. Most scholars argue that better diets and better health care are the likely environmental agents responsible for pushing the onset of puberty earlier into the life course. Yet scientists were left to speculate as to the exact genetic triggers that stimulate the endocrine system. Recent findings, though, have radically reshaped our understanding of what causes puberty in humans.

A unique disorder prevents 1 in every 50,000 people from entering puberty. Known as idiopathic hypogonadotropic hypogonadism (IHH), this genetic malfunction seems to prevent the stimulation of the endocrine system. With this information at hand, scientists examined a Saudi Arabian family strongly affected by IHH. They also examined mice, and through a series of "knock out" studies—that is, where they "knock out" a gene through selective breeding—found that in mice and humans, the GPR54 gene was responsible for triggering the onset of puberty. Their study, one of the most important in the area of human biology, demonstrates how the use of animal models informs research into humans. More importantly, their study was the first to identify the gene responsible for the onset of puberty in humans.

Puberty actually starts well before the telltale signs emerge, such as pubic hair. For girls, endocrine secretions of female hormones begin to enlarge the ovaries between the ages of 8 and 11. For boys, however, the onset of puberty occurs roughly 2 years later, when testosterone begins to influence the development of the testes. Throughout their pubertal development, boys and girls differ in the timing of onset, the hormones to which they are exposed, and the effects these hormones have on their body.

Geoff Malta (www.puberty101.com) describes five stages of pubertal growth for males and females. For females,

Stage 2 usually occurs between the ages of 11 and 12, and includes the development of pubic hair, increased breast growth, and the onset of a substantial growth spurt.

Stage 3 occurs on average between ages 12 and 13. This stage can see the onset of menstruation and the darkening of pubic hair.

Stage 4 usually begins between the ages of 14 and 15. During this stage, ovulation begins, hair develops on other areas of the body, and substantial height and weight gains occur.

Stage 5, with an average age of 15, occurs when a monthly cycle is developed, and when gains in height have reached their maximum threshold. Although this process is usually complete by age 15, some girls are fully mature by age 12, whereas others are not fully mature until late in their teens.

Whereas for males,

Stage 2 usually begins between the ages of 12 and 13. Visibly, males in this stage begin to acquire greater muscle mass. Their testes and scrotum also continue to mature and to enlarge.

Stage 3 occurs, on average, between the ages of 13 and 14. During this stage the male penis will begin to grow, as will pubic hair. A male's voice will also begin to deepen, resulting in that well-known "cracking" sound.

Stage 4 has an average onset between ages 14 and 15. Boys will usually experience their first ejaculation during this time period ("wet dreams"), and hair will become visible under their arms and on their face. It is not uncommon for boys to also begin to experience acne during this stage as their skin becomes oilier.

Stage 5 happens around age 16. At this stage, the average male has gained roughly 80 to 100 pounds of weight and has increased in height from 6 inches to more than 1 foot on average. His muscles, moreover, have become biochemically stronger, and they can more efficiently process cellular waste products, such as lactic acid.

Boys and girls thus experience puberty very differently and at different times. The processes that lead to sexual maturation are both hidden (the activation of the pituitary gland and the gonads) and visible (the development of secondary sex characteristics). Differences between males and females were graphically depicted by Beaver and Wright (2005) in their analysis of data from the National Longitudinal Adolescent Health Survey (AddHealth). Beaver and Wright used self-reports from adolescents to form a composite scale that measured the overall physical maturation process. Their results are shown in Figure 11.1.

The differences between males and females in their average levels of physical development are fairly obvious. For males, their development continues to occur across the grades measured, with a steady linear increase occurring over time. Their physical maturation thus takes relatively longer to complete than that for females.

Quite a different pattern, however, is shown for females. Data from the AddHealth survey indicate that by the ninth grade, female pubertal development has largely plateaued. Unlike their male counterparts, females tend to mature more rapidly.

The Effects of Sexual Maturation

Studying the effects of puberty on human development presents us with an optimal situation to study the factors that produce changes in behaviors and/or that promote continuity in maladaptive behavior. Puberty represents a fundamental

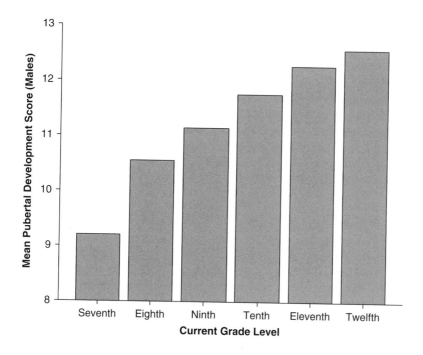

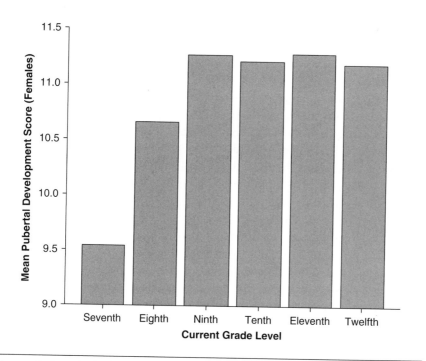

Figure 11.1   Physical Maturation by Grade Level and Gender

transition in the life course—a transition that unfolds over the course of years and leads to dramatic changes in physical appearance and ability. The transition, as we will see, is multifaceted and affects a range of other factors that can lead to more conduct problems.

Although it would be tempting to argue that puberty affects everyone equally, research evidence tells us that the effects of puberty are varied and dependent on a host of conditions. Graber and Brooks-Gunn (1996) lay out six models by which the transition through puberty can best be understood. We examine three of these models.

Timing Within Transitional Periods

Recall from the previous chapters that we stated that the earlier the onset of problem behavior, the more likely the behavior is to remain stable over time. This fact draws attention to the timing of onset within the life course. Understanding the effects of puberty is no different. Numerous studies, conducted primarily on females, have revealed that the timing of puberty in the life course has consequential effects on the transition from adolescence to adulthood.

Early onset of puberty begins a process that ultimately sets individuals apart from one another, biologically and socially. Compared to "on-time" youth, early-maturing youths are less likely to have had time to develop effective coping skills, or to have had enough experiences to have learned how to navigate complex social relationships. These social relationships become all the more important because early-maturing youths are more likely to associate with older, and presumably more experienced, adolescents. Moreover, early maturation also seems to be associated with reductions in synaptic growth and lateralization between the spheres of the brain. For these reasons, and more, off-time maturation may lead to a number of transitional problems.

Data indicate that timing does, indeed, matter. On one hand, girls appear to be more affected by an early onset of puberty than boys. That is, the effects of puberty are more pervasive. Early maturation in females is associated with increased risk for depression (Ge, Conger, & Elder, 1996, 2001), conduct problems (Haynie, 2003), low self-esteem, eating disorders, early sexual intercourse, suicide (Beaver & Wright, 2005; Caspi, Lynam, Moffitt, & Silva, 1993), and association with delinquent others (Beaver & Wright, 2005; Haynie, 2003).

On the other hand, early or late onset of puberty extends consequences for boys. In particular, off-time males are at a substantially elevated risk for risk taking (Anderson & Magnusson, 1990), and there is consistent evidence that puberty is linked to increases in delinquency and criminal behavior (Graber, Lewinsohn, Seeley, & Brooks-Gunn, 1997; Rutter & Smith, 1995), and to increases in other forms of deviance, including drinking and drug use (Duncan, Ritter, Dornbusch, Gross, & Merrill Carlsmith, 1985; Flannery, Rowe, & Gulley, 1993; Lanza & Collins, 2002; Stattin & Magnusson, 1990; Tschann et al., 1994).

The consistency in findings indicates that off-time maturation is associated with a range of problem behaviors and consequences. Of particular interest is the association between puberty and aggression and violence. On this, the data are clear: Off-time maturation is a substantial risk factor for maladaptive behavior. Indeed, in one study of the AddHealth data, Felson and Haynie (2002) concluded by stating that "Its [pubertal development's] effects are comparable in strength to the effects of peer delinquency and school performance. . . . Its effect is stronger than the effects of socioeconomic status, race, and family structure" (p. 982). The pattern of findings has led some scholars to question whether the effects of puberty are a better predictor of aggression and violence than age (Keenan & Shaw, 1997; Rutter, Giller, & Hagell, 1998).

Accentuation During Transitional Periods

When individuals are placed under immediate and intense stress, they tend to behave in ways that they have behaved before—even if it is to their own detriment. A person who usually reacts with anger to every situation will, when faced with a stressful experience, typically react with anger. This illustration highlights how previously acquired cognitive and behavioral structures and individual traits interact during transitional periods; periods that can generate an abundance of stress and anxiety.

For individuals, transitions initially represent novel experiences, experiences where new behaviors can emerge or where old behaviors continue to be used. Evidence indicates that adaptation to novel situations and transitions depends partly on an individual's prior behaviors and personality characteristics and partly on the structure of the environment. Environments that are less structured tend to allow a greater range of behaviors to emerge.

Perhaps owing to the stability of maladaptive behavior, studies indicate that aggressive and problematic youths tend to respond to novel, unrestricted social settings with aggression and negativity. In essence, their prior behaviors and traits become accentuated in response to the stress and ambiguity associated with the situation or transition (Caspi & Moffitt, 1991). Change, although possible, is less likely when maladaptive characteristics override the potential changing influences found in the transition or the environment. However, it is not just that continuity in individual differences remains through periods of transition; it is that the transitions can amplify or worsen these initial conditions. A conduct-disordered child with a very difficult temperament, for example, may become physically violent during the transition through puberty. Even in the highly restricted environments found in the military, for example, research has found that men with prior criminal records are more likely to go AWOL, and they are more likely to be arrested and punished by military authorities (Sampson & Laub, 1993; Wright, Carter, & Cullen, 2005). Children removed from abusive and neglectful homes and placed into foster care remain more likely to drop out of school, to use drugs, and to be arrested—even though their home environment has changed substantially (Wertheimer, 2002).

Accentuation thus reduces the likelihood that periods of transition will produce changes in problem behavior. Indeed, counter to the idea that transitions are breeding grounds for the development of new behaviors and adaptive psychological structures, the available data indicate that many people employ familiar behaviors and cognitive processes to meet new challenges. The failure to adapt appropriately, to meet the demands of the transition, can further embed an individual in a pathway of problem behavior and can further erode the chances of changing his or her behavior in the future. As this applies to the puberty transition, it takes no stretch of the imagination to understand what can happen to a conduct-disordered, hyperactive, and impulsive young male once he is greeted by the onset of puberty and the accompanying physical growth (Beaver & Wright, 2005).

Perturbation

Exposure to transitional pathways, like puberty, can lead even well-adjusted youths to display behaviors they otherwise wouldn't. Criminologists have known for a long time that problem behaviors increase in the teenage years and decline precipitously over time. Moffitt (1993) emphasizes this trend by arguing that most youthful offenders can best be described as "adolescent limited." Offending, especially engaging in behaviors that are not very serious or life-threatening, emerges during adolescence and lasts only a few years. The limited frequency and duration of these types of problem behaviors makes them more of a perturbation in the life cycle rather than a prolonged pattern of maladaptive behavior. As Moffitt notes, engaging in low levels of delinquent behavior is very normal during this period of development, and youths who do not "seek out and break some boundaries" are also the youths who are more at risk for internalized problems, such as depression, anxiety, and social withdrawal.

Perturbations in behavioral patterns have been tied to the puberty transition. Indeed, much of the lore and common wisdom view adolescents as moody, troubled, and difficult to get along with. Because youths are being flooded with hormones, their behaviors and emotional states can become more tenuous and unstable. Girls, for example, are significantly more likely to experience situations as stressful, and they are more likely to be affected by mood disorders, especially depression (Brooks-Gunn & Warren, 1989; Kipke, 1999). During puberty, many boys become more risk taking and thrill seeking, which often leads to conflict with school authorities, parents, and even the police.

These temporally limited periods of maladjustment are not inherently problematic, although history is replete with examples where teenagers engaged in foolish behavior, such as speeding, and paid the ultimate price. For many youths, however, this period of their lives is where they build a new social reputation; become more integrated into their social niches; and develop new skills, interests, and talents. The mostly minor problem behaviors in which youths engage during this transition also help them acquire new cognitive structures, ideas, and values that can aid them in their transition to adulthood. The point is, perturbations in behavior and emotional states often act as precursors to more effective and adaptive lifestyles and thinking patterns.

The effects of any transition, be it puberty or entrance into a job or marriage, thus can be highly variable. For some, the transition through puberty offers opportunities for growth and exploration, whereas for others, the transition only heightens the number of problems they encounter and create. Although the general effects of puberty on human development may be somewhat deleterious, most youths make the transition relatively unscathed and ready to assume adult roles. For those who don't, their life course becomes even more circumscribed as their risk for arrest, incarceration, drug abuse, and premature mortality increases substantially.

Adolescent Development

Puberty sets the stage for a host of changes that adolescents will encounter. Some of these changes are obvious, such as being exposed to drugs and alcohol, whereas other changes are not visible but nonetheless important. How well youths encounter and react to these changes, how well they respond to their broadening social world as well as to their physiological development, foreshadows the type and quality of life they will live as adults.

Adolescence is a time of social change, but it would be incorrect to say that it can best be characterized as a time of personal upheaval. Most adolescents make the transition through adolescence with little difficulty. For these youths, the transitions embedded in adolescence are navigated with a degree of skill and planning that ultimately lead to advantages in adulthood. They typically graduate from high school and enter college, where their characteristics continue to propel them toward the accumulation of advantage. For other youths, however, the transition through adolescence is difficult. They encounter stress and emotional upheaval, as well as have difficulty finding their social niche. Yet for most of these youths, who represent about 20% of all adolescents, their difficulties are transitory and will pass with time and maturity. They may be "roughed up" by their adolescent experiences, but their adaptive skills eventually direct them to a pathway of conformity and social approval.

The same cannot be said for other youths, however. For a small percentage of adolescents, roughly 3% to 10%, adolescence is a period of severe pathology and the continuation of social failure. These youths suffer from a range of problems that seem to balloon as they get older. During this time, it is not unusual for these youths to fail in or drop out of school, become addicted to drugs, be homeless, be sexually active with a wide range of partners, be arrested or incarcerated, or suffer from any number of mental illnesses. For these youths, adolescence is the time period where their pathologies and problems become publicly visible, and where the consequences of their misbehavior cut them off from pathways that accumulate social and personal benefits. In short, their lives become embedded in crime and disrepute.

Why do youths take such divergent paths? Before we answer that question, it is important to first set the context for understanding adolescence as a period of stability and change. In many ways, adolescence can be viewed as the continuation of a developmental cycle whose roots date back more than a decade. All the experiences, behaviors, language patterns, cognitive templates, and friends that one has acquired from childhood continue to exert influence throughout the adolescent years. In this way, the origins of maladaptive and adaptive pathways have already been established prior to a youth entering this stage of the lifespan. In other words, adolescence can be viewed as the continuation of preexisting developmental pathways.

Recall from the chapter on childhood that we made the point that to understand future development, you must first understand *initial conditions.* That is, to forecast future behavioral problems, you must first be aware of prior levels of behavioral adjustment. Initial conditions create variation in childhood temperament and social development, so it should not be too surprising that initial conditions can also help predict successful and unsuccessful transitions into and during adolescence. Children with severe conduct disorders, for example, are likely to greet adolescence with a long list of identifiable problems, whereas youths who have already acquired the ability to integrate into social groups and regulate their impulses and behaviors, and who have acquired a reasonable degree of knowledge, will encounter adolescence well armed.

Yet there are important changes, outside of puberty, that make adolescence a period ripe with peril and problems for many youths. As we already mentioned, some environments restrict certain behavioral responses, whereas other environments tend to promote a wide range of behavioral adaptations. For most, adolescence is a time when they experience a wide range of environments and relationships that require youths to engage in complex behaviors. They move from the restricted environments of school and home to the largely unrestricted environments offered when driving privileges are gained. They enter into complex, didactic romantic relationships that require innumerable skills to navigate, and they experience, sometimes for the first time, many of the emotions that come out of those relationships and environments.

Successfully navigating these myriad obstacles brings positive and negative consequences. Youths who acquire the skills necessary to assimilate into various groups, move from one environment to the next, and hold on to and terminate romantic relationships will be better prepared as adults to assume work and marriage roles. It is not that these youths will be completely free from problems, or that they will not suffer from stressful or emotionally taxing events, or even that they will not engage in minor acts of delinquency, but in general, they will not suffer from the accumulation of negative consequences. In short, they will make the transition to adulthood and will lead relatively prosocial and productive lives.

The accumulation of negative consequences, however, will define the life course of some adolescents. As Sampson and Laub (1993) tell us, some negative consequences knife off future opportunities for personal growth and social advancement. Perhaps no other transition is as important as graduating from high school. Without a diploma, a youth is likely to find the transition to adult roles difficult, largely because a high school diploma is now a required credential for many jobs, entrance into the military, and continued education. Moreover, without a diploma, an individual is highly likely to find him- or herself cemented to the bottom of the economic ladder. A single decision, to drop out of school, brings with it any number of negative consequences that accumulate social disadvantage over the life course.

Choice and the Structure of Life

To answer the question "Why do youths take such divergent pathways?" we must begin to understand the choices that youths make and why some adolescents do not learn from their past choices.

First, adolescence is a period of development where many youths encounter for the first time an unrestricted range of choices and opportunities to exercise choice. No longer are they always under the supervision of their parents or neighbors; their lives instead begin to be encompassed by spending time with friends, dating, working, and playing. Instead of their choices being restricted by their parents, they begin to exercise choice independently. In so doing, their choices illustrate not only independence from their parents, but more importantly, they represent the expression of their own emotional preferences and character traits. Some of these choices are subtle, such as what kind of clothes they want to purchase, whereas other choices are more pronounced, such as their choice to use drugs. Although adolescents vary tremendously in their traits and talents, interests and convictions, it is their choices that begin to determine the course their lives will take. In this sense, the human organism integrates with and operates on the immediate environment. From this point forward, it is the freedom to engage in action, to make choices and to respond to the consequences, both positive and negative, of those choices that will further shape and mold their lives.

Perhaps nobody else has so elegantly studied how choice circumscribes the life course of developing youths as John Clausen (1991). Clausen's work followed individuals from the Berkeley Longitudinal Studies well into their 60s. Clausen was interested in how "planned competence"—a term he used to describe how well youths planned out their future, how dependable they were, and how intellectually involved they were—placed youths on pathways that led to the accumulation of social capital. For Clausen, youths who showed early signs of planned competence would be more likely to know where they wanted their lives to go—that is, whether they wanted to attend college or enter the military. These youths would understand themselves, have a stable self-identity, and be able to be counted on. If youths demonstrated these signs of competence early in the life course, hypothesized Clausen, they would be more likely to be successful and happy as adults. Those who reached competence later in their lives, and especially those who never reached a level of planned competence, would face more troubling prospects.

Clausen's work documented how the choices made in adolescence influenced youths' educational attainment, career stability, and marital stability over the course of their adult lives. Clausen's findings showed that those who demonstrated early levels of planned competence (in high school) eventually led easier lives, had better jobs and more job stability, and were more satisfied later in life as adults. Interestingly, Clausen's data also revealed that those who showed early competence were the least likely to change—that is, the more competent individuals were as adolescents, the more competent they would be 50 to 60 years later! To quote Clausen (1991):

Those who were most mature and competent tended to assess the options available to them; they made more considered choices and were better prepared to work through the problems of adaptation that marriage and careers require. Their competence led to superior opportunities and superior achievements. Men who were in adolescence less planful, mature, and competent had much less orderly lives. Many of these men attained mature competence in the early adult years, but others never found a job that brought lasting satisfaction or a wife with whom they could live in harmony. It was in this group that recurrent life crises most often occurred, crises due to career disruption, to marital conflict and marital dissolution, and to feelings of alienation and depression. (p. 835)

Choices that are made, even relatively early in life, extend advantages (or disadvantages) across the life course. In many ways, as Clausen points out, choice structures the life course. Youths who have clear and reasonable goals, think about how best to achieve those goals, and engage in behaviors that further their goals then create and seize opportunities. These youths are not the haphazard victims of chance, but are instead the architects of their own lives. They come from varied backgrounds; some are wealthy and others are poor, but in the end, their lives are rich in texture and embedded in trusting and caring relationships. In short, although their backgrounds may have differed, they eventually end up successful.

Of course, other youths do not fare as well. Even early in life, the choices they make run counter to their long-term health and welfare. More importantly, some youths tend to replicate these types of bad choices across time and across situations, further divorcing themselves from prosocial opportunities and helpful others. Instead of learning that certain choices bring about negative consequences, these youths are able to neutralize their motives, rationalize away their guilt, and shift blame onto others with remarkable consistency.

In Chapter 3, we discussed the issue of continuity and how individuals interact in their environment. The fact that individuals are partly the architects of their own lives becomes all the more clear in adolescence. Like their more prosocial colleagues, antisocial adolescents experience environments that offer more choices, less supervision, and fewer rules. Under these conditions, the choices they make are allowed to be fully exposed. They will yell at and threaten teachers, insult police officers, and get into fights with other youths. When they attend school, which isn't frequently, they sleep, don't pay attention, or get into trouble. When on their own or with friends, they are significantly more likely to smoke cigarettes and marijuana, drink alcohol, drive recklessly, and have sex with multiple partners. They are provocative, they have a strong tendency to see the world through an antisocial lens, and they select friends and situations that support and encourage their behaviors and views.

Their antisocial behavior continues even though the consequences pile up and become more serious over time. Their behavior continues even though tragedy may strike because of their actions, such as when a friend dies or is seriously injured, and it continues even when serious harm is brought to them.

Adolescents develop along a continuum from socially competent to noncompetent. At one end are those who will achieve good jobs, good marriages, and reasonably happy adult lives. At the other end are those who will populate our jails and prisons; have unstable or no job histories; have few marketable skills; have multiple children and no means of support; and, for all intents and purposes, be socially maladaptive. Choice, as we have seen, is a key component to understanding how people differ in terms of their social competence. Yet choice does not occur in a vacuum; rather, it is circumscribed by internal and external factors.

Brain Development, Choice, and Adolescent Functioning

Chad Trulson and his colleagues (Trulson, Marquart, Mullings, & Caeti, 2005) identified the "worst 2 percent" of juvenile offenders in the Texas Department of Corrections (TDOC). Most of these youths were first referred to the TDOC at age 13, after they had already been adjudicated for at least two other felony arrests. Over the course of 5 years, Trulson followed almost 2,500 of these youths, average age of 17 at time of release, as they made the transition from secure institutions to life in free society. Within 5 years from their time of their release, 1,876 (77%) were rearrested for another *felony.* Of those rearrested, 56% were rearrested for a nonviolent felony, and 44% were rearrested for a violent assault. About 60% of those youths who were rearrested were eventually reincarcerated. Only 23% of the youths who emerged from the Texas Department of Corrections remained arrest free over the course of the 5-year follow-up. Only 23%! Even this relatively low number may be too high an estimate, however; certainly, some have remained arrest free only because they have yet to be caught again!

The TDOC is not known for being soft on offenders, young or old. Yet the vast majority of the youths in Trulson's sample reoffended not long after gaining their freedom. The choices they made in early adulthood, when they were between the ages of 18 and 23, were the same types of choices they exercised when they were younger, the same types of choices that led to arrest and incarceration.

In dramatic fashion, Trulson's results highlight the high degree of continuity in antisocial behavior. Clearly, youths committed to the TDOC as juveniles represent a small but criminally active subset of all juveniles. For the most part, their lives have been embedded in social maladjustment, and their decision-making skills typically have been quite marginal. Numerous studies show that these serious, violent youths have substantial deficits in self-regulation. They are impulsive, hedonistic, and hyperactive, and they lack empathy for others.

Some scholars interpret this as evidence that internal biological factors become resistant to change relatively early in life, usually before the age of 10, and that once solidified, their biology does not change. Indeed, Gottfredson and Hirschi (1990) maintain that self-control has to emerge prior to age 10 or youths risk never acquiring those skills. Fortunately, the view that youths are complete in their biological and social maturation by age 10 is, as modern science has revealed, incorrect.

As we discussed in Chapter 5, myelin is a fatty substance that wraps itself around axons. It acts as a conductor of electricity, increasing the speed at which an electrical charge travels down an axon almost a hundredfold. Myelination is a process that appears to begin at different times in development. Early in life, sensory and motor regions of the brain are completely myelinated. This likely aids the child in gaining an understanding of his or her environment, as well as learning how to coordinate his or her limb movements so that objects in the environment can be manipulated and so he or she can crawl, toddle, and finally walk. These parts of the brain, such as the occipital and motor lobes, mature at a significantly faster rate than the frontal cortex

Brain development is much more asymmetrical than originally understood. Primarily through the use of brain imaging studies, scientists have found that myelin continues to form and to coat axons in the frontal cortex into the early 20s (Blakemore & Choudhury, 2006). Whereas other parts of the brain have matured in terms of synaptic density and myelination, the frontal cortex takes extra time and seems to be dependent on puberty to initiate the process. The continued myelination of the frontal cortex, where rational thought and planning occurs, increases neural processing speed and thus accuracy and precision of thought. Theoretically, this should allow adolescents greater control in managing their emotional impulses, managing and prioritizing their time, and evaluating the future consequences of their behavior.

In a review of imaging studies, Blakemore and Choudhury (2006) note that differences in gray and white matter density are dependent on the age of the subject. Young children, for example, show significantly higher levels of gray matter volume than do adolescents or adults. In turn, it is during adolescence that the ratio of white matter (myelination) to gray matter is reversed.

These differences can be viewed overall, and within specific regions of the brain. The corpus callosum, which allows communication between the left and right hemispheres of the brain, contains an estimated 180 million myelinated axons. Changes in the corpus callosum from the end of childhood through the beginning of adulthood are dramatic. The corpus callosum is particularly important to healthy brain functioning because it links the left and right cerebral hemispheres and is thus connected to subhemispheric regions. Because it links different regions of the brain, it is involved in the integration and organization of complex information; memory retrieval; and attention, language, and complex cognitive tasks. As Giedd (2004) notes, these abilities increase throughout adolescence. The corpus callosum undergoes changes in the density of visible white matter by 1.3% per year. However, in a surprising discovery, Giedd and his colleagues found that the corpus callosum "matures" from front to back—that is, the anterior part of the brain (think of your eyes as the front or anterior part of the brain) matures prior to the mid and posterior sections.

The adolescent brain has been described as a symphony in need of practice. What this means is that the various parts of the adolescent brain are not completely developed (like the skills of the violinists), and that they are not completely synchronized with each other (the brass section may come in too early or too late). This lack of synchrony can be seen in the regions that link the cortex to Wernicke's and Broca's areas (the parts of the brain responsible for speech and language processing). These regions, especially the left arcuate fasciculus, undergo substantial alterations during adolescence that will link the language processing areas together more efficiently. This process is critical because it allows for more efficient use of language but also because the language centers are deeply connected to the frontal cortex. Language generation and comprehension are part of the executive functions that allow humans greater control over and understanding of their environment. It is not at all uncommon for serious delinquents to have substantial deficits in vocabulary, language comprehension, and impulse control.

The available evidence thus indicates that the adolescent brain is under relatively constant change. In the frontal cortex, gray matter increases with the onset of puberty. It will decline throughout the rest of adolescence and into adulthood. However, axons in the region will eventually become myelinated and thus more efficient. Continued pruning of synaptic pathways that are unused or unneeded results in gray matter decreases, but these decreases are offset and balanced by the strengthening of signal processing pathways that remain (Giedd et al., 1999). Many of these changes are not only age specific, but also sex specific.

As Figures 11.2a and 11.2b show, males are more likely to have increased gray matter in the frontal, temporal, and parietal lobes, as well as in the caudate nucleus. Females have about 11% more neurons in the language and hearing areas of the brain, and they have significantly increased hippocampal volume compared to men. Giedd (2004) also notes that for females, cortical gray matter reaches a peak at 11.0 years, compared to 12.1 years for males; temporal gray matter peaks at about 16.7 years for females compared to 18 years for males; and parietal lobe gray matter peaks at 10.2 years in girls compared to 11.8 years in males. Males, on the other hand, experience significant increases in amygdala volume throughout adolescence. In each sex, however, the last part of the adolescent brain to develop is the

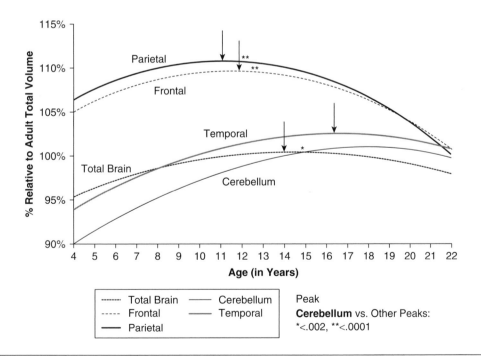

Figure 11.2a   Brain Development by Anatomic Region (145 Children and Adolescents Aged 4–22 Years Who Underwent 243 MRI Scans)

SOURCE: Reprinted by permission from Macmillan Publishers, Ltd: Nature Neuroscience (Giedd et al. "Brain development during childhood and adolescence: A longitudinal MRI study.") 1999.

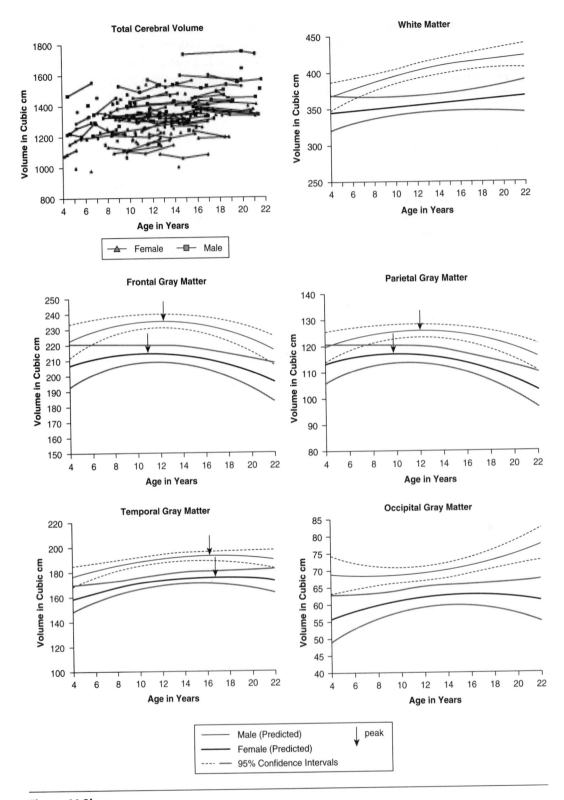

Figure 11.2b

SOURCE: Reprinted from *Molecular and Cellular Endocrinology*, Vol. 254–255, Giedd et al., "Puberty-related influences on brain development." (2006), with permission from Elsevier.

dorsolateral prefront cortex (DLPC) and the superior temporal gyrus. The DLPC, according to Giedd (2004), is "linked to the ability to inhibit impulses, weigh consequences of decisions, prioritize, and strategize" (p. 83).

The clear implication from these studies is that morphological and structural changes in the brain beginning at puberty and extending through the mid-20s should correlate with observable changes in behaviors. Anecdotally, parents have for some time described their young adolescents as moody, irritable, hyper, and lazy. There is, of course, empirical evidence that many adolescents fit these labels, at least for a brief period of time. Youths frequently self-report finding certain behaviors very difficult, such as awaking early, concentrating through class, and controlling the range of emotions they experience throughout the day.

Adolescents and their parents are likely not exaggerating what they observe, especially considering the fact that study after study finds that parent-child conflict usually escalates in adolescence. To parents, adolescents demonstrate behaviors and emotions that are of concern because they can jeopardize the life chances of their child. Adolescents, moreover, may not fully realize the social consequences of their behaviors, nor may they understand completely how their negative or unpredictable attitudes and emotional outbursts affect those around them. Adolescents, it seems, have a unique ability to provoke others. However, for the majority of youths, these behaviors are a state (not a trait) that will change as they gain greater neurological control over their internal emotional impulses.

Adolescent Decision Making

We again return to the concept of "executive functions" to further describe how changes in the brain affect the behavior of adolescents. Executive functions refer to the highest order cognitive skills that humans possess. These include voluntary verbal and behavioral inhibition, planning for the future, evaluating options and consequences, filtering out unnecessary environmental and internal stimuli while simultaneously focusing on a task, and exercising control over powerful emotional impulses (Bradshaw, 2001). Executive functions, as we mentioned earlier, are located in the frontal lobes—the last part of the brain to develop.

Conventional wisdom holds that adolescents are notoriously bad at understanding risk and connecting the possible consequences of their actions with their risk-taking behavior. As various scholars point out, nowhere is this more evident than in the tragic statistics that show an unacceptably high mortality rate among adolescent drivers. Research solidly documents that young drivers are more likely to speed, speed in excess, drive with others who have been drinking, drive in hazardous conditions, drive recklessly, and not wear their seat belts. Males are significantly more likely to engage in these risky behaviors than are females, and they are at an elevated likelihood of dying (Insurance Institute for Highway Safety, 2005).

Driving serves as a good example of how adolescent brain development interacts with the social development for at least two reasons. First, learning to drive requires the accumulation and mastery of several skills. A beginning driver must learn to manage the controls of the vehicle, such as the gas pedal and brake. He or she must learn how to coordinate the movement of his or her hands, arms, legs, feet, and eyes. Distances must be estimated, closure rates accurately assessed, and time-distance intervals understood. Laws of the road and driving behaviors specific to certain types of driving conditions and environments must be acquired, practiced, and assimilated. For these reasons, and more, driving taxes severely the developing brain.

Second, driving is, for most youths, a social experience. That is, youths drive to places largely out of convenience and so they can share time with other youths. Unfortunately, research has shown that the risks for injury and death increase significantly with each additional adolescent passenger who is within the car. This fact was highlighted nicely in an experiment by Gardner and Steinberg (2005). Their experiment involved adults and adolescents driving on a computer simulator. The simulator presented them with a range of driving hazards, such as a light changing from green to yellow, and kept score of how many times the driver engaged in a risky behavior. On the whole, adults and adolescents scored about equally on the simulator test. However, when the researchers had the adolescent's friends watch and participate in the simulation, risky driving increased substantially. This experiment suggests that youth process social information differently in the presence of peers (a gene × environment interaction).

There can be little doubt that adolescents take more risks with their lives, and the lives of others, than do adults. However, is it true, as conventional wisdom holds, that adolescents are crippled when it comes to understanding risks and benefits, or that they are simply incapable of making adult-like decisions? According to Valerie Reyna and Frank Farley (2006), convention wisdom is, yet again, wrong.

Reyna and Farley's review of studies on risk taking indicates that adolescents do not see themselves as impervious to problems or that they are invulnerable. Numerous studies show that adolescents tend to overestimate many risks, such as the likelihood of getting HIV from a single sexual encounter, and accurately estimate others, such as the likelihood of being injured in a traffic accident. Indeed, if there is a group to be labeled as "risk takers," it has to be young children. Several laboratory controlled studies have found that children are far more likely to take risks than are adolescents or adults. The developmental trend, argue Reyna and Farley (2006), is for a relatively constant reduction in the toleration of risk and the preference for risk over time—that is, children prefer risk more than adolescents, who prefer risk more than adults.

Most adolescents can make adult-like decisions, but the efficiency and precision of these decisions appears to be more subject to the immediate context (Steinberg, 2004). Many adolescents, for example, are better drivers than are some adults. Again referring to Reyna and Farley (2006), adolescent decision making becomes less accurate and less efficient than adult decision making when

- adolescents are in hot emotional states, such as anger or jealousy, or when they are sexually aroused;
- a decision needs to be made immediately;
- behavioral restraint is necessary for good outcomes;
- the cost/benefit estimation favors long-term negative consequences;
- they are in the presence of friends.

Under these conditions, adolescent decision making becomes more subject to error. Contrary to conventional wisdom, scientists such as Steinberg (2004) and Reyna and Farley (2006) show that the idea that adolescents misunderstand the risks associated with certain behaviors is largely incorrect. For the most part, adolescents, especially those around the ages of 15 to 16, appear just as capable of assessing risk as adults. Steinberg (2004) argues that what differentiates adolescents from adults is the influence of contextual factors, such as the presence of peers, and/or their inability to inhibit initial impulses. Unlike rational actors who weigh the costs and benefits of any action, adolescents may, under certain circumstances, simply act without regard to the costs. A similar conclusion has been reached by Reyna (2004), who argues that adolescents may accurately estimate risk, but simultaneously overestimate reward.

Neuroscience has reinvigorated the study of adolescence, and it has played a pivotal role in shaping legal and public opinion about adolescent behavior. The past 20 years have witnessed remarkable new insights into the ontological development of youths and young adults. Where our earlier understanding of adolescence was shaped largely by political, cultural, and social values, a contemporary understanding of adolescence has to be informed by the biology of puberty and brain structure and functioning.

Adult Criminals

The movement away from adolescence and into adulthood represents a critical transition in the life course development of individuals. Upon graduating from high school, most youths take one of several paths; some will enter military service, some will enter or remain in the world of work, some will get married, and some will go to college. For these youths, the process of growing up is, in some ways, beginning again. They will encounter novel situations that require sophisticated, adaptive responses; they will be expected to conform to adult rules and expectations, and they will be expected to manage their own lives. In short, their lives take on all the trappings of adulthood—that is, independence, self-sufficiency, autonomy, self-direction, social responsibility, and the creation of new family and friend networks.

As life has taught us, however, even youths relatively low in criminality will encounter a variety of personal difficulties along the way. Divorce, bankruptcy, death of significant others, loss of a job, alcoholism, drug addiction, loneliness, mental health issues and an assortment of other problems are likely to be experienced during the adult life course. Even so, the majority of individuals have terminated their involvement in criminal conduct prior to or immediately after entrance into adulthood. Regardless of the stresses and strains that accompany the adult life course, the vast majority of adults never commit serious acts of crime. The same cannot be said of all adults, however.

Armed robbery is one of the most serious crimes that can be committed. Individuals who commit armed robbery are some of the most predatory individuals in society. They usually plan their crime; confront their victim face-to-face, usually threatening violence or loss of life; and usually are armed with a weapon. But what are armed robbers like—that is, how do they think, how do they live their lives, and why do they elect to engage in violence?

Research by Wright and Decker (1997) provided valuable insight into these questions. Using traditional qualitative methods, Wright and Decker interviewed 86 active armed robbers from the St. Louis, Missouri, area. In some ways, their findings converged with other criminological studies (see Figure 11.3). Even among active offenders, for example, some were more active than others: Thirty-six percent of their sample reported having committed more than 49 robberies each. Moreover, their criminal behavior was pervasive: Sixty-two percent reported other forms of theft, 58% reported engaging in drug distribution, and 62% reported engaging in burglary.

In other ways, however, their work sheds light on the daily existence of active offenders. Many offenders were labeled as "urban nomads" by Wright and Decker (1997, p. 38) because they rarely slept in the same place night after night. Instead, they wandered from street to street, from alley to alley, and from apartment to apartment. Their lives had no geographic center outside of the broad confines of the inner city. Moreover, their findings revealed that, contrary to most sociological theories, offenders did not commit armed robbery because of any long-term goals to achieve an elevated standard of living. "Even when offenders had a substantial sum of money," note Wright and Decker, "their disdain for long-range planning coupled with their desire to live for the present often encouraged them to spend it with reckless abandon" (p. 39). For these offenders, money was used to purchase and consume alcohol and drugs, to purchase the "right" clothes, and to participate in a party culture.

Armed robbery is also fun, or at least exhilarating. Armed robbers in Wright and Decker's sample consistently reported that the act of intimidating others, terrorizing the unsuspecting, and taking total control of the situation was often accompanied by feelings of superiority and glee. Even more disturbing, however, was the

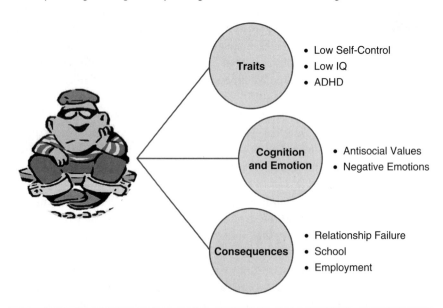

Figure 11.3   Compilation of Criminal Characteristics

fact that "even in casual conversations," armed robbers' "strong propensity for sudden violence seemed to lurk just below the surface" (Wright & Decker, 1997, p. 57). Active robbers reported that they not only enjoyed engaging in robbery but that they also enjoyed the violence that often accompanied the crime. According to one armed robber, "It just be fun when we do the robbery cause we'll beat the person's ass bad, make 'em suffer. It just be so fun." And another stated, "We try not to kill [our victims]. If we can avoid killing them, then we try not to. But if they force your hand, then you have to kill them. It's just that simple" (p. 57).

The criminality voiced by Wright and Decker's subjects stands as a testament to the danger these men pose. It also graphically highlights the social and personal pathology that circumscribes their lives. They are unreliable as friends and spouses, they are untrustworthy as neighbors, and they habitually manipulate others. More importantly, these men commit crime, sometimes very serious crime, because their attitudes, values, and lifestyles encourage and support criminal behavior. They have few or no moral or internal restraints, and they relish the rewards that street culture brings to those who are criminal enough or violent enough to gain a street reputation.

Not all adult offenders are criminally violent or deeply embedded in criminal conduct. Some are, in the words of Neal Shover (1996), "fuck-ups." Shover's ethnographic study into the lives of persistent thieves provides another stark account into the criminal underworld and the personal pathology that accompanies most criminally active men. Shover classified the men in his sample as "fuck-ups," "dope fiends and crackheads," "outlaws," "hustlers," and "thieves."

"Fuck-ups" is a label used by Shover to describe men who are criminally and personally inept. Their ineptitude typically leads to arrest and incarceration as they often fail to adequately plan their crimes. "Dope fiends and crackheads," as Shover's label describes, steal primarily to support their drug habit. They steal when the opportunity is present, and they steal from anyone around them. "Thieves," on the other hand, usually confine their stealing to incidents that are well planned out and where there is the opportunity for a sizable return on their risky behavior. "Hustlers" do just that—they hustle to create opportunities for criminal action. Hustlers are often quite entrepreneurial and dedicate their energy to making ends meet through criminal behavior. Finally, "outlaws" are, according to Shover, men who have fully and completely internalized the criminal lifestyle. Much like Wright and Decker's armed robbers, Shover's outlaws participate in crime and violence as part of their everyday existence. These men can be brutal and dangerous.

Adults with high levels of criminality can pose a serious problem for any community, and they pose a serious threat to those around them. They help to destroy the quality of life in the local area by eroding the social trust required for good social order. However, as we have endeavored to make clear, the precursors to their criminal actions were likely visible early in their life course, and most followed a general antisocial pathway that has led them to this point in their lives. If they continue to survive—because many die a premature, violent death—their lives will be littered with arrests, bouts of incarceration, limited to no employment skills, drug addiction, homelessness, mental health problems, and relationship failures. A life of crime, a life of criminal involvement, is not a life that can be sustained. It is not healthy, socially or psychologically, and it places a great burden on society. In the end, criminality, fully exposed, is nothing more than a life of wasted opportunities.

BOX 11.1 The Continuing Saga of Stanley: A Not-So-Happy Follow-Up at Age 70

An excellent follow-up to Stanley's development was completed approximately 50 years later (published in 1982 by Lexington Books) by Jon Snodgrass, along with commentary by highly respected criminological experts (including Gilbert Geis, James F. Short, and Solomon Kobrin). In this follow-up, Snodgrass had Stanley discuss various key events in his life over that 50-year period. Notably, Stanley gave his dedication for the book to one person: Clifford R. Shaw, who was key in documenting not only his story, but also his efforts at rehabilitation.

Regarding the time period since the publication of the original book, Stanley revealed that he had a number of negative occurrences in his life. These included the demise of his first marriage, his movement from one job to another, an attempted holdup of a businessman (which led to only a misdemeanor charge even though he had discharged a weapon five times), a period of depression and physical alterations, his stay at a state hospital, a second marriage (in which he admitted to physically hitting her), and his move to California. However, there were some high times as well. For example, he made a significant amount of money at certain jobs, made a number of friends, and had some stable employment during some of these 50 years. However, Stanley also made clear that he had major issues with some of his employers and was trying to pursue legal options for getting certain wages.

In the end, largely through interviews done by Snodgrass, Stanley appeared not to have changed much. Specifically, regarding incidents in which Stanley was aggressive to others (in this particular case, it was to a taxi driver), Snodgrass asked him (p. 100): "Is there a noteworthy instance where you didn't act aggressively?" Stanley then replied: "Well, nothing, uh [long pause]." Thus, it appears that although Stanley had moved away from his proactive, violent activity, his ability to adapt to the daily frustrations in everyday life had not improved much.

This is supported by the fact that Stanley, even at the approximate age of 70, appeared defiant when asked about confrontations with others. For example, regarding the previous incident with the taxi driver, Stanley said, "To myself I say, 'That sonofabitch, I should've broke his neck,' or something like that" (p. 100). In another incident that occurred at a bar in California, Stanley claimed that when a female bartender got "nasty" with him, he said: "Listen, you bitch. . . . You say another goddamn word, I'll throw this goddamn drink right in your face and kick your cunt in on top of it" (p. 110). Her boyfriend, who happened to be there, approached Stanley, and as Stanley claimed,

> *I kicked his fuckin' head in. I kicked him unmercifully. He was just lucky I didn't have these shoes on, I'da killed him and I didn't give a shit. But I had those light tan shoes on and I just kicked his face in and his head and I wanted to kill the son-ofabitch. (p. 110)*

Although there are many other examples provided in Snodgrass' follow-up to Stanley's story, these passages make it clear that he was not a good citizen in society. This supports the stability of criminality among individuals. Although it may take numerous forms, especially as people age, it appears that persons who have a high propensity toward violence and other criminal behaviors are often unable to escape such tendencies, even as they age. Furthermore, although Shaw suggests at the close of the original publication of *The Jack-Roller* that the story of Stanley had a happy ending, this appears not to be the case in Snodgrass' follow-up 50 years later. Rather, Stanley appears to be a bitter, violent man who is not remorseful for his actions and is a bad fit for conventional society.

CHAPTER 12

Policy Recommendations

W e arrive at the last chapter cautiously hopeful. If we have done our job, you should have a better sense of the complexity of criminality. You should also have a better understanding of how biological and social variables combine and interact, in some cases, to produce pathological behavior, and in other cases, to produce human resilience.

We are also optimistic. We are optimistic because a biosocial understanding of the development of criminality points to opportunities for effective intervention and prevention. Indeed, there is now consistent empirical evidence that a range of planned and directed efforts can prevent criminality or can reduce criminal behavior once criminality emerges. By pinpointing critical periods of development, dynamic risk factors, and sources of potential, it is possible to help children avoid a lifetime of problem behaviors, as well as to reduce the number of victims of crime in society.

We cannot help but point out that a biosocial approach to understanding criminality does not inevitably lead to harsh, repressive state interventions, as critics of biosocial approaches claim. Quite the contrary, understanding the interrelationships between biological and social development illuminates a range of humane interventions along the life course. More importantly, this understanding can come closer to attacking the root causes of criminality than can theories that locate the causes of crime far from the individual.

In this chapter, we lay out specific policy recommendations that emerge from biosocial criminology. We make no claims that the policies we put forward are exhaustive, as new techniques for intervention and prevention continue to evolve. However, we do note that most of our recommendations have some degree of empirical support—that is, research evidence shows that these efforts have been successful.

Contextual Factors

Remove Environmental Toxins

Healthy human development cannot occur in polluted areas. Still, today, in many inner cities, children are exposed to toxic levels of environmental pollutants that can have disastrous effects on their brains and their development. The deleterious effects are known, pervasive, and unalterable. From our point of view, there is no justification for the continued poisoning of children. The financial costs may be steep, but they are outweighed by the costs to human life.

Share Information Across Service Providers

If it takes a community to raise a child, then it follows that members of that community need to talk to each other. Unfortunately, service providers, such as social workers, teachers, police officers, and psychologists, are often legally forbidden to communicate with each other. Laws pertaining to confidentiality should be changed to better facilitate the exchange and flow of information. One of the secrets of many service providers is that they all deal with the same individuals and families. Insights and information garnered from one group, however, usually cannot be shared with another group that is also working with the family. It is time to rethink this arrangement.

Parenting Classes for All Serious Felons

Having criminal parents elevates the risk of antisocial behavior in children. The causal mechanisms are likely a mix of genetic, biological, and social variables, but there is little doubt that criminal parents represent a serious risk to the healthy development of children. Empirical data also confirm that seriously criminal individuals also produce an above-average number of offspring.

This group of individuals is known and identifiable. They pose serious problems to society and, more importantly, to the healthy development of their children. We recommend that this information be used to help ameliorate these risks, prepare these individuals for parenthood, help them with medical and psychological problems, and teach them how to be reasonably good parents.

Rework the Foster Care System

One of the dirty little secrets of the social service arena is that the foster care system is in dire need of reorganization. Children placed in the foster care system are usually of very high risk for a range of behavioral and psychological problems. Many foster parents are not prepared or adequately trained for dealing with these types of youths. Moreover, too many foster parents also have serious behavioral problems, including lengthy criminal histories, patterns of drug abuse, and mental health issues. Foster parents should be better screened and evaluated, better trained and supervised, and supported in their efforts to support children.

Victim Counseling

As criminologists, we tend to focus on offenders, but as the empirical evidence has shown, being a victim of crime can have serious consequences. Victims of crime face financial losses; psychological trauma; and, sometimes, serious physical hardships. Innocent victims of violent crime deserve more than waiting years for a trial, they deserve more than the pain and misery imposed on them by another, and they deserve help to regain their lives. Ignoring their pain only serves to victimize them once again.

Better Training and Education of Justice Professionals

As a rule, many individual justice professionals, such as police officers, counselors, and probation and parole agents, are well intentioned, decent, and hard working. They believe they are making society safer. With that said, too many are still lacking in even the most basic understanding of human development and the principles of effective interventions.

From our viewpoint, justice professionals should be exposed to the full range of knowledge about human development and about what works in intervening in the lives of individuals. Moreover, there needs to be greater accountability for those who provide direct services to offenders. Too many programs have been implemented that have been doomed from the outset because they did not follow what is known about changing behavior. Too many programs do not work and too many make the conduct of offenders worse instead of better. We advocate more research into effective interventions and we advocate greater accountability for those who work with offenders both young and old.

Later School Hours

Much crime occurs immediately after youths leave school for the day—usually between 2 p.m. and 3 p.m. Most parents, indeed, most adults are not home during these hours. This makes no sense. As a matter of practical social control, schools should extend their operating hours until closer to the time when parents leave work.

Continued Research Into
Pharmaceutical Therapies for Behavioral Disorders

Medication has saved the lives of countless individuals with mental disorders, and it has given new opportunities for children with attention deficit hyperactivity disorder to live lives without the range of problems associated with the disorder. Certain individuals need medications such as selective serotonin reuptake inhibitors to function normally. We believe it is past time for criminologists to advocate for increased research into effective pharmaceutical interventions for individuals with behavioral disorders.

Prior to Birth

Health Care, Including Mental Health Care, for Pregnant Women and Infants

Health care for pregnant women is critical for the healthy development of the fetus and mother. We recognize the debate surrounding health care in America, but we believe that all interest groups would view providing quality health care to all pregnant women, but especially to those with high-risk pregnancies, as money well spent. Moreover, because many high-risk pregnancies are accompanied by maternal and paternal mental health issues, we also believe that the best interventions would be holistic, including counseling and psychiatric support services when necessary.

Once the infants are born, we would also advocate for universal health care coverage for all children in the United States. Although federal bills addressing this issue have been proposed in recent years, they have encountered strong political opposition in recent years. However, medical studies have consistently shown that each dollar spent on prevention saves at least $10 in future treatment, not to mention the financial and societal impact that such early health care would have on reducing crime rates.

Legally Mandated Intervention for Drug-Addicted Pregnant Women

This is a difficult issue in a democratic country. Its difficulty, however, should no longer deter us from taking this issue seriously. The ingestion of neurotoxins by the mother poses serious health and developmental risks to the developing fetus. The current debates surrounding abortion, when life begins, and the extension of constitutional guarantees to unborn children do not deny the horrible harm that is done when pregnant addicts subject their fetuses to high levels of drugs and alcohol. Instead of taking a laissez-faire approach to this serious issue, we believe it is time to take it seriously and to intervene on behalf of the child. We have laws that prevent smoking in public places because of our understanding of the deleterious effects of secondhand smoke; surely we could pass laws banning the induction of nicotine and narcotics into a developing child.

At Birth

Intensive Social Work for High-Risk Pregnancies

Almost all children born in the United States are now born in hospitals. This offers an incredible opportunity to target services to high-risk families and to families in need. A broad array of information is typically collected at the birth of a child. This information should be used to help identify those at the highest risk for health and behavioral problems. Relatedly, we believe that it is time for prognostic information to be provided to new parents. Children born too early or born underweight are at risk for a range of cognitive and behavioral problems. New parents should be informed of this and instructed on what to watch for and what to do if problems emerge. Evaluation of all children in at-risk families should be undertaken.

After Birth

Systematic Early Intervention

Interventions should not stop once the child is born. For those in need, services should be provided for free through the age of 8. We envision a comprehensive set of services that could be housed in a single building—a one-stop shop designed to evaluate the development of at-risk youths. Children who fall behind developmentally, display an early onset of behavioral pathology, or manifest indicators of future behavioral problems would be able to obtain comprehensive interventions to help them overcome any developmental deficit.

Flagging At-Risk Kids in Doctors' Offices

All children in the United States visit a doctor's office. This is again an opportunity to flag children and families in need of services. Children with serious behavior problems should be referred to service providers just as children with cancer are referred to cancer specialists. It is time for the medical community to take behavior problems as seriously as they take health-related problems.

Training for Parents

Parenting is hard, difficult, and rewarding work. Most parents offer an environment with sufficient stimulation and stability. However, some parents struggle to be good parents but have only a limited understanding of effective parenting. These parents benefit from parent training, and parent training has been shown to reduce problem behavior in youths and adolescents.

Other parents, however, are selfish, callous, abusive, and neglectful. We believe the research evidence is of sufficient quality and quantity to warrant taking abuse and neglect more seriously. Abusive and neglectful parents should face the full penalty of law, but they should also be provided opportunities to become reasonable parents. For those who do not take their responsibilities seriously, or who pose a threat to their children, their parental rights should be terminated and their children placed with highly trained "professional" parents.

Child Development

Universal Preschool With Full Developmental Evaluations

The most serious offenders typically have an early onset of problem behavior, and they do not tend to "age out" of the use of physical aggression. This information is meaningful as it points to the critical need for early intervention. Preschool settings are natural social arenas where children interact with authority figures other than their parents, as well as with other children. With an eye toward the early onset of problematic behavior, we see it as reasonable that every child be evaluated continuously from preschool through at least third or fourth grade. This should allow adequate time for the accumulation of evidence showing that a child is seriously at risk for a life course of problem behavior.

Along these lines, we can envision a system of continual assessment from pre-K through at least fourth grade. Children with behavioral problems, self-control problems, and/or language problems could be identified, given help, and tracked so that they do not "fall between the cracks" or fail before entering middle school.

Males and Females Are Different

Normal behavior for males may not be normal behavior for females. Males tend to be more aggressive in their play, more hierarchical in their relationships, and more status oriented. These qualities are not immoral, bad, or "wrong." Elementary and middle schools, however, tend to equate these behaviors and orientations as disruptive and/or masculine. It is difficult to argue that some male-type behaviors are not disruptive in certain environments, but it would be wrong to conclude that normative male behavior is always criminogenic. We are not advocating the enforcement of old and outdated social roles, simply the awareness that the male "world" is different from the female world. Males should understand the limits of aggression, but they should not be socially neutered.

Adolescence

Free Mental Health and Drug Counseling

Adolescents are usually forced to rely on their parents' insurance to receive counseling services. This means that they have to approach their parents to receive these services, get their permission to receive these services, and face their parents while divulging potentially embarrassing information. This arrangement makes it very difficult for adolescents to get the help they need. Barriers to obtaining services should be removed.

Zero Tolerance Is Foolish

Many schools have enacted "zero tolerance" policies that ban certain types of behaviors. Youths in violation of these policies are typically expelled from school. Although dangerous kids clearly pose a problem for school officials and have to be managed accordingly, most kids are not dangerous nor are their behaviors seriously threatening. Youths, especially teenage males, will get into physical altercations; most of the time, these altercations are minor and involve merely pushing and shoving. This should not be considered criminal conduct. We recommend replacing "zero tolerance" policies with the application of "maximum reason."

Juvenile Justice Should Hold Youths Accountable and Try to Rehabilitate Them

Juvenile justice systems must balance the public mandate to dispense justice and the public mandate to rehabilitate youths. Unfortunately, many juvenile systems do both equally poorly. There is no individual accountability, and efforts to reform youths border on the ridiculous.

Adulthood

Treatment and Punishment

Some individuals are too dangerous to be free. Other individuals may not be dangerous but may commit so much crime that jail or prison is necessary. Criminologists sometimes underestimate the degree of pathology embedded in many adult criminals. We see incarceration as a tool that can be used to reduce crime, at least in the margins, and as a tool for the distribution of justice. Its use should be limited primarily to serious and chronic offenders. Even here, however, we see the opportunity for rehabilitation and reform. The empirical evidence does show, quite consistently, that rehabilitation programs that target high-risk individuals, address criminogenic needs, and provide cognitive-behavioral treatment can reduce recidivism by 20% to 30% on average. Punishment and rehabilitation are not mutually exclusive.

Caveats

Our recommendations cross the political spectrum—that is, some will appeal to liberals and some to conservatives. Although we do not see the passage of these changes as insurmountable, we are keenly aware that many intractable policy differences exist. On one hand, it has been our experience that liberals will accuse us of wanting to widen the net of social control, targeting the poor or minorities, and labeling young people as potential offenders. On the other hand, conservatives will accuse us of wanting the state to take on a burden it should not handle, be it parenting classes or health care for children. We find these criticisms to be politically based and without empirical merit.

From our point of view, it is time for rigorous science to trump political ideology. We can no longer ignore the central findings in this book, namely, that criminality is produced by a complex intermingling of genetic, biological, and social factors; criminality can be stable across time and place; criminality emerges early in the life course; and, ultimately, criminality leads to incarceration, a life of misery, or premature death. Criminality should be taken as seriously as cancer because the effects can be equivalent. Caregivers, child care providers, teachers, counselors, school resource officers, social workers, judges, probation officers, and direct service providers should understand that criminality should not be ignored out of fear that any intervention will "widen the net of social control," or that it will disproportionately affect a minority group. Children of any color sometimes need help. To ignore their developmental needs out of a sense of saving them from an invisible label is tantamount to malign neglect or malpractice. The science to help is there. The only real obstacle for its implementation is us.

Closing Thoughts

This chapter was written immediately after the Virginia Tech college shootings. We were struck by the emotional callousness of the shooter, but more importantly, we were struck by the visible, telltale signs that the shooter had serious behavioral and psychological problems long before he ever acted violently. More information about the shooter will eventually surface, but suffice it to say that many of the biological and social risk factors we discussed in this book were clearly visible to anyone who knew the shooter.

Our desire is that the information presented in this book will be used for the betterment of society. As we noted above, a biosocial understanding of serious, pathological behavior can lead to a better understanding of the causes of maladaptive conduct. More importantly, a biosocial understanding of the development of criminality can also lead to a range of effective prevention and intervention programs. Empirically validated interventions targeted to those at the highest risk of criminality can reduce offending behaviors and thus ultimately reduce the number of crime victims.

Victims of crime do not care if the causes of an offender's conduct were biological, genetic, or social. They care only about picking up the pieces of their lives. As students of human behavior, we should follow suit and quit enforcing disciplinary boundaries that favor certain perspectives while simultaneously demonizing others. Human development, especially criminality, is highly complex. We need all the help we can get to better understand it.

References

Achenbach, T. M., Edelbrock, C., & Howell, C. T. (1987). Empirically based assessment of the behavioral/emotional problems of 2- and 3- year-old children. *Journal of Abnormal Child Psychology, 15*(4), 629–650.

Achenbach, T. M., Howell, C. T., Quay, H. C., & Conners, C. K. (1991). National survey of problems and competencies among four- to sixteen-year-olds: Parents' reports for normative and clinical samples. *Monographs of the Society for Research in Child Development, 56*(3), 1–131.

Akers, R. L. (2000). *Criminological theories: Introduction, evaluation, and application.* Los Angeles: Roxbury.

Alexander, G. M., & Hines, M. (2002). Sex differences in response to children's toys in non-human primates (*Cercopithecus aethiops sabaeus*). *Evolution and Human Behavior, 23*(6), 467–479.

Alwin, D. F. (1994). Aging, personality, and social change: The stability of individual differences over the adult life span. In D. L. Featherman, R. M. Lerner, & M. Perlmutter (Eds.), *Life span development and behavior* (pp. 135–185). Hillsdale, NJ: Lawrence Erlbaum.

Ames, E. W. (1997). *The development of Romanian orphanage children adopted to Canada: Final report.* Burnaby, BC, Canada: Simon Fraser University.

Ames, E., & Carter, M. (1992). A study of Romanian orphanage children in Canada: Background, sample, and procedure. *Canadian Psychology, 33,* 503.

Anderson, E. (1999). *Code of the street: Decency, violence, and the moral life of the inner city.* New York: Norton.

Anderson, T. S., & Magnusson, D. (1990). Biological maturation in adolescence and the development of drinking habits and alcohol abuse among males: A prospective longitudinal study. *Journal of Youth and Adolescence, 19,* 33–42.

Archer, J. (1991). The influence of testosterone on human aggression. *British Journal of Psychology, 82*(1), 1–28.

Arrigo, B. A., & Shipley, S. L. (2004). *Introduction to forensic psychology.* St. Louis, MO: Elsevier.

Arseneault, L., Tremblay, R. E., Boulerice, B., & Saucier, J. F. (2002). Obstetrical complications and violent delinquency: Testing two developmental pathways. *Child Development, 73*(2), 496–508.

Asberg, M., Traskman, L., & Thoren, P. (1976). 5-HIAA in the cerebrospinal fluid: A biochemical suicide predictor? *Archives of General Psychiatry, 33*(10), 1193–1197.

Asendorpf, J. B. (1992). Continuity and stability of personality traits and personality patterns. In J. B. Asendorpf & J. Valsiner (Eds.), *Stability and change in development: A study of methodological reasoning* (pp. 116–154). Thousand Oaks, CA: Sage.

Audesirk, G., & Audesirk, G. (1989). *Biology: Life on Earth.* Upper Saddle River, NJ: Prentice Hall.

Bagwell, C. L., Coie, J. D., Terry, R. A., & Lochman, J. E. (2000). Peer clique participation and social status in preadolescence. *Merrill-Palmer Quarterly, 46*(2), 280–305.

Bandura, A. (1979). The social learning perspective: Mechanisms of aggression. In H. Toch (Ed.), *Psychology of crime and criminal justice* (pp. 298–336). New York: Holt, Rinehart and Winston.

Banich, M. T., & Heller, W. (1998). Evolving perspectives on lateralization of function. *Current Directions in Psychological Science, 7*(1), 1–2.

Barkley, R. A. (1997). *ADHD and the nature of self-control.* New York: Guilford.

Barkley, R. A. (1998). *Attention-deficit hyperactivity disorder* (2nd ed.). New York: Scientific American.

Baron-Cohen, S. (2004). *The essential difference: Male and female brains and the truth about autism.* New York: Basic Books.

Beatty, J. (2001). *The human brain: Essentials of behavioral neuroscience.* Thousand Oaks, CA: Sage.

Beaver, K. M., & Wright, J. P. (2005). Biosocial development and delinquent involvement. *Youth Violence and Juvenile Justice, 3,* 168–192.

Becker, H. S. (1963). *Outsiders: Studies in the sociology of deviance.* New York: Free Press.

Begley, S. (2001a). In search of the roots of evil. *Newsweek, 137*(21), 30–35.

Begley, S. (2001b). Religion in the brain. *Newsweek, 137*(19), 50–56.

Belfrage, H., Lidberg, L., & Oreland, L. (1992). Platelet monoamine oxidase activity in mentally disordered violent offenders. *Acta Psychiatrica Scandinavica, 85*(3), 218–221.

Benasich, A. A., Curtiss, S., & Tallal, P. (1993). Language, learning, and behavioral disturbances in childhood: A longitudinal perspective. *Journal of the American Academy of Child and Adolescent Psychiatry, 32*(3), 585–594.

Benjamin, J., Li, L., Patterson, C., Greenberg, B. D., Murphy, D. L., & Hamer, D. H. (1996). Population and familial association between the D4 dopamine receptor gene and measures of novelty seeking. *Nature Genetics, 12*(1), 81–84.

Benson, M. L. (2002). *Crime and the life course: An introduction.* Los Angeles: Roxbury.

Berson, D. M., Dunn, F. A., & Takao, M. (2002). Phototransduction by retinal ganglion cells that set the circadian clock. *Science, 295*(5557), 1070–1073.

Biederman, J., Newcorn, J., & Sprich, S. (1991). Comorbidity of attention deficit hyperactivity disorder (ADHD). *American Journal of Psychiatry, 148,* 564–577.

Bishop, K. M., & Wahlsten, D. (1997). Sex differences in the human corpus callosum: Myth or reality? *Neuroscience and Biobehavioral Review, 21*(5), 581–601.

Bjork, J. M., Knutson, B., Fong, G. W., Caggiano, D. M., Bennett, S. M., & Hommer, D. W. (2004). Incentive-elicited brain activation in adolescents: Similarities and differences from young adults. *Journal of Neuroscience, 24*(8), 1793–1811.

Black, I. B. (1991). *Information in the brain: A molecular perspective.* Cambridge: MIT Press.

Blakemore, S. J., & Choudhury, S. (2006). Development of the adolescent brain: Implications for executive function and social cognition. *Journal of Child Psychology and Psychiatry, and Allied Disciplines, 47*(3–4), 296–312.

Blumer, D., & Benson, D. F. (1975). Personality changes with frontal and temporal lobe lesions. In D. F. Benson & D. Blumer (Eds.), *Psychiatric aspects of neurologic disease* (pp. 151–170). New York: Grune & Stratton.

Blumstein, A., Cohen, J., & Farrington, D. P. (1988). Criminal career research: Its value for criminology. *Criminology, 26*(1), 1–35.

Blumstein, A., Cohen, J., Roth, J. A., & Visher, C. A. (1986). *Criminal careers and career criminals.* Washington, DC: National Academy Press.

Blundell, J. (1975). *Physiological psychology.* London: Methuen.

Boldizar, J. P., Perry, D. G., & Perry, L. C. (1989). Outcome values and aggression. *Child Development, 60*(3), 571–579.

Booth, A., & Osgood, D. W. (1993). The influence of testosterone on deviance in adulthood: Assessing and explaining the relationship. *Criminology, 31,* 93–117.

Bouchard, T. J., Jr. (1987). *Environmental determinants of IQ similarity in identical twins reared apart.* Paper presented at the 17th annual meeting of the Behavior Genetics Association, Minneapolis, MN.

Bradshaw, J. L. (2001). *Developmental disorders of the frontostriatal system: Neuropsychological, neuropsychiatric, and evolutionary perspectives.* Philadelphia: Taylor & Francis.

Brennan, P. A., Grekin, E. R., & Mednick, S. A. (1999). Maternal smoking during pregnancy and adult male criminal outcomes. *Archives of General Psychiatry, 56*(3), 215–219.

Brinton, B., & Fujiki, M. (1993). Language, social skills, and socioemotional behavior. *Language, Speech, and Hearing Services in Schools, 24*(4), 194–198.

Brody, G. H., Stoneman, Z., & Burke, M. (1988). Child temperament and parental perceptions of individual child adjustment: An intrafamiliar analysis. *American Journal of Orthopsychiatry, 58*(4), 532–542.

Brook, J. S., & Newcomb, M. D. (1995). Childhood aggression and unconventionality: Impact on later academic achievement, drug use, and workforce involvement. *Journal of Genetic Psychology, 156*(4), 393–410.

Brooks-Gunn, J., & Warren, M. P. (1989). Biological and social contributions to negative affect in young adolescent girls. *Child Development, 60*(1), 40–55.

Brown, G. L., Goodwin, F. K., Ballenger, J. C., Goyer, P. F., & Major, L. F. (1979). Aggression in humans correlates with cerebrospinal fluid amine metabolites. *Psychiatry Research, 1*(2), 131–139.

Brown, S., Esbensen, F., & Geis, G. (2006). *Criminology: Explaining crime and its context* (5th ed.). Cincinnati, OH: Anderson.

Brunner, H. G., Nelen, M., Breakefield, X. O., Ropers, H. H., & van Oost, B. A. (1993). Abnormal behavior associated with a point mutation in the structural gene for monoamine oxidase A. *Science, 262*(5133), 578.

Buka, S. L., Tsuang, M. T., & Lipsitt, L. P. (1993). Pregnancy/delivery complications and psychiatric diagnosis: A prospective study. *Archives of General Psychiatry, 50*(2), 151–156.

Buss, A. H., & Plomin, R. (1984). *Temperament: Early developing personality traits.* Hillsdale, NJ: Lawrence Erlbaum.

Buss, D. M., Block, J. H., & Block, J. (1980). Preschool activity level: Personality correlates and developmental implications. *Child Development, 51*(2), 401–408.

Buydens-Branchey, L., & Branchey, M. H. (1992). Cortisol in alcoholics with a disordered aggression control. *Psychoneuroendocrinology, 17*(1), 45–54.

Cadoret, R. J., Leve, L. D., & Devor, E. (1997). Genetics of aggressive and violent behavior. *Psychiatric Clinics of North America, 20*(2), 301–322.

Cairns, R. B., & Cairns, B. D. (1994). *Lifelines and risks: Pathways of youth in our time.* Cambridge, UK: Cambridge University Press.

Cairns, R. B., Cairns, B. D., & Neckerman, H. J. (1989). Early school dropout: Configurations and determinants. *Child Development, 60*(6), 1437–1452.

Campbell, S. B. (1990). *Behavior problems in preschool children: Clinical and developmental issues.* New York: Guilford.

Campbell, S. B. (1995). Behavior problems in preschool children: A review of recent research. *Journal of Child Psychology and Psychiatry and Allied Disciplines, 36*(1), 113–149.

Campbell, S. B. (1997). Behavior problems in preschool children: Developmental and family issues. *Advances in Clinical Child Psychology, 19,* 1–26.

Campbell, S. B. (2002). *Behavior problems in preschool children.* New York: Guilford.

Campbell, S. B., & Breaux, A. M. (1983). Maternal ratings of activity level and symptomatic behaviors in a nonclinical sample of young children. *Journal of Pediatric Psychology, 8*(1), 73–82.

Campbell, S. B., Breaux, A. M., Ewing, L. J., & Szumowski, E. K. (1984). A one-year follow-up study of parent-referred hyperactive preschool children. *Journal of the American Academy of Child Psychiatry, 23*(3), 243–249.

Campbell, S. B., & Ewing, L. J. (1990). Follow-up of hard-to-manage preschoolers: Adjustment at age 9 and predictors of continuing symptoms. *Journal of Child Psychology and Psychiatry and Allied Disciplines, 31*(6), 871–889.

Campbell, S. B., March, C. L., Pierce, E. W., Ewing, L. J., & Szumowski, E. K. (1991). Hard-to-manage preschool boys: Family context and the stability of externalizing behavior. *Journal of Abnormal Child Psychology, 19*(3), 301–318.

Campbell, S. B., Pierce, E. W., March, C. L., Ewing, L. J., & Szumowski, E. K. (1994). Hard-to-manage preschool boys: Symptomatic behavior across contexts and time. *Child Development, 65*(3), 836–851.

Campbell, S. B., Shaw, D. S., & Gilliom, M. (2000). Early externalizing behavior problems: Toddlers and preschoolers at risk for later maladjustment. *Development and Psychopathology, 12*(3), 467–488.

Canli, T., Desmond, J. E., Zhao, Z., & Gabrieli, J. D. E. (2002). Sex differences in the neural basis of emotional memories. *Proceedings of the National Academy of Sciences, 99,* 10789–10794.

Caplan, P. J., Crawford, M., Hyde, J. S., & Richardson, J. T. E. (1997). *Gender differences in human cognition.* New York: Oxford University Press.

Carey, G. (2003). *Human genetics for the social sciences.* Thousand Oaks, CA: Sage.

Carmichael, M. (2003). Mother knows best. *Newsweek, 142*(20), 8.

Carmichael, M. (2007). Stronger, faster, smarter. *Newsweek, 149*(13), 38–46.

Carnegie Corporation of New York. (1995). *Great transitions: Preparing adolescents for a new century.* New York: Author.

Cases, O., Seif, I., Grimsby, J., Gaspar, P., Chen, K., & Pournin, S. (1995). Aggressive behavior and altered amounts of brain serotonin and norepinephrine in mice lacking MAOA. *Science, 268*(5218), 1763–1766.

Caspi, A., & Bem, D. J. (1990). *Personality continuity and change across the life course.* New York: Guilford.

Caspi, A., Bem, D. J., & Elder, G. H.,Jr. (1989). Continuities and consequences of interactional styles across the life course. *Journal of Personality, 57*(2), 375–406.

Caspi, A., Henry, B., McGee, R. O., Moffitt, T. E., & Silva, P. A. (1995). Temperamental origins of child and adolescent behavior problems: From age three to age fifteen. *Child Development, 66*(1), 55–68.

Caspi, A., & Herbener, E. S. (1990). Continuity and change: Assortative marriage and the consistency of personality in adulthood. *Journal of Personality and Social Psychology, 58*(2), 250–258.

Caspi, A., Lynam, D., Moffitt, T. E., & Silva, P. A. (1993). Unraveling girls' delinquency: Biological, dispositional, and contextual contributions to adolescent misbehavior. *Developmental Psychology, 29*(1), 19–30.

Caspi, A., McClay, J., Moffitt, T. E., Mill, J., Martin, J., & Craig, I. W. (2002). Role of genotype in the cycle of violence in maltreated children. *Science, 297,* 851–854.

Caspi, A., & Moffitt, T. E. (1991). Individual differences are accentuated during periods of social change: The sample case of girls at puberty. *Journal of Personality and Social Psychology, 61*(1), 157–168.

Caspi, A., & Moffitt, T. E. (1993). When do individual differences matter? A paradoxical theory of personality coherence. *Psychological Inquiry, 4*(4), 247–271.

Caspi, A., & Moffitt, T. E. (1995). The continuity of maladaptive behavior: From description to understanding in the study of antisocial behavior. In D. Cicchetti & D. Cohen (Eds.), *Manual of developmental psychopathology* (pp. 472–511). New York: Wiley.

Caspi, A., & Silva, P. A. (1995). Temperamental qualities at age three predict personality traits in young adulthood: Longitudinal evidence from a birth cohort. *Child development, 66*(2), 486–498.

Caspi, A., Sugden, K., Moffitt, T. E., Taylor, A., Craig, I. W., Harrington, H., et al. (2003). Influence of life stress on depression: Moderation by a polymorphism in the 5-HTT gene. *Science, 301*(5631), 386–389.

Caspi, A., Wright, B. R. E., Moffitt, T. E., & Silva, P. A. (1998). Early failure in the labor market: Childhood and adolescent predictors of unemployment in the transition to adulthood. *American Sociological Review, 63*(3), 424–451.

Centers for Disease Control and Prevention (CDC). (2005). Varicella-related deaths—United States, January 2003-June 2004. *Morbidity and Mortality Weekly Report, 54*(11), 272–274.

Champion, L. A., Goodall, G., & Rutter, M. (1995). Behaviour problems in childhood and stressors in early adult life: A 20 year follow-up of London school children. *Psychological Medicine, 25*(2), 231–246.

Chandler, M., & Moran, T. (1990). Psychopathy and moral development: A comparative study of delinquent and nondelinquent youth. *Development and Psychopathology, 2,* 227–246.

Chess, S., & Thomas, A. (1977). Temperamental individuality from childhood to adolescence. *Journal of the American Academy of Child Psychiatry, 16*(2), 218–226.

Christiansen, K. O. (1977). A preliminary study of criminality among twins. In S. A. Mednick & K. O. Christiansen (Eds.), *Biosocial bases of criminal behavior* (pp. 89–108). New York: Gardner.

Chugani, H. T., Behen, M. E., Muzik, O., Juhasz, C., Nagy, F., & Chugani, D. C. (2001). Local brain functional activity following early deprivation: A study of postinstitutionalized Romanian orphans. *NeuroImage, 14*(6), 1290–1301.

Citrome, L., & Volavka, J. (1997). Psychopharmacology of violence, Part I: Assessment and acute treatment. *Psychiatric Annals, 27,* 691–695.

Clark, W. R., & Grunstein, M. (2000). *Are we hardwired? The role of genes in human behavior.* New York: Oxford University Press.

Clausen, J. S. (1991). Adolescent competence and the shaping of the life course. *American Journal of Sociology, 96*(4), 805–842.

Coccaro, E. F., Bergeman, C. S., & McClearn, G. E. (1993). Heritability of irritable impulsiveness: A study of twins reared together and apart. *Psychiatry Research, 48*(3), 229–242.

Coccaro, E. F., Lawrence, T., Trestman, R., Gabriel, S., Klar, H. M., & Siever, L. J. (1991). Growth hormone responses to intravenous clonidine challenge correlate with behavioral irritability in psychiatric patients and healthy volunteers. *Psychiatry Research, 39*(2), 129–139.

Coccaro, E. F., & Murphy, D. L. (1990). *Serotonin in major psychiatric disorders.* Washington, DC: American Psychiatric Press.

Cohen, A. K. (1955). *Delinquent boys: The culture of the gang.* New York: Free Press.

Cohen, D. B. (1999). *Strangers in the nest: Do parents really shape their child's personality, intelligence, or character?* New York: Wiley.

Cohen, J. (1986). Research on criminal careers: Individual frequency rates and offense seriousness. In A. Blumstein, J. Cohen, J. A. Roth, & C. A. Visher (Eds.), *Criminal careers and career criminals* (pp. 292–418). Washington, DC: National Academy Press.

Coie, J. D., Terry, R., Lenox, K. F., Lochman, J. E., & Hyman, C. (1995). Peer rejection and aggression as predictors of stable risk across adolescence. *Development and Psychopathology, 7,* 697–713.

Collier, D. A., Stober, G., Li, T., Heils, A., Catalano, M., & Di Bella, D. (1996). A novel functional polymorphism within the promoter of the serotonin transporter gene: Possible role in susceptibility to affective disorders. *Molecular Psychiatry, 1*(6), 453–460.

Collins, D. W., & Kimura, D. (1997). A large sex difference on a two-dimensional mental rotation task. *Behavioral Neuroscience, 111*(4), 845–849.

Collins, W. A., Maccoby, E. E., Steinberg, L., Hetherington, E. M., & Bornstein, M. H. (2000). Contemporary research on parenting: The case for nature and nurture. *American Psychologist, 55*(2), 218–232.

Conley, J. J. (1984). The hierarchy of consistency: A review and model of longitudinal findings on adult individual differences in intelligence, personality and self-opinion. *Personality and Individual Differences, 5*(1), 11–25.

Coren, S. (1992). *The left-hander syndrome.* New York: Free Press.

Coren, S. (1993). *The left-hander syndrome* (1st Vintage Books ed.). New York: Vintage.

Cornely, P., & Bromet, E. (1986). Prevalence of behavior problems in three-year-old children living near Three Mile Island: A comparative analysis. *Journal of Child Psychology and Psychiatry and Allied Disciplines, 27*(4), 489–498.

Crowther, J. H., Bond, L. A., & Rolf, J. E. (1981). The incidence, prevalence, and severity of behavior disorders among preschool-aged children in day care. *Journal of Abnormal Child Psychology, 9*(1), 23–42.

Cummings, E. M., Iannotti, R. J., & Zahn-Waxler, C. (1989). Aggression between peers in early childhood: Individual continuity and developmental change. *Child Development, 60*(4), 887–895.

Dabbs, J. M., Jr., & Hargrove, M. F. (1997). Age, testosterone, and behavior among female prisoners. *Psychosomatic Medicine, 59,* 477–480.

Dabbs, J. M., Jr., Jurkovic, G. J., & Frady, R. L. (1991). Salivary testosterone and cortisol among late adolescent male offenders. *Journal of Abnormal Child Psychology, 19*(4), 469–478.

Dalgaard, O. S., & Kringlen, E. (1976). A Norwegian study of criminality. *British Journal of Criminology, 16,* 213–232.

Damasio, A. R. (1994). *Emotion, reason and the human brain.* New York: Grosset Putnam.

Damasio, A. R., Tranel, D., & Damasio, H. (1990). Individuals with sociopathic behavior caused by frontal damage fail to respond autonomically to social stimuli. *Behavioural Brain Research, 41*(2), 81–94.

Damasio, H., Grabowski, T., Frank, R., Galaburda, A. M., & Damasio, A. R. (1994). The return of Phineas Gage: Clues about the brain from the skull of a famous patient. *Science, 264*(5162), 1102–1105.

Daniels, M., & Tibbetts, S. G. (2005, February). *Personality differences in predicting assault and binge drinking: Variation across explanatory factors and gender.* Paper presented at the annual meeting of the Western Society of Criminology in Honolulu, Hawaii. Available from S. G. Tibbetts at California State University, San Bernardino.

Davidson, R. (2004). What does the prefrontal cortex "do" in affect: Perspectives on frontal EEG asymmetry research. *Biological Psychology, 67,* 219–234.

Davidson, R. J., Shackman, A. J., & Maxwell, J. S. (2004). Asymmetries in face and brain related to emotion. *Trends in Cognitive Sciences, 8*(9), 389–391.

Davies, W. (1982). *Developments in the study of criminal behaviour* (Vol. 2). New York: Wiley.

Day, N. L., Leech, S. L., Richardson, G. A., Cornelius, M. D., Robles, N., & Larkby, C. (2002). Prenatal alcohol exposure predicts continued deficits in offspring size at 14 years of age. *Alcoholism, Clinical and Experimental Research, 26*(10), 1584–1591.

Dean, C., Leakey, M. G., Reid, D., Schrenk, F., Schwartz, G. T., Stringer, C., et al. (2001). Growth processes in teeth distinguish modern humans from *Homo erectus* and earlier hominins. *Nature, 414,* 628-631.

DeBellis, M. D. (1997). Posttraumatic stress disorder and acute stress disorder. In R. T. Ammerman & M. Hersen (Eds.), *Handbook of prevention and treatment with children and adolescents: Intervention in the real world context* (pp. 455–494). New York: Wiley.

Delaney-Black, V., Covington, C., Templin, T., Ager, J., Nordstrom-Klee, B., Martier, S., et al. (2000). Teacher-assessed behavior of children prenatally exposed to cocaine. *Pediatrics, 106*(4), 782–791.

DeLisi, M. (2005). *Career criminals in society.* Thousand Oaks, CA: Sage.

DeLisi, M. (2006). Zeroing in on early arrest onset: Results from a population of extreme career criminals. *Journal of Criminal Justice, 34*(1), 17–26.

Diamond, M. C., Scheibel, A. B., & Elson, L. M. (1985). *The human brain.* New York: HarperPerennial.

Dietrich, K. N., Ris, M. D., Succop, P. A., Berger, O. G., & Bornschein, R. L. (2001). Early exposure to lead and juvenile delinquency. *Neurotoxicology Teratology, 23,* 511–518.

DiLalla, L. F., & Gottesman, I. I. (1989). Heterogeneity of causes for delinquency and criminality: Lifespan perspectives. *Development and Psychopathology, 1,* 339–349.

Dionne, G., Tremblay, R., Boivin, M., Laplante, D., & Perusse, D. (2003). Physical aggression and expressive vocabulary in 19-month-old twins. *Developmental Psychology, 39*(2), 261–273.

Dodge, K. A. (1980). Social cognition and children's aggressive behavior. *Child Development, 51*(1), 162–170.

Dodge, K. A. (1986). Social information processing variables in the development of aggression and altruism in children. In C. Zahn-Waxler, M. Cummings, & M. Radke-Yarrow (Eds.), *The development of altruism and aggression: Social and biological origins* (pp. 280–302). New York: Cambridge University Press.

Dodge, K. A. (1990). The structure and function of reactive and proactive aggression. In D. Pepler & K. H. Rubin (Eds.), *The development and treatment of childhood aggression.* Hillsdale, NJ: Erlbaum.

Dodge, K. A., & Newman, J. P. (1981). Biased decision-making processes in aggressive boys. *Journal of Abnormal Psychology, 90*(4), 375–379.

Domhoff, G. W. (2003). *The scientific study of dreams: Neural networks, cognitive development, and content analysis.* Washington, DC: American Psychological Association.

Dugdale, R. L. (1877). *"The Jukes": A study in crime, pauperism, disease, and heredity: Also further studies of criminals.* New York: Putnam.

Duncan, P. D., Ritter, P. L., Dornbusch, S. M., Gross, R. T., & Merrill Carlsmith, J. (1985). The effects of pubertal timing on body image, school behavior, and deviance. *Journal of Youth and Adolescence, 14*(3), 227–235.

Dutton, D. G. (2002). Personality dynamics of intimate abusiveness. *Journal of Psychiatric Practice, 8*(4), 216–228.

Eccles, J. C. (1989). *Evolution of the brain: Creation of the self.* New York: Routledge.

Egeland, B., Kalkoske, M., Gottesman, N., & Erickson, M. F. (1990). Preschool behavior problems: Stability and factors accounting for change. *Journal of Child Psychology and Psychiatry and Allied Disciplines, 31*(6), 891–909.

Eisenberger, N. I., Lieberman, M. D., & Williams, K. D. (2003). Does rejection hurt? An FMRI study of social exclusion. *Science, 302*(5643), 290–292.

Elder, G. H. (1985). *Life course dynamics: Trajectories and transitions, 1968–1980.* Ithaca, NY: Cornell University Press.

Elder, G. H. J., & Rockwell, R. C. (1979). The life-course and human development: An ecological perspective. *International Journal of Behavioral Development, 2*(1), 1–21.

Elliott, D. S. (1994). Serious violent offenders: Onset, developmental course, and termination: The American Society of Criminology 1993 presidential address. *Criminology, 32*(1), 1–21.

Elliott, D. S., Huizinga, D., & Ageton, S. (1985). *Explaining delinquency and drug abuse.* Beverly Hills, CA: Sage.

Ellis, L., & Walsh, A. (2000). *Criminology: A global perspective.* Boston: Allyn and Bacon.

Elmen, J., & Offer, D. (1993). Normality, turmoil, and adolescence. In P. H. Tolan & B. J. Cohler (Eds.), *Handbook of clinical research and practice with adolescents* (pp. 5–19). New York: Wiley.

Ennis, E., & McConville, C. (2004). Stable characteristics of mood and seasonality. *Personality and Individual Differences, 36*(6), 1305–1315.

Epstein, E., & Guttman, R. (1984). Mate selection in man: Evidence, theory, and outcome. *Social Biology, 31*(3–4), 243–278.

Eysenck, H. J., & Gudjonnson, G. H. (1989). *The causes and cures of crime.* New York: Plenum.

Faden, V. B., & Graubard, B. I. (2000). Maternal substance use during pregnancy and developmental outcome at age three. *Journal of Substance Abuse, 12*(4), 329–340.

Farrington, D. P. (1978). The family backgrounds of aggressive youths. *Book supplement to the Journal of Child Psychology and Psychiatry, 1*(1), 73–93.

Farrington, D. P. (1982). Longitudinal analyses of criminal violence. In M. E. Wolfgang & N. Weiner (Eds.), *Criminal violence.* Beverly Hills, CA: Sage.

Farrington, D. P. (1987a). Early precursors of frequent offending. In J. Q. Wilson & G. C. Loury (Eds.), *From children to citizens: Families, schools, and delinquency prevention* (pp. 27–50). New York: Springer-Verlag.

Farrington, D. P. (1987b). Implications of biological findings for criminological research. In S. A. Mednick, T. E. Moffitt, & S. A. Stack (Eds.), *The causes of crime: New biological approaches* (pp. 42–64). New York: Cambridge University Press.

Farrington, D. P. (1991). Childhood aggression and adult violence: Early precursors and later-life outcomes. In D. J. Pepler & K. Rubin (Eds.), *The development and treatment of childhood aggression* (pp. 5–29). Hillsdale, NJ: Erlbaum.

Farrington, D. P. (1997). The relationship between low resting heart rate and violence. In A. Raine, P. A. Brennan, D. P. Farrington, & S. A. Mednick (Eds.), *Biosocial bases of violence* (pp. 89–105). New York: Plenum.

Farrington, D. P. (2005). Childhood origins of antisocial behavior. *Clinical Psychology & Psychotherapy, 12*(3), 177–190.

Farrington, D. P., Jolliffe, D., Loeber, R., Stouthamer-Loeber, M., & Kalb, L. (2001). The concentration of offenders in families, and family criminality in the prediction of boys' delinquency. *Journal of Adolescence, 24*(5), 579–596.

Farrington, D. P., Loeber, R., Elliott, D. S., Hawkins, J. D., Kandel, D. B., Klein, M. W., et al. (1990). Advancing knowledge about the onset of delinquency and crime. *Advances in Clinical Child Psychology, 13,* 283–342.

Farrington, D. P., Snyder, H. N., & Finnegan, T. A. (1988). Specialization in juvenile court careers. *Criminology, 26*(3), 461–485.

Farrington, D. P., & West, D. J. (1990). The Cambridge study in delinquent development: A long-term follow-up of 411 London males. In H. J. Kerner & G. Kaiser (Eds.), *Criminality: Personality, behavior, and life history* (pp. 115–138). Berlin: Springer-Verlag.

Federici, R. S. (1998). *Help for the hopeless child: A guide for families.* Alexandria, VA: Federici & Associates.

Felson, R. B., & Haynie, D. L. (2002). Pubertal development, social factors, and delinquency among adolescent boys. *Criminology, 40*(4), 967–988.

Fergusson, D. M., Horwood, L. J., & Lynskey, M. T. (1995). The stability of disruptive childhood behaviors. *Journal of Abnormal Child Psychology, 23*(3), 379–396.

Fergusson, D. M., Woodward, L. J., & Horwood, L. J. (1998). Maternal smoking during pregnancy and psychiatric adjustment in late adolescence. *Archives of General Psychiatry, 55*(8), 721–727.

Fischer, M., Rolf, J. E., Hasazi, J. E., & Cummings, L. (1984). Follow-up of a preschool epidemiological sample: Cross-age continuities and predictions of later adjustment with internalizing and externalizing dimensions of behavior. *Child Development, 55*(1), 137–150.

Fishbein, D. H. (1990). Biological perspectives in criminology. *Criminology, 28*(1), 27–72.

Fishbein, D. H. (1992). The psychobiology of female aggression. *Criminal Justice and Behavior, 19*(2), 99–126.

Fishbein, D. H. (2001). *Biobehavioral perspectives in criminology.* Belmont, CA: Wadsworth/Thomson Learning.

Fisher, L., Ames, E. W., Chisholm, K., & Savoie, L. (1997). Problems reported by parents of Romanian orphans adopted to British Columbia. *International Journal of Behavioral Development, 20*(1), 67–82.

Fitch, R. H., & Denenberg, V. H. (1998). A role for ovarian hormones in sexual differentiation of the brain. *Behavioral and Brain Sciences, 21*(3), 311–327.

Flannery, D. J., Rowe, D. C., & Gulley, B. L. (1993). Impact of pubertal status, timing, and age on adolescent sexual experience and delinquency. *Journal of Adolescent Research, 8*(1), 21–40.

Forth, A., & Hare, R. D. (1990). The contingent negative variation in psychopaths. *Psychophysiology, 26,* 676–682.

Franklin, J. (1987). *Molecules of the mind: The brave new science of molecular biology.* New York: Atheneum.

Frechette, M., & Leblanc, M. (1979). *La délinquance cachée à l'adolescence [Hidden delinquency at adolescence].* Montreal, QC: Université de Montréal.

Frick, P. J., & Hare, R. D. (2001). *The psychopathy screening device.* Toronto: Multi-Health Systems.

Fried, P. A., Watkinson, B., & Gray, R. (1998). Differential effects on cognitive functioning in 9- to 12-year-olds prenatally exposed to cigarettes and marihuana. *Neurotoxicology and Teratology, 20*(3), 293–306.

Furstenberg, F. F., Jr. (1976). *Unplanned parenthood: The social consequences of teenage childbearing.* New York: Free Press.

Fuster, J. M. (1989). *The prefrontal cortex.* New York: Raven.

Gabel, S., Stadler, J., Bjorn, J., & Shindledecker, R. (1995). Homovanillic acid and dopamine-beta-hydroxylase in male youth: Relationships with paternal substance abuse and antisocial behavior. *American Journal of Drug and Alcohol Abuse, 21*(3), 363–378.

Gage, F. H. (2002). Neurogenesis in the adult brain. *Journal of Neuroscience, 22*(3), 612–613.

Gardner, M., & Steinberg, L. (2005). Peer influence on risk taking, risk preference, and risky decision making in adolescence and adulthood: An experimental study. *Developmental Psychology, 41*(4), 625–635.

Garnett, E. S., Nahmias, C., Wortzman, G., Langevin, R., & Dickey, R. (1988). Positron emission tomography and sexual arousal in a sadist and two controls. *Sexual Abuse: A Journal of Research and Treatment, 1*(3), 387–399.

Ge, X., Conger, R. D., & Elder, G. H., Jr. (1996). Coming of age too early: Pubertal influences on girls' vulnerability to psychological distress. *Child Development, 67*(6), 3386–3400.

Ge, X., Conger, R. D., & Elder, G. H., Jr. (2001). The relation between puberty and psychological distress in adolescent boys. *Journal of Research on Adolescence, 11*(1), 49–70.

Gerra, G., Zaimovic, A., Avanzini, P., Chittolini, B., Giucastro, G., & Caccavari, R. (1997). Neurotransmitter-neuroendocrine responses to experimentally induced aggression in humans: Influence of personality variable. *Psychiatry Research, 66*(1), 33–43.

Giancola, P. R., Martin, C. S., Moss, H. B., Pelham, W. E., & Tarter, R. E. (1996). Executive cognitive functioning and aggressive behavior in preadolescent boys at high risk for substance abuse/dependence. *Journal of Studies on Alcohol, 57,* 57–72.

Gibson, C. L., Piquero, A. R., & Tibbetts, S. G. (2001). The contribution of family adversity and verbal IQ to criminal behavior. *International Journal of Offender Therapy & Comparative Criminology, 45*(5), 574–592.

Gibson, C., & Tibbetts, S. G. (2000). A biosocial interaction in predicting early onset of offending. *Psychological Reports, 86,* 509–518.

Giedd, J. N. (2004). Structural magnetic resonance imaging of the adolescent brain. *Annals of the New York Academy of Sciences, 1021,* 77–85.

Giedd, J. N., Blumenthal, J., Jeffries, N. O., Castellanos, F. X., Liu, H., Zijdenbos, A., et al. (1999). Brain development during childhood and adolescence: A longitudinal MRI study. *Nature Neuroscience, 2,* 861–863.

Gilbertson, M. W., Shenton, M. E., Ciszewski, A., Kasai, K., Lasko, N. B., & Orr, S. P. (2002). Smaller hippocampal volume predicts pathologic vulnerability to psychological trauma. *Nature Neuroscience, 5,* 1242–1247.

Gindis, B. (1999). Language-related issues for international adoptees and adoptive families. In T. Tepper, L. Hannon, & D. Sandstrom (Eds.), *International adoption: Challenges and opportunities* (pp. 98–107). Meadowlands, PA: First Edition.

Glaser, R., Kennedy, S., Lafuse, W. P., Bonneau, R. H., Speicher, C., Hillhouse, J., et al. (1990). Psychological stress-induced modulation of interleukin 2 receptor gene expression and interleukin 2 production in peripheral blood leukocytes. *Archives of General Psychiatry, 47*(8), 707–712.

Glennen, S. (2002). Language development and delay in internationally adoped infants and toddlers: A review. *American Journal of Speech-Language Pathology, 11*(4), 333–339.

Glover, V., & O'Connor, T. G. (2002). Effects of antenatal stress and anxiety: Implications for development and psychiatry. *British Journal of Psychiatry, 180,* 389–391.

Glueck, S., & Glueck, E. (1950). *Unraveling juvenile delinquency.* Cambridge, MA: Harvard University Press.

Goddard, H. H. (1914). *Feeble-mindedness: Its causes and consequences.* New York: Macmillan.

Gopnik, A., Meltzoff, A. N., & Kuhl, P. K. (1999). *The scientist in the crib: Minds, brains, and how children learn.* Fairfield, NJ: Morrow.

Gottesman, I. I. (1963). Heritability of personality: A demonstration. *Psychological Monographs, 77*(9), 1–21.

Gottfredson, M., & Hirschi, T. (1990). *A general theory of crime.* Palo Alto, CA: Stanford University Press.

Gould, E. (1999). Serotonin and hippocampal neurogenesis. *Neuropsychopharmacology, 21*(Suppl.), 46S-51S.

Goyer, P. F., Andreason, P. J., Semple, W. E., Clayton, A. H., King, A. C., & Compton-Toth, B. A. (1994). Positron-emission tomography and personality disorders. *Neuropsychopharmacology, 10*(1), 21–28.

Graber, J. A., & Brooks-Gunn, J. (1996). Transitions and turning points: Navigating the passage from childhood through adolescence. *Developmental Psychology, 32*(4), 768–776.

Graber, J. A., Lewinsohn, P. M., Seeley, J. R., & Brooks-Gunn, J. (1997). Is psychopathology associated with the timing of pubertal development? *Journal of the American Academy of Child and Adolescent Psychiatry, 36*(12), 1768–1776.

Grasmick, H. G., Bursik, R., & Arneklev, B. (1993). Reduction in drunk driving as a response to increased threats of shame, embarrassment, and legal sanctions. *Criminology, 31*(1), 41–67.

Gray, J. A. (1981). A critique of Eysenck's theory of personality. In H. J. Eysenck (Ed.), *A model of personality* (pp. 246–276). New York: Springer.

Gray, J. A. (1987). Perspectives on anxiety and impulsivity: A commentary. *Journal of Research in Personality, 21,* 493–509.

Gray, J. A. (1994). Three fundamental emotion systems. In P. Ekman & R. Davidson (Eds.), *The nature of emotion: Fundamental questions* (pp. 243–247). New York: Oxford University Press.

Gray, P. B., Kahlenberg, S. M., Barrett, E. S., Lipson, S. F., & Ellison, P. T. (2002). Marriage and fatherhood are associated with lower testosterone in males. *Evolution and Human Behavior, 23,* 193–201.

Greenough, W. T., Black, J. E., & Wallace, C. S. (1987). Experience and brain development. *Child Development, 58*(3), 539–559.

Grove, W. M., Eckert, E. D., Heston, L., Bouchard, T. J., Jr., Segal, N., & Lykken, D. T. (1990). Heritability of substance abuse and antisocial behavior: A study of monozygotic twins reared apart. *Biological Psychiatry, 27*(12), 1293–1304.

Gunnar, M. (1996). *Quality of care and the buffering of stress physiology: Its potential in protecting the developing human brain.* Minneapolis: University of Minnesota Institute of Child Development.

Gur, R. C., Gunning-Dixon, F., Bilker, W. B., & Gur, R. E. (2002). Sex differences in temporolimbic and frontal brain volumes of healthy adults. *Cerebral Cortex, 12*(9), 998–1003.

Gur, R. C., Mozley, L. H., Mozley, P. D., Resnick, S. M., Karp, J. S., & Alavi, A. (1995). Sex differences in regional cerebral glucose metabolism during a resting state. *Science, 267*(5197), 528–531.

Guterl, F. (2002). What Freud got right. *Newsweek, 140*(48), 50–53.

Guyton, A. C., & Hall, J. E. (2006). *Textbook of medical physiology* (11th ed.). St. Louis, MO: Elsevier.

Hagan, J., Simpson, J., & Gillis, A. R. (1987). Class in the household: A power-control theory of gender and delinquency. *American Journal of Sociology, 92*(4), 788–816.

Hall, C. S. (1954). *A primer of Freudian psychology.* New York: New American Library.

Hall, J. G. (1996). Twins and twinning. *American Journal of Medical Genetics, 61,* 202–204.

Hallikainen, T., Saito, T., Lachman, H. M., Volavka, J., Pohjalainen, T., & Ryynanen, O. P. (1999). Association between low activity serotonin transporter promoter genotype and early onset alcoholism with habitual impulsive violent behavior. *Molecular Psychiatry, 4*(4), 385–388.

Halpern, D. F. (2000). *Sex differences in cognitive abilities.* Mahwah, NJ: Lawrence Erlbaum.

Hamer, D., & Copeland, P. (1999). *Living with our genes.* New York: Doubleday.

Harris, J. R. (1995). Where is the child's environment? A group socialization theory of development. *Psychological Review, 102*(3), 458–489.

Harris, J. R. (1998). *The nurture assumption: Why children turn out the way they do.* New York: Free Press.

Hart, B., & Risley, T. R. (1995). *Meaningful differences in the everyday experience of young American children.* Baltimore, MD: Brookes.

Hart, B., & Risley, T. R. (2003). The early catastrophe: The 30 million word gap by age 3. *American Educator, 22,* 4–9.

Hastings, P. D., Zahn-Waxler, C., Robinson, J., Usher, B., & Bridges, D. (2000). The development of concern for others in children with behavior problems. *Developmental Psychology, 36*(5), 531–546.

Hay, D. F., Castle, J., & Davies, L. (2000). Toddlers' use of force against familiar peers: A precursor of serious aggression? *Child Development, 71*(2), 457–467.

Hay, D. F., Zahn-Waxler, C., Cummings, E. M., & Iannotti, R. J. (1992). Young children's views about conflict with peers: A comparison of the daughters and sons of depressed and well women. *Journal of Child Psychology and Psychiatry and Allied Disciplines, 33*(4), 669–683.

Haynie, D. L. (2003). Contexts of risk? Explaining the link between girls' pubertal development and their delinquency involvement. *Social Forces, 82*(1), 355–397.

Heck, C., & Walsh, A. (2000). The effects of maltreatment and family structure on minor and serious delinquency. *International Journal of Offender Therapy and Comparative Criminology, 44*(2), 178.

Henry, B., Moffitt, T. E., Robins, L., Earls, F., & Silva, P. (1993). Early family predictors of child and adolescent antisocial behaviour: Who are the mothers of delinquents? *Criminal Behaviour and Mental Health, 3,* 97–118.

Heynen, A. J., Yoon, B. J., Liu, C. H., Chung, H., Huganir, R. L., & Bear, M. F. (2003). Molecular mechanism for loss of visual cortical responsiveness following brief monocular deprivation. *Nature Neuroscience, 6*(8), 854–862.

Hines, M. (1990). Gonadal hormones and human cognitive development. In J. Balthazart (Ed.), *Hormones, brain and behaviour in vertebrates: Sexual differentiation, neuroanatomical aspects, neurotransmitters, and neuropeptides* (pp. 51–63). Basel, Switzerland: Karger.

Hines, M., Chiu, L., McAdams, L. A., Bentler, P. M., & Lipcamon, J. (1992). Cognition and the corpus callosum: Verbal fluency, visuospatial ability, and language lateralization related to midsagittal surface areas of callosal subregions. *Behavioral Neuroscience, 106*(1), 3–14.

Hirschi, T. (1969). *Causes of delinquency.* Berkeley: University of California Press.

Hirschi, T., & Gottfredson, M. R. (1994). *The generality of deviance.* London: Transaction.

Hirschi, T., & Gottfredson, M. R. (1995). Control theory and the life-course perspective. *Studies on Crime and Crime Prevention, 4,* 131–142.

Holloway, R. L. (1998). Relative size of the human corpus callosum redux: Statistical smoke and mirrors? *Behavioral and Brain Sciences, 21*(3), 333–335.

Hooten, E. A. (1939). *The American criminal: An anthropological study.* Cambridge, MA: Harvard University Press.

Horney, J., Osgood, D. W., & Marshall, I. H. (1995). Criminal careers in the short-term: Intra-individual variability in crime and its relation to local life circumstances. *American Sociological Review, 60*(5), 655–673.

Howard, P. J. (2006). *Owner's manual for the brain: Everyday applications from mind-brain research.* Dallas, TX: Bard.

Hsu, Y. P., Powell, J. F., Sims, K. B., & Breakefield, X. O. (1989). Molecular genetics of the monoamine oxidases. *Journal of Neurochemistry, 53*(1), 12–18.

Hucker, S., Langevin, R., Wortzman, G., Bain, J., Handy, L., & Chambers, J. (1986). Neuropsychological impairment in pedophiles. *Canadian Journal of Behavioral Science, 18,* 440–448.

Huesmann, L. R., Eron, L. D., Lefkowitz, M. M., & Walder, L. O. (1984). Stability of aggression over time. *Developmental Psychology, 20,* 1120–1134.

Hyman, S. E., & Nestler, E. J. (1993). *The molecular foundations of psychiatry.* Washington, DC: American Psychiatric Press.

Innocenti, G. M. (1994). Some new trends in the study of the corpus callosum. *Behavioural Brain Research, 64*(1–2), 1–8.

Insurance Institute for Highway Safety. (2005). *Status report,* vol. 40, no. 9. Retrieved from http://www.iihs.org/sr/default.html

Jackson, D. C., Mueller, C. J., Dolski, I., Dalton, K. M., Nitschke, J. B., Urry, H. L., et al. (2003). Now you feel it, now you don't: Frontal EEG asymmetry and individual differences in emotion regulation. *Psychological Science, 14,* 612–617.

Jancke, L., & Steinmetz, H. (1994). Interhemispheric transfer time and corpus callosum size. *Neuroreport, 5*(17), 2385–2388.

Jessor, R. (1998). *New perspectives on adolescent risk behavior.* New York: Cambridge University Press.

Johnson, D., & Dole, K. (1999). International adoptions: Implications for early intervention. *Infants and Young Children, 11*(4), 34–45.

Jolliffe, D., & Farrington, D. P. (2004). Empathy and offending: A systematic review and meta-analysis. *Aggression & Violent Behavior, 9*(5), 441–476.

Kagan, J. (2003). Biology, context, and developmental inquiry. *Annual Review of Psychology, 54,* 1–23.

Kagan, J., Reznick, J. S., & Snidman, N. (1987). The physiology and psychology of behavioral inhibition in children. *Child Development, 58*(6), 1459–1473.

Kandel, E., Brennan, P. A., & Mednick, S. A. (1990). *Minor physical anomalies and parental modeling of physical aggression predict adult violent offending.* Unpublished manuscript, University of Southern California, Los Angeles.

Kandel, E., & Freed, D. (1989). Frontal-lobe dysfunction and antisocial behavior: A review. *Journal of Clinical Psychology, 45*(3), 404–413.

Kandel, E. R., Schwartz, J. H., & Jessel, T. M. (1991). *Principles of neuroscience.* Norwalk, CT: Appleton and Lange.

Kantrowitz, B. (2002). In search of sleep. *Newsweek, 140*(3), 38–40.

Kapit, W., & Elson, L. M. (2002). *The anatomy coloring book* (3rd ed.). New York: HarperCollins.

Karr-Morse, R., & Wiley, M. S. (1997). *Ghosts from the nursery: Tracing the roots of violence.* New York: Atlantic Monthly Press.

Katz, J. (1988). *Seductions of crime: Moral and sensual attractions in doing crime.* New York: Basic Books.

Kaufer, D., Friedman, A., Seidman, S., & Soreq, H. (1998). Acute stress facilitates long-lasting changes in cholinergic gene expression. *Nature, 393*(6683), 373–377.

Kaufman, J., Plotsky, P. M., Nemeroff, C. B., & Charney, D. S. (2000). Effects of early adverse experiences on brain structure and function: Clinical implications. *Biological Psychiatry, 48*(8), 778–790.

Keenan, K., Loeber, R., Zhang, Q., Stouthamer-Loeber, M., & Van Kammen, W. B. (1995). The influence of deviant peers on the development of boys' disruptive and delinquent behavior: A temporal analysis. *Development and Psychopathology, 7*(4), 715–726.

Keenan, K., & Shaw, D. (1997). Developmental and social influences on young girls' early problem behavior. *Psychological Bulletin, 121*(1), 95–113.

Kellogg, R. T. (1995). *Cognitive psychology.* Thousand Oaks, CA: Sage.

Kestenbaum, R., Farber, E. A., & Sroufe, L. A. (1989). Individual differences in empathy among preschoolers: Relation to attachment history. *New Directions for Child Development, 44*(44), 51–64.

Kinsley, C. H., Madonia, L., Gifford, G. W., Tureski, K., Griffin, G. R., & Lowry, C. (1999). Motherhood improves learning and memory. *Nature, 402*(6758), 137–138.

Kipke, M. D. (1999). *Adolescent development and the biology of puberty: Summary of a workshop on new research.* Washington, DC: National Academy Press.

Kokko, K., & Pulkkinen, L. (2000). Aggression in childhood and long-term unemployment in adulthood: A cycle of maladaptation and some protective factors. *Developmental Psychology, 36*(4), 463–472.

Kolb, B., & Milner, B. (1981). Performance of complex arm and facial movements after focal brain lesions. *Neuropsychologia, 19*(4), 491–503.

Kolb, B., & Whishaw, I. Q. (1990). *Fundamentals of human neuropsychology* (3rd ed.). New York: Freeman.

Kolb, B., & Whishaw, I. Q. (1998). IQ: Brain plasticity and behavior. *Annual Review of Psychology, 49,* 43–64.

Kuypers, H. (1981). Motor control. In J. M. Brookhart & V. B. Mountcastle (Eds.), *Handbook of physiology, section 1: The nervous system* (pp. 54–76). Bethesda, MD: American Physiological Society.

Lange, J. (1931). *Verbrechen als Schiskal.* London: Unwin.

Langevin, R., Wortzman, G., Dickey, R., Wright, P., & Handy, L. (1988). Neuropsychological impairment in incest offenders. *Sexual Abuse: A Journal of Research and Treatment, 1*(3), 401–415.

Lanza, S. T., & Collins, L. M. (2002). Pubertal timing and the onset of substance use in females during early adolescence. *Prevention Science, 3*(1), 69–82.

Larson, J., Lynch, G., Games, D., & Seubert, P. (1999). Alterations in synaptic transmission and long-term potentiation in hippocampal slices from young and aged PDAPP mice. *Brain Research, 840*(1–2), 23–35.

Laub, J. H., & Lauritsen, J. L. (1993). Violent criminal behavior over the life course: A review of the longitudinal and comparative research. *Violence and Victims, 8*(3), 235–252.

Laub, J. H., Nagin, D. S., & Sampson, R. J. (1998). Trajectories of change in criminal offending: Good marriages and the desistance process. *American Sociological Review, 63*(2), 225–238.

LeBlanc, M., & Fréchette, M. (1989). *Male criminal activity from childhood through youth: Multilevel and developmental perspectives.* New York: Springer-Verlag.

Lefkowitz, M. M., Eron, L. D., Walder, L. O., & Huesmann, L. R. (1977). *Growing up to be violent: A longitudinal study of the development of aggression.* New York: Pergamon.

LeMarquand, D., Pihl, R. O., & Benkelfat, C. (1994). Serotonin and alcohol intake, abuse, and dependence: Clinical evidence. *Biological Psychiatry, 36*(5), 326–337.

LeVay, S. (1991). A difference in hypothalamic structure between heterosexual and homosexual men. *Science, 253*(5023), 1034–1037.

Levenson, R. (2003). Blood, sweat, and fears: The autonomic architect of emotion. *Annals of the New York Academy of Sciences, 1000,* 348–366.

Leventhal, A. G., Wang, Y., Pu, M., Zhou, Y., & Ma, Y. (2003). GABA and its agonists improved visual cortical function in senescent monkeys. *Science, 300*(5620), 812–819.

Levin, H. S., Eisenberg, H. M., & Benton, A. L. (1991). *Frontal lobe function and dysfunction.* Oxford: Oxford University Press.

Levy, F., Hay, D. A., McStephen, M., Wood, C., & Waldman, I. (1997). Attention-deficit hyperactivity disorder: A category or a continuum? Genetic analysis of a large-scale twin study. *Journal of the American Academy of Child and Adolescent Psychiatry, 36*(6), 737–744.

Lewis, D. O. (1992). From abuse to violence: Psychophysiological consequences of maltreatment. *Journal of the American Academy of Child and Adolescent Psychiatry, 31*(3), 383–391.

Lewis, M. (1992). *Shame: The exposed self.* New York: Macmillan.

Lidberg, L., Modin, I., Oreland, L., Tuck, J. R., & Gillner, A. (1985). Platelet monoamine oxidase activity and psychopathy. *Psychiatry Research, 16*(4), 339–343.

Lieberman, M. D., & Eisenberger, N. I. (2005). A pain by any other name (rejection, exclusion, ostracism) still hurts the same: The role of dorsal anterior cingulate in social and physical pain. In J. T. Cacioppo, P. Visser, & C. Pickett (Eds.), *Social neuroscience: People thinking about people* (pp. 167–187). Cambridge: MIT Press.

Linnoila, M., Virkkunen, M., George, T., Eckardt, M., Higley, J. D., Nielsen, D., et al. (1994). Serotonin, violent behavior and alcohol. *EXS, 71,* 155–163.

Linnoila, M., Virkkunen, M., Scheinin, M., Nuutila, A., Rimon, R., & Goodwin, F. K. (1983). Low cerebrospinal fluid 5-hydroxyindoleacetic acid concentration differentiates impulsive from nonimpulsive violent behavior. *Life Sciences, 33*(26), 2609–2614.

Liu, X., & Kaplan, H. B. (1996). Gender-related differences in circumstances surrounding initiation and escalation of alcohol and other substance use/abuse. *Deviant Behavior, 17*(1), 71–106.

Loeber, R. (1982). The stability of antisocial and delinquent child behavior: A review. *Child Development, 53*(6), 1431–1446.

Loeber, R., & Hay, D. (1997). Key issues in the development of aggression and violence from childhood to early adulthood. *Annual Review of Psychology, 48,* 371–410.

Loeber, R., & Leblanc, M. (1990). Towards a developmental criminology. In M. Tonry & N. Morris (Eds.), *Crime and justice: A review of research* (pp. 375–473). Chicago: University of Chicago Press.

Loeber, R., & Stouthamer-Loeber, M. (1996). The development of offending. *Criminal Justice and Behavior, 23*(1), 12.

Loehlin, J. C., & Nichols, R. C. (1976). *Heredity, environment, and personality: A study of 850 sets of twins.* Austin: University of Texas Press.

Lombroso, C. (1876). *L'uomo delinquente [The criminal man].* Florence, Italy: Frateli Bocca.

Lombroso-Ferrero, G. (1972). *Lombroso's Criminal Man.* Montclair, NJ: Patterson Smith.

Lorenz, K. (1935). Der Kumpan in der Umwelt des Vogels. *Journal of Ornithology, 83*(2), 137–213.

Lund, T. D., Rhees, R. W., Setchell, K. D., & Lephart, E. D. (2001). Altered sexually dimorphic nucleus of the preoptic area (SDN-POA) volume in adult Long-Evans rats by dietary soy phytoestrogens. *Brain Research, 914*(1–2), 92–99.

Lutwak, N., & Ferrari, J. R. (1996). Moral affect and cognitive processes: Differentiating shame from guilt among men and women. *Personality and Individual Differences, 21*(6), 891–896.

Lynam, D., Moffitt, T., & Stouthamer-Loeber, M. (1993). Explaining the relation between IQ and delinquency: Class, race, test motivation, school failure, or self-control? *Journal of Abnormal Psychology, 102*(2), 187–196.

Lyons, M. J., True, W. R., Eisen, S. A., Goldberg, J., Meyer, J. M., Faraone, S. V., Eaves, L. J., & Tsuang, M. T. (1995). Differential heritability of adult and juvenile antisocial traits. *Archives of General Psychiatry, 52*(11), 906–915.

Maccoby, E. E., & Jacklin, C. N. (1983). The "person" characteristics of children and the family as environment. In D. Magnusson & V. L. Allen (Eds.), *Human development: An interactional perspective* (pp. 75–91). New York: Academic Press.

MacLean, P. D. (1990). *The triune brain in evolution: Role in paleocerebral functions.* New York: Plenum.

Magnusson, D. (1988). *Individual development from an interactional perspective: A longitudinal study.* Hillsdale, NJ: Lawrence Erlbaum.

Magnusson, D., Stattin, H., & Duner, A. (1983). Aggression and criminality in a longitudinal perspective. In K. Teilman van Dusen & S. A. Mednick (Eds.), *Prospective studies of crime and delinquency* (pp. 277–301). Boston: Kluwer-Nijhoff.

Mann, J. J. (1998). The neurobiology of suicide. *Nature Medicine, 4*(1), 25–30.

Marcovitch, S., Goldberg, S., Gold, A., Washington, J., Wasson, C., Krekewich, K., et al. (1997). Determinants of behavioural problems in Romanian children adopted in Ontario. *International Journal of Behavioral Development, 20*(1), 17–31.

Marks, V. (1976). The measurement of blood glucose and the definition of hypoglycemia. *Hormone and Metabolic Research, 6*(Suppl. 5), 1–6.

Martin, G. N. (1998). *Human neuropsychology.* London: Prentice-Hall Europe.

Masters, R. D. (1999). *Poisoning the well: Neurotoxic metals, water treatment, and human behavior.* Plenary address to the annual conference of the Association for Politics and the Life Sciences.

Mathiesen, K. S., & Sanson, A. (2000). Dimensions of early childhood behavior problems: Stability and predictors of change from 18 to 30 months. *Journal of Abnormal Child Psychology, 28*(1), 15–31.

Matza, D. (1964). *Delinquency and drift.* New York: Wiley.

Mayberg, H., Lozano, A., Voon, V., McNeely, H., Seminowicz, D., Hamani, C., et al. (2005). Deep brain stimulation for treatment-resistant depression. *Neuron, 45*(5), 651–660.

McCanne, T. R., & Milner, J. S. (1991). Physiological reactivity of physically abusive and at-risk subjects to child-related stimuli. In J. S. Milner (Ed.), *Neuropsychology of aggression* (pp. 147–166). Norwell, MA: Kluwer.

McCord, J. (1983). A longitudinal study of aggression and antisocial behavior. In K. T. van Dusen & S. A. Mednick (Eds.), *Prospective studies of crime and delinquency* (pp. 269–275). Boston: Kluwer-Nijhoff.

McCord, J., & McCord, W. (1959). A follow-up report on the Cambridge-Somerville Youth Study. *Annals of the American Academy of Political and Social Science, 322*(1), 89–96.

McEwen, B. S. (2000). Effects of adverse experiences for brain structure and function. *Biological Psychiatry, 48*(8), 721–731.

McGee, R., Partridge, F., Williams, S., & Silva, P. A. (1991). A twelve-year follow-up of preschool hyperactive children. *Journal of the American Academy of Child and Adolescent Psychiatry, 30*(2), 224–232.

McGivern, R. F., Huston, J. P., Byrd, D., King, T., Siegle, G. J., & Reilly, J. (1997). Sex differences in visual recognition memory: Support for a sex-related difference in attention in adults and children. *Brain and Cognition, 34*(3), 323–336.

McGloin, J. M., & Pratt, T. (2003). Cognitive ability and delinquency behavior among inner-city youth: A life-course analysis of main, mediating and interaction effects. *International Journal of Offender Therapy and Comparative Criminology, 47*(3), 253–271.

McGue, M. (1997). A behavioral-genetic perspective on children of alcoholics. *Alcohol Health and Research World, 21*(3), 210–217.

Mednick, S. A., Gabrielli, W. F., Jr., & Hutchings, B. (1984). Genetic influences in criminal convictions: Evidence from an adoption cohort. *Science, 224*(4651), 891–894.

Mednick, S. A., Gabrielli, W. F., Jr., & Hutchings, B. (1987). Genetic factors in the etiology of criminal behavior. In S. A. Mednick, T. E. Moffitt, & S. A. Stack (Eds.), *The causes of crime: New biological approaches* (pp. 74–91). Cambridge, UK: Cambridge University Press.

Meltzoff, A. N., & Moore, M. K. (1977). Imitation of facial and manual gestures by human neonates. *Science, 198*(4312), 74–78.

Meltzoff, A. N., & Moore, M. K. (1983). Newborn infants imitate adult facial gestures. *Child Development, 54*(3), 702–709.

Mereu, G., Fà, M., Ferraro, L., Cagiano, R., Antonelli, T., Tattoli, M., et al. (2003). Prenatal exposure to a cannabinoid agonist produces memory deficits linked to dysfunction in hippocampal long-term potentiation and glutamate release. *Proceedings of the National Academy of Sciences, 100*(8), 4915–4920.

Merton, R. K. (1938). Social structure and anomie. *American Sociological Review, 3*(5), 672–682.

Meshorer, E., & Soreq, H. (2006). Virtues and woes of Ach alternative splicing in stress-related neuropathologies. *Trends in Neurosciences, 29*(4), 216–224.

Miles, D. R., & Carey, G. (1997). Genetic and environmental architecture of human aggression. *Journal of Personality and Social Psychology, 72,* 207–217.

Milstein, V. (1988). EEG topography in patients with aggressive violent behavior. In T. E. Moffitt & S. A. Mednick (Eds.), *Biological contributions to crime causation* (pp. 40–54). Dordrecht, the Netherlands: Martinus Nijhoff.

Mirsky, A. F., & Siegel, A. (1994). The neurobiology of violence and aggression. In A. J. Reiss, Jr., K. A. Miczek, & J. A. Roth (Eds.), *Understanding and preventing violence* (Vol. 2, pp. 59–173). Washington, DC: National Academies Press.

Mitchell, S., & Rosa, P. (1981). Boyhood behaviour problems as precursors of criminality: A fifteen-year follow-up study. *Journal of Child Psychology and Psychiatry and Allied Disciplines, 22*(1), 19–33.

Moffitt, T. E. (1990). Juvenile delinquency and attention deficit disorder: Boys' developmental trajectories from age 3 to age 15. *Child Development, 61*(3), 893–910.

Moffitt, T. E. (1993a). Adolescence-limited and life-course-persistent antisocial behavior: A developmental taxonomy. *Psychological Review, 100,* 674–701.

Moffitt, T. E. (1993b). The neuropsychology of conduct disorder. *Development and Psychopathology, 5*(1–2), 135–151.

Moffitt, T. E. (1996). Measuring children's antisocial behaviors. *Journal of the American Medical Association, 275*(5), 403–404.

Moffitt, T. E. (1997). Neuropsychology, antisocial behavior, and neighborhood context. In J. McCord (Ed.), *Violence and childhood in the inner city* (pp. 116–170). Cambridge, UK: Cambridge University Press.

Moffitt, T. E., Caspi, A., Belsky, J., & Silva, P. A. (1992). Childhood experience and the onset of menarche: A test of a sociobiological model. *Child Development, 63*(1), 47–58.

Moffitt, T. E., Caspi, A., Dickson, N., Silva, P., & Stanton, W. (1996). Childhood-onset versus adolescent-onset antisocial conduct problems in males: Natural history from ages 3 to 18 years. *Development and Psychopathology, 8*(2), 399–424.

Moffitt, T. E., Caspi, A., Rutter, M., & Silva, P. A. (2001). *Sex differences in antisocial behaviour.* Cambridge, UK: Cambridge University Press.

Mosovich, A., & Tallaferro, A. (1954). Studies on EEG and sex function orgasm. *Diseases of the Nervous System, 15*(7), 218–220.

Nagin, D. S., & Land, K. C. (1993). Age, criminal careers, and population heterogeneity: Specification and estimation of a nonparametric, mixed Poisson model. *Criminology, 31*(3), 327–362.

Nagin, D. S., & Paternoster, R. (1991). On the relationship of past to future delinquency. *Criminology, 29*(4), 163–189.

Nagin, D. S., & Paternoster, R. (1993). Enduring individual differences and rational choice theories of crime. *Law & Society Review, 27*(3), 467–496.

Nagin, D., & Paternoster, R. (2000). Population heterogeneity and state dependence: State of the evidence and directions for future research. *Journal of Quantitative Criminology, 16*(2), 117–144.

Nagin, D., & Tremblay, R. E. (1999). Trajectories of boys' physical aggression, opposition, and hyperactivity on the path to physically violent and nonviolent juvenile delinquency. *Child Development, 70*(5), 1181–1196.

New, A. S., Gelernter, J., Yovell, Y., Trestman, R. L., Nielsen, D. A., Silverman, J., et al. (1998). Tryptophan hydroxylase genotype is associated with impulsive-aggression measures: A preliminary study. *American Journal of Medical Genetics, 81*(1), 13–17.

Newman, J. P. (1987). Reaction to punishment in extraverts and psychopaths: Implications for the impulsive behavior of disinhibited individuals. *Journal of Research in Personality, 21*(4), 464–480.

Newman, J. P., Kosson, D. S., & Patterson, C. M. (1992). Delay of gratification in psychopathic and nonpsychopathic offenders. *Journal of Abnormal Psychology, 101*(4), 630–636.

Newth, S. J., & Corbett, J. (1993). Behaviour and emotional problems in three-year-old children of Asian parentage. *Journal of Child Psychology and Psychiatry and Allied Disciplines, 34*(3), 333–352.

Nichols, R. C. (1978). Twin studies of ability, personality, and interests. *Homo, 29,* 158–173.

Nielsen, D. A., Goldman, D., Virkkunen, M., Tokola, R., Rawlings, R., & Linnoila, M. (1994). Suicidality and 5-hydroxyindoleacetic acid concentration associated with a tryptophan hydroxylase polymorphism. *Archives of General Psychiatry, 51*(1), 34–38.

Nilsen, L. S., Hansen, V., & Olstad, R. (2004). Improvement in mental health over time in northern Norway: A prospective study of a general population followed for 9 years, with special emphasis on the influence of darkness in winter. *Social Psychiatry and Psychiatric Epidemiology, 39*(4), 273–279.

Nofzinger, E. A., Buysee, D. J., Germain, A., Carter, C., Luna, B., Price, J. C., et al. (2004). Increased activation of anterior paralimbic and executive cortex from waking to rapid eye movement sleep in depression. *Archives of General Psychiatry, 61,* 695–702.

Nowicki, S., & Duke, M. P. (1994). Individual differences in the nonverbal communication of affect: The diagnostic analysis of nonverbal accuracy scale. *Journal of Nonverbal Behavior, 18*(1), 9–35.

O'Conner, T. G., Rutter, M., Beckett, C., Keaveney, L., & Kreppner, J. M. (2000). The English and Romanian adoptees study team. The effects of global severe privation on cognitive competence: Extension and longitudinal follow-up. *Child Development, 71,* 376–390.

O'Connor, M., Foch, T., Sherry, T., & Plomin, R. (1980). A twin study of specific behavioral problems of socialization as viewed by parents. *Journal of Abnormal Child Psychology, 8*(2), 189–199.

O'Connor, T. G., McGuire, S., Reiss, D., Hetherington, E. M., & Plomin, R. (1998). Co-occurrence of depressive symptoms and antisocial behavior in adolescence: A common genetic liability. *Journal of Abnormal Psychology, 107*(1), 27–37.

O'Dwyer, J. M. (1997). Schizophrenia in people with intellectual disability: The role of pregnancy and birth complications. *Journal of Intellectual Disability Research, 41*(3), 238–251.

Ollendick, T. H., Weist, M. D., Borden, M. G., & Greene, R. W. (1992). Sociometric status and academic, behavioral, and psychological adjustment: A five-year longitudinal study. *Journal of Consulting and Clinical Psychology, 58,* 126–129.

Olson, S. L., Bates, J. E., Sandy, J. M., & Lanthier, R. (2000). Early developmental precursors of externalizing behavior in middle childhood and adolescence. *Journal of Abnormal Child Psychology, 28*(2), 119–133.

Olweus, D. (1979). Stability of aggressive reaction patterns in males: A review. *Psychological Bulletin, 86,* 852–875.

Olweus, D. (1987). Testosterone and adrenaline: Aggressive antisocial behavior in normal adolescent males. In S. A. Mednick, T. E. Moffitt, & S. A. Stack (Eds.), *The causes of crime: New biological approaches* (pp. 263–282). New York: Cambridge University Press.

Onalaja, A. O., & Claudio, L. (2000). Genetic susceptibility to lead poisoning. *Environmental Health Perspectives, 108*(Suppl. 1), 23–28.

Oppenheim, J. S., Skerry, J. E., Tramo, M. J., & Gazzaniga, M. S. (1989). Magnetic resonance imaging morphology of the corpus callosum in monozygotic twins. *Annals of Neurology, 26*(1), 100–104.

Orvaschel, H. (1990). Early onset psychiatric disorder in high risk children and increased familial morbidity. *Journal of the American Academy of Child and Adolescent Psychiatry, 29*(2), 184–188.

Osborn, S. G., & West, D. J. (1978). The effectiveness of various predictors of criminal careers. *Journal of Adolescence, 1*(2), 101–117.

Owen, D. R., & Sines, J. O. (1970). Heritability of personality in children. *Behavior Genetics, 1*(3), 235–248.

Pagnoni, G., Zink, C. F., Montague, P. R., & Berns, G. (2002). Activity in human ventral striatum locked to errors of reward prediction. *Nature Neuroscience, 5,* 97–98.

Pallone, N. J., & Hennessy, J. J. (1998). Brain dysfunction and criminal violence. *Society, 35*(6), 21–27.

Patterson, G. R. (1980). Children who steal. *Understanding Crime: Current Theory and Research, 18,* 411–455.

Patterson, G. R. (1982). *Coercive family process.* Eugene, OR: Castilia.

Patterson, G. R. (1986). Performance models for antisocial boys. *American Psychologist, 41,* 432–444.

Patterson, G. R., DeBaryshe, B. D., & Ramsey, E. (1989). A developmental perspective on antisocial behavior. *American Psychologist, 44*(2), 329–335.

Paul, D. B. (1998). *The politics of heredity: Essays on eugenics, biomedicine, and the nature-nurture debate.* Albany: State University of New York Press.

Pepler, D. J., & Sedighdeilami, F. (1998). *Aggressive girls in Canada* (Government Document W-98–30E). Applied Research Branch, Strategic Policy, Human Resources Development Canada. Retrieved from http://www.hrsdc.gc.ca/en/cs/sp/sdc/pkrf/publications/research/1998-000127/w-98-30e.pdf

Perry, B. D. (1994). Neurobiological sequelae of childhood trauma: PTSD in children. In M. M. Murburg (Ed.), *Catecholamine function in posttraumatic stress disorder: Emerging concepts* (pp. 233–255). Washington, DC: American Psychiatric Press.

Perry, B. D. (2000). *Violence and childhood.* Houston, TX: Child Trauma Academy.

Perry, B. D. (2001). The neurodevelopmental impact of violence in childhood. In D. Schetky & E. Benedek (Eds.), *Textbook of child and adolescent forensic psychiatry* (pp. 221–238). Washington, DC: American Psychiatric Press.

Perry, B. D., & Pollard, D. (1997, October). *Altered brain development following global neglect in early childhood.* Paper presented at the annual meeting of the Society for Neuroscience, New Orleans, LA.

Petersilia, J. (1980). Criminal career research: A review of recent evidence. *Crime and Justice, 2,* 321–379.

Pew Research Center for People and the Press. (2003, October). Women much happier than men: Survey. Retrieved from http://pewglobal.org/commentary/display.php?AnalysisID=71

Pfefferbaum, A., Sullivan, E. V., Swan, G. E., & Carmelli, D. (2000). Brain structure in mean remains highly heritable in the seventh and eighth decades of life. *Neurobiology of Aging, 21,* 63–74.

Pierce, E. W., Ewing, L. J., & Campbell, S. B. (1999). Diagnostic status and symptomatic behavior of hard-to-manage preschool children in middle childhood and early adolescence. *Journal of Clinical Child Psychology, 28,* 44–57.

Pike, A., McGuire, S., Hetherington, E. M., Reiss, D., & Plomin, R. (1996). Family environment and adolescent depressive symptoms and antisocial behavior: A multivariate genetic analysis. *Developmental Psychology, 32*(4), 590–603.

Pinker, S. (2002). *The blank slate: The modern denial of human nature.* New York: Viking.

Piquero, A., & Tibbetts, S. (1996). Specifying the direct and indirect effects of low self-control and situational factors in offenders' decision making: Toward a more complete model of rational offending. *Justice Quarterly, 13*(3), 481–510.

Piquero, A., & Tibbetts, S. (1999). The impact of pre/perinatal disturbances and disadvantaged familial environment in predicting criminal offending. *Studies on Crime and Crime Prevention, 8*(1), 52–70.

Plomin, R. (1990). *Nature and nurture: An introduction to human behavioral genetics.* Pacific Grove, CA: Brooks/Cole.

Plomin, R. (1994). *Genetics and experience: The interplay between nature and nurture.* Thousand Oaks, CA: Sage.

Plomin, R., & Daniels, D. (1987). Why are children in the same family so different from one another? *Behavioral and Brain Sciences, 10,* 1–60.

Plomin, R., Reiss, D., Hetherington, E. M., & Howe, G. W. (1994). Nature and nurture: Genetic contributions to measures of the family environment. *Developmental Psychology, 30*(1), 32–43.

Pratt, T. C., & Cullen, F. T. (2000). The empirical status of Gottfredson and Hirschi's general theory of crime: A meta-analysis. *Criminology, 38,* 931–964.

Pratt, T. C., Cullen, F. T., Blevins, K. R., Daigle, L., & Unnever, J. D. (2002). The relationship of attention deficit hyperactivity disorder to crime and delinquency: A meta-analysis. *International Journal of Police Science and Management, 4,* 344–360.

Pulkkinen, L. (1982). Self-control and continuity from childhood to late adolescence. *Life-Span Development and Behavior, 4,* 63–105.

Quinton, D., Pickles, A., Maughan, B., & Rutter, M. (1993). Partners, peers, and pathways: Assortative pairing and continuities in conduct disorder. *Development and Psychopathology, 5*(4), 763–783.

Raine, A. (1989). Evoked potentials and psychopathy. *International Journal of Psychophysiology, 8*(1), 1–16.

Raine, A. (1993). *The psychopathology of crime: Criminal behavior as a clinical disorder.* San Diego, CA: Academic Press.

Raine, A. (2002). Biosocial studies of antisocial and violent behavior in children and adults: A review. *Journal of Abnormal Child Psychology, 30,* 311–326.

Raine, A., Brennan, P., & Mednick, S. A. (1997). Interaction between birth complications and early maternal rejection in predisposing individuals to adult violence: Specificity to serious, early-onset violence. *American Journal of Psychiatry, 154*(9), 1265–1271.

Raine, A., Buchsbaum, M., & LaCasse, L. (1997). Brain abnormalities in murderers indicated by positron emission tomography. *Biological Psychiatry, 42*(6), 495–508.

Raine, A., Lencz, T., Bihrle, S., LaCasse, L., & Colletti, P. (2000). Reduced prefrontal gray matter volume and reduced autonomic activity in antisocial personality disorder. *Archives of General Psychiatry, 57*(2), 119–127.

Raine, A., Meloy, J. R., Bihrle, S., Stoddard, J., LaCasse, L., & Buchsbaum, M. S. (1998). Reduced prefrontal and increased subcortical brain functioning assessed using positron emission tomography in predatory and affective murderers. *Behavioral Sciences & the Law, 16*(3), 319–332.

Raine, A., O'Brien, M., Smiley, N., Scerbo, A., & Chan, C. J. (1990). Reduced lateralization in verbal dichotic listening in adolescent psychopaths. *Journal of Abnormal Psychology, 99*(3), 272–277.

Raine, A., Phil, D., Stoddard, J., Bihrle, S., & Buchsbaum, M. (1998). Prefrontal glucose deficits in murderers lacking psychosocial deprivation. *Neuropsychiatry, Neuropsychology, and Behavioral Neurology, 11*(1), 1–7.

Raine, A., Reynolds, C., Venables, P. H., Mednick, S. A., & Farrington, D. P. (1998). Fearlessness, stimulation-seeking, and large body size at age 3 years as early predispositions to childhood aggression at age 11 years. *Archives of General Psychiatry, 55*(8), 745–751.

Rasanen, P., Hakko, H., Isohanni, M., Hodgins, S., Jarvelin, M. R., & Tiihonen, J. (1999). Maternal smoking during pregnancy and risk of criminal behavior among adult male offspring in the Northern Finland 1966 Birth Cohort. *American Journal of Psychiatry, 156*(6), 857–862.

Reiss, A. J., Jr., & Farrington, D. P. (1991). Advancing knowledge about co-offending: Results from a prospective longitudinal survey of London males. *Journal of Criminal Law and Criminology, 82*(2), 360–395.

Reiss, A. J., Jr., Miczek, K. A., & Roth, J. A. (1994). *Understanding and preventing violence* (Vol. 2). Washington, DC: National Academies Press.

Reiss, D. (2001). *Child effects on family systems: Behavioral genetic strategies.* Paper presented at the Penn State University National Symposium "Children's Influence on Family Dynamics: The Neglected Side of Family Relationships," State College, PA.

Reiss, D., Neiderhiser, J. M., Hetherington, E. M., & Plomin, R. (2000). *The relationship code: Deciphering genetic and social influences on adolescent development.* Cambridge, MA: Harvard University Press.

Reneman, L., Booij, J., de Bruin, K., Reitsma, J. B., de Wolff, F. A., & Gunning, W. B. (2001). Effects of dose, sex, and long-term abstention from use on toxic effects of MDMA (ecstasy) on brain serotonin neurons. *Lancet, 358*(9296), 1864–1869.

Retz, W., Retz-Junginger, P., Supprian, T., Thome, J., & Rosler, M. (2004). Association of serotonin transporter promoter gene polymorphism with violence: Relation with personality disorders, impulsivity, and childhood ADHD psychopathology. *Behavioral Sciences & the Law, 22*(3), 415–425.

Revelle, W. (1995). Personality processes. *Annual Review of Psychology, 46*(1), 295–328.

Reyna, V. F. (2004). How people make decisions that involve risk: A dual-processes approach. *Current Directions in Psychological Science, 13*(2), 60–66.

Reyna, V. F., & Farley, F. (2006). Risk and rationality in adolescent decision making: Implications for theory, practice, and public policy. *Psychological Science in the Public Interest, 7*(1), 1–44.

Reznikoff, M., & Honeyman, M. S. (1967). MMPI profiles of monozygotic and dizygotic twin pairs. *Journal of Consulting Psychology, 31,* 100.

Richman, N., Stevenson, J., & Graham, P. J. (1982). *Pre-school to school: A behavioural study.* London: Academic Press.

Rintoul, B., Thorne, J., Wallace, I., Mobley, M., Goldman-Fraser, J., & Luckey, H. (1998). *Factors in child development: Part I: Personal characteristics and parental behavior.* Report prepared for the Centers for Disease Control and Prevention, Atlanta. Retrieved from http://www.rti.org/pubs/child-development.pdf

Ritter, M. (2002, November 4). Brain cell production. *Associated Press.*

Robins, L. N. (1966). *Deviant children grown up.* Baltimore, MD: Williams and Wilkins.

Robins, L. N. (1978). Sturdy childhood predictors of adult antisocial behaviour: Replications from longitudinal studies. *Psychological Medicine, 8*(4), 611–622.

Ross, G., Lipper, E. G., & Auld, P. A. (1990). Social competence and behavior problems in premature children at school age. *Pediatrics, 86*(3), 391–397.

Rowe, D. C. (1981). Environmental and genetic influence on dimensions of parental perception: A twin study. *Developmental Psychology, 17,* 203–208.

Rowe, D. C. (1983). Biometrical genetic models of self-reported delinquent behavior: A twin study. *Behavior Genetics, 13*(5), 473–489.

Rowe, D. C. (1985). Sibling interaction and self-reported delinquent behavior: A study of 265 twin pairs. *Criminology, 23*(2), 223–240.

Rowe, D. C. (1986). Genetic and environmental components of antisocial behavior: A study of 265 twin pairs. *Criminology, 24*(3), 513–532.

Rowe, D. C. (1994). *The limits of family influence: Genes, experience, and behavior.* New York: Guilford.

Rowe, D. C. (2002). *Biology and crime.* Los Angeles: Roxbury.

Rowe, D. C., & Plomin, R. (1981). The importance of nonshared (E_1) environmental influences in behavioral development. *Developmental Psychology, 17*, 517–531.

Rubin, K. H., LeMare, L. J., Lollis, S., Asher, S. R., & Coie, J. D. (1990). *Peer rejection in childhood.* New York: Cambridge University Press.

Ruden, R. A. (1997). *The craving brain: The biobalance approach to controlling addictions.* New York: HarperCollins.

Rutter, M., Giller, H., & Hagell, A. (1998). *Antisocial behavior by young people.* Cambridge, UK: Cambridge University Press.

Rutter, M. L., Kreppner, J. M., & O'Connor, T. G. (2001). Specificity and heterogeneity in children's responses to profound institutional privation. *British Journal of Psychiatry, 179*(2), 97–103.

Rutter, M., & Quinton, D. (1984). Parental psychiatric disturbance: Effects on children. *Psychological Medicine, 14*, 853–880.

Rutter, M., & Smith, D. J. (1995). *Psychosocial disorders in young people: Time trends and their causes.* Chichester, UK: Wiley.

Sampson, R. J., & Groves, W. B. (1989). Community structure and crime: Testing social-disorganization theory. *American Journal of Sociology, 94*(4), 774–802.

Sampson, R. J., & Laub, J. H. (1990). Crime and deviance over the life course: The salience of adult social bonds. *American Sociological Review, 55*(5), 609–627.

Sampson, R. J., & Laub, J. H. (1993). *Crime in the making: Pathways and turning points through life.* Cambridge, MA: Harvard University Press.

Sampson, R. J., & Laub, J. H. (1994). Urban poverty and the family context of delinquency: A new look at structure and process in a classic study. *Child Development, 65*(2 Spec No.), 523–540.

Sampson, R. J., & Laub, J. H. (1995). Understanding variability in lives through time: Contributions of life-course criminology. *Studies on Crime and Crime Prevention, 4*, 143–158.

Sapolsky, R. M. (2000). Glucocorticoids and hippocampal atrophy in neuropsychiatric disorders. *Archives of General Psychiatry, 57*(10), 925–935.

Scarr, S. (1988). How genotypes and environments combine: Development and individual differences. In N. Bolger, A. Caspi, G. Downey, & M. Moorehouse (Eds.), *Persons in context: Developmental processes* (pp. 217–244). New York: Cambridge University Press.

Scerbo, A., & Raine, A. (1992). *Neurotransmitters and antisocial behavior: A meta-analysis.* Manuscript submitted for publication; available from A. Raine at University of Southern California (raine@usc.edu).

Schalling, D. (1978). Psychopathy-related personality variables and the psychophysiology of socialization. In R. D. Hare & D. Schalling (Eds.), *Psychopathic behavior: Approaches to research* (pp. 85–106). Chichester, UK: Wiley.

Schalling, D. (1993). Neurochemical correlates of personality, impulsivity, and disinhibitory suicidality. In S. Hodgins (Ed.), *Mental disorder and crime* (pp. 208–226). Newbury Park, CA: Sage.

Schleifer, M., Weiss, G., Cohen, N., Elman, M., Cvejic, H., & Kruger, E. (1975). Hyperactivity in preschoolers and the effect of methylphenidate. *American Journal of Orthopsychiatry, 45*(1), 38–50.

Seguin, J. R., Pihl, R. O., Harden, P. W., Tremblay, R. E., & Boulerice, B. (1995). Cognitive and neuropsychological characteristics of physically aggressive boys. *Journal of Abnormal Psychology, 104*(4), 614–624.

Seidlitz, L., & Diener, E. (1998). Sex differences in the recall of affective experiences. *Journal of Personality and Social Psychology, 74*(1), 262–271.

Shannon, L. W. (1976). *Predicting adult careers from juvenile careers.* Unpublished manuscript.

Shannon, L. W. (1982). *Assessing the relationship of adult criminal careers to juvenile careers: A summary.* Washington, DC: Government Printing Office.

Shapiro, S. K., Quay, H. C., Hogan, A. E., & Schwartz, K. P. (1988). Response perseveration and delayed responding in undersocialized aggressive conduct disorder. *Journal of Abnormal Psychology, 97*(3), 371–373.

Shaw, C. R. (1930). *The jack-roller: A delinquent boy's own story.* Chicago: University of Chicago Press.

Shaw, C. R., & McKay, H. D. (1942). *Juvenile delinquency and urban areas.* Chicago: University of Chicago Press.

Shaw, D. S., Gilliom, M., Ingoldsby, E. M., & Nagin, D. S. (2003). Trajectories leading to school-age conduct problems. *Developmental Psychology, 39*(2), 189–200.

Shaw, D. S., Owens, E. B., Vondra, J. I., Keenan, K., & Winslow, E. B. (1996). Early risk factors and pathways in the development of early disruptive behavior problems. *Development and Psychopathology, 8*(4), 679–699.

Shaywitz, B. A., Shaywitz, S. E., Pugh, K. R., Constable, R. T., Skudlarski, P., & Fulbright, R. K. (1995). Sex differences in the functional organization of the brain for language. *Nature, 373*(6515), 607–609.

Sheline, Y. I., Mittler, B. L., & Mintun, M. A. (2002). The hippocampus and depression. *European Psychiatry, 17*(Suppl. 3), S300–S305.

Shonkoff, J. P., & Phillips, D. A. (2000). *From neurons to neighborhoods: The science of early childhood development.* Washington, DC: National Academy Press.

Shore, R. (1997). *Rethinking the brain: New insights into early development.* New York: Families and Work Institute.

Shover, N. (1996). *Great pretenders: Pursuits and careers of persistent thieves.* Boulder, CO: Westview.

Siegel, D. J. (1999). *The developing mind: Toward a neurobiology of interpersonal experience.* New York: Guilford.

Silberg, J., Rutter, M., Meyer, J., Maes, H., Hewitt, J., Simonoff, E., et al. (1996). Genetic and environmental influences on the covariation between hyperactivity and conduct disturbance in juvenile twins. *Journal of Child Psychology and Psychiatry and Allied Disciplines, 37*(7), 803–816.

Silva, P. A. (1987). Epidemiology, longitudinal course and associated factors: An update. In W. Yule & M. Rutter (Eds.), *Language development and disorders* (pp. 1–15). London: MacKeith Press/Blackwell Scientific.

Silverman, I., Phillips, K., & Silverman, L. K. (1996). Homogeneity of effect sizes for sex across spatial tests and cultures: Implications for hormonal theories. *Brain and Cognition, 31*(1), 90–94.

Single-sex classes increasing. (2004, October 5). *San Bernardino County Sun.*

Skinner, B. F. (1953). *Science and human behavior.* New York: Macmillan.

Slaby, R. G., & Guerra, N. G. (1988). Cognitive mediators of aggression in adolescent offenders: 1. Assessment. *Developmental Psychology, 24*(4), 580–588.

Smith, D. A., & Paternoster, R. (1987). The gender gap in theories of deviance: Issues and evidence. *Journal of Research in Crime and Delinquency, 24*(2), 140–172.

Snodgrass, J. (1982). *The jack-roller at seventy: A fifty-year follow-up.* Lanham, MD: Lexington Books.

Snyder, H. N., & Sickmund, M. (2006). *Juvenile offenders and victims: 2006 national report.* Washington, DC: U.S. Department of Justice, Office of Justice Programs, Office of Juvenile Justice and Delinquency Prevention.

Solms, M. (2004). Freud returns. *Scientific American, 290*(5), 82–89.

Sommer, I. E. C., Ramsey, N. F., Graafmans, D., Mandl, R. C. W., & Kahn, R. S. (2002). How identical are monozygotic twins? An fMRI study on language lateralization. *European Psychiatry, 17*(Suppl. 1), S11.

Sood, B., Delaney-Black, V., Covington, C., Nordstrom-Klee, B., Ager, J., Templin, T., et al. (2001). Prenatal alcohol exposure and childhood behavior at age 6 to 7 years: I. Dose-response effect. *Pediatrics, 108*(2), E34.

Soubrie, P. (1986). Reconciling the role of central serotonin neurons in human and animal behavior. *Behavioral and Brain Sciences, 9*(2), 319–364.

Sowell, E. R., Thompson, P. M., Welcome, S. E., Henkenius, A. L., Toga, A. W., & Peterson, B. S. (2003). Cortical abnormalities in children and adolescents with attention-deficit hyperactivity disorder. *Lancet, 362*(9397), 1699–1707.

Speltz, M. L., McClellan, J., DeKlyen, M., & Jones, K. (1999). Preschool boys with oppositional defiant disorder: Clinical presentation and diagnostic change. *Journal of the American Academy of Child and Adolescent Psychiatry, 38*(7), 838–845.

Spitz, R. A., & Wolf, K. M. (1946). Anaclitic depression: An inquiry into the genesis of psychiatric conditions in early childhood. *Psychoanalytic Study of the Child, 2,* 313–342.

Stallard, P. (1993). The behaviour of 3-year-old children: Prevalence and parental perception of problem behaviour: A research note. *Journal of Child Psychology and Psychiatry and Allied Disciplines, 34*(3), 413–421.

Stark, R. (2002). Physiology and faith: Addressing the "universal" gender difference in religious commitment. *Journal for the Scientific Study of Religion, 41*(3), 495–507.

Starr, C., & Taggart, R. (1987). *Biology: The unity and diversity of life* (4th ed.). Belmont, CA: Wadsworth.

State of New Jersey. (2004). *Uniform crime report.* West Trenton: State of New Jersey, Division of State Police, Uniform Crime Reporting Unit.

Stattin, H., & Klackenberg-Larsson, I. (1993). Early language and intelligence development and their relationship to future criminal behavior. *Journal of Abnormal Psychology, 102*(3), 369–378.

Stattin, H., & Magnusson, D. (1989). The role of early aggressive behavior in the frequency, seriousness, and types of later crime. *Journal of Consulting and Clinical Psychology, 57*(6), 710–718.

Stattin, H., & Magnusson, D. (1990). *Pubertal maturation in female development.* Hillsdale, NJ: Erlbaum.

Steinberg, L. (2004). Risk taking in adolescence: What changes and why? *Annals of New York Academy of Sciences, 1021,* 51–58.

Steinberg, L., & Lerner, R. M. (2004). The scientific study of adolescence: A brief history. *Journal of Early Adolescence, 24*(1), 45–54.

Steinberg, M. S., & Dodge, K. A. (1983). Attributional bias in aggressive adolescent boys and girls. *Journal of Social and Clinical Psychology, 1*(4), 312–321.

Steiner, H., & Dunne, J. E. (1997). Summary of the practice parameters for the assessment and treatment of children and adolescents with conduct disorder. *Journal of the American Academy of Child and Adolescent Psychiatry, 36*(10), 1482–1485.

Steinmetz, H., Staiger, J. F., Schlaug, G., Huang, Y., & Jancke, L. (1995). Corpus callosum and brain volume in women and men. *Neuroreport, 6*(7), 1002–1004.

Stevens, D., Charman, T., & Blair, R. J. (2001). Recognition of emotion in facial expressions and vocal tones in children with psychopathic tendencies. *Journal of Genetic Psychology, 162*(2), 201–211.

Stratton, K. R., Howe, C. J., & Battaglia, F. C. (1996). *Fetal alcohol syndrome: Diagnosis, epidemiology, prevention, and treatment.* Washington, DC: Committee to Study Fetal Alcohol Syndrome, Institute of Medicine.

Straus, M. A., Gelles, D. R., & Steinmetz, S. K. (2006). *Behind closed doors: Violence in the American family.* New York: Transaction Books.

Sutherland, E. (1947). *Principles of criminology* (4th ed.). Philadelphia: Lippincott.

Swaab, D. F., & Fliers, E. (1985). A sexually dimorphic nucleus in the human brain. *Science, 228,* 1112–1115.

Swaab, D. F., Zhou, J. N., Fodor, M., & Hofman, M. A. (1997). Sexual differentiation of the human hypothalamus: Differences according to sex, sexual orientation, and transsexuality. In L. Ellis & L. Ebertz (Eds.), *Sexual orientation: Toward biological understanding* (pp. 129–150). New York: Praeger.

Tangney, J. P. (1995). Recent advances in the empirical study of shame and guilt. *American Behavioral Scientist, 38*(8), 1132.

Tangney, J. P., & Fischer, K. W. (1995). *Self-conscious emotions: The psychology of shame, guilt, embarrassment, and pride.* New York: Guilford.

Teicher, M. H., Ito, Y., Glod, C. A., Schiffer, F., & Gelbard, H. (1994). Early abuse, limbic system dysfunction, and borderline personality disorder. In J. Osofsky (Ed.), *Children in a violent society* (pp. 177–207). New York: Guilford.

Tellegen, A., Lykken, D. T., Bouchard, T. J., Jr., Wilcox, K. J., Segal, N. L., & Rich, S. (1988). Personality similarity in twins reared apart and together. *Journal of Personality and Social Psychology, 54*(6), 1031–1039.

Thomas, W. I., & Thomas, D. S. (1928). *The child in America: Behavior problems and programs.* New York: Knopf.

Thompson, P. M., Cannon, T. D., Narr, K. L., van Erp, T., Poutanen, V. P., & Huttunen, M. (2001). Genetic influences on brain structure. *Nature Neuroscience, 4*(12), 1253–1258.

Thornberry, T. (1987). Toward an interactional theory of delinquency. *Criminology, 25,* 863–891.

Thornberry, T. (1997). *Developmental theories of crime and delinquency.* Edison, NJ: Transaction Books.

Tibbetts, S. G. (1997). Gender differences in students' rational decisions to cheat. *Deviant Behavior, 18*(4), 393–414.

Tibbetts, S. G. (1997). Shame and rational choice in offending decisions. *Criminal Justice and Behavior, 24*(2), 234.

Tibbetts, S. G. (2002). *Gender, emotions, and criminal offending.* Paper presented at the annual meeting of the Academy of Criminal Justice Sciences, Anaheim, CA. Available from S. G. Tibbetts at California State University, San Bernardino.

Tibbetts, S. G. (2003). Self-conscious emotions and criminal offending. *Psychological Reports, 93*(1), 101–126.

Tibbetts, S. G., & Herz, D. C. (1996). Gender differences in factors of social control and rational choice. *Deviant Behavior, 17*(2), 183–208.

Tibbetts, S. G., & Piquero, A. (1999). The influence of gender, low birth weight, and disadvantaged environment in predicting early onset offending: A test of Moffitt's interactional hypothesis. *Criminology, 37,* 843–877.

Tiihonen, J., Kuikka, J., Bergstrom, K., Hakola, P., Karhu, J., & Ryynanen, O. P. (1995). Altered striatal dopamine re-uptake site densities in habitually violent and non-violent alcoholics. *Nature Medicine, 1*(7), 654–657.

Tolan, P. H. (1987). Implications of onset for delinquency risk identification. *Journal of Abnormal Child Psychology, 15,* 47–65.

Tramo, M. J., Loftus, W. C., Stukel, T. A., Green, R. L., Weaver, J. B., & Gazzaniga, M. S. (1998). Brain size, head size, and intelligence quotient in monozygotic twins. *Neurology, 50*(5), 1246–1252.

Tremblay, R. E. (2006). Tracking the origins of criminal behavior: Back to the future. *Criminologist, 31*(1), 1, 3–7.

Tremblay, R. E., Japel, C., Perusse, D., McDuff, P., Boivin, M., Zoccolillo, M., et al. (1999). The search for the age of "onset" of physical aggression: Rousseau and Bandura revisited. *Criminal Behavior and Mental Health, 9*(1), 8–23.

Tremblay, R. E., Loeber, R., Gagnon, C., Charlebois, P., Larivee, S., & LeBlanc, M. (1991). Disruptive boys with stable and unstable high fighting behavior patterns during junior elementary school. *Journal of Abnormal Child Psychology, 19*(3), 285–300.

Tremblay, R., Masse, L., Pagani, L., & Vitaro, F. (1996). From childhood physical aggression to adolescent maladjustment: The Montreal prevention experiment. In R. D. Peters & R. J. McMahon (Eds.), *Preventing childhood disorders, substance abuse and delinquency* (pp. 268–298). Thousand Oaks, CA: Sage.

Tremblay, R. E., Pihl, R. O., Vitaro, F., & Dobkin, P. L. (1994). Predicting early onset of male antisocial behavior from preschool behavior. *Archives of General Psychiatry, 51*(9), 732–739.

Trulson, C. R., Marquart, J. W., Mullings, J. L., & Caeti, T. J. (2005). In between adolescence and adulthood: Recidivism outcomes of a cohort of state delinquents. *Youth Violence and Juvenile Justice, 3*(4), 355–387.

Tschann, J. M., Adler, N. E., Irwin, C. E., Jr., Millstein, S. G., Turner, R. A., & Kegeles, S. M. (1994). Initiation of substance use in early adolescence: The roles of pubertal timing and emotional distress. *Health Psychology, 13*(4), 326–333.

U.S. Department of Justice. (2005). *Crime in the United States, 2004.* Washington, DC: Author.

Underwood, A. (2002). How to lift the mind. *Newsweek, 140,* 67.

Van Voorhis, P., Braswell, M., & Lester, D. (2000). *Correctional counseling & rehabilitation.* Cincinnati, OH: Anderson.

Venables, P. H. (1988). Psychophysiology and crime: Theory and data. In T. E. Moffitt & S. A. Mednick (Eds.), *Biological contributions to crime causation* (pp. 78–97). Dordrecht, the Netherlands: Martinus Nijhoff.

Venables, P. H., & Raine, A. (1987). Biological theory. In B. McGurk, D. Thornton, & M. Williams (Eds.), *Applying psychology to imprisonment: Theory and practice* (pp. 3–28). London: Her Majesty's Stationery Office.

Virkkunen, M. (1982). Reactive hypoglycemic tendency among habitually violent offenders: A further study by means of the glucose tolerance test. *Neuropsychobiology, 8*(1), 35–40.

Virkkunen, M., & Linnoila, M. (1990). Serotonin in early onset, male alcoholics with violent behaviour. *Annals of Medicine, 22*(5), 327–331.

Virkkunen, M., Nuutila, A., & Huusko, S. (1976). Effect of brain injury on social adaptability: Longitudinal study on frequency of criminality. *Acta Psychiatrica Scandinavica, 53*(3), 168–172.

Volavka, J. (1995). *Neurobiology of violence.* Washington, DC: American Psychiatric Press.

Volavka, J. (1999). The neurobiology of violence: An update. *Journal of Neuropsychiatry and Clinical Neurosciences, 11*(3), 307–314.

Volkow, N. D., & Tancredi, L. (1987). Neural substrates of violent behavior: A preliminary study with positron emission tomography. *British Journal of Psychiatry, 28,* 728–732.

Volpe, J. J. (1992). Effect of cocaine use on the fetus. *New England Journal of Medicine, 327*(6), 399–407.

Wachs, T. D. (2000). *Necessary but not sufficient: The respective roles of single and multiple influences on individual development.* Washington, DC: American Psychological Association.

Wallis, C. (2004). What makes teens tick. *Time, 163*(19), 56–65.

Walsh, A. (1995). Genetic and cytogenetic intersex anomalies: Can they help us to understand gender differences in deviant behavior? *International Journal of Offender Therapy and Comparative Criminology, 39*(2), 151–166.

Walsh, A. (2002). *Biosocial criminology: Introduction and integration.* Cincinnati, OH: Anderson.

Walters, G. D. (1992). A meta-analysis of the gene-crime relationship. *Criminology, 30*(4), 595–613.

Walters, G. D. (2002). Developmental trajectories, transitions, and nonlinear dynamical systems: A model of crime deceleration and desistance. *International Journal of Offender Therapy and Comparative Criminology, 46*, 30–44.

Wang, Y., Fujita I., Tamura, H., & Murayama, Y. (2002). Contribution of GABAergic inhibition to receptive field structures of monkey inferior temporal neurons. *Cerebral Cortex, 12*(1), 62–74.

Ward, D. A., & Tittle, C. R. (1994). IQ and delinquency: A test of two competing explanations. *Journal of Quantitative Criminology, 10*(3), 189–212.

Warr, M. (1998). Life-course transitions and desistance from crime. *Criminology, 36*, 183–216.

Warr, M. (2002). *Companions in crime: The social aspects of criminal conduct.* New York: Cambridge University Press.

Wertheimer, R. (2002). *Youth who "age out" of foster care: Troubled lives, troubling prospects.* Washington, DC: Child Trends.

West, D. J., & Farrington, D. P. (1977). *The delinquent way of life: Third report of the Cambridge Study in Delinquent Development.* London: Heinemann.

White, J., Moffitt, T. E., Earls, F., Robins, L. N., & Silva, P. A. (1990). How early can we tell? Predictors of childhood conduct disorder and adolescent delinquency. *Criminology, 28*(4), 507–553.

Whitley, B. E., Nelson, A. B., & Jones, C. J. (1999). Gender differences in cheating attitudes and classroom cheating behavior: A meta-analysis. *Sex Roles, 41*(9), 657–680.

Willoughby, M., Kupersmidt, J., & Bryant, D. (2001). Overt and covert dimensions of antisocial behavior in early childhood. *Journal of Abnormal Child Psychology, 29*(3), 177–187.

Wilson, J. Q., & Herrnstein, R. (1985). *Crime and human nature: The definitive study of the causes of crime.* New York: Simon & Schuster.

Wilson, S. L. (2003). Post-institutionalization: The effects of early deprivation on development of Romanian adoptees. *Child and Adolescent Social Work Journal, 20*(6), 473–483.

Wismer-Fries, A. B., Ziegler, T. E., Kurian, J. R., Jacoris, S., & Pollak, S. D. (2005). Early experience in humans is associated with changes in neuropeptides critical for regulating social behavior. *Proceedings of the National Academy of Science, 102*(47), 17237–17240.

Wolf, O. T., Schommer, N. C., Hellhammer, D. H., McEwen, B. S., & Kirschbaum, C. (2001). The relationship between stress induced cortisol levels and memory differs between men and women. *Psychoneuroendocrinology, 26*(7), 711–720.

Wolfgang, M. E., Figlio, R. M., & Sellin, J. T. (1972). *Delinquency in a birth cohort.* Chicago: University of Chicago Press.

Wright, J. P., Carter, D. E., & Cullen, F. T. (2005). A life-course analysis of military service in Vietnam. *Journal of Research in Crime & Delinquency, 42*(1), 55–83.

Wright, P., Nobrega, J., Langevin, R., & Wortzman, G. (1990). Brain density and symmetry in pedophilic and sexually aggressive offenders. *Sexual Abuse: A Journal of Research and Treatment, 3*(3), 319–328.

Wright, R., & Decker, S. H. (1997). *Armed robbers in action: Stickups and street culture.* Boston: Northeastern University Press.

Yeudall, L. T., Fromm-Auch, D., & Davies, P. (1982). Neuropsychological impairment of persistent delinquency. *Journal of Nervous and Mental Disease, 170,* 257–265.

Zametkin, A. J., Nordahl, T. E., Gross, M., King, A. C., Semple, W. E., & Rumsey, J. (1990). Cerebral glucose metabolism in adults with hyperactivity of childhood onset. *New England Journal of Medicine, 323*(20), 1361–1366.

Zoccolillo, M., Pickles, A., Quinton, D., & Rutter, M. (1992). The outcome of childhood conduct disorder: Implications for defining adult personality disorder and conduct disorder. *Psychological Medicine, 22*(4), 971–986.

Index

About the Authors

John Paul Wright is Associate Professor of Criminal Justice in the Division of Criminal Justice at the University of Cincinnati. He earned his undergraduate degree in criminology from Indiana State University and his PhD from the University of Cincinnati. He has published extensively in criminology, psychology, behavioral genetics, and molecular genetics journals and is a frequent lecturer to professional organizations interested in the development of serious, violent offending. He teaches in the area of life course development and biosocial criminology.

Stephen G. Tibbetts is Associate Professor in the Department of Criminal Justice at California State University, San Bernardino. He earned his undergraduate degree in criminology and law at the University of Florida, and his master's and doctoral degrees at the University of Maryland, College Park. For more than a decade, he worked as an Officer of the Court (Juvenile) in both Washington County, Tennessee, and then for San Bernardino County, California, in which he provided recommendations for disposing numerous juvenile court cases. He has published more than 30 scholarly articles in scientific journals (including *Criminology* and *Justice Quarterly*), as well as several books, all examining various topics regarding criminal offending or policies to reduce such behavior. His recent research interests include developmental and biosocial factors in predicting offending, particularly factors that affect brain function, as well as testing traditional theoretical models of criminal offending and gang intervention/prevention strategies. His most recent book is a coedited anthology, *American Youth Gangs at the Millennium* (Waveland Press, 2005), which was given a Choice award by the American Library Association as an Outstanding Academic Title.

Leah E. Daigle is Assistant Professor in the Department of Criminal Justice at Georgia State University. She received her PhD in criminal justice from the University of Cincinnati. Her most recent research has focused on the development and continuation of offending and victimization over time, the sexual victimization of college women, and gender differences in the antecedents to and consequences of criminal victimization and participation across the life course. Her recent publications have appeared in *Justice Quarterly, Journal of Research in Crime and Delinquency,* and *Journal of Interpersonal Violence.*